The Heritage Crusade and the Spoils of History

DAVID LOWENTHAL

PUBLISHED BY THE PRESS SYNDICATE OF THE UNIVERSITY OF CAMBRIDGE
The Pitt Building, Trumpington Street, Cambridge CB2 1RP, United Kingdom

CAMBRIDGE UNIVERSITY PRESS
The Edinburgh Building, Cambridge CB2 2RU, United Kingdom   htt:p://www.cup.cam.ac.uk
40 West 20th Street, New York, NY 10011–4211, USA   http://www.cup.org
10 Stamford Road, Oakleigh, Melbourne 3166, Australia

First published in Great Britain by Viking 1997
First published in the USA by The Free Press 1996
as *Possessed by the Past: The Heritage Crusade and the Spoils of History*
ISBN 0 684 827980

First paperback edition by Cambridge University Press 1998

Printed in the United Kingdom at the University Press, Cambridge

Typeset in Monotype Bembo   [SE]

A catalogue record for this book is available from the British Library

Library of Congress Cataloguing in Publication data

Lowenthal, David.
  [Possessed by the past]
  The heritage crusade and the spoils of history / David Lowenthal.
    p.   cm.
  Originally published: Possessed by the past. New York : Free
Press, c.1996.
  Includes bibliographical references and index.
  ISBN 0 521 63562 4
  1. History – Philosophy.   I. Title.
D16.9.L636   1998
901–dc21 97-44370 CIP

ISBN 0 521 635624 paperback

For Mary Alice

"The free-ranging master of Heritage Studies . . . has managed to coax an extraordinary inventory of heritage pathology into a coherent, lucid argument."

Patrick Wright, *THE INDEPENDENT*

"David Lowenthal has done us a service by demystifying the new religion of the past, the cult of heritage, second only to health as the great moral absolute of our time."

Clive Aslet, *LITERARY REVIEW*

"Wry and hugely learned analysis . . . Will surely provoke changes of attitude, and deeper self-knowledge, in all who read it." Jill Paton Walsh, *Books of the Year, THE TABLET*

"Perceptive and provocative . . . explores the many perversities of the heritage cult – and its absolute irresistibility." Michael Kerrigan, *THE SCOTSMAN*

"*The Past Is a Foreign Country* is a wild and magnificent book; *The Heritage Crusade* is its equally glorious successor . . . a keen eye for what is often comical in the pretensions of 'patrimonialists'." Jo Tollebeek, *DE VOLKSKRANT* (Amsterdam)

"Absorbing book . . . spectacular demolition job on the cult of heritage . . . highly recommended." Frank McLynn, *GLASGOW HERALD*

"Lowenthal's entertaining and enthralling study succeeds brilliantly. It deserves to be placed on the shelves of every olde gifte shoppe in the kingdom."

Ben Pimlott, *THE GUARDIAN*

"Steeped in wit and sensitivity . . . [T]his acute savant's tone, at once severe and benevolent, with an irony devoid of venom and spite, on every page reminds me of Montaigne."

Charles Edouard Racine, *LA DISTINCTION* (Lausanne)

"*The Heritage Crusade* and *The Past Is a Foreign Country* together provide the intellectual underpinning and wider context that any understanding of preservation's meaning and direction requires." Robert Wilson, *PRESERVATION* (U.S. National Trust)

"David Lowenthal knows more about the uses and abuses of the past than anyone I know . . . It is the strength of Lowenthal's book that he shows us how heritage is deeply antithetical to history, yet inseparable from it."

John R. Gillis, *REVIEWS IN AMERICAN HISTORY*

CONTENTS

PREFACE TO THE PAPERBACK EDITION, 1998

To PEN A NEW PREFACE FOR A BOOK less than two years old is a privilege granted few authors. Yet it is symptomatic of my topic that even this brief lapse of time commends a new look at how we engage with the past— or rather our manifold pasts. For each person, each group, each nation has its own views, views traditionally rooted yet also in ceaseless flux, of its particular past and, by extension, of history in general.

It is fitting that this paperback edition is issued by Cambridge University Press, which thirteen years ago published my forerunner. Having *The Heritage Crusade and the Spoils of History* under the same publishing roof as *The Past is a Foreign Country* prompts me to stress today's craving to domesticate that past: face to face with the past's foreignness, we are apt to wonder how we and our world could ever have come from so strange a place. My earlier book traced how historians had jettisoned assumptions that human nature was everywhere and always the same; comparative scrutiny showed that denizens of other times thought and acted in ways and for reasons unlike our own. But this insight is not shared by most cultures, nor widely accepted even in the West. We mainly idealize or demonize the past not as a foreign country, but as close kin to our own present-day homeland.

Three conjoined aims led me to write *The Heritage Crusade and the Spoils of History*. One was to assess and account for the growth, exponential in pace and global in sweep, of current obsessions with the past, above all with what we enjoy or endure as patrimonial legacies. Our ever more magnified attachments to heritage have myriad consequences, some lauded as life-enhancing, others detested as lamentable or even lethal, still others viewed askance as a *mélange* of good and evil. Britain's Millennium

ix

Dome at Greenwich, intended as a "lasting legacy" to the arts of our age, is just as apt, some fear, to become a lasting legacy to the environmental harm caused by the plastic dome's ozone-destructive emissions. Heritage displays untold similar instances of benefits commingled with ill effects. How should we judge a realm at once so beneficial and so harmful?

My second aim was to explore the tensions generated by heightened patrimonial concerns. Rival claimants seem hell-bent on aggrandizing their own heritage goods and virtues, to the exclusion or detriment of all others. Disputes about who should own and interpret heritage are endemic, tarnishing many legacies with acquisitive greed. Heritage is mainly sought and treasured as our own; we strive to keep it out of the clutches of others we suspect, often with good reason, of aiming to steal it or to spoil it. Indeed, heritage stewardship is intrinsically possessive: only those pledged to their clients' exclusive cause can be relied on as stewards. An heir must be sure his trustees acts solely on his behalf, a state that national custodians will yield no part of the domain. No wonder global stewardship of culture and environment makes but glacial headway against entrenched interests, private and corporate.

My third aim was to distinguish between heritage and history. These two routes to the past are habitually confused with each other, yet they are also defined as antithetical. Heritage is apt to be labeled as false, deceitful, sleazy, presentist, chauvinist, self-serving—as indeed it often is. But such charges, I suggest in this book, are usually leveled on the mistaken assumption that heritage is "bad" history. In fact, heritage is not history at all; while it borrows from and enlivens historical study, heritage is not an inquiry into the past but a celebration of it, not an effort to know what actually happened but a profession of faith in a past tailored to present-day purposes.

My third aim has notably vexed many readers. Surely, they rejoin, I exaggerate the gulf between heritage and history. Instead of the exclusive dichotomy I posit, do not these two realms continually merge and interact along a continuum of everyday experience? Are we not all sometimes heritage-mongers, at other times historians, at still others both at once?

My critics are right. No aspect of heritage is wholly devoid of historical reality; no historian's view is wholly free of heritage bias. As I myself stress, just as yesterday's heritage becomes today's history, so we in turn embrace as heritage what our precursors took as history. At this moment, the death of Diana, Princess of Wales, is transforming a history into a heritage. Yet history too is a heritage. The history we normally accept without demur stems from seldom-tested faith in the cumulative probity of historians, even when we know their chronicles were forged—often trumpeted—in the crucible of self-interest.

Rather than stressing the gulf that divides history and heritage, my critics want partisans of both enterprises to acknowledge that, despite their differences, theirs is truly a common cause. We need at one and the same time to know the past as truth and as faith, as enlightened reality and as amazed inspiration. But can heritage managers negotiate the manifold fictions integral to mass entertainment, without being castigated for historical *lèse-majesté*? And can historians come to terms with the reality that most of the history we learn—including that authoritatively taught in schools and textbooks—is gleaned from heritage sources? Indeed, to purge heritage from what is taught as history would be impossible, perhaps inconceivable, certainly self-defeating. To paraphrase Caroline Walker Bynum's 1997 American Historical Association presidential address, teachers of history must above all strive to astonish, students aspire to be astonished.

All the more reason, in my view, to underscore distinctions between aims proper to heritage and those proper to history. The two enterprises are inextricably conjoined. But it is crucial to underscore their dissimilar intents. The historian, however blinkered and presentist and self-deceived, seeks to convey a past consensually known, open to inspection and proof, continually revised and eroded as time and hindsight outdate its truths. The heritage fashioner, however historically scrupulous, seeks to design a past that will fix the identity and enhance the well-being of some chosen individual or folk. History cannot be wholly dispassionate, or it will not be felt worth learning or conveying; heritage cannot totally disregard history, or it will seem too incredible to command fealty. But the aims that animate these two enterprises, and their modes of persuasion, are contrary to each other. To avoid confusion and unwarranted censure, it is vital to bear that opposition in mind.

History and heritage are both here to stay, despite recurrent forecasts of their demise and crusades to expunge them from public life. In Britain the cult of heritage seems such an incubus that the new government jettisons the old name of the Department of National Heritage—the word "heritage" is now too backward looking. But at the same time Britain rejoins UNESCO, which cherishes the global heritage of culture and nature. "That's history," say Americans dismissively, hoping they can get the past off their backs. Yet at the same time America is riven by disputes over whether to commemorate Little Bighorn as Custer's Last Stand or as Indian slaughter, whether to memorialize Franklin D. Roosevelt as a cigarette-smoking cripple, and whether to proffer a national apology for black slavery.

Ancestral iniquities are nowadays everywhere retracted, as if Salisbury's anguished cry in Shakespeare's *Richard II*, "O, call back yesterday—bid time return," might actually be achieved. The Papacy rehabilitates Galileo, Britain's prime minister apologizes for the Irish Famine, Japanese schoolbooks regret long-denied wartime atrocities, Sweden condemns the last generation's eugenic sterilizations as indefensibly "barbaric." It is ever more common to hold figures from the past accountable for not thinking and acting as right-minded people do today. But the current habit of chastising ancestral villains, no less than traditional chauvinist glory in ancestral virtues, disserves history and heritage alike. Legacies become more useful and more bearable when we refrain from saddling their begetters with our own views, and cease invoking ancestral myths to justify present ends.

INTRODUCTION

ALL AT ONCE HERITAGE IS EVERYWHERE—in the news, in the movies, in the marketplace—in everything from galaxies to genes. It is the chief focus of patriotism and a prime lure of tourism. One can barely move without bumping into a heritage site. Every legacy is cherished. From ethnic roots to history theme parks, Hollywood to the Holocaust, the whole world is busy lauding—or lamenting—some past, be it fact or fiction.

To neglect heritage is a cardinal sin, to invoke it a national duty. Even as I write, American presidential aspirant Pat Buchanan champions the flag of the southern Confederacy because "everyone should stand up for their heritage." And in early 1996 British Defense Secretary Michael Portillo, pilloried for want of "pride in our national heritage," was forced to rescind a proposed sale of Aston Webb's majestic but now moribund and otiose 1910 Admiralty Arch.

Why this rash of backward-looking concern? What makes heritage so crucial in a world beset by poverty and hunger, enmity and strife? We seek comfort in past bequests partly to allay these griefs. In recoiling from grievous loss or fending off a fearsome future, people the world over revert to ancestral legacies. As hopes of progress fade, heritage consoles us with tradition. Against what's dreadful and dreaded today, heritage is *good*—indeed, the first known use of the term is Psalm 16's "goodly heritage."

Yet much that we inherit is far from "goodly," some of it downright diabolical. Heritage brings manifold benefits: it links us with ancestors and offspring, bonds neighbors and patriots, certifies identity, roots us in time-honored ways. But heritage is also oppressive, defeatist, decadent.

Miring us in the obsolete, the cult of heritage allegedly immures life within museums and monuments. Breeding xenophobic hate, it becomes a byword for bellicose discord. Debasing the "true" past for greedy or chauvinist ends, heritage is accused of undermining historical truth with twisted myth. Exalting rooted faith over critical reason, it stymies social action and sanctions passive acceptance of preordained fate.

With its benefits hyped and its perils exaggerated, heritage by its very nature excites partisan extremes. Ready recourse to patrimony fills many vital needs. But it also glamorizes narrow nationalism. Vainglory vindicates victors and solaces the vanquished, justifying jingoism and inflaming partisan zeal.

Three sets of aims animate this book. One is to see why heritage is now such a growth industry and to clarify the problems its popularity generates. A second is to assess what we expect from history and heritage and to show where these linked enterprises fulfill (or fail) our hopes. The third is to understand why possessive rivalry cripples cooperation, subverting our will and thwarting our ability to care for common global legacies.

Heritage passions impact myriad realms of life today. They play a vital role in national and ethnic conflict, in racism and resurgent genetic determinism, in museum and commemorative policy, in global theft, illicit trade, and rising demands for repatriating art and antiquities. Decisions about what to conserve and what to jettison, about parenthood and adoption, about killing or converting or cosseting those of rival faiths all invoke heritage to explain how we feel and to validate how we act.

A decade ago, my *The Past Is a Foreign Country* traced changing perceptions of the past. Initially, people had thought human nature universal and changeless; past motives and events were explained in the same terms as those of today. But the last two centuries of turmoil have revolutionized historical awareness. Denizens of the past now seem to inhabit alien worlds, to act in ways and for reasons other than our own. The past has become a foreign and exotic place where people did things differently. And despite advances in science and scholarship that tell us more than ever about former times, the past frustrates understanding: its events seem unfathomable, its denizens inscrutable. However much we know *about* the past, we can never really know *how* it was for those who lived back then.

This is what historians now tell us. But how many really share their doubts? I suspect few take historians' cautions to heart; so alien a past is too hard to bear, especially when we treasure it as our own possession. The precursors we conjure up continue to seem folk much like ourselves. Probably most people, most of the time, view the past not as a foreign but a deeply domestic realm.

In domesticating the past we enlist it for present causes. Legends of origin and endurance, of victory or calamity, project the present back, the past forward; they align us with forebears whose virtues we share and whose vices we shun. We are apt to call such communion history, but it is actually heritage. The distinction is vital. History explores and explains pasts grown ever more opaque over time; heritage clarifies pasts so as to infuse them with present purposes.

Critics who confuse the two enterprises condemn heritage as a worthless sham, its credos as fallacious, even perverse. But heritage, no less than history, is essential to knowing and acting. Its many faults are inseparable from heritage's essential role in husbanding community, identity, continuity, indeed history itself. If for one Australian historian "heritage is the cuckoo in the historian's nest," another prizes heritage as the fount of historical evidence.[1] In trying to explain why this is so, I seek to resolve the conundrums that encumber heritage when it is misconceived as history. Because heritage concerns are passionately partisan, they are also seamed with paradox.

Thus we mourn worlds known to be irrevocably lost—yet more vividly felt, more lucid, more real than the murky and ambiguous present. We yearn for rooted legacies that enrich the paltry here and now with ancestral echoes, yet also encumber us with outworn relics and obsolete customs. We see what has happened as inalterable (not even God can change the past) and cleave to timeless tradition, yet we ever reshape what we inherit for current needs. Treasuring heritage as authentic history, we blind ourselves to our own legacy's biased limits. We acclaim heritage as a universal requisite, yet disdain and derogate legacies that differ from or compete with our own. We avow concern for the sanctity of all heritage, yet strip it of context and debase its meaning. Devoted inheritors, we kill the legator and cripple our legacy.

The relics of time help us both to know the past and to bend it to our own uses. Such remains, on the ground and in the mind, are more and more extracted and enjoyed. Under the rubric of heritage ever more is revered in theory and ruined in practice. Stewardship saves the past from decay—and robs it of majesty and mystery. Heritage aims to convert historical residues into witnesses that attest our own ancestral virtues. The past thus coerced renders up the spoils of history on untold altars of aggrandizement. History not effaced is despoiled.

The spoils of history lie all around us—in developers' debris, in the sacked remains of prehistoric tombs, in the ravaged ruins of Mostar and Sarajevo, in the fetishes of restorers and reenactors, in the paraphernalia of cultural tourism. They proliferate too in patriotic credos and self-serving anachronisms, in the certitudes of school history, in the delusory dreams of Disney, in the squabbles of rival claimants to relics and emblems.

Such feuds make heritage a menacing minefield as well as a nourishing marvel. We need to understand what impulses drive us, heritage crusaders all, to ravage the past in the very act of revering it and to censure others for faults equally our own. Yet we should also realize that in thus corrupting we also enhance the spoils of history, breathing new life into them for ourselves and our inheritors by fabricating heritage anew.

One such fabrication, described by the historian Patrick Geary, illumines my point and sets my stage. In 1162, Milan fell to Frederick Barbarossa. As a reward for his help in the conquest, archbishop-elect Rainald of Cologne pillaged Milan's relics. Rainald's most notable coup was the remains of the Magi, legendarily brought to Milan from Constantinople (with Constantine's consent) by St. Eustorgio in an oxcart in 314.

Now the Magi were on the move again. Though waylaid en route by minions of Pope Alexander III, the three coffins with their sacred booty reached Cologne unharmed. In Nicolas of Verdun's splendid golden shrine (c. 1200) they become Cologne's main patrons. By the 13th century the Three Kings were a royal cult, emperors coming to venerate them after being crowned in Aachen. Otto IV of Brunswick had himself portrayed on the reliquary as the Fourth King. Belatedly, the Milanese lamented the theft. The 16th-century Archbishop St. Carlo Borromeo campaigned for their return; in 1909 a few Magi fragments were actually sent from Cologne to Milan.

But they were *not* sent *back*; they had never been in Milan. The whole story—Constantine, Eustorgio, removal to Cologne—had been fabricated by Rainald. Every mention of the Magi in Milan traces to the archbishop's own self-serving account. No wonder the Milanese were tardy in recognizing the theft; only in the late 13th century did Rainald's tale reach them. Milan then mourned the loss of relics it had never had.

Rainald's purpose was clear: to promote the power of the emperor and the glory of Cologne. Relics of the Savior were the most precious the Franks got from Italy and the Holy Land. As symbols of Christ's lordship and of divine kingship, the Magi trumped vestiges of Church Fathers and Roman martyrs. But they needed a pedigree; a legacy of veneration was vital to their efficacy in Cologne. Hence Constantine, the oxcart, stewardship in Milan, their incorruptible state en route. And it worked. It worked even in Milan, where Visconti patronage of the lamented Magi helped scuttle both republicanism and Torriani family rivals accused of exposing the Magis' hiding place to Frederick Barbarossa.[2]

This fabrication was multiply worthy. It confirmed the Holy Roman Empire's sacred roots. It updated and enlarged a useful biblical legend (little before was known of the Magi, even how many they were). It became an exemplar of other sacred translations—fragments of bone and dust that were easy to fake, easy to steal, easy to move, easy to reassign to new saints as needed. It begot great value from wishful fantasy. It destroyed nothing, not even faith when the fake was found out.

Today things are different. We still steal, forge, and invent much of our heritage. But we are no longer confident it is right to do so. That the legacies we cherish, whether inherited or re-created, are so pliable and corruptible seems to us sacrilegious. We yearn instead for fixed verities.

At its best, heritage fabrication is both creative art and act of faith. By means of it we tell ourselves who we are, where we came from, and to what we belong. Ancestral loyalties rest on fraud as well as truth and foment peril along with pride. We cannot escape dependency on this motley and peccable heritage. But we can learn to face its fictions and forgive its flaws as integral to its strengths.

Chapter 1

HERITAGE ASCENDANT

THE WORLD REJOICES IN A NEWLY POPULAR FAITH: the cult of heritage. To be sure, heritage is as old as humanity. Prehistoric peoples bequeathed goods and goals; legacies benign and malign suffuse Homeric tales, the Old Testament, and Confucian precepts. But only in our time has heritage become a self-conscious creed, whose shrines and icons daily multiply and whose praise suffuses public discourse.

Regard for roots and recollection permeates the Western world and pervades the rest. Nostalgia for things old and outworn supplants dreams of progress and development. A century or even fifty years ago the untrammeled future was all the rage; today we laud legacies bequeathed by has-beens. Once the term patrimony implied provincial backwardness or musty antiquarianism; now it denotes nurturance and stewardship.

Devotion to heritage is a spiritual calling "like nursing or being in Holy Orders," as James Lees-Milne termed his own career of rescuing historic English country houses for the National Trust. A successor's verbal slip as he spoke with me, "When I joined the Church—I mean, the Trust," echoed the analogy. The Trust's supreme tidiness recalls those Victorian restorers who scraped medieval churches and cathedrals clean of the debris of time and neglect, so as to perfect their divinity. The English, however, are not the only such devotees; heritage awakens piety the world over. Australians are said to "spend more of their spiritual energy" in quests for enshrined symbols of identity than in any other pursuit; "worship of the past in Australia [is] one of the great secular religions."[1]

The creed of heritage answers needs for ritual devotion, especially

1

where other formal faith has become perfunctory or mainly political. Like religious causes, heritage fosters exhilarating fealties. For no other commitment do peoples so readily take up arms. Once a dilettante pastime, the pursuit and defense of patrimonial legacies is now likened to the Crusades—bitter, protracted, and ruthless.

The religious analogy extends to modes of belief: heritage relies on revealed faith rather than rational proof. We elect and exalt our legacy not by weighing its claims to truth, but in feeling that it *must* be right. The mainstay is not mental effort but moral zeal. "You can't be taught jazz," says American singer Cassandra Wilson, "it's a legacy."

As doctrine, heritage is mandatory. It comes to us willy-nilly and cannot be shed, however shaming it may be. To share a legacy is to belong to a family, a community, a race, a nation. What each inherits is in some measure unique, but common commitments bind us to others within our group. Inheritors are fellow countrymen—not just patriots but *com*patriots. Mutual identity demands mutual allegiance. Those deprived of a legacy are rootless and bereaved; those who seek to reject one are unnatural ingrates. Nations bereft of birthrights today lament their loss much as Esau did in the book of Genesis. Whatever its burdens, a heritage ought never be denied: self-respect requires us to accept, husband, and transmit it.

The traits that align heritage with religion help explain its potent pull, but they also pose serious risks. A dogma of roots and origins that must be accepted on faith denies the role of reason, forecloses compromise, and numbs willpower. Credence in a mythic past crafted for some present cause suppresses history's impartial complexity. Touting our own heritage as uniquely splendid sanctions narrow-minded ignorance and breeds belligerent bigotry.

Benign and baneful consequences are alike manifold, and heritage vice is inseparable from heritage virtue. This is little understood, though; because few realize how heritage actually functions, most are content either to admire or traduce it. Devotees ignore or slight its threats, while detractors deny its virtues and suppose that simply cursing heritage can excise its ills.

The current craze for heritage seems to me likely to last and hence essential to understand. Its potential for both good and evil is huge. On the one hand, it offers a rationale for self-respecting stewardship of all we hold dear; on the other, it signals an eclipse of reason and a regression to embattled tribalism. I aim to show how and why heritage has come to matter so much, to caution that heritage credos are by their very nature manipulative, and to counsel that we learn to control heritage lest it control us.

HERITAGE RAMPANT

Heritage is not our sole link with the past. History, tradition, memory, myth, and memoir variously join us with what has passed, with forebears, with our own earlier selves. But the lure of heritage now outpaces other modes of retrieval. If our era heralds the end of history, as pundits like Francis Fukuyama contend, perhaps the eclipse of history heralds the rise of heritage. Heritage may be heir to the "continuous nourishing tradition" that the historian Carl Schorske, by no means alone, fears history has abdicated.[2]

Yet these diverse routes to the past are neither fixed nor firmly bounded; they overlap and shift their focus. Much that was once termed history or tradition is now heritage, as shown in Chapter 5. But neither history nor tradition ever commanded the ubiquitous reach that heritage has today.

Never before have so many been so engaged with so many different pasts. Spanning the centuries from prehistory to last night, heritage melds Mesozoic monsters with Marilyn Monroe, Egyptian pyramids with Elvis Presley. Memorials and monuments multiply, cities and scenes are restored, historic exploits are reenacted, flea-market kitsch is elevated into antiques. Retro-fashion rages and camcorders memorialize yesterday. Historic sites multiply from thousands to millions; 95 percent of existing museums postdate the Second World War. Budapest, for instance, boasts museums of everyday life that enshrine the telephone and the tram, pastries and pharmaceuticals, advertising and animal husbandry; nothing seems too recent or trivial to commemorate. Invoking heritage justifies any collector's obsession. "I do love pigs," a self-styled fanatic in England defends his rare-breeds hobby, "but after all pigs are part of our heritage."

Fifty years back, book titles and indexes suggest, heritage dwelt mainly on heredity, probate law, and taxation; it now features antiquities, roots, identity, belonging. The French near-equivalent "patrimony" shows the same shift: the Larousse definition of *patrimoine* has expanded from "goods inherited from parents" to embrace bequests from remote forebears and cultural legacies in general. "We derive all we possess as an inheritance from our forefathers," held Edmund Burke two centuries ago; these days that inheritance determines our very selves. Prior possession once primarily legitimated title to land or lucre; today it sanctions claims to sites and relics. Stressing traditions that are especially our own, heritage magnifies self-esteem and bolsters communal ardor.

Modern preoccupation with heritage dates from about 1980, alike in Reagan's America, Thatcher's Britain, and Pompidou's France. In France, 1978's Year of the Woman and 1979's Year of the Child made a Year of Patrimony in 1980 a logical successor. Nostalgia was everywhere: in 1975 Hélias's *The Horse of Pride*, an elegy for rural Brittany, and Le Roy Ladurie's *Montaillou*, an intimate glimpse of a medieval Languedoc village, won these scholars popular fame; the annals of the hitherto unsung spread fast and far. Patrimony graduated from construing the civil code to celebrating the national estate.[3]

The pull of the past differs from place to place, and each tongue has its own nuance—French *patrimoine* is more personal than English *heritage*, German *Erbgut* more patriotic than Italian *làscito*. Each people supposes their newly inflated heritage concerns to be unique, reflecting some trait of character or circumstance, some spirit of veneration or revenge that is peculiarly their own. Some impute these concerns to patriotic ardor, some to nostalgic fancy, others to specific needs for mourning or celebrating. Vaunting our own legacy, we are unaware how strikingly concurrent it often is with those of our neighbors. Here is a typical list of unique heritage goodies from a 1994 Canadian travel brochure:

> Chestnut canoes . . . O Canada! . . . Emily Carr . . . golden wheat fields of the prairies . . . Blackfoot medicine wheels . . . moss-covered Haida totem poles . . . fishing villages such as Joe Batt's Arm on Fogo Island . . . donning skates on a crisp winter's morning . . . Northern Lights . . . Anne of Green Gables . . . soapstone carvings . . . loons . . . igloos . . . toboggans . . . maple syrup . . .

These items are Canadian, to be sure. But the resonant words and the stress on wilderness, ethnicity, and childhood typify heritage anywhere.

Maxims current in Manchester and Minneapolis, Madagascar and the

Marquesas stress similar communal concerns. "If wealth is lost, nothing is lost," says Sikhs; "if health is lost, something is lost. If character is lost, much is lost. If *heritage* is lost, *you* are lost." To a Cameroon diplomat heritage is "beyond price, beyond value; it unifies the tribe [and] is the spirit of the nation, what holds us together." Canada's Inuits and Indians, like France's Minister of Culture, claim that "everything is part of our heritage." UNESCO protocols enthrone heritage as the sovereign core of collective identity and self-respect, a nutriment as necessary as food and drink.[4]

Global popularity homogenizes heritage. Its aims and traits are assessed in similar terms in Bergen and Beirut, Tonga and Toronto. The same concerns with precedence and antiquity, continuity and coherence, heroism and sacrifice surface again and again, nurturing family bonds, strengthening fealty, and stressing stewardship. Most heritage is amassed by particular groups, but media diffusion and global networks make these hoards ever more common coin.

Heritage care and conveyance conjoin the stewardship of relics of nature and culture unique to Australia or Amazonia, New Mexico or New Guinea. Display and tourism layer diverse legacies with common facades. The same multinationals finance restoration in Prague and Peru, using techniques devised in Rome and London. Legacies of nature, prehistory, art, and architecture are hyped in terms ever more alike. Exotic dragonflies and endangered dialects are not yet priced alongside Old Master paintings in Sotheby's salesbooks, but their collectors and protectors talk the same legacy lingo.

The language of heritage that suffuses the world is mainly Western. The first historic monuments meeting in 1931 engaged Europeans alone; Tunisia, Mexico, and Peru joined in 1964; in 1979 eighty nations from all continents crafted the World Heritage Convention.[5] The remotest village in Vanuatu may vaunt Sotheby's auction schedule. Swedish, Japanese, and German firms built the "living" Shona village and replica of Old Bulawayo at Zimbabwe's Heritage Centre. Under the aegis of national patrimony looms a multinational enterprise.

CAUSES OF MODERN HERITAGE CONCERN

Why does heritage loom so large today? Answers differ from place to place. Heritage in Britain is said to reflect nostalgia for imperial self esteem and other bygone benisons, in America to requite economic and social angst and lost community, in France to redress wartime disgrace, in Australia to replace the curse of recency to forge indigenous pride.[6] But no explanation specific to one people can account for a trend so contagious. What is involved is a cluster of trends whose premises, promises, and problems are truly global.

These trends engender isolation and dislocation of self from family, family from neighborhood, neighborhood from nation, and even oneself from one's former selves. Such changes reflect manifold aspects of life—increasing longevity, family dissolution, the loss of familiar surroundings, quickened obsolescence, genocide and wholesale migration, and a growing fear of technology. They erode future expectations, heighten past awareness, and instill among millions the view that they need and are owed a heritage.

Dismay at massive change stokes demands for heritage. Market forces swiftly outdate most things now made or built; migration uproots millions from familiar locales; technology transforms familiar scenes at shocking speed. The intricate texture of downtown Boston visible in 1930s photos is today totally effaced by packing-crate office blocks; the old Massachusetts State House, a minuscule survivor among overgrown monsters, becomes an ornamental snuff box in a museum case. Landscape itself is replaced ever sooner: London's trees, the mighty oaks and majestic limes Victorians planted to endure, give way to fast-growing, short-lived species.

Beleaguered by loss and change, we keep our bearings only by clinging to remnants of stability. Hence preservers' aversion to letting anything go, postmodern manias for period styles, cults of prehistory at megalithic sites. Mourning past neglect, we cherish islands of security in seas of change. "In a throwaway society where everything is ephemeral," a London College of Arms spokesman explains the rise of ancestor hunts, people "begin to look for something more lasting." The passing of close-knit families spurs such searches. Since "grandparents no longer take the youngsters on their knee and tell them about *their* grandparents," noted an American genealogist in 1974, youngsters have had to find them for themselves.[7]

Legacies at risk are cherished for their very fragility. The heritage of rural life is exalted because everywhere at risk, if not already lost. So rapid is French scenic and social decay that tourists were urged in 1993 to "see France while it is still there." Landscape is Britain's archetypal legacy; two centuries of city celebrants made country life a metaphor for the national soul, yearning to "win back a share in the common heritage filched from them with Enclosure and the Industrial Revolution." The historian Herbert Butterfield lauded Englishmen's "inescapable heritage" of Whig history as "part of the landscape of English life, like our country lanes or our November mists or historic inns." The glossy magazine *Heritage* is subtitled "British Life and *Countryside*." Landscape-as-heritage stresses time-honored verities at risk.[8]

Modern genocide and iconoclasm magnify needs for legacies to outlast ourselves. Doomed Jews resolved to leave witnesses attesting to the Holocaust. Along with human slaughter we mourn art that cannot be replaced: Harold Nicolson in 1944 would have sacrificed himself to save Giotto's frescoes and would have given up his sons sooner than St. Mark's, Venice.[9] The ruin of Mostar's bridge built to outlast the centuries, or of a minaret's poignant reach toward eternity, truncates our own lives as well.

Such losses now seem graver than ever before. A pace of change "peculiar to our times," declared UNESCO in 1972, menaced mankind's cultural and natural heritage and mandated its protection. English curriculum caretakers in 1993 lauded time-honored lore as a "cultural link with the long-valued past [essential] in these turbulent times."

Yet horror at upheaval is not new; each generation since the French Revolution has felt buffeted by turbulent times. Marx's 1848 *Communist Manifesto* noted the "constant revolution of productions, the uninterrupted disturbance of all social relations, ideas becoming obsolete before they can ossify." Our great-great-grandparents were more severed from their past than are we—heirs to two centuries of change, schooled to expect and until recently even to welcome innovation.

After Napoleon, by contrast, many felt stranded between a past when life had been much the same from eon to eon and a present that sundered each year from the last. They were the first to mourn the recent as beyond recall and to limn a childhood unimaginable to their own children. This total rupture of experience was just what the Jacobins intended: a new order expunging all the old, from priests and patricians to customary practices. Discontinuity was their deliberate bequest to the next generation, savagely disjoining them, as many attested, from any familiar past.[10]

It is a common belief that technical invention has soared without precedent in recent decades. But is it true? Have television, computers, nuclear power, and space flights altered life more in our time than did the auto, telephone, electric light, airplane, radio, and cinema between 1900 and 1950? Or the railroads, gaslights, steamships, telegraph, factory-made clothing, and household goods that transformed the Western world between 1800 and 1860?[11] No one from the 1750s could have imagined the new world of 1800; in contrast, no one from the 1950s would find most present-day scenes unfamiliar—"blink, today, and you could *be* in the 1950s," wrote a journalist in 1992. While the 1890s· seemed like the Dark Ages in 1945, fifty years later 1945 seems like only yesterday, laptop computers and seatbelts aside.

Our precursors were no less estranged by novelty, rueing lost familiar vistas just as we do. But they were less ceaselessly reminded of their loss. Nor did a socially certified nostalgia sanction their yearnings; on the contrary, they were enjoined to praise the new and take change in their stride. They suffered change more violent than ours, but we *perceive* ourselves to be its unexampled victims.

Modern media magnify the past's remoteness. We digest and domesticate written accounts as we read them, but even recent visual images (street scenes, home decor, hairstyles, and clothing) at once strike us as anachronistic. Everything in the 1940s movie *Brief Encounter*—morals, fashion, etiquette, and language—is staggeringly different from its 1985 renewal *Falling in Love*. Old photos, posed in studios, seem inconceivably remote. Our great-grandparents look more like foreigners than forebears; they resemble Jonathan Raban's ancestral portraits of people who "might have been anyone's distant relations. They certainly didn't look related to *us*."[12]

Growing longevity cuts us off even from our own pasts. Many who reach ninety are "punished for their great age," a columnist suggests, "by being reminded that they are out of touch with the world." Bereft of familiar scenes and companions, their memories grow unrecognizable. "If you age a lot, there is finally almost nobody left who shared your vast experience" of a bygone world. You look around for "*anyone* of the older generation . . . to satisfy your curiosity about some detail of the landscape of the past. There is no longer any older generation. You have become it, while your mind was mostly on other matters," notes William Maxwell.[13] "I went to the kitchen to fix a cup of coffee when I was 59," goes the tale; "when I came out I suddenly found I was 84."

Those poised between two worlds, two ways of thinking and acting, find heritage of crucial import. "My Breton-speaking contemporaries will perhaps be the very last people to have spoken Breton on their mothers' laps," says the folklorist Hélias. Hence their stewardship duty transcends that of their predecessors and successors. "The former were not much concerned with the fate of their idiom"; the latter will condemn us for failing to protect their heritage.[14] Thus we feel uniquely accountable. Previous generations likewise looked back to a congenial world just gone, but their laments were formulaic; ours harden into heritage doctrine.

Massive migration also sharpens nostalgia. This century's diaspora have suffered incomparable displacement. Fleeing violence, hatred, and hunger, tens of millions seek refuge in lands not their own. Mass exodus has many precedents, to be sure; famine made exile and emigration customary in Ireland 150 years ago, when more Irish lived outside their country than in it. But refugee exodus, up tenfold in twenty years, is now a global commonplace. Over half of all Palestinians, Liberians, Rwandans, and Bosnians, one in three Lebanese, one in four Poles, Mozambicans, Eritreans, and Afghans mourn lost homes. So do billions of rural folk forced into cities. "Displaced persons are displaced not just in space but in time; they have been cut off from their own pasts," writes Penelope Lively, severed from her own Egyptian childhood by removal to England. "If you cannot revisit your own origins—reach out and touch them from time to time—you are for ever in some crucial sense untethered."[15]

Quests for roots reflect this trauma; heritage is invoked to requite displacement. Provincial newcomers to French cities haunt archival registers for family links, and tame alien milieus with rural furnishings and old farm tools. "The more people are on the move," observes a columnist, "the more they will grasp at tangible memorials of their collective past."[16] Much as bereft parents enshrine the rooms of departed children, so mementos of bygone lifestyles console those torn from native scenes.

Diaspora are notably heritage-hungry. Five out of six ancestry searches in Italy are made by Italian-Americans. Dublin is deluged with inquiries from Sons of Erin abroad, some seeking a long-lost legacy or an heir on whom to bestow one, others just hoping to find someone who remembers Uncle Seamus. So many Jews today seek memories of *shtetl* forebears that East Europeans call them "roots people."

Emigrés are also vital in sustaining ancestral heritage. West Indian, Hebridean, Dodecanese, and Polynesian islanders abroad nourish homeland traditions. Armenia's diaspora celebrate the ancient nation's past glories and bewail its griefs. The most ardent patriots are returned exiles; Fresno-born foreign minister Rafi Hovannisian is termed "the best Armenian in the world."[17] Diaspora nostalgia refreshes heritage for those at home. Returnees from North America reanimate traditional Ukrainian *bandura* music that is close to dying out. Remittance-dependent Ithacans revive obsolete folkways to give visiting American kinsfolk a nostalgic "taste of home."

To identify a past as heritage one need not have known it firsthand. "I come from Rotuma," says a Fijian who has never been in Rotuma; home is where the ancestors came from. Up to the 1950s, fourth-generation New Zealanders spoke of Britain as "home" with no intention of ever living there. Descendants of Southern planters who fled with their slaves to Brazil still cleave to ancestral Dixieland ways: "Preserving our heritage helps us pass cherished values on to future generations."[18]

Heritage is also nurtured by technophobia: an idealized past replaces a discredited future. The horrors of fascism, the failure of Marxism, the threat of nuclear and biological catastrophe, and the rise of factional animus have put paid to the ideology of progress. Many doubt their leaders' vision or ability to sustain a livable globe; dismayed by technology, they hark back to a simpler past whose virtues they inflate and whose vices they ignore. We show chronic affection for anything apart from the present, clutching at the outworn and the obsolete.

Those who express such dismay are newly legion. Heritage expands especially because more people now have a share in it. In times past, only a small minority sought forebears, amassed antiquities, enjoyed Old Masters, or toured museums and historic sites. Such pursuits now lure the multitude. No longer are only aristocrats ancestry-obsessed, only the super-rich antique collectors, only academics antiquarians, only the gentry museum visitors; millions now hunt their roots, protect beloved scenes, cherish mementos, and generally dote on times past.

Heritage growth thus reflects traumas of loss and change and fears of a menacing future. "How many preservationists does it take to change a light bulb?" runs the adage. "Four: one to change the bulb, one to document the event, and two to lament the passing of the old bulb." Heritage cannot be equated solely with felt decline; it also allures celebrants of success. On balance, though, obsessive concern with rooted legacies is more backward- than forward-looking.

HAZARDS OF HERITAGE GLUT

Our newly augmented heritage answers a congeries of needs, but the magnitude and momentum of its growth are also alarming and in the end self-defeating. Heritage of every kind accumulates to counter the transience of everything else. We cordon off more and more against the rapid demise of the disposable. A mounting legacy of protected sites and objects links us with the past; heritage thrives as the felt opposite of obsolescence. Salvaging ever more from erosion and discard, we seek to redress the balance between the ephemeral and the enduring.[19] Fending off irreversible change, we preserve, restore, or replicate. Any extinction, even of pestilential germs, becomes a crime against the legacy of diversity.

Crusades to save endangered heritage take little heed of custodial resources. For example, archaeologists bemoan sites plundered or lost to developers, yet by the mid-1970s so much prehistory was being salvaged that scholars and museums could not handle it, and more and more of what has been excavated languishes unseen and awaiting analysis.[20] Thus the accretion of archives has multiplied holdings a thousandfold within decades. Each American president's papers are said to outnumber those of all his predecessors combined.

Every enterprise becomes memorable; not only banks and bureaucrats but bakeries and beauty shops file dossiers, notes Pierre Nora.

No epoch has deliberately produced so many archives as ours, due alike to technical advances in reproduction and conservation and to our superstitious

respect for these traces. As traditional memory fades, we feel obliged reli-
giously to accumulate the testimonies, documents, images, and visible signs
of what was, as if this ever-proliferating dossier should be called on as evidence in some tribunal of history. Hence the inhibition against destroying,
the retention of everything. . . . In classical times, only great families, the
church, and the state kept records; today memories are recorded and memoirs written not only by minor actors in history but by their spouses and
doctors.

Once reproached for saving too much, archivists are now adjured to
keep everything. The glut causes chaos: reduced publication and maintenance funds make the augmented heritage ever less accessible. New
acquisitions go unrecorded, lacking even rudimentary maintenance,
their very existence unknown to the public lest some seek to use
them.[21] Inheriting a growing legacy of unsorted verbiage, chroniclers
often feel, like Tristram Shandy, that they are losing ground all the time.

The problem of heritage overload is not entirely new, to be sure.
"The world is accumulating too many materials for knowledge," observed Hawthorne after a day at the British Museum in 1855. "We do
not recognize for rubbish what is really rubbish; & under this head
might be reckoned almost everything one sees at the British Museum;
and as each generation leaves its fragments & potsherds behind it, such
will finally be the desperate conclusion of the learned."[22]

Only in our time, though, has the glut become suffocatingly unman-
ageable. Yet heritage is such a sacred cow that few will heed a call to halt
its growth. For example, Italy is so stuffed with heritage that only a fraction of it is catalogued, let alone cared for, least of all open to the public.[23]
Everyone knows this, yet no steward dares publicly affirm the unpalatable
facts. To query a worthy cause goes against the grain. As a heritage activist
I myself almost instinctively applaud the renewal of pride in ancestral
roots, the protection of relics threatened by erosion or plunder, and the
rescue of cherished legacies from purblind greed.

Hapless stewardship is one of many heritage dilemmas. Tangible mementos and documentary traces threaten to swamp creative life. Worship of a bloated heritage invites passive reliance on received authority,
imperils rational inquiry, replaces past realities with feel-good history,
and saps creative innovation, as I discuss in later chapters. Yet the fact

remains that heritage expands, and goes on expanding, in response to new needs. What are these needs, and how do they change the character of heritage?

FACETS OF GROWTH

Until modern times most peoples trusted tradition, lived in accordance with what was constant and consistent, and customarily communed with ancestors. Handing down modes of life and thought to descendants was more a matter of ingrained habit than of deliberate effort; the inheritance of land and livestock, lineage, and repute was socially codified and largely closed to personal decision. Few clung to artifacts that had outlasted practical or spiritual use. By contrast, heritage now reflects not just habit but conscious choice. Ways of valuing the past that arose in Renaissance and Enlightenment Europe and were bolstered by nationalism and populism have now become commonplace the world over.

Earlier folk largely fused past with present. Stability and cyclical recurrence muted marks of change and averted the breaches that now sunder old from new, useful from obsolete, the dead from the living. Spirits of the departed remained intimately involved with everyday life, bonding what could be seen and touched with what was veiled or imagined. For most peoples, the past was not a foreign country but their own.

While in our world the new replaces the old, in theirs the new was but another aspect of the eternal; as the book of Ecclesiastes put it, there was nothing new under the sun. Hence few desired to preserve what was old. The only vestiges of the past medieval Europeans systematically conserved were princely talismans and spiritual icons—the vestments and bodily traces of saints and sovereigns. Ancient edifices were allowed to decay or were demolished with little sense of loss.

The razing and rebuilding of St. Peter's in Rome in the 1500s was wholly consonant with stewardship as then seen. The old stones meant nothing in themselves; it was the site that signified the Church's indestructible permanence. Hence the visible legacy going back twelve centuries to Constantine was supplanted with little regret. To be sure, ancient Roman buildings still in use (the Pantheon, Castel Sant' Angelo, the Capitol) were kept up by repair. But old structures bereft of utility mattered only as examples to emulate, and such lessons were better conveyed in words or images than in bricks and stones.[24]

Over ensuing centuries, as will be seen in Chapter 3, material relics played an increasing role as emblems of power and piety, then of popular purpose. Heritage today is more substantial, more secular, and more social. Three dimensions of its enlargement merit attention: from the elite and grand to the vernacular and everyday; from the remote to the recent; and from the material to the intangible.

VERNACULAR BENTS

Like its new clientele, the past doted on is populist. Formerly about grand monuments, unique treasures, and great heroes, heritage now also touts the typical and evokes the vernacular. The homes and haunts of Everyman and Everywoman have spread from Scandinavian open-air museums into historical theme parks the world over. The humble English half-timbered, mock-Tudor, semidetached house—the cartoonist Osbert Lancaster's "Bypass Variegated"—is lauded for "epitomizing the traditions of the race." Colonial Williamsburg fosters dirt, ruin, and decay (unmown grass, peeling paint, and horse manure) in an everyday scene more authentic, and hence more virtuous, than the genteel fictions of previous restorers. To their disgust, Williamsburg craftsmen now have to make shoddy replicas true to supposed 18th-century prototypes.[25]

Traditionally controlled by the well-born and the well-off, heritage remains more an elite than a folk domain. But if palaces are more lavishly stewarded than folk haunts, the latter are better loved. Historic-house visitors nowadays flock to kitchens and servant and slave quarters; folk museums stress the humdrum over the exquisite, the ordinary in place of the unusual, the popular rather than the patrician. In reenacting the past, peasants and artisans now get pride of place.

Auction prices attest the value of folk legacies, with the bibelots of Everyman as pricey as those of princes. The bedroom carpet and plastic houseplant from Elvis Presley's Graceland mansion are his fans' Mona Lisa and Elgin Marbles. Old baseball cards, beer cans, Coke bottles, and barbed wire thrill ten times as many collectors as Queen Anne chairs or mahogany highboys. Genre scenes, decoy ducks, and mangle boards that once cluttered lofts and attics get reclaimed as art. Liverpool tourists throng Beatles' locales—Strawberry Fields, Eleanor Rigby's headstone, olden haunts of Lennon and McCartney. All pop memorabilia are treasured, however trivial or tawdry.

The more who engage with a heritage, the less esoteric and exacting it becomes. The grass roots fertilized in journals like *Foxfire* suggest that if the weak and the meek have not inherited the earth, they at least become the keepers of its castoffs. Vestiges of folkways formerly seen as backward are now prized as quaint. Once a stigma, Italian-American cooking now signals legacy pride: "Starting in her kitchen, my mother found her way back to her heritage."[26]

Sanctuaries that used to be exclusively elite now cater to the hoi polloi. The Victoria & Albert Museum hypes New Age grunge and "street cred." New York's Metropolitan Museum shows a Honus Wagner 1909 baseball card "worth" $1.2 million (card collectors spend $2 billion annually). The generals and grandees glowering along the walls of Britain's National Portrait Gallery are now outfaced by grinning athletes, pop stars, and media celebrities.

To be sure, some decry such plebeian trends. "Can a perfectly ordinary house in a perfectly ordinary town really be a part of our national heritage?" carped a critic in 1993, when England's National Trust was bequeathed a Victorian semidetached house in Worksop, Nottinghamshire, that had been kept in a time warp for sixty years by its reclusive tenants. Rather than "a worm's-eye view" of the past, the Trust should "illustrate the *finest* examples of architecture and furnishings."[27] Yet heritage lovers had already made *Our Grimy Heritage* (1971) and SAVE Britain's Heritage's *Satanic Mills* (1984) coffee-table best-sellers.

The populist trend is worldwide. In 1980s France, a Socialist regime legitimated a wide range of working-class legacies. A heritage once wholly patrician now includes 20th-century factories and merely familiar locales; "a simple oven or a village lavatory elicits the patrimonial ardour once given an artistic masterpiece."[28] Populist in theory since the Revolution, American heritage became visibly proletarian after the Civil War, when (as noted in Chapter 6), George Washington got repackaged from austere aristocrat into common man.

Australians zealously promote the folk past with museums dwelling on migration and newcomers, the poor and homeless, and events within living memory. Australian populism reflects a general view that they *have* no elite past worth notice. No monuments to wealthy taste, no heroic episodes, no significant events like Magna Carta come to mind. Australian history "consists of happenings so small, so everyday, so endlessly repeatable that they draw no attention to themselves," avers the writer David Malouf. Anything pompous gets mercilessly mocked. Gallipoli and Aborigines apart, heritage is more apt to be sent up than extolled. Authority figures—governors, judges, admirals, clerics—are ridiculed at reenactments.[29]

Genealogy typifies the populist trend. Millions of roots-seekers swamp registries. In America, fallout from *Roots* and the national bicentenary by the mid-1980s spawned fifty thousand family-tree experts. "Not long ago most Europeans would have stared blankly if asked to give their great-grandmother's name," noted a 1988 survey, and "genealogy was a hobby for aristocrats, maiden aunts, and eccentrics." Now all our forebears are upgraded to ancestors; Americans on Debrett "Roots" tours dine at their own British ancestral homes. In the last two decades, France's three hundred authorized genealogists grew to twenty thousand, and hunting for ancestors has become "a veritable national sport."[30]

In these quests, humble origins are newly chic. Bastards once hidden now festoon the family tree. "When I was a boy at Harrow School in the 1920s," the architectural historian Sir John Summerson told me sixty years later, "I did all I could to prevent *any*one finding out my grandfather was a common labourer. Today I'd make sure *every*one knew." The writer Jonathan Raban relates his father's switch from genteel to rougher roots. In the 1950s he mounted an "antique truffle hunt [for] an unbroken arc of pure ancestry, a trail of blood [from] helmeted centurions [and] Anglo-Saxons in mead halls" down through army officers and minor gentry. But by the 1980s Raban *père* was digging up "our criminal past," ancestors "engaged in smuggling, privateering and the slave trade," showing that "rapine, plunder, fiddling the books and dealing under the counter ran in our blood."[31]

Only now do Antipodeans reclaim ancestral black sheep. Even in the 1970s, as Tasmania's chief archivist told me, respected figures used to rip out pages of convict records bearing their forebears' names. When a young assistant told his father of these goings-on, the father paled: "That's all very well, my boy; but you must never let the aunts know." The aunts now all know, but they no longer mind. Convict forebears who once disgraced Australian descendants now lend them radical chic. Some limits remain: "Murder, rape—no, we wouldn't brag about that," said Norma Tuck of the Society of Australian Genealogists in 1988. "We would brag about highway robbery, though; . . . *that* was fun."

It is more typical of heritage populism, though, that most family historians hope to find either fellow-sufferers or "simple, honest, law-abiding" ancestors, in Carol Shields's words, whose "robustly rounded" lives will compensate for their own complex fears and doubts.[32]

INSTANT TRADITION

Once confined to a distant past—pre-1750 buildings, centuries-old antiques, Old Master paintings—heritage now spreads into yesterday. Houses become "historic" in mere decades, school history takes on events within living memory, a "Heritage" car is one made before 1970. The commemorative pace quickens from centennials to fiftieth and twenty-fifth anniversaries. Mere weeks after the Gore-Perot North Atlantic Free Trade Agreement debate in 1994, television host Larry King donated to Planet Hollywood's souvenir collection the green suspenders he had worn at the event; they already had the hoary aura of memorabilia.

Heritage today hails even the living. Fans of Dan Quayle boast the first museum honoring an extant U.S. vice president, featuring baby and Bible-school snapshots, a fifth-grade report card, and his Little League baseball uniform: "A lot of people wait 50 years, after the person is gone, but we had all his stuff lying right here, so why not do it while he's still living?" The 1993 inaugural opening coincided with a plastic duck race, the annual highlight of "Heritage Days" in Huntington, Indiana. A New Jersey museum of Bruce Springsteen memorabilia opens *and* closes while the rock star yet lives. Hits from the 1980s become relics while they still reverberate.

Stress on recent heritage mirrors the shift to mass clienteles. Especially for those with little schooling, things within living memory have a relevance absent from remoter times. Replacing steam engines with diesel in the 1950s gave rise to England's most popular preservation mania—for steam railways.[33] And recent souvenirs soon gain scarcity value: fountain pens and vintage cameras are already rare, antique TV sets the latest collectibles.

Novelties at first decried in the end gain legacy status, and the end is nigh ever sooner. From hated eyesores Victorian railway viaducts mutated into beloved scenic features defended with the same zeal as castles and abbeys. The transit from horror to heritage that once took a century now happens in two decades. The Fylingdale Beacons, Cold War strategic warning outposts on the North York Moors, were "monstrous intrusions" when erected in 1964. Obsolete by 1992, these giant golf balls were esteemed so scenic that English Heritage was on the point of saving them until they were disqualified as 1980s replacements, not 1960s originals. Verandas proscribed by Australian towns through the 1950s as shabby reminders of a hated past, by the 1970s became treasured heritage; in the 1980s they were being added to buildings that had never had verandas, as "typically Victorian."[34] The golden arches of McDonald's eateries are concurrently a detested novelty in Hampstead and a cherished legacy in California.

New heritage is in turn soon superseded. A Long Islander in 1990 stripped off the late-Victorian porch tacked on to his 1790s house; local heritage officials forced him to rebuild a replica porch. What had thirty years back been an excrescence was now a sacrosanct relic of East Hampton's Boarding-house Era; in thirty more years, sliding glass doors and jalousie windows might well be preserved as archetypally 1950s.

Like populism, the vogue for recency shows that heritage is open to change. A mean or meager legacy can always be augmented, a too-limited time span lengthened. Today's new clients supplant or supplement preexisting legacies with icons of their own. "Other great Americans will be born whose birthdays will force their way in to the calendar," cautioned a 1911 essay against a fixed ancestral canon. "Our boundaries of national gratitude are not finally set."[35] They never are. As shown in Chapter 7, rosters of historic persons and places ever annex what becomes newly relevant and shed what loses pertinence.

The pace of heritage replacement does exact costs. Fads for things barely past, like those for vernacular culture, hasten the attrition of historical memory and diminish shared canonical legacies. American students today are said to find even such 20th-century icons as Faulkner, Fitzgerald, and Hemingway as remote as Dickens or Fielding. Thus, as heritage expands its range, it becomes less consensual and more ephemeral.

Moreover, accruing ever more recent relics makes heritage harder to demarcate from the ongoing present. Yesterday's traces merge with those of antiquity and modernity; conserved legacies coalesce with current locales. Proximity to the present makes heritage ever more relevant to, but ever less distinct from, today's world. At length all that distinguishes heritage is its history of previous use. For all the stone-washing and sandblasting meant to make new blue jeans seem old, a German wholesaler finds that "used jeans simply look better and feel better"— especially if pre-worn by fabled, ill-starred American athletes.

LIVING FOLKWAYS

Along with the recent and the vernacular, heritage today stresses intangible folkways—kinship, language, poetry, music. Such concerns are not new: Homeric lineages sustained feudal perquisites; folk legacies generated European nation-states. Indeed, two centuries ago the philosopher Herder made language and folklore the crux of collective heritage. Yet during the 19th and early 20th centuries, national patrimony came to inhere more and more in tangible monuments and memorials, with material preservation an overriding concern. Even now, heritage crusades are more apt to conjure up images of castles and cathedrals than of quatrains or cookery.

But legacy concerns now refocus on ideas and images. This shift reflects improved techniques of enhancing the quality and value of images. It also reflects the influence of cultures that do not share the Western mania for material objects as heritage. For example, Korea cherishes masked plays, musical genres, and skills like knot making, brass smelting, and pot glazing, supporting master performers and craftsmen. Japan's Living Cultural Treasures enact similar roles in a culture that admires ancient forms and skills but shuns old buildings (save for sacred shrines) as *furukusai*—so old they stink.

Poland speedily restored Nazi-razed historic centers felt to be crucial to the national identity, but Polish heritage today is more concerned with the thoughts and memories such buildings evoke. And peoples who build or make little meant to long endure find Western conservation zeal bizarre. Emphasis on original materials in UNESCO's canonical Venice Charter of 1966 is said to "leave other cultures and traditions ill at ease, [for] *they* place more emphasis on spiritual values, on authenticity of thought, than on material symbols."[36]

Cultural heritage stresses words over things above all in China, where esteem for tradition goes hand in hand with recurrent destruction of material remains. Mao's orders to demolish most of China's ancient monuments proved easy to carry out, for few historic structures had survived the dynastic iconoclasm of past millennia. Revering ancestral memory and calligraphy, the Chinese hold the past's purely physical traces in small regard; indeed, old works must perish so that new ones can take their place. Memory of art, not its physical persistence, suffuses Chinese consciousness and spurs new creations. The "capacity for metamorphosis and adaptation" over three and a half millennia, Pierre Ryckmans suggests, "may well derive from the fact that this tradition never let itself be trapped into set forms, static objects and things, where it would have run the risk of paralysis and death."[37]

Famed old Soochow has no ancient ruins. "We in the West tend to equate the antique presence with authentically ancient physical objects," observes a Sinologist. "China has no ruins comparable to the Roman Forum, or even to Angkor Wat," not for want of skills "but because of a different attitude about how to achieve an enduring monument." Ancient cities became sites of heritage through "a past of words, not of stones." Soochow's Maple Bridge is famed as a locus but not for its looks. "No single poem refers to its physical presence"; what mattered "was not the stones forming the span" but its associations realized in words.[38] The Chinese gain immortality not with imperishable monuments but with imperishable words exalting others' enduring thoughts.

Sentiments linked with sites override tangible concerns elsewhere, too. In western North Carolina a folklorist found many old family homesteads empty and neglected, but often used for family reunions; what mattered was "the memory of the experiences within and the meanings attached to the homeplace, . . . not the walls, the roof, and the foundation. [They] preserve stories about old houses better than they preserve the structures themselves."[39] Family feeling outlasts other tangible heirlooms. Inheriting no more than a soup pot and a roasting pan, a woman finds her vital Thanksgiving legacy in recipes and in an "appetite for togetherness."

The marginalized are most apt to demote material legacies. Preserving old houses is a serious threat to working-class or ethnic neighborhoods that risk being gentrified. Heritage to them is more likely to mean folkways (faiths, foods, forms of music and dance) than fabric, performance more than product. Until America's National Trust enlarged its sphere of concern, it made little headway among minorities who gave priority to intangible folkways.[40]

Intangible folkways now gain mainstream patrons. Copying Japan and Korea, the U.S. National Endowment for the Arts awards annual heritage fellowships; 1995 recipients include a blues guitarist, a cowboy balladeer, a basket weaver, a step dancer, a luthier, a quiltmaker, and a blacksmith. A publican, a thatcher, a cheese-monger, and an umbrella-handle maker figure among *Country Life* magazine's monthly "living national treasures." More than bricks and mortar, Britons hanker after old moralities, the "amalgam of faith, diligence, loyalty, independence and authority" immortalized in the novels of Anthony Trollope.[41]

That heritage can be sustained only by a living community becomes an accepted tenet. To sustain a legacy of stones, those who dwell among them also need stewardship. "*We* are the heritage," declaimed the mayor of Dijon in 1980 of plans to conserve that indigent city; the French government should "extend patrimonial solicitude to us." Though their crafts revive, Georgia's Sea Islanders are beleaguered by tourist development: "We, the black native population of these islands, have become the new endangered species."[42] As modes of active life fade away, material remnants become mere curiosa.

HERITAGE DEPRIVATION, HERITAGE POSSESSION

Hunger for heritage takes diverse forms. The poor and the powerless market any antiquities they can unearth; millions of Guatemalans, Mexicans, Peruvians, Italians, Lebanese, and others eke out meager livelihoods by selling off ancestral pasts. "To be rich, dig up an ancient tomb," runs a Chinese peasant saying; "to make a fortune, open a coffin." Against such acts legal codes are impotent and moral entreaty otiose. Why should the indigent not hawk their heritage to feed their families?

Indeed, how can they view it as their heritage at all? A local leader about to loot the pre-Incan Lord of Sipán's newfound gravesite was persuaded first to view it, then asked if he dared "steal from the ancestors" and "sack his father's sacred tomb." Instead of just a storeroom of gold, awed villagers gazed raptly on an esteemed ancestor. But such local veneration is rarely evoked; prehistorians in Peru still require armed police. Mayan descendants in Yucatan were told that in plundering pre-Columbian sites they were destroying their legacy; they were unrepentant. "The ancient people made it," they said; "it is not a part of what we are."[43]

Only a heritage that is clearly ours is worth protecting. "The issue is ownership and control," says a civil-rights veteran battling both Hollywood and the National Park Service for interpretive stewardship of the movement and its sites. "If we don't tell the story or control the telling, then it is no longer about us." Egyptians whose antiquities have mostly ended up in Europe, and Jamaicans whose beaches are fenced off for exclusive tourist use, cannot suppose these legacies truly their own.

Such dispossessions are legion. Westernized Javanese sundered from indigenous roots under Dutch rule felt like exiles in their own land; "living in a hotel owned by others, we seek neither to improve nor equip it as we do not feel that it is ours." Sicily remains "always a colony, never a country"; a chronicler details Sicilians' corrosive sense "that none of these riches—the Greek temples, the Byzantine mosaics, the Catalan-Gothic churches—are really" theirs. Near Syracuse, the faceless, limbless stumps of a dozen statues of the goddess Cybele, hacked to pieces by a peasant tired of tourists trampling his onions, attest "the danger presented by a people that feels that its past doesn't belong to it."[44]

Even those intimately attached to their past may sell it. Expert tomb robbers in Sicily and Tuscany feel fully justified in smuggling their heritage to Swiss dealers. "They consider that these tombs contain the bodies of their ancestors and they are therefore entitled to the contents," explains a Sicilian antiquities official. Tuscan tomb robbers claim communion with and sanctions from Etruscan forebears who tell them when and where to dig, while leaving certain sacred tombs inviolate. The skills of *tombaroli* specialists are passed on within particular families, but they share proceeds with the whole community.[45]

Others eager to slough off past social constraints find legacies crippling. "In an egalitarian culture like ours," says an American folklorist, "people don't want to be tied to the past." Heritage gets transmitted only in "dead countries, or secure and by-passed ones—where men can cherish the past and think of passing on furniture and china to their heirs"—places like Sweden and Canada, imagines V. S. Naipaul. "Everywhere else . . . the past can only cause pain."[46]

One reason is that conquerors persuaded others they *had* no proper patrimony. Children in French Africa were taught to revere "our ancestors, the Gauls." All over the Caribbean, in Jamaica Kincaid's rebuke, British colonizers built schools and libraries, "and in both of those places you distorted or erased my history and glorified your own," leaving millions with "no motherland, no fatherland, no gods, no mounds of earth for holy ground, . . . no tongue." The glory of earlier legacies is little solace. "No periods of time over which my ancestors held sway, no documentation of complex [African] civilisations, is any comfort to me." To reconvert such lost legacies into national heritage today is harder still. Third World efforts to regain attributes or forge emblems of tradition are mocked as imitative and obsolete, an opéra-bouffe parading of flags and folk costumes, not authentic heritage.[47]

The point of heritage, in a British custodian's words, is "not that the public should learn something but that they should *become* something." Merely to inherit is not enough; people must realize they are "heirs to the past, heirs to the collections which they own, free to decide for themselves what they are going to do with the past, what it means for them now and what it may mean for them in the future."[48] Choices are constrained, to be sure; most heritage comes already packaged by precursors. But to secure the past to our present lives, we must feel that its legacies have become our very own.

The signal value of heritage possession was the point made by soldier-scholar-mythmaker Yigael Yadin to Israeli army recruits sworn in at the Dead Sea fortress of Masada:

When Napoleon stood among his troops next to the pyramids of Egypt, he declared: "Four thousand years of history look down upon you." But what would he not have given to be able to say: "Four thousand years of *your own* history look down upon you."

What is our own matters most. But we have a stake in what others care for, too. "History did not need to be mine in order to engage me," writes a Haitian scholar. "It just needed to relate to someone, anyone. It could not just be The Past. It had to be someone's past."[49]

VULNERABLE AND VALUABLE LEGACIES

We value our heritage most when it seems at risk; threats of loss spur owners to stewardship. Just as impending civil war impelled the 17th-century antiquary Thomas Dugdale to record England's imperiled ecclesiastical monuments, so did the menace of the Second World War mobilize the art historian Kenneth Clark's colleagues to record the national legacy. "Heritage never means more to us," remarked a British art historian viewing Constable paintings at Yale, "than when we see it inherited by someone else."

Only when the English spoke of dismantling ruined Norman abbeys and shipping them across the Channel did the French rescue them from further neglect; only when a London museum bought the 's Hertogenbosch 17th-century rood-loft did the Dutch rally to defend their national legacy; only when Americans were about to export Tattershall Castle brick by brick did Britain in 1913 legislate to protect its built heritage. When J. P. Morgan bought a staircase from Burgos's Casa de Miranda, the outraged Spanish were told to be glad Americans had prodded them into heritage pride.[50] The Tower of London in 1836 casually disposed of two Hanoverian state crowns. Their whereabouts were long unknown, their very absence unremarked. But in 1995 widespread dismay greeted the news that this "purest national heritage of priceless importance" might be sold abroad. (A Brunei prince rescued the crowns for Britain.)

Sneers at a lack of heritage impel efforts to retrieve or re-create it. Voltaire's slur that "German is a language for horses and servants" spurred Herder's quest for "the ancient German soul" in tribal lore. Gibbon's taunt about debased Athenians "incapable of admiring the genius of their predecessors" kindled philhellene pride in the classical legacy. Lord Durham's dismissal of French Canadians as "a people with no history, and no literature" catalyzed Québécois militancy.[51]

England's heritage owes much to a student binge at historic Rousham, Oxfordshire, about 1930. Helplessly watching his drunken host take potshots at garden statuary and slash family portraits with a hunting crop roused in James Lees-Milne "some deep atavistic compassion for ancient architecture so vulnerable and transient, and some paternal instinct to protect and safeguard all tangible works of art." Thus inspired, he became the guiding spirit of the National Trust country-house crusade, limned in Chapter 3.[52]

Conservation efforts are commonly couched in terms of some national legacy at risk. Groombridge villagers decried the 1991 breakup of their estate as the loss of "part of the feudal system." Fending off animal-rights advocates, fox hunting is defended as a quintessential rural ritual. Pig fanciers note with alarm the decline of stewardship. "Once there was a strong link between the aristocracy and swine," snuffles *The Ark*, the farm breeders' bible, but by 1995 breeds were dying out for want of elite support. The aristocracy itself feels endangered: "We are now down to 25 breeding dukes," warned the Duke of Buccleigh in 1992. "At this rate we shall soon need our own rare breed society."

For living icons, extinction seems always imminent. In World Wildlife Fund appeals every species of bird is on the brink, every mammal all but doomed. So scarce was the bald eagle, America's national bird, that corporations launched a costly (and successful) 1980s drive to restock eaglets. To save shrinking rain forests, conservers cry havoc over acreage felled and species lost.

As developers ravage and robbers ransack prehistoric sites, the world's material legacy shrinks as fast as the rain forest. So does its cerebral patrimony. Nine-tenths of the world's six thousand existing languages are thought soon to succumb to global media forces. Such fears are not chimerical; many dwindling legacies do seem destined to die out. But as shown in Chapter 10, alarmism is part and parcel of the heritage mindset. Attrition is usually exaggerated. "Hurry. The bulldozers are coming. Historic buildings are falling. The best of our past is being sacrified," warned America's National Trust in 1970; similar pleas were common in 1870. Britons fear their patrimony is fast diminishing—yet theirs is perhaps the world's best protected national legacy. Distressed by the drain of treasures to Japan and the Getty, they forget the flux was ever thus. "Precious things are going out of our distracted country," agonized a Henry James grandee a century ago, "at a quicker rate" than they ever came in.[53]

Heritage loss and recovery are better understood as ongoing routine than as perilous plight. To expunge the obsolete and restore it as heritage are, like disease and its treatment, conjoined processes less discordant than symbiotic. When a nuclear accident destroys Britain, in David Ely's tale, a massive campaign restores the whole peopled island, "every stick and stone, every blade of grass, every hedge and bush, every mansion, palace, hut and hovel. . . . Insects, too, and even vermin. Everything." Restoration justifies destruction. "The vaporization of Britain was logically necessary to express the dual impulse of our age—vast devastation coupled with equally vast reconstruction." It brought manifold benefits: history learned, relics conserved, stewardship lauded, and global tensions abated. It might be useful "to vaporize and then restore one nation every generation. That would ease the population pressure and provide a harmless outlet for human energy both at the same time."[54]

The facts of history had presaged this fiction. The Nazis gutted Old Warsaw to obliterate an icon of Polish identity that postwar Poles speedily rebuilt as a symbol of communal care. The world's greatest technocrats combined a genius for annihilation with an instinct to preserve: the inventor of dynamite, long the globe's most destructive agency, is now best recalled for the Nobel Peace Prize; Henry Ford and John D. Rockefeller, whose juggernauts doomed older modes of life, became exemplary collectors and custodians of the heritage their oil and engines outdated, as Ford's Old Dearborn and Rockefeller's Colonial Williamsburg bear witness.

Heritage that affronts new orthodoxies is jettisoned in turn. The heroic Soviet statues recently blasted or carted away are just the latest victims of cycles of veneration and iconoclasm, chronic from the Hittites to Hitler. "Bolsheviks topple czar monuments, Stalin erases old Bolsheviks, Khrushchev tears down Stalin, Brezhnev tears down Khrushchev . . . no difference," says artist Vitaly Komar. "This is classic old Moscow technique: either worship or destroy. . . . Each time it is history, the country's true past, which is conveniently being obliterated. And usually by the same people!"[55]

Heritage also succumbs to those who love it to death. Devotees wear down old floors, abrade ancient stones, erode prehistoric trackways. Banning hobnail boots and stiletto heels merely retards inevitable decay.

Only withdrawal from use avails; as a town clerk said when asked to replace park benches, "benches will not wear out so fast if people do not sit on them." The more we learn of the ill effects of light, the less can old fabrics and watercolors be displayed. Since breath is lethal to the cave paintings, legacies like Lascaux are closed to public view; to see Leonardo's *Last Supper* visitors today must first be decontaminated.

To prevent heritage being ravished by admirers proves all but impossible. Eco-friendly tourism swamps the fragile sites it was designed to safeguard. To protect Galápagos tortoises and birds, an annual ceiling of twelve thousand visitors was set two decades ago; this "ultimate environmental experience" now disastrously lures five times that many. In Donald Hall's "Scenic View," each snapshot eats up scenery:

> Every year the mountains
> get paler and more distant—
> trees less green, rock piles
> disappearing—as emulsion
> from a billion Kodaks
> sucks color out.
> In fifteen years,
> Monadnock and Kearsarge,
> the Green Mountains
> and the White will turn
> invisible, all
> tint removed,
> atom by atom to albums
> in Medford and Greenwich,
> while over the valleys
> the still intractable granite
> rears with unseeable peaks
> fatal to airplanes.[56]

"The White Cliffs of Dover Experience" heritage center arises from the ruins of the legacy it celebrates. A 1995 superstore in Dorchester, England, is festooned with Edwardian views of the bustling city center the new shop signally destroyed.

The best intentions prove lethal; the more heritage is appreciated, the more it decays or turns to dross. Public concern boomerangs when structures denoted as historic are surrepticiously weakened or hastily torn down to avoid burdens of care. Ending military hostilities may actually heighten the risk to prized legacies. During Lebanon's civil war, Druze forces saved the 1500-year-old Cedars of Lebanon from being chopped down for firewood. Peace left them more precarious, at the mercy of tourists who trampled new shoots and took cuttings from the ancient trees.

Stonehenge, Britain's heritage archetype and a major global site, typifies such dilemmas. First a fearsome pagan relic, Stonehenge has been ascribed to Satan, to Phoenicians, and to Druids, among others. Demonized by the medieval Church, fount of Tudor sovereign claims, and icon of Welsh nationalism, Stonehenge has served (and suffered for) myriad purposes. Locals took stones for fencing and building and rented tools to visitors to chip off bits of sarsen—one antiquary grumbled at being "Obliged with a Hammer to labour hard three Quarters of an Hour to get but one Ounce and a half."[57]

National property since the First World War, Stonehenge is now shared by English Heritage (the stone circle) and the National Trust (the surrounding land). A decade's joint stewardship has spawned a self-confessed national disgrace. Safe from religious zealots, farmers, and souvenir hunters, Stonehenge now suffers ceaseless custodial folly. Access is through a dank concrete tunnel; barbed wire intermittently festoons the stones; car parks and lavatories, a cramped gift shop, and a dingy cafe's Sarsen Sandwiches degrade the ambience. "We've managed to separate the stones from their setting," English Heritage's chief seems to brag; "we've surrounded a great monument to the genius of the early British with the worst excesses of the 20th century."[58]

Cult groups and commercial pressure aggravate these woes. Stonehenge is sacred to modern Druids and hippies, celebrants at the solstice rituals since the 1950s. The few Druids posed little threat, but their dawn vigils lumped them with a motley crew of New Age cultists, commune nostalgists, ley-line mystics, and drug addicts. To farmers' mingled dismay and profit, thousands camped in nearby fields, got stoned and laid, and left behind condoms, needles, and excrement. To make Stonehenge seemly for paying tourists, its custodians in 1983 banned solstice visits and set Wiltshire police on would-be intruders. Over three summers convoys and encampments for miles around were broken up, heads smashed, hippies jailed.

Razor-wired, dog-patrolled, and arc-lit, Stonehenge was cleansed of riffraff by 1987. The sole solstice celebrants were police, who ensured no one else got in. Weirder than Druids, cops in spiked helmets stared up at their ceremonial helicopter, circling over the sarsens to spy out subversion. Meanwhile English Heritage pledged a purified Stonehenge as honeypot and sanctuary. But making it over from "national disgrace" to "eighth wonder of the world" fell foul of the Transport Ministry, Wiltshire county, archaeologists, the disabled, and six million in cars whom a proposed tunnel would deprive of prized views from the road.[59]

Barred from worshippers and bereft of magic, Stonehenge remains squalid and minatory, its splendors at once hawked and subverted by fearful custodians. But Stonehenge's woes are not unique; they reflect confusion over heritage goals and means common to many famous sites. Popularity equally degrades Mont-Saint-Michel. Bandits drawn by the antiquities market machine-gun their way into Angkor Wat, ill protected even when floodlit and wired like a concentration camp; tourists must evade land mines planted to halt plunder. Hyping Cycladic figurines led to looting thousands of graves and a flood of fakes from the Dodecanese. Florence's Uffizi Gallery and Roman sites were bombed by terrorists who, custodians wryly noted, seemed uniquely appreciative of Italy's heritage.

A million and a half ritual and cultural objects from five hundred American museums will go back to Indian tribes under the Native American Graves and Repatriation Act of 1991. Half of them will be reburied, exposed to the elements, or destroyed for purposes of purification, as happened with bones and grave goods repatriated to Australian Aborigines after 1984. Some argue that such returns will deprive indigenes' own better-educated (in other words, Westernized) descendants of an invaluable legacy. One archaeologist predicts that "Aboriginal people may come to acknowledge the good fortune that European collectors preserved fragments of their cultural heritage."[60]

Or they may continue to deplore preservation. Aborigines who have schooled themselves to accept loss remark that "white people don't know what to remember and what to forget, what to let go of and what to preserve." Unsure how to relate to their past, whites need to keep it all. An American curator recalls a meeting where anthropologists were arguing against reburial because knowledge might be lost:

Finally one Native American activist said, "Why do you white people need to know all this stuff? Why can't you just let it go?" Listening, I had such a visceral reaction of horror, I knew he had hit on something very sacred to *my* culture. The thought of deliberately letting knowledge perish was as sacrilegious to me as the thought of keeping one's ancestors on a museum shelf was sacrilegious to the Indians in the audience.[61]

Such disputes are now endemic. They can be resolved, I suggest in Chapter 10, only by understanding what heritage means to myriad claimants, whose desires differ with culture, time, and circumstance.

The past feels more accessible, more controversial, and more vulnerable than ever before. Heritage appetites outpace heritage growth. Awareness of its fragility endears what we inherit, but our very embrace dooms it; we kill what we love. Ever more popular, heritage becomes ever more perishable. When possession and stewardship are contested, as discussed in Chapter 10, risks to heritage are heightened.

What heritage means for us as individuals and as members of families, and how our personal concerns link with national and ethnic legacies, is shown in Chapters 2 and 3. How heritage needs reshape old and invent new pasts, spurning historical fact, occupies Chapters 4 through 7.

Chapter 2

PERSONAL LEGACIES

HERITAGE STARTS with what individuals inherit and bequeath. Along with the national legacy cited in Chapter 1, Heritage Canada offers an evocative personal inventory:

> Memories . . . old photographs . . . family words and tales . . . grandmother's old quilt . . . a locket with a picture of a long-forgotten aunt . . . smells that trigger past events . . . an old wedding dress . . . father's pocket watch . . . our ancestral cemetery . . . special holiday meals . . . treasured tea sets . . . a favourite teddy bear . . . a tree you climbed as a child . . . your dad's baseball mitt . . . a lullaby . . .

Lineal linkage justifies holding on to possessions; to keep all we gain may seem selfish, but to keep what we inherit is a family duty, binding us in a chain of caretakers. An heirloom is, as the word suggests, a device for interweaving generations. Nowadays heirlooms smack of things folkloric or outworn—Penelope's plaiting and unraveling, an obsolete tool, an ornament that was once an amulet. They may seem mere frills or encumbrances. Yet we continue to treasure and transmit things and thoughts handed down to us, tokens of times remembered and of lives linked with ours.

Material bequests are commonly likened to offspring. "I love them with a passion, and I want them to stay together after I'm gone," said Walter Annenberg of the Old Master paintings he gave New York's Metropolitan Museum in 1991, chiding would-be Japanese buyers for "asking me to sell members of my family." Selling a family portrait is censured as unfilial in a Henry James tale; "respectable people don't lop off the branches" of their family trees. Offspring themselves are our

31

most enduring legacies. "Houses rot, villages are moved, empires fall," in the customary view, "but the great faith is that the lineage . . . will endure forever."[1]

Memories embedded in heirlooms outlast their testators. "One tries to cure such possessions of their obsession with the past by giving them a new home, a new frame, a new coat of paint," writes Hugo Williams, but "they go on muttering their old owners' names." They remain "something which used to belong to my mother" until we too pass them on and they become, for our children, things that used to belong to us.[2] Stewardship rewards those who inherit and those who bequeath.

We bequeath and inherit more than goods. Personal legacies of love and duty remain crucial to being born, growing up, parenting, and aging. And the fundaments of collective heritage derive from family affections, habits, and obligations. This chapter reviews what legatees and legators seek from each other, why legacy aims change, and how personal bequests link—or conflict—with public endowment.

THE BLESSINGS OF INHERITANCE

In the narrow legal sense, we normally inherit on the death of parents or other kin. But their bequests are only a fraction of a larger legacy of teachings, precepts, and habits drummed into or emulated by us since infancy. These hopes, fears, and customs reach us throughout life. They come not only from progenitors but from myriad mentors and models.

When Isaac denied Esau the birthright due him as firstborn son, loss of the blessing was more grievous than that of lands and chattels. The main worth of what we inherit is social or psychic. The heir in Compton-Burnett's *A Heritage and Its History* looks forward not to wealth or grandeur but only to his rightful place in the family lineage. "Family land" in the West Indies today, as in medieval England, seldom sustains a livelihood; it is a locus of communal comfort whose fruits all kinsfolk are entitled to harvest, a potential refuge for any descendant. "My grandfather said the land should not be sold," says a Jamaican of the symbolic acre bought when slavery ended. "It is for his heritage going down. It must go from children to grandchildren, right down the line."[3]

One need not be royal to reap riches from a legacy handed down.

Continuity enhances all manner of inherited careers. It was long common to pass on family callings by apprenticeship. Skills transmitted from parents to children bound rural clothworkers in early industrial England in a trans-generation trust.[4] Inheriting vocations remains routine in many societies; in Tasmania and Trinidad I have heard men boast of being sixth or seventh in a line of island doctors or lawyers or farmers.

Rugged individualists take pride in owing nothing to family or society, habit or tradition. But we are all in debt to legacies. "Whether I like it or not, whether I recognize it or not," in a philosopher's words, "what I am is in key part what I inherit." That no one is self-made is the moral of Karen Fields's mastery of her new bicycle after being taught by her grandfather:[5]

> The day I got the knack, I ran yelling into the house, "I DID it! I did it ALL BY MYSELF." Spoken like a true American, but the sentiment did not suit him: in Dixie nobody got by as an isolated individual, "all by myself" . . . It was sure very nice that I could ride now. But listen here, didn't my uncle Al hold me up sometimes? . . . And wasn't it my parents who bought the training wheels? Yes. Didn't other children try to show me what to do? Uh huh. So why did I want to say, now, "all by myself"?

Chattels and clothing, books and bibelots benefit heirs beyond their ongoing use. More than mementos in attic and album, they connect us with childhood, mend missing linkages, revivify bygone life. The bric-à-brac atop the poet Seamus Heaney's dresser is "not just inert rubbish but dormant energies"; a previous era "was vestigially alive in them, [bringing] you out of yourself and close to yourself all at once." In her living room an elderly Norwegian finds that "every single thing has its history, its memories," bridging her with those gone. "When I look at my things, I talk to the people I associate them with."[6] The links lengthen and strengthen identity.

Lineages of master and apprentice, teacher and pupil, transmit legacies of skill and insight. Violinists trace mentors back to Mozart, analysts their own analysts back to Freud. "The farther back you went, the more exalted it became," recalls a pianist of 1930s Vienna. "You could trace yourself through Liszt all the way to Beethoven."[7]

Such pedagogic precursors may deservedly be more cherished than genetic forebears; a child's true parent, in John Locke's definition, is not the one who brings it into the world but the one who forms its mind. Locke's precept held special appeal for Americans, who revered the childless Washington as the Father of His Country. Having severed their bonds with autocratic English monarchs, they made patriarchs of New World pioneers, revering the Plymouth colonists not just as Pilgrims but as Pilgrim *Fathers*.[8]

Yet familial roots remain our most essential legacy. "To understand the learning of your ancestors," exhort Maori elders, you must "learn to trace your descent lines to all your ancestors."[9] As shown in the previous chapter, recovering forebears has special urgency for folk brutally sundered from their past—descendants of slaves, Aboriginal victims, Holocaust survivors. A huge hunger for roots fueled Alex Haley's legendary search for his African antecedents.

It is noteworthy that black Americans, deprived by bondage of ancestral annals, inaugurated popular quests since diffused the world over. Tracing African progenitors supplied a self-respect long denied by servitude. Hence heritage pride in Africans as "biologically, genetically, and historically the mother and father of all the disciplines, all the sciences," became crucial to much black self-esteem. History is typically hyped to justify grandiloquent legacy claims: unlike the flotsam and jetsam from Europe, conjectures a black historian, many enslaved Africans were aristocrats, America's "only royal immigrants. By now a majority of black Americans may have the blue blood of African royalty and aristocracy in their veins."[10]

Rooted elites likewise magnify mythic forebears. American Mayflower Descendants trace ancestral roots "to establish a unique and respectable personality." Finding "a long line of ancestors who were deeply religious, honorable, brave and desirable" thrills one woman sure she had "inherited similar worthy and noble traits." Mayflower boasts are blatant: "I never hesitate to brag about my ancestors," they aver; "the heritage I have makes me feel strong in crises." Though ignorant of any specifics about her adulated forebears, one Descendant proudly passes their legacy on to her children as a token of "the continuity and hence stability of our nation."[11] The family legacy betokens faith in the national heritage, its worthiness a mythic affirmation of American history.

FINDING PARENTS, KEEPING CHILDREN

Knowing our own antecedents is for many the most crucial legacy. The common focus of parentage is intensely genetic; the orphan's search for true parents is a central childhood myth. Adoptees are pitied as amputees, condemned to search forever for their lost selves. "There's a hole inside me that only this guy who made me can fill," says an American boy of his missing father. Known genesis is held crucial for self-knowledge. "To feel that I'm *authentic*," says a 28-year-old in search of birth parents, "I need to be like every other human being who knows where he came from and where he belongs." A young girl wants "to see my birth mother, so I'll know what I'll look like when I get older." Any detail helps. "You *know* something," exults a woman who finds her father had been exactly six feet one, "I could go home, mark a spot on the wall, and proclaim a victory. There, there is my *father*."

Ancestral data may be literally crucial. Finding natural parents can truly save one's life; those ignorant of family ills may succumb to hereditary ills. Dread of a hidden genetic defect stops some adoptees from becoming parents. "It's one thing to be a second-class citizen oneself," says a woman, "quite another to condemn one's children to no information or heritage." Some feel sullied by the very fact of abandonment, others that it would make them bad parents. "I would be a terrible mother; . . . a child who has no mother can mother no child."[12] Like carriers of genetic defects, many Nazi offspring shunned passing on bad seed. "I must not have any children," said an "incurably tainted" young German. "This line must come to an end with me. . . . I lived with my parents too long, who knows what evil I carry within me? It mustn't be handed down." Family legacy is often assessed as inescapable fate.

Loving adoptive parents do not annul needs for lineage links. "There was always this dark shadow behind my happy childhood; where did I come from? Who were my parents? Why didn't they want me?" Tracing them gave their daughter "a deep sense of security." Finding her mother after a fifteen-year probe made another adoptee "a lot happier now I know where I came from. I used to feel I came from the moon."[13]

Today's heritage goals validate such quests. "All people who walk the face of the earth," declares a family therapist, "possess the inalienable right to know their history and to meet the man and woman from whom they drew breath."[14] While fewer than half actively seek natural parents, most adoptees engage in a psychic search for roots, some from childhood, many when forming their own families. As stigma of race and illegitimacy dwindle, so do constraints on finding genetic parents. Sources of donor insemination are still withheld lest genetic fathers be dunned for child support or "birth" fathers be shamed as infertile. But even this is apt to yield to offspring who demand to know their "roots"—roots apt to be automatically equated with biological lineage.

Parental flaws seldom negate these benefits. Realizing that her belatedly revealed father, the philosopher A. J. Ayer, was a selfish egoist did not detract from his daughter thereby becoming more securely herself. Germaine Greer's hunt for her father brought both grief and gratitude; unearthing his unending deceptions augmented Greer's insight into her childhood.[15] The bleakest newfound family link may become a solace, as with American drifter pals who proved to be father and son. Abandoned when three, John Earl found his dad by a fluke in an Illinois homeless mission seventeen years later in 1992. At first John wanted to punish his father: "I liked you better before I knew you were my dad." But they then rebuilt their relationship. "Parents may make mistakes," says the son, "but there's always a chance for renewal."

Some lost legacies impel lifelong search for a potent buried secret; others surface abruptly, as with Oedipus, during some rite of passage. A friend of mine long out of touch with his father felt humiliated when his mother died and he could not certify if she was or was not a widow. Chagrin provoked a hunt for the facts; he found his father had died a few years before. Elated by his act of retrieval, he went on to trace earlier forebears through parish records. Locating great-grandparents, he himself palpably changed. Each discovery filled him out, augmented his stature. Regaining an ancestral legacy enlarged his sense of himself. Triggered by traumas of loss and grief, such searches often encourage the amateur genealogist to feel in possession of an identity, "knowing exactly who I am and where I came from."[16]

Another English friend of half-Jamaican parentage knew almost nothing of her Caribbean roots and never saw Jamaica until she was fifty. "Having 'passed for white' over many years," she later wrote, she felt "a compulsion to explore my Jamaican identity and discover my extended family, as a pilgrimage that needed to be done at some point in my life." A two-week research visit to Jamaica gained her a clutch of cousins, firsthand memories of a fabled grandfather, a whole, richly textured family milieu. Finding "lost" forebears and kinsfolk earned her amplitude, confidence, and status vis-à-vis her English family and colleagues.[17]

Even an unsought or long-rejected ancestry can in the end fructify a heritage. Uprooted from and taught to disdain tribal ways, Sally Morgan's mixed-race grandmother and mother lived in semiseclusion lest their ancestry shame their "white" offspring. Only when Sally coaxed them into vivid remembrance did the older women reembrace their Aboriginal legacy. Another child of mixed parentage, made a state ward at the age of four and imbued with white values, was returned to her Aboriginal community five years later. "The train pulled up and I was lookin' for a white grandmother and grandfather," she recalled, "and the next minute I saw these old black arms stretched out to me, and I said, 'I'm not goin' with them.' I was frightened of them blacks 'cause it was the first time I had ever seen blackfellers." But among loving kin the 9-year-old soon came to cherish her Aboriginal origins.[18]

Not all retrievals work; many memoirists resent being returned to incompatible kin. Horrific predicaments confront children of Argentine "disappeareds," adopted and raised by the very men who tortured and killed their parents. In the last few years genetic markers have revealed kinship links. Bent on reclaiming their "disappeared" children's offspring, the "Grandmothers of the Plaza de Mayo" have won suits to reunite fifty grandchildren with their "real" heritage. "The captors think they own these children, and they say they love them," says a Plaza de Mayo advocate. "You can't love a child who you robbed and are still lying to about who they are." But the shock of learning that "two people they have called Mommy and Daddy all their lives are not really Mommy and Daddy—in fact they killed Mommy and Daddy"— traumatized adolescents who balked at quitting the only families they knew to rejoin unknown and vengeful grandparents in alien milieus.[19] The claims of lineage here are natural and virtuous, but invoking that legacy is calamitous.

Compared with child raising, the effort of propagation is brief: a few minutes of coupling, a few months of gestation, a few hours of labor. More arduous and more bonding are the tasks of imparting family and group heritage over many years of childhood. As life spans lengthen long past child rearing, handing on skills and customs beyond the realm of immediate kin occupies us more and more.[20]

Yet giving birth is still our overriding urge. In times past, having many children signaled power, prosperity, and fealty; some still view off-spring as a group resource, a communal legacy. Even where they are more burden than benefit, children are still craved. Some who yield to such yearning are at a loss to explain it. When a fertility doctor in Virginia who had impregnated scores, if not hundreds, of women with his own sperm was asked why he had done it, all he said was "I know I'm healthy." Not even the risk of incest fazed this proudly unrepentant propagator.

Adoption advocate Elizabeth Bartholet dismisses this urge as futile. "Not much is gained by leaving a genetic legacy. You do not in fact live on just because your egg or sperm has contributed to another life." But Bartholet herself cites the stockpiling of sperm, donor eggs, and em-bryos as marks of procreative zeal.[21] Some today bequeath fortunes to children to be hatched from their embryos in the distant future.

Eagerness to pass on genes peaks when risk to life is imminent, as eve-of-battle pregnancies attest. To sire posthumous children strikes some as selfish and irresponsible, but the practice gains public accep-tance; Gulf War combatants and death-row prisoners in America froze sperm to perpetuate their lineage and console widows and grandpar-ents. To inherit sperm and eggs is seen more and more as a conjugal right, a compensation for untimely widowhood.

A writer wonders why hospital mix-ups of newborn babies are so traumatic:

> Does it really matter which baby you take home? We feel that it does; throughout history there's been little difference that mattered more. [But] *why* does it matter that this is the child of my loins, rather than somebody else's? Why would my attitude to the child change if I knew this particular configuration of cells wasn't "mine"?[22]

One reason is paternal vainglory: impregnation is equated with man-hood and fatherhood. A man fails to bond with an adopted son because the son "was not of his bloodline; . . . he wanted me to be a miniature of him." Our own loins, we assume, yield the sweetest fruit. But there is nothing innate about such a tie; as anthropologists have shown, fatherhood in every society is socially defined, and basing fatherhood on biological links may be of no import or rejected as spurious.[23]

For mothers, biology is less deniable. Pregnancy and parturition tend to bond women with offspring, who may store fetal memories. From girlhood on, many envisage their future babies, and after giving birth they dote on recognizable features. Family legacies best resonate through a lineage, a child's look or temper held to resemble this or that forebear. The babies frantically sought at IVF (in vitro fertilization) clinics are genetic offspring of at least one parent. As with yeast saved to bake new bread, suggests Jerome Bruner, "you need a piece of the past to make the present."[24] Such homilies support the embedded view that legacies are biological in essence. Claims that inheritance is inborn and innate mirror the organic mystique of collective heritage (see Chapter 3) and widespread endorsement of racial and genetic determinism (Chapter 9).

DISPUTED AND UNWELCOME LEGACIES

We are owed our just deserts, including parental inheritance as a matter of right. Yet many are incensed to get less patrimony than they feel they deserve, so legacies are in chronic dispute. Disgruntled heirs make bequests a byword for discord. They see their inheritance frittered away by undue liberality to a second family or some megalomaniac cause, or too lavish a lifestyle. The father in Fleetwood's *Relative Duties* (1705), who consumes his heirs' whole estate in "Gaming, Drinking, Riot, Luxury, and sinful Pleasures,"[25] has modern counterparts in the heiress Pamela Harriman and building magnate Peter Palumbo. How on earth, wondered Lord Palumbo's older children in 1994, did he spend two millions of their trust fund on *wine*—bathing in it, perhaps?

No longer are legacy squabbles confined to the rich or the landed. Families that once had "nothing but granny's silver-boat to bicker about" now have the same problems as the old elite, notes a journalist: "dilemmas about death duties, gifts, and the rival claims of ageing children, second spouses, and illegitimate offspring." The most equitable will provokes litigious envy, the most trifling heirlooms incite lasting animus; baubles bequeathed to others become jewels. A six-year feud over model locomotives took two sons to the High Court in 1992. "My half-brother has always had everything," recalled one. "I was jealous of his electric train when I was ten, and I'm bloody furious about the will now." Rivals since Horace's *Satires* have accused one another of flaunting false pedigrees, filching the affections or addling the wits of senile legators, or being ingrates apt to defame or dissipate the legacy.

Inheritance can impoverish as well as enrich heirs. Like the bankrupt sons of Robert Maxwell, many endure unwanted legacies—the "damnable heritage" of Roman bequests whose debts exceeded their assets. Entire societies can be crippled by forebears' unwise undertakings. Tobacco growers' debts in colonial Virginia, regretted Thomas Jefferson, "had become hereditary from father to son for many generations."[26] Needy heirs, compelled to husband family mansions in terminal decay and mortgaged to the hilt, today typify the plight of onerous inheritance. Stewards of family legacies find that living among ancestral echoes paralyzes present action.

Lois Roget, heir to a seventh-generation Canadian farmhouse crammed with family memorabilia, is a case in point. She feels it her curatorial duty to protect, display, and hand on this legacy intact, eschewing new furnishings that would not blend in. At family gatherings she hands around objects from ancestral childhoods, hoping to bind her grandchildren to the same stewardship. But her offspring resist caretaking that would constrain them beyond their mother's lifetime. Like the heirs in Hawthorne's *House of the Seven Gables*, they prefer to forgo inherited goods and begin anew with a blank slate in places unburdened by history.[27]

Dubious legacies abound. A writer is glad not to inherit "half-moroccoed rubbish I shall never read" or a rosewood spinet he cannot play. Nor is he stuck with "this grandfather's gigantic bureau bookcase, or that aunt's vast and melancholy study of cart-horses approaching Utrecht." Breton youngsters in the 1920s came to rue the khaki uniforms their fathers and uncles had brought back from lice-infested trenches; strutting about in army castoffs, they inherited the lice as well. Job hunters in Paris felt their Breton tongue a stigma of poverty and ignorance, all but "cursing their parents" for a patrimony "more deplorable than a hereditary physical disability."[28]

Inherent handicaps are notorious among inbred elites, from the fava-bean madness of the pharaohs to the hemophilia of the Romanovs. The gout of Dickens' Sir Leicester Dedlock had "come down, through the illustrious line, like the plate, or the pictures, or the place in Lincolnshire." Today's Dedlocks are less smugly content. With their estates, the Earls of Bristol accrue by heredity or example two centuries of cruelty, vanity, debauchery, and drug addiction. Heirs of Admiral Byng, court-martialed for losing Minorca in 1756, feel so haunted by his legacy of cowardice that they are regularly driven to acts of foolhardy courage. Nightmares about weaknesses transmitted from convict ancestors led Australians well into the 1970s to prove fitness through fortitude, even self-sacrifice, in sports and warfare.[29]

Medicine cannot cure nor miracles rid us of most unwanted legacies. In vain do we rue the dark skins, long noses, or bandy legs, the propensity to obesity or heart disease left us by progenitors. Nor can humanity as a whole quicken the glacial pace of mutation that lumbers us with Pleistocene-model, fat-craving bodies.

Quite to the contrary, demographic trends make parental legacies ever more onerous. Old age lengthened by medical science encumbers dwindling numbers of active earners and caregivers. "Have you no children to help look after you?" a 95-year-old acquaintance was asked at her nursing home. "Well, I have these two boys, but I think they're both senile." No sooner are their children grown than the middle-aged are saddled with the care of elderly parents. The ratio of those over 85 to the middle-aged has tripled since 1950 and will triple again by 2050. One hears grim forecasts of 120-year-olds looked after by 90-year-old children. The senescent prospect makes one envy the Eskimo, reputed to deposit granny on an ice floe before she is decrepit to ensure that she gets reborn in good shape in the next world.

Expectant heirs may fret at parental endurance like Dickens' Jonas Chuzzlewit, who impatiently viewed "his parent as a certain amount of personal estate, which had no right whatever to be going at large, but ought to be secured in . . . a coffin, and banked in the grave."[30] Longevity irks heirs as geriatric care erodes legacies. That testators live so long shifts the sense of what is due to whom. "We respect old grandmothers," runs the old German adage, "but we hope they'll die soon and leave us a rich and unencumbered legacy." Some are callously prodded to do so. "One old couple," recounts a will-making lawyer, "had clearly been brought into my office with the aid of levers and goads."[31]

Belated legacies are also less useful to offspring who are no longer young. Eight of ten adults in a 1994 British survey "really don't want to inherit anything." They prefer current release from arduous care to nest-egg promises. "I want my inheritance *now*," said one woman. She wished her mother would spend it on a cleaner "so I don't feel obliged to go round after work and help her wash the kitchen floor."

To disown a heritage is commonly held to be indecent, but heirs may find it unavoidable. When Alex Haley's estate was auctioned off in 1992, the dispersal of his literary legacy dismayed African-American scholars. But only thus, as he explained, could Haley's brother and executor settle all the debts, "rid himself of Alex's world, and move on with his own life."

Heirs may well look askance at testaments designed to keep them dependent on parental goodwill and jockeying for favor. As in Montaigne's day, donors "exploit their wills as sticks and carrots to punish or reward every little action of those who may claim an interest in the inheritance." Aged or infirm legators often delay or encumber legacies to exact attentive care while still alive; such demands often outweigh the benefits of inheritance. Some refuse legacies to avoid the "grisly blackmail [of] time spent with people you don't like in the greedy hope of one day getting your hands on artefacts you do." Others forfeit claims by defying testators' provisos about whom to marry, where to live, what faith to practice, or having to cosset the cats.[32]

Heirs regret inheriting for other reasons, too. Some are crippled by self-doubt: could they ever have made it on their own? Others are wearied by the weight or soured by the habit of long stewardship; still others fear being imprisoned by outworn expectations. A heritage of family fame is of dubious worth, above all when it is commandeered by outsiders. Offspring resent sharing a legacy with acolytes and followers or feel betrayed when their childhood becomes public property. "My father had got to where he was by climbing upon my infant shoulders," concluded A. A. Milne's son Christopher; "he had filched from me my good name and left me with nothing but the empty fame of being his son." And because they belonged to all the world, his father's famous tales left Christopher unsure whether he had any legacy of his own.[33]

Like Christopher, as later chapters will show, heirs to collective legacies often feel cheated by rival claimants, lack security as stewards, and
are driven to disown legators and refashion their bequests after their
own fancy.

LEGATEES AND LEGATORS

How we deal with our inheritance changes as we grow up. At first we
follow parents' footsteps and yearn to match their feats, but soon we
are torn between submission and selfhood, reverence and rebellion.
While youngsters copy parents as a matter of course, adolescents reject
them as stigmas of dependency. Even in maturity we never wholly outgrow the need to slough off things and thoughts made by others and
hence beyond our control. To banish such burdens, some scant parental
influence, others renounce it.

Only in midlife do we begin to see that we willy-nilly recapitulate
our parents. "At sixteen, you still think you can escape from your father," in Salman Rushdie's phrase; "you aren't [yet] listening to his voice
speaking through your mouth, you don't see how your gestures already
mirror his." Later, you "hear his whisper in your blood." Taking parents'
places as we age shows how they survive within us. Instead of his father's
selfhood having "vanished into the grave with him," a memoirist "had
incorporated and re-created" it.[34]

That we cannot attain our legacy without killing the legator is the
common Oedipal quandary. "I did not want to hate my father," writes
a psychoanalyst's son; "yet, by failing to hate him, I should repudiate his
creed." Succession always includes a legacy of loss. "Each place is hereditary, and it can be held only by the death of the forerunner," in the ancient Chinese perspective. The inheritor is forced to recognize himself
also as usurper.[35]

Strategies for surviving parental legacies differ. "One way is to ignore them, another way is elegy," notes a scholar; a third is to make
them "elements in a discourse . . . they could not have foreseen." Being
born after our ancestors, we know more than they did, to paraphrase T.
S. Eliot; and perhaps the most important thing we know is them. Since
"we understand them better than they did themselves," loving acquaintance with forebears might, surmised Olaf Stapledon, become "our

supreme act of filial piety." But it cannot cancel the war of legator and legatee, a battle perennially renewed that leaves its scar on each new generation's heritage.[36]

Leaving what we have to others is innate to mortal life. "There is a time to be born, and a time to die," Ecclesiastes (3:2, 6) reminds us, "a time to keep, and a time to cast away." Yet casting away is sorrow as well as solace. We are loath to give up what cost much to create or acquire, is long enmeshed with our lives, and may requite mortality. It is hard to slough off even the outworn. Before being bundled off to the Salvation Army, old clothes may have to be divested of personal bonds by being boxed away for a year or two in closet or cellar.[37] Reluctance to part with accumulated clutter often encumbers heirs and executors for months, years, even decades.

One of the hardest possessions to part with is our own children, who are parental property emotionally if not economically. Children in medieval and early-modern Europe were explicitly owned, and often hired out or sold, by fathers who held authority even over grown offspring. Children owed manifold debts to parents, but parents few to children beyond ensuring rites of passage such as baptism.[38] Needy parents in many lands still sell children into slavery and prostitution.

Many words for children denoted inferiors, just as slaves, servants, and subject peoples were called "boy" or "girl." Even those who hated slavery approved of parental possession; for the abolitionist Harriet Beecher Stowe, slaveholding stood in iniquitous contrast with fathers' moral right to "own" their children. Like slaveowners, family autocrats enjoyed control over offspring wholly at their mercy: Louis XIV favored his bastard sons, whose obedience could be relied upon *because* they were illegitimate.[39]

One mode of treating children as property was the medieval practice of oblation, turning them into holy gifts. It became customary to endow monastic orders with offspring whom parents could not or chose not to rear themselves. While some came with dowries or bequests for upkeep, many were cast on the cloister like unwanted kittens. Bequeathing children under the guise of piety was often frankly self-serving, like a son given to the Benedictines "so that he may implore the mercy of God for me and his mother and all his relatives."[40]

Children are now apt to be cherished to realize parental ambitions or reap the fruits of their efforts—looked to, often urged, to fulfill parental dreams. In the Dickens novel, Dombey's son, "the little image by inheritance," is his father's alter ego. "Wind up a son," writes John Fuller, "and watch him act out the elusive perfection of your own muddled career! Light candles before the image of your daughter, and love itself might be restored to its first purity!" Children become surrogates for national as for family goals.[41] Asked why so many fine Americans sacrificed their talents to politics, John Adams famously replied, "We devote ourselves to government so that our sons may become scientists and their sons poets."

By contrast, other parents withhold material legacies in their children's supposed moral interest. Anxiety about the ill effects of inherited wealth persuades some to delay or to cancel bequests. A self-made pioneer "wants my children to start from nothing, the way we did." Hardship and toil may be the best legacy: "I'd rather have my grandsons see what I saw and feel what I felt in the conquest of these prairies, than to get up by their radiators, step into their baths, whirl themselves away in their cars, and go to their universities." A rich father explains, "Everything I have, son, I have because your grandfather left it to me. I see now that that was a bad thing."[42] As in most dynasties, Dad remains the boss. A man may clutch his son and say: "Some day all this will be yours," but he will be obliged to add, if he is honest, "But for the time being, it's mine."

Solicitude lest heirs have things too easy may mask envy. "We are jealous of seeing [our children] cut a figure in this world, able to enjoy it just when we are on the point of leaving it," noted Montaigne. "This makes us miserly and close-fisted towards them: it irritates us that they should come treading on our heels, as if to summon us to take our leave." Reluctance to bequeath may betoken resentment of heirs whose mere existence presages our own death. A popular 18th-century play depicts a father who "so hated posterity" that he "wished the world were to expire with himself."[43]

Progeny of the mind, the "lovelier and less mortal" creations of Plato's *Symposium*, please some parents better than genetic offspring. Lovers of poetry should be "more gratified at fathering the Aeneid than the fairest boy in Rome," thought Montaigne, who would "much rather have given birth to one perfectly formed son by commerce with the Muses than by commerce with my wife." Products of "a part more noble than the body and more purely our own," the offspring of "our wisdom and our talents" are more apt to exalt their begetters than are the fruit of their loins, who often disappoint parental goals.[44]

Whether parents prefer flesh-and-blood children or progeny of the mind, however, most legators seek to convert their own goods, deeds, and memories into durable legacies.

EMBLEMS OF ENDURANCE: SALVATION, DYNASTY, FAME

Bequests are as manifold in their aims as their forms. To endow is to care about what outlasts us; as death nears, many strive to leave something that will survive them. Some seek salvation in the hereafter, others to speed its advent, like the £276,000 recently willed to Christ in anticipation of the Second Coming. Many aspire to immortality in arts or acts; it was wise to "use your life to acquire eternal glory," Petrarch exhorted Charles of Bohemia.[45] Others enjoin commemoration, like the 1852 benefaction in Edington, Wiltshire, allotting one shilling and sixpence "to the sexton if he shall keep free from dust & dirt the Monuments of George Tayler & members of his Family."

Legators' goals reflect their cultures and circumstances. Memorial inscriptions and statues obsessed imperial Romans; ascetic medieval testators renounced worldly goods and goals, ended life in mendicant seclusion, and bade heirs pray for their souls' repose. From early medieval times the Church aggrandized its holdings by exhorting renunciation; better that children suffer in this world than parents be damned in the next. Clerical curbs on marriage and remarriage, adoption, and entail made it harder to keep family property. Lack of legal secular heirs and fear of eternal damnation enlarged Church holdings by the late Middle Ages to a quarter or more of landed wealth, often surpassing lay rulers.[46]

Reversing this trend, the Reformation enriched secular legatees at sacred expense. Individualism promoted desires for earthly remembrance along with heavenly salvation. Renaissance worthies attached their names to benefactions and memorials, had their likenesses limned by renowned artists, and entailed estates to lineal descendants. To gain immortal fame and glory or to secure property or ancestry, they spared no expense to be long remembered.

To ensure their estates remained intact, testators in some lands restricted landed property to just one heir. Many English estates were entailed entirely to eldest sons, their siblings often signally deprived. Only the English were said to "tolerate the dominion of a bygone generation over the greater part of the national soil,"[47] but much of Europe subordinated personal ambition to family and communal aims.

Bequests in wills cited by Samuel Cohn from Renaissance Italy combined these aims—aiding prospects of salvation, exalting earthly fame, and sheltering lineage. Symoneus of Arezzo's donation bound Dominican friars to pray for him, his relatives, business associates, servants, and benefactors. All but two of Signoria of Pisa's 148 bequests celebrated his own life. Many commissioned altarpieces and church ornaments in their name or affixed family regalia and coats of arms to gifts of schools, hospitals, and fountains. A Florentine testator required the nunnery he endowed to accept without further dowry any girl of his lineage.

Legators disinherited any who failed to perpetuate their names. Unless a cobbler's property was kept within his lineage "until the infinite degree," it would pass to Florentine hospitals. Landucius of Arezzo insisted his house, with his coat of arms visible from the street, "stand in perpetual memory of the testator and his ancestors"; were it sold, his family would forfeit the proceeds to the Misericordia.[48]

Such bequests often proved vexedly at odds. Unlike otherworldly testators unconcerned about securing their memory or enriching descendants, most now craved worldly fame or sought to benefit their successors. Juggling self-glory against the welfare of offspring, many made wills mainly to perpetuate their own power. Many still do so. Just as Montaigne mocked French grandees who "foresee a ridiculous eternity for our family name," so American courts centuries later banned far-reaching entails to prevent any legator from "trying to rule the world," in an estate lawyer's words, "by perpetuating his ego as far down his tree as he can get it."[49]

Abiding self-memory today seems most legators' prime aim—a penchant for eternal fame mocked in Amanda Filipacchi's popular performer whose fortune goes for rotas of claques to stand by her grave, applauding her forever. "We all like to be remembered—by a new species, by the next generation, even by ourselves," says an ad for personal time capsules; we "bury our past and hope that others will dig it up in years to come." Bequests to museums and colleges aim to enshrine donors in posthumous permanence, often like Annenberg demanding the collection be kept together in perpetuity.[50] Few may match Samuel Lefrak's faith that his $10 million gift to New York's Guggenheim Museum was "a passport to Heaven." But a cult of named professorships now augments Athena's lure of eternity; faculty members are barely visible in the penumbra of generous patrons, like "Dr. John Doe, Hermione & Herman Higginbotham Memorial Professor of Hotel Studies." That "Hermione" shares center stage as legator reflects another shift—the rising recognition of women's heritage role.

GENDER

Heritage is traditionally a man's world, inheritance largely a matter of fathers and sons. "Everyone loves his own country's manners and languages [just as] he does his wife and children," intoned Herder two centuries ago, "not because they are the best in the world but because they are absolutely his own." No less sexist was the American psychologist William James: "A man's Self is the sum total of all that he can call his own, not only his body and his psychic powers, but his wife and his children, his ancestors and his friends, his reputation and works, his clothes and his house, his lands and horse and yacht and bank–account."[51] That women are part of heritage, not sharers in it, is still a common view.

Male chauvinism is by no means confined to the West; it is flagrant in India and above all in China, where sons alone worship ancestors, inherit property, and (in theory) support parents. Chinese female abortion and infanticide are rife, girls often given numbers, not names, at birth as tokens of their precarious hold on life.

Gender inequality is embedded in the very language of inheritance. It is "patrimony," never "matrimony," that we get as persons and nations. Traditionally only men have birthrights, only men inherit, only men acquire the wealth and power that accompany heritage. Men alone also inherit the anxiety of patrimonial displacement, the classical urge to kill their fathers. The 19th-century term "governor" (colloquially "guv'nor"), used only by sons, hinted at paternal authority subverted and to be supplanted.

Women are not simply excluded from men's heritage: they belong to it. Like the rest of a man's estate, women are chattels, property, things; in many cultures married women must take their husbands' names but are entitled to little if any of their property. In English law until 1870 married women could own or bequeath nothing save personal paraphernalia (literally, things that came with their dowries); husband and wife were one person, and that person was the husband. Growing animus against women as landowners whittled away the old common law that entitled widows to a third of their husbands' property; by the 18th century, acts of settlement all but ended women's formal role in transmitting landed estates. "An ancient estate should always go to a male," as Samuel Johnson put it. "It is mighty foolish to let a stranger have it because he married your daughter."[52]

Wives did have one vital role: they were the *carriers* of heritage, bearing and birthing the men who succeeded to it. The right to women's reproductive capacity, expressed in the Roman *jus genitricum*, was legitimized in the practice of husbandry—in the blunt phrase of the Prophet, "Your wives are your furrows."[53] Patriarchal transmission of a man's name through his sons (never daughters) and women's happiness in "giving" their husbands sons still suffuse many societies.

Among matrilineal groups, to be sure, women figure prominently as progenitors and legators. Trobriand Islanders, in Malinowski's classic depiction, denied males any role in engendering; a child's father was simply the mother's husband. The *couvade*, in which men enact a ritual of childbearing, affirms paternity and gives fathers a social equivalent of motherhood. But inheritance in most societies, traditional and modern, has been patrilineal. Biblical texts made men procreators, women profane vessels for sacred male legacies. Early Christian annals show sons inheriting flesh and blood, habits and skills, names, powers, blessings, and even souls from fathers alone. Lineage traced back to fore*fathers*; only males emerge from the Tree (or body) of Jesse. Not until the 17th century was women's procreative (as distinct from gestational) role even acknowledged in the West.[54]

Surnames, diffusing throughout Europe from the 15th century, reified male lineage; save in Iceland, children inherited fathers' names, and wives adopted those of husbands. Gender parity is still rare, with nominal use of the mother's lineage a mainly Hispanic exception. Elsewhere only a handful of feminists keep natal names and bestow them on daughters, though this usage is growing among professional elites.

In male-centered societies certified paternity was vital; a man dowered with his wife's property had to ensure that her children were also his. But such assurance meant either blind faith or chained wives. Whether to attest Jewishness or slave status, maternity customarily mattered more than paternity. Only motherhood, verified by witnesses at childbirth, offered sure proof of lineage; paternal doubts are ingrained in popular imagery from Shylock to Lloyd George.

In Freud's view, the very uncertainty of fatherhood lent it prestige. He saw the shift from matriarchy to patriarchy as a victory of intelligence over sensuality, "since maternity is proved by the evidence of the senses while paternity is [only] a hypothesis." Yet the dubiety of fatherhood resurfaces in the Oedipus complex, the son's yearning to replace the "false" father. Supposed fathers are still termed "putative genitors." Asked which parent's race a child should declare, the U.S. Census Bureau ruled the mother's, for "we always know who the mother is and not always the father."[55]

Differing heritage concerns reflect the gender disparity. The mother–child bond has no innate parallel for fathers, who are lamed by "genealogical uncertainty." Hence in their bequests men are more apt to dwell on fame, women on family. "My wife has her children," a modern physician echoes Montaigne, "but I need something tangible— like my name in the medical literature." Virginia Woolf expressed envy of her sister Vanessa's talent as a painter; inasmuch "as you have the children, the fame by rights belongs to me." As makers of babies rather than works of art, argues Simone de Beauvoir, women have less to show for their labors, since people are perishable while creative masterpieces are immortal. This sees women as caring and nurturing because physiology *joins* them with nature. By the same token, men's obsession with finding roots and proving origins reflects their *distance* from nature, reflecting "a displacement of patrimonial anxiety."[56]

Men have likewise generally monopolized the transmission of history. To the historian Michelet, women embodied the eternal non-historical; in Macaulay's opinion, their habitual stress on specific details showed women unable to reason historically. History training seminars in European and American universities from the 1870s explicitly invoked male virility and "manly" debate, as distinct from the passive female salon. Just as women's role in history remains mostly hidden, so their role as historians is still marginalized by stereotypes that deny them a capacity for rigorous and objective modes of analysis, or that ascribe to them a maternal attitude to the past, "wanting to bring people to life again as a mother would want to bear children."[57]

Economic shifts and modern feminism have begun to rectify these gender inequities. The past century has greatly enlarged women's role in personal legacies; in Britain and the United States, women transmit and inherit more than half of all property. Experience as widows and trustees intensifies a custodial bent already common among women deeply involved with household and personal effects, memorably limned in Henry James's *Spoils of Poynton*. And they continue their primary role in handing on ancestral data. Female stewardship of family genealogy is a byword alike among Australian Aborigines and Mayflower Descendants, just as medieval potentates relied on women to tap a reservoir of memorial lore.[58]

Yet, if medieval women were specialists in remembering the dead, it was husbands and sons who were recalled and mourned, not the women themselves, notes Patrick Geary, speaking of 10th-century Europe. "The role of women was to be the custodian of men's life and soul, [but] men did not play the same role for women," who were mere vessels for preserving and transmitting the legacy of the lineage. A thousand years later, the same disparity persists. Acknowledging women's special role in "creating and preserving life," parliamentarian Enoch Powell urges that British citizenship be passed only through fathers, the nation's fighters. Though grandmothers survive longer and relay most family annals, male forebears remain more memorialized and better remembered; women are victims of genealogical amnesia. "How can we think back through our mothers," asks a folklorist, "if we don't know who they are?"[59]

The dearth of women depicted in the Washington Capitol Rotunda frieze outrages historian Caroline Sparks. "All those powerful male figures, and the women are simply absent"—save for Martha Washington watching George in action, and a few terrified, scantily clad squaws. "The overwhelming message is that women don't count." Statues echo the message, with great men upstairs, suffragettes in the crypt: "forefathers in the living room, foremothers in the basement."[60]

The names of long-reigning queens like Elizabeth and Victoria are synonymous with period authenticity. But men's continuing preponderance in most positions of power and prominence confines women's roles in heritage mainly to generic rather than individual recognition.

STEWARDSHIP AND SELF-INDULGENCE

In the past, legacies, like reputations, were meant to be handed down intact; estates were not spent, they were stewarded. Except among environmentalists, stewardship is now out of fashion. Instead of conserving family heritage, we consume it. Inheriting and transmitting give way to self-indulgence, since many find any future too uncertain to be worth planning for. Nuclear fears led some young people in the 1950s to reject parenthood, to eschew mortgages and life insurance—even refusing, Alan Brien recalls, to "make any appointments of any kind more than a week ahead." So imminent seemed the end that it was pointless to think of heritage. Gloomy prognoses still militate against postmortem planning; one American high school student in three, surveyed in the late 1980s, expected nuclear or biological annihilation within their lifetime.[61]

Weakened family bonds and disposable wares curtail the handing on of household goods. "Virtually no one buys a home with the idea that it might become a 'family seat,'" writes McCracken; few household items endure beyond two generations. Even the ultra-rich no longer dream of lineal glory or plan elaborate dynastic strategies; family-minded Rockefellers make way for atomistic Trumps and Gettys. Unlike our forebears, we rarely envisage descendants as replicas of ourselves.[62]

Decline of belief in a sentient hereafter also weakens posthumous concerns. Few conjure up images of heirs enjoying the legacies we have left them. Instead we muse like mummified Egyptians on what to take with us to the grave: a crowbar and a mobile phone, in case death proves premature; a fire extinguisher, in case divine justice miscarries; or, cannily, a proof of longevity, such as a 100th-birthday telegram from Buckingham Palace. Treasures are stored up less for heirs than for our own futures. "Posterity!" scoffed an American senator when urged to set aside national lands for future use, "what's posterity ever done for me?" Self-regard supplants intergenerational generosity.

The shift from stewardship to self-gratification is summed up in a cartoon that shows expectant heirs at a reading of the deceased's will: "Being of sound mind and body, I blew it all." The connoisseur who once aimed to leave his children a noble cellar no longer buys wine that will mature after his death; indeed, in the absence of cool cellars and long credit, little wine is now put down to age. The tailor or shoemaker who once clinched a sale with "This will see you out" today has customers who prefer to outlast their wardrobes. "I don't want long-term bonds," an old woman tells her broker; "I'm so old I don't even buy green bananas any more." To survive long enough means having a future short enough to need no plans.

Taking longevity as our inborn right, we feel like Woody Allen, who saw no solace in bequeathing films to posterity: "I don't want to be immortal by leaving a great legacy; I want to be immortal by living forever." A service called Cards from Beyond will send your posthumous birthday greetings, with messages like "Take joy in the fact that those of us who have gone on before would give anything to be in your shoes." A few hopeful souls await being thawed from cold storage when a cure is found for what today would have killed them. Cryonic salesmen reckon most people would opt to be frozen if assured they could resume conscious life, however far in the future.[63]

Self-absorption also reflects widespread attrition of kinship bonds. We seek roots and origins, but the search is apt to be a respite from rather than a link with our current concerns. The family portraits on the mantel that once endowed these ties with familial sanctity often now have the opposite effect, distancing forebears and kinsfolk in a standardized antique decor. Indeed, figures on some family altars are in fact *other* people's more picturesque ancestors, available at bargain prices already framed.

Family heritage, long the staple of fiction, has ceased to engage most writers' attention. "Families have been banished, houses have no heads," writes a literary historian; with Samuel Beckett, most writers put parents in the dustbin. Oedipus endures, but Odysseus is obsolete; few testators now would say, with Tennyson, "This is my son, mine own Telemachus/To whom I leave the sceptre and the isle." All but extinct is the filial piety that formerly persuaded inheritors to abide by the provisos of such legacies.[64]

What displaced or supplanted family obligations and expectations was commitments to wider communities. Dynasties of landed dukes and democratic entrepreneurs alike gave way in public importance to the legacies of national and ethnic groups. Heritage over the past two centuries, most notably over the last two decades, has come to denote what we inherit and bequeath less as individuals than as collective entities. To this shift and its sequels I now turn.

Chapter 3

COLLECTIVE LEGACIES

AT FIRST YOURS OR MINE, heritage soon becomes inherently collective. We share what we inherit among colleagues and communities, nations and faiths. Rooted in many allegiances, we may simultaneously be carpenters, communists, Catholics, and Croatians. We are shaped by a congeries of disparate but overlapping legacies; allegiance compels painful choices. Personal bequests conflict with collective patrimonies also at odds. How important is being Pennsylvania Dutch or Navaho, asks a historian, relative to being "also an American, a molecular biologist, a woman, and a Baptist?"[1] Each attachment, whether fixed at birth or freely chosen, presumes our fealty.

Choices among personal and collective legacies vary with culture and stage of life. Rebel youth and rugged individuals stress being self-made, owing nothing to family, society, or tradition. Democracy let Americans forget their ancestors and "imagine that their whole destiny is in their own hands," Tocqueville observed. Echoing Benjamin Franklin's pride in having "never inherited a shilling from any ancestor or relative," 19th-century Americans boasted of being the architects of their own fortunes, of making it on their own without patronage or family influence. Emerson's "imperial self" discarded filiations of memory and custom; the American was a new Adam "emancipated from history, happily bereft of ancestry, untouched and undefiled by the usual inheritances of family and race," in R. W. B. Lewis's words, "an individual standing alone, self-reliant and self-propelling."[2]

Collective roots in America ever fray in the face of private interests. Few common lands or communal rights outlasted colonial regimes; corporate concerns yield to personal ones. Connecticut townsfolk seeking historical data for their 1958 bicentennial were blocked by a local worthy who refused to share his documentary hoard. "The history of the Town of Bethel is my own personal business," he told them. "A man has a right to what is his." His magpie sweep left few hostages: "I got all the oldest newspapers I could find, took down what I wanted and then burned them. It's all mine now. Why should I tell you or anybody else? It is mine for my book."[3] Private claims erode collective heritage in the Old World, too. Stone Age cave paintings lately found in the Ardèche have for six centuries been part of "the land of our ancestors," say residents bent on keeping this prehistoric heritage (and any tourist bonanza) out of state hands.

By contrast, personal legacies in Britain customarily coalesce with collective heritage. Landed elites have long merged individual and ancestry, property and place. "Sir Leicester and the family credit are one," says Tulkinghorn in *Bleak House*. "Sir Leicester and the baronetcy, Sir Leicester and Chesney Wold, Sir Leicester and his ancestors and his patrimony are . . . inseparable." Stewardship implied abnegation as well as aggrandizement. Landed gentry preferred "to go unknown and leave behind . . . an arch, a potting shed, a wall where peaches ripen," in Virginia Woolf's phrase, "than to burn like a meteor and leave no dust. [They] never forgot to set aside something for those who come after." To perpetuate family and community they "were content to go down into obscurity with the molecatcher and the stone-mason." English readiness to stunt self for lineage amazed Americans. "The man who died yesterday, or ever so long ago, walks the village street today," wrote Hawthorne from the heart of England in 1862, "and must be buried again, tomorrow, under the same kindred dust that has already covered him half a score times."[4]

Heirs on opposite Atlantic shores still stress divergent goals. The American mogul William A. V. Cecil told a bi-national heritage meeting at Leeds Castle, Kent, in 1980 how he had transformed his North Carolina estate, Biltmore, from debt-laden encumbrance to lucrative honeypot by moving out of the house. This horrified the custodial English, bent on tenanting their stately homes even if bankrupt. Britons cared about *living* in their homes, Americans about *owning* them.

In England in the early 1960s I was amazed how few university colleagues could trace great-grandparents—some did not even know their grandparents' names. Told that Americans made a point of knowing (or inventing) all their forebears back to New World arrivals, they retorted, "Well, we don't need those family details; we have a secure *national* identity." Britishness in the 1990s is less potent and family history far more popular, but for many the collective heritage still takes precedence over the grandparental. This chapter traces how personal and family legacies have come to intertwine with national and minority heritage.

PERSONAL ROOTS, GROUP ALLEGIANCE

The nature of collective heritage and the feelings it arouses reflect its personal origins. Group ownership and fealty are rooted in family legacies. Heritage's stress on unique and exclusive possession harks back to family heirlooms; terms like patrimony, birthright, and roots evoke its inherently personal character. Building on parental bequests, group heritage bonds us with forebears' communal passions and patriotisms. Willingness to die for a collective cause is the supreme seal of national faith, the archetype of allegiance, in a Boer War correspondent's lines:

> A nation is never a nation
> Worthy of pride of place
> Till the mothers have sent their first born
> To look death in the field in the face.

"The Fatherland is the land of our fathers, the soil cleared and defended by them," the French nativist Le Pen put it in 1984; "the foreigner . . . can be integrated into the Fatherland only by a sacrificial act: the spilling of his blood."[5]

Collective legacies enmesh us even before birth, with tribal histories declaimed to babes in the womb. Along with mother's milk, the infant imbibes a litany of names, signs, symbols, and legends, notes Harold Isaacs:

> Before he can "know" it, the baby is tagged with labels and enveloped in the past he has inherited. Before he can "hear" it, he is told the story of his origins, . . . the "facts" about the world he has entered, the "history" of those who have gone before him, the myths to believe about what it all means.

Experience fortifies these linkages, making us aware of being "someone's son or daughter, someone else's cousin or uncle, citizen of a city, member of a guild or profession," writes Alisdair MacIntyre. "I inherit from the past of my family, city, tribe, nation a variety of expectations, and obligations . . . I am born with a past and can't cut myself off from it."[6]

Family ties embed personal lives in communal fates. Visiting his father's ancestral Armenia, the American writer Michael Arlen wondered if the slaughtered Armenians might have been too subservient to the Turks. His guide berates him for defaming his own father's memory: "You want to tear down your father." "It has nothing to do with my father." "Of course it has . . . Fatherland, father. It is the same thing. . . . Not like a proper son!" Childhood recall had denied ethnic memory, but Arlen's family legacy now merges with tribal belonging.[7] Among natives, national pride and family nurture readily converge. When I misheard a Tasmanian patriarch termed "patriot," he approved the conflation: "Patriot, patriarch, it's just the same."

Filial and parental metaphors abound; collective heritage remains ancestor-ridden. We trace admired group traits to ancestral deeds and seeds. Roots and birthrights, legacy and patrimony are the common parlance of nation-states. The king is a fond father, the populace his children, the country maternal, life a gift from mother nature. Organic analogies liken corporate to individual careers, "inherited" traits limn nations and races, and terms like brother and sister stress unity against outsiders. Heroes incarnate the state and personify its heritage. "As most people feel a need for ancestry," a historian puts it, "so most countries feel a need for national mythology."[8]

Private purposes coalesce into communal commitments. Personal legacies become collective, things at first exclusive to one person become generic or corporate. Deceased Trobriand Islanders are shorn of kinship connections to be forged anew when they are reborn as descendants.[9] Most societies, however they view life after death, phase out personal remnants in favor of collective relics. Mortal remains at first separately interred are later reburied in composite graves.

Like amalgamated bones, memories of the dead by and by coalesce. "After three or four generations, the faces of ancestors staring out from photograph albums look no different from the faces you see in history books," notes a memoirist; by then, few remember their individual careers.[10] As time effaces personal fame we recall the famous collectively: particular Greek pundits become classically plural, Lorenzo is replaced by a congeries of Medicis, specific poets and painters are subsumed in generic schools and styles.

Artistic creations likewise pass from private heirs into public possession soon after their authors' death, if not before; outliving the rights to much of his music, Irving Berlin was most upset when at 98 his theme song, "Alexander's Ragtime Band," went into the public domain. The premise of such transfers is that intellectual, unlike other, property belongs not to creators' heirs but to an admiring world. The writer William Manchester traces this anomaly to misreading "gifted" as though creative talent were literally a free gift, rather than the outcome of long tutelage and arduous effort.

Celebrities themselves become public legacies while still alive or just barely dead. "No one has any right to his or her own life," notes Jonathan Yardley; "everything is raw material for the insatiable machines of mass market entertainment." Pleas for posthumous reticence are ignored; the media crave any minutiae of the well-known. "In the end (and especially after the end) they no longer belong to themselves but to us," in the common view; hence Philip Larkin, "being fully aware of his own importance to 20th century British poetry," is held to have had no right to destroy his diaries and notebooks. Privacy ends at the grave; family efforts can no longer keep Nixon's self-condemning tapes being made public.

Public appropriation of private lives is a chronic literary cross. "One *ought* to be let alone while one's alive," lamented Elizabeth Barrett Browning when Mary Mitford exposed her intimate feelings; "the vultures *should* wait a little until the carrion is ready, & not pluck out the living eyes." But few can expect to maintain any privacy after death. "A personality as big as Margaret Aubyn's belongs to the world," Edith Wharton says of her protagonist. "It's the penalty of greatness—one becomes a *monument historique*. Posterity pays the cost of keeping one up, but on condition that one is always open to the public."[11]

The heroic dead are essential to the collective heritage. No martyrdom unified a nation more than Abraham Lincoln's, whose cortège across the country, viewed by millions, broadcast the nation's reborn unity to the whole world. But Lincoln was not mourned because he

was a national symbol; he became a hero by being mourned, notes
Barry Schwartz. A cleric truly gauged that "Lincoln dead may yet do
more for America than Lincoln living," and the press acclaimed "the
rich treasures we have inherited through the assassination."[12]

FROM COMMUNITY TO NATION

Heritage more and more denotes what we hold jointly with others—the
blessings (and curses) that belong to and largely define a group. The last
two centuries spread legacies from personal to public domains; the last
two decades made heritage popular as well as public. Collective legacies
have long lent pride and purpose to locale, creed, and trade. But their
customary arena is now larger: ethnic group, nation-state, sovereign people. What triggered the diffusion from family to broader realms?

Heritage was always of moment to the fortunate who had it and the
envious who craved it. In earlier epochs only a tiny minority aspired to
wealth and power. The properties and perquisites they inherited bespoke their privileged position. To be sure, underlings inherited chattels, skills, bonds with kinsfolk and masters, codes of behavior. But this
was not heritage. Heritage constituted the goods and rights of princes
and prelates, magnates and merchants.

Until modern times, communal fealty was narrowly bounded.
Approximating Aristotle's ideal state, viewable in toto by all of its 5,040
inhabitants, the Renaissance city-state was long a European paragon. A
few thousand folk within a few square miles encompassed most people's
known world. Except for religious faith their links were local, rooted in
tribe, village, and neighborhood. Communal allegiance grew from
family networks. Corporate awareness among ancient Jews or Greeks
seldom transcended, say, Judean or Theban loyalties. Only a handful in
the world's empires consciously partook of imperial heritage. Serfs,
slaves, and subjects were barely aware of being Babylonian, Egyptian,
Roman, or Chinese.

Allegiance beyond immediate locales was limited to European elites
until well after the Enlightenment. Notions of French, German, and
Polish nationhood in Rousseau's *Social Contract* (1762), for example, ignored the masses. To 19th-century patriots the Russian "people" and
the Polish "nation" meant only nobles and gentry. Japanese national

feeling was exclusive to aristocrats until the 1868 Meiji Restoration. American immigrants required to renounce fidelity to foreign powers had no difficulty in doing so, for few were conscious of any such ties. A scant century ago many rural French could not name villages ten miles distant, spoke only regional dialects, and knew as "national" only the tax collector, the recruiting sergeant, and the judge. Exiled in southern Italy in the 1930s, Carlo Levi noted the utter absence of all but local ties; nation and region meant nothing to villagers who relied solely on a web of kinship.[13] To this day, the chief legacies of many rural Europeans remain local or regional.

Restricted by status and by geography, heritage in the past differed from today's in makeup and meaning. Hallowing power and privilege, it endowed select possessors with dominion over the land and lives of others. The spiritual realm mirrored the secular: church relics and regalia bespoke inherent status. Rulers *deserved* heritage; it defined them and confirmed their rule. Its loss or absence spelled impotence.

Emblems of nationhood in post-medieval Europe likewise stressed noble origins and echoed elite traits. "Objects attesting to nobility," notes Paul Connerton, could not be "acquired either by proxy or in haste." Cherished antiques, fine wines, hunting skills: "These competences are ancient, they can be learned only slowly, they can be enjoyed only by those who take their time, they manifest a concern for things that last."[14] Heritage of this kind typified the old regime.

Such heritage forms and functions are not wholly defunct. The Stone of Scone still attests British sovereignty; the hue and cry after its theft by Scottish nationalists in the 1950s shows its symbolic vitality. English manorial lordships now embody no rents or rights, yet these tokens of extinct benefits command high prices. Wannabes the world over covet aristocratic titles; old elites command respect in ex-communist lands; Ralph Lauren's English trappings lend well-heeled Americans squirearchical credentials.

But beyond such quirky exceptions traditional heritage is mostly obsolete. It has succumbed to secularism, to the decline of inherited status, and to the rise of populist nationalism.

First, secularism: faith in the hereafter and the eternal spirit is of ever less consequence in everyday life. Up to the Reformation and the Enlightenment, the dead played an active role in the affairs of the living—

saints interceding for them with God, the deceased aiding or admonishing them to ensure they themselves were properly remembered. But the Reformation rejected the involvement of the dead in ongoing everyday life, and the Enlightenment and the rise of science banished the non-living to passive impotence.[15]

Few now prepare for an afterlife. Churches, cathedrals, and religious art are stewarded less as sacred legacies than as objects of national pride and secular profit. Fundamentalism is on the rise, but present politics rather than past relics are its main focus. Beyond the rare creed or cult, few in the West promote or placate ancestral spirits. Instead of looking after dead souls, as noted in Chapter 2, legators transmit legacies to the living or the unborn, or else memorialize themselves.

The second change lethal to olden heritage is the decline of family heirlooms as status symbols. When status required generations of gentility, patinas of age and use attested inherited rank. But capital entrepreneurs, imperial markets, and factory production created instant wealth. A deluge of new luxury goods made for a cult of novelty that supplanted the merit of antiquity; patina gave way to personal fashion. "What men and women had once hoped to inherit from their parents," Neil McKendrick sums up 18th-century England, "they now expect[ed] to buy for themselves." Though snobs still snubbed those who had to buy their own furniture, furnishings for the most part ceased to sustain family heritage. "They now rarely move from one generation to another, and rarely are they useful in memorializing past generations."[16]

As wealth displaced lineage, social hierarchy became less rigid, inheritance less a mark of gentility. More people left legacies, but heirlooms figured in fewer of them. The blurring of status lines and the abundance of high-class manufactures deprived inherited chattels of their old role as social icons. Things handed down ceased to bolster status; their worth now was largely nostalgic or lucrative. Patinaed heirlooms may still accredit antiquity, but they no longer exalt their inheritors. Nor was genealogy so crucial when it too could be bought anew. "So long as high society knows the amount of your fortune," Balzac wrote of Paris in 1830, "no one asks to see your family tree, because everyone knows how much it costs."[17] Instant wealth supplanted the old power of family lineage with new elites of energy and money.

Third, 19th-century nationalism roused mass allegiance to icons of collective identity, including architecture, music, folklore, and language. From emblems of persons and property, flags became symbols of national soil. Treasures once in private hands came under state control; patrimony spelled patriotism. State stewards protected national legacies from neglect and pillage. Owners formerly free to dispose of property as they liked were increasingly constrained by heritage codes prohibiting demolition or even alteration. As patrimony passed from private to public domains, heritage creators—architects, painters, poets—came to rely on the state more than on personal patronage.

Both inspired and justified by popular fervor, the new national heritage exalted vernacular culture. Folklore, the authentic voice of unlettered ancestors, became a prime facet of 19th-century patrimony, folksong an agent of chauvinism, potsherds a spur to patriotism. Princely collections were converted into public museums. Each national heritage stemmed from a checklist of essentials: a common language, past, future, fate, folk culture, values, tastes, landscape.[18]

Commemoration shifted from personal to collective, elite to popular subjects; patriotism demanded democratic memorials. Statues of local worthies and of Marianne, the maiden Republican icon, festooned French communes. American Civil War monuments elevated ordinary soldiers above famed commanders. Statues the world over paid homage to the anonymous fallen. Elbowing out generals and admirals, the Unknown Warrior occupies pride of place at Westminster Abbey; each new monarch approaches the throne over the grave of the nameless commoner who gave his life to save the kingdom.[19]

VARIETIES OF NATIONAL HERITAGE

Private legacies became public patrimonies in ways that differed with place and people. Thus the French national heritage stems from one climactic event: the Revolution. All remnants of the *ancien régime*—châteaux and cathedrals, archives and antiquities, paintings and royal tombs—instantly became odious as props of seigneurial and clerical repression, their end decreed by newly freed citizens. But public possession soon raised these relics from reminders of aristocratic rule to emblems of an inclusive national saga. Private archives initially consigned

to the flames were salvaged as significant *public* documents. Relics and
art at first vilified as icons of privilege gained acclaim as national patrimony. Converted from iconoclast to conserver, the revolutionary Abbé
Grégoire strove to save France's heritage from vandals. Only "barbarians
and slaves . . . destroy monuments of art," he declared in 1794, "free
men love and conserve them."[20]

Though vandalism and neglect were rife, many French treasures
fared better under national aegis than they had in regal or noble
hands. Slated for demolition by Louis XVI, Vincennes and Blois
châteaux were reprieved by the Revolution. National pride spurred
the conservation of history and prehistory; literature and painting were
consecrated as patriotic bequests. But the most inspiring new legacy
was participation: a general consciousness of being partners in a great
nation. It was patently "more beneficial" to the Breton or the Basque
to become a French national citizen, judged John Stuart Mill, "than to
sulk on his own rocks, the half-savage relic of past times, revolving in
his own little mental orbit." The historian Jules Michelet exalted the
filial bonds of *la belle France*'s children. Painting and fiction glorified
Chauvin, the rustic soldier-laborer whose sword defended and whose
plough nourished ten thousand hamlets. Emblematic of a plebeian
France renewed by its very setbacks, Chauvin incarnated Michelet's
nation of embattled citizen-farmers.[21]

Misfortune continued to cement French unity. Defeat by Germany
in 1870 impelled pedagogues to promote French language unity as patrimony. Regional dialects and other local legacies succumbed to nationalist mystique. "The fatherland is like a great family," exhorted an 1878
directive. It "is not your village, your province, it is all of France," its
whole chronicle thus sanctified. Love of France, held the school-
historian Lavisse, must be inculcated through heroic legends:

> If the schoolboy does not carry away with him the living memory of our
> national glories, if he does not know that our ancestors have fought on
> countless battlefields for noble causes, if he has not learned how much blood
> . . . it has taken to make the unity of our fatherland . . . , if he does not be-
> come a citizen imbued with his duties and a soldier who loves his flag, the
> teacher will have wasted his time.[22]

Unlike France, heritage in Britain was nationalized by gradual devolution from landed elites, who instead of being beheaded became beholden to the people (not least for staunch allegiance against Napoleon). Private property blurs into public patrimony; privilege entails stewardship; noblesse oblige is a living precept. They "have a common freemasonry of blood," a 19th-century radical said of the landed elite, "a common education, common pursuits, common ideas, a common dialect, a common religion, and . . . a common prestige . . . conceded, and even, it must be owned, secretly liked by the country at large."[23]

Stately Home and Grand Tour legacies turned private owners into public curators. Exhibiting treasures built at home and bought abroad, great houses opened their doors on occasion even to the hoi polloi. From the early 19th century, private treasures came to be seen as British *national* heritage, notes Linda Colley: "aristocratic property was in some magical and strictly intangible way *the people's property also*." Some collections, like Sir Hans Sloane's at the British Museum, were in large measure bequeathed to the nation; others, like Lord Elgin's Parthenon frieze, were purchased for the patrimony. Victorian and Edwardian magnates endowed state and municipal museums with the proceeds of family legacies.

Proprietorship bred patriotism among the elite. Entreated to husband his heirlooms for the national good, Henry James's Lord Theign at first demurs. "It's one thing to keep our possessions for ourselves—it's another to keep them for other people." But the mutuality of family and nation then dawns on him: "Who in the world's England, unless I am?" As his friend says of her own ancestor's portrait, "we don't want any more of our national treasures (for I regard my great-grandmother as national) to be scattered about the world." Theign leaves his legacy of Old Masters to the National Gallery, as do many actual grandees.[24]

Ancestral estates themselves have become national. In the 1930s and 1940s scores of hard-up country-house owners ceded family estates to the National Trust in return for continued tenancy and a promise of loving care. "The great houses of England were brought into public ownership by confident delegation, by mild nepotism, . . . by leaning on the great and the good," *The Times* put it. "This was the old-boy network's finest hour . . . the noblest nationalisation." It worked because "Trust officials were manifestly of the same class and stock" as the donors: "The aristocracy of England yielded up its finest possessions . . .

into the care of like-minded guardians. . . . They shared assumptions, friends, even families."

Some dispossessed dukes act as if they still own the estates they tenant: "only the English," comments an American, "would think it possible to go on living in a house after you've given it away." Lord Scarsdale, who occupies a 23-room family wing with servants' flats at Kedleston rent free, is not the only beneficiary of an ancestral gift to the nation. At Uppark the Meade-Fetherstonhaughs "continued to dine in the dining room and sit in the sitting rooms even on the open days, reading *Country Life* or drinking claret while the unconsidered . . . paying visitors milled, amazed, around them."[25]

The British national legacy now embraces the entire countryside. Great estates are to be kept intact, with owners expected to forgo present profits for the nation's sake. Sales are seen as "theft from a hoard which belongs to us all," in a journalist's phrase; the public do not "ask for whom the auctioneer's hammer falls: they are convinced that it falls on their own heritage." At Blenheim, the poet Peter Levi's "perfect ducal paradise," visitors mingle "puritanic disapproval of the past, furious resentment of the old, complacent upper classes, [with] the odd illusion that all these landscapes and lakes and palaces are 'our inheritance,' that they belong to us and they represent our creative powers."[26] When Blenheim in 1994 risked spoliation by the spendthrift Marquis of Blandford, national spokesmen insisted that "what a grateful nation gave the Duke of Marlborough in 1706 remains forever a treasure of the nation."

When Winston Churchill's estate trustees bruited selling his archives abroad, they were exhorted to keep intact at home a record of British valor comparable to America's Declaration of Independence; duty to the nation outweighed obligations to family heirs. Their purchase by the National Heritage Memorial Fund for £12.5 million in 1995 evoked relief at their rescue—and resentment at the family windfall from what was by right the nation's anyway. "To own part of a nation's heritage is not an absolute liberty," said *The Times* in chastising Japanese owners of London's County Hall for barring the British Royal Legion's customary VJ-Day ceremony there in 1995. "It involves a duty of custodianship [and] a degree of moral responsibility."

Britain conjoins family and nation, personifying the national heritage, stamping public treasures with a private imprimatur. "Phrases such as 'The Rokeby Venus,' 'The Portland Vase,' 'The Elgin Marbles'" held, for Shirley Hazzard's Christian Thrale, "more than passing proprietary meaning. They summarized a proper custody and appeared to state a desirable case." The elite take for granted control of that legacy. "Hereditary peers like me are very conditioned," said Lord Gowrie, bowing out as Arts Minister in 1985; "you look upon a spell in government as lending a hand."[27]

English paternalism struck even a famous egalitarian as benevolent. Emerson "pardoned high park-fences, when I saw that besides does and pheasants, these have preserved Arundel marbles, Townley galleries, Howard and Spenserian libraries, Warwick and Portland vases, Saxon manuscripts, monastic architectures, millennial trees, and breeds of cattle elsewhere extinct." England's noble gatekeepers embellished a heritage not just their own but everyone's: "These lords are the treasurers and librarians of mankind, engaged by their pride and wealth to this function." Collective heritage in turn fortifies family legacies. Landed estates sustain old dynasties more by reverence than revenue. "Without Chatsworth, Hatfield or Woburn," concludes a scholar, "Cavendishes, Cecils and Russells would have lost their identity."[28]

Patrimony everywhere ceases to be exclusive to elites; in principle it is open to all. To be sure, some inherit much, others little or nothing. But heritage now mainly denotes what belongs to and certifies us as communal members. We are all its owners. The same agencies that nationalize heritage—compulsory schooling, open access, media pervasion—at the same time democratize it. Past monuments are not ours to do whatever we like with, insisted Ruskin, but a sacred trust to hand on intact. Besides fidelity to their creators, Ruskin also meant to stress that cherished legacies were common, not private, property: they merited public use and care for the benefit of *all* successors. Not the nabob collector but the citizen proprietor sanctioned stewardship.[29] That heritage must be a general good is now a general faith.

The distinction between private and public legacies is the point of an American cartoon. "Why so sad?" a man asks a friend. "Well, the National Trust said to 'celebrate your inheritance,' and I don't have any to celebrate." "Cheer up! It's celebrate your *heritage*, not your inheritance." Few expect a sizeable personal legacy, but most are now conceded full shares in communal inheritance. Such legacies are defining traits of ethnic, religious, and other groups, above all of national states. Extension to mass clienteles magnifies their felt worth. As linchpins of communal identity, legacies become birthrights that none can do without. Whatever is now prized gets traced back to collective antecedents.

VAINGLORIOUS VICTORS

Prizing heritage as our very source of being, we cherish traits attributed to tribal, ethnic, and national precursors. Lauding triumphs and lamenting tragedies, patriots also claim unique endowments: America's Manifest Destiny, the French *mission civilisatrice*, the Whig version of English history, Australia as the Lucky Country. Like the ancient Jews, each people feels specially chosen in a fashion uniquely its own.

Heritage both celebrates victory (success, conquest, supremacy) and consecrates loss (defeat, misery, degradation). The legacies of victors are protean. This section offers selected samples of national vainglory and shows how the legacies that peoples most admire often alter over time. (Two widespread facets of heritage pride, priority and innateness, are reserved for treatment in Chapters 8 and 9.)

Self-congratulation for inherited virtues is the global norm. Rebels and reactionaries, dictators and democrats alike acclaim ancestral deeds. Emblematic icons buttress claims to superiority. For Greeks the Acropolis is the world's sublime masterpiece, for Americans the Declaration of Independence is democracy's supreme document. Bretons term their *Barzaz-Breiz* folk saga greater than the Iliad; Provençal partisans hail Mistral's pastoral epic *Mirèio* as a legacy the equal of the Aeneid. Stonehenge is Britain's "Anabasis, our Exodus, our Kon Tiki," writes a columnist. Architectural legacies serve as awesome and enduring archetypes. Britain, France, Italy, and Germany each boast matchless medieval castles, the finest Gothic cathedrals, the grandest mansions, the best vernacular buildings. Heritage boasts in other realms—archaeology, art, folklore, philosophy—are no less perfervid.

To treat each aspect of heritage would be otiose; I take language as one trait prized by most peoples ever since Babel. Folk unified by speech share legacies of lore and literature opaque to outsiders. Ancient tongues are marks of pride among modern Greeks and Israelis; verbal uniqueness signals autonomy to Bretons and Catalans. Language legacies demand acts of faith: those born to a tongue must wholly retain it, others must acquire and perfect it. Linguistic affiliation bespeaks a community, perpetuates its heritage, and alienates outsiders. With few exceptions, a common language is felt to be a crucial criterion of nationhood.

Unity and uniqueness are not enough; each also thinks his own tongue best, thanks to ancestral bequest, natural law, or divine fiat. So sweet was French that God's angels were said to speak it in heaven; patriots found Dutch, German, and Swedish the mother tongues of paradise. Because of being absent at Babel, they also escaped dispersal and corruption; the names Adam and Noah were said to be intelligible only in Dutch, a truly "natural" language spoken without strain or vehemence. Some tongues fuse myriad merits: English "gather[ed] the honey" of others' good traits, leaving them with "the dreggs"; Russian combined "the majesty of Spanish, the vivacity of French, the firmness of German, the delicacy of Italian, and the richness and concise imagery of Greek and Latin." Russians claimed roots, untarnished by the mundane, in spiritual Church-Slavonic.[30]

Every people thinks its own speech near to nature, since the merest child learns it with ease. Flawless vocabulary and grammar made French the vehicle of Cartesian clarity, its syntax the very mirror of innate infant thought. Indeed, it inherited every virtue. Fecund, jovial, judicious, versatile, spoken in "a relaxed manner with a relaxed body," French excelled in literature, reason, diplomacy, and everyday speech. Flexibly responsive to new needs, French yet kept its integral shape, leaving its literary legacy uniquely accessible; other tongues changed beyond recognition. "To read Dante one needs a commentary," noted an 18th-century linguist; "to read Pascal, good sense suffices." Lively repartee and fluent phrasing gave French converse "a charm and ease that please all peoples," held Voltaire. "Social freedom and gentility . . . long common only in France [lent] a delicacy of expression and a natural finesse hardly to be found elsewhere." From Druid bards to the songs of Roland, from Montaigne to Sartre, French authors have been national heroes; public figures fancy becoming Proustian *littérateurs*.[31] Culture minister Jacques Toubon's 1990s language crusade reasserted this legacy's abiding merits.

Linguistic chauvinism peaked in the 17th century, but similar views remain current. To this day, the writer Franz Stark acclaims German as a "highly precise yet graphic and emotional language of clear and direct expression" and creative force, *the* tongue of science and intellect. Dutch and Portuguese speakers boast a range of speech sounds that lets them master any language. English, the current lingua franca, inspires Voltairean accolades. "Our infinitely adaptable mother tongue," intones Simon Jenkins, citing linguists, is globally dominant due not to imperial diffusion but inherent merit—"no clicks, tones or implosives," a phonetic alphabet, creative flexibility; "the sooner the world speaks English, the happier and more prosperous it will be." Thus language seems an inherited blessing unique to us, yet at the same time a nonpareil that others should adopt or emulate.

What is striking about such claims is how alike they are. Other traits, too, are praised in markedly similar ways, but they combine in unique heritage syntheses that stem from each people's special circumstances. For example, Swiss self-pride derives from confederating autonomous cantons to which most Swiss owe primary fealty. To cope with dual allegiance (and language diversity), the national heritage becomes an obligatory credo; everyone is duty bound to express patriotic ardor. Anything specially Swiss is sanctioned, even rewarded, by the deity: for example, heroic self-isolation explains why God spared the Swiss the horrors of both world wars. Every supposed Swiss virtue—autonomy, piety, miniaturization, even the Alps—demands perpetual acclaim; anyone who dares criticize is "accused not only of heresy but indecency."[32] The Swiss cling with special intensity, as shown in Chapter 6, to founding myths known to be fabulous.

American self-praise is equally sweeping but periodically punctuated by self-doubt. Freedom-loving, hardworking, egalitarian, generous—such traits typify the self-declared legacy. "There is nothing wrong with America that cannot be cured by what is right in America," says the Bill Clinton robot in Florida's Disney World, "and there is nothing wrong in the world that cannot be cured by the ideals that created America." Disney's proposed Historyland showed "the United States the best of all possible places, the best of all possible systems." Such tenets must not be queried; "AMERICA: LOVE IT OR LEAVE IT," bumper stickers bluster. Heritage faith means tunnel vision. "I don't need to visit other countries," says a Florida schools' head, "to know that America is the best country in the world." Yet Americans recurrently bewail the present for falling short of professed heritage ideals. And they lack the intense conviction of "belonging to a nation of fathers and forefathers," as Pope John Paul II put it after his 1969 American visit—a conviction manifest, say, in his native Poland.

French patrimonial pride is exemplified in the Gallic tongue, as noted above, and in cathedrals, gastronomy, and wine. Cathedrals are both supreme Christian art *and* hallmarks of rational order: Victor Hugo's icons of national heroism, Michelet's "houses of the people," Viollet-le-Duc's exemplars of pathos, Rodin's aesthetic essence. Cathedrals elsewhere simply reflect French models, with Cologne a copy of Amiens, Toledo a replica of Bourges. Metz, Reims, and Strasbourg cathedrals served as enduring emblems of French wartime traumas.

Cuisine epitomizes French superiority, the French palate termed the "rampart of the most prestigious socio-cultural heritage of humanity" in a 1994 Paris weekly. "Only in France does one know how to eat," averred Brillat-Savarin; "France alone breeds chefs, other lands produce cooks." The Revolution diffused gastronomy throughout the populace without diluting its perfection. Patriots are said no longer to die but to dine for their country—"la France une et indivisible" becomes "une France à la carte, carte menu et carte Michelin." The wine legacy stresses stewardship and maturation; vignerons inherit ancestral palates, patience, and expertise. Process and product rely on dynastic continuities. As with food, global supremacy is assumed. "Through its wines," runs an ad, France "has immortalized the history of the world."[33]

French heritage thus exhibits four generic traits: a felt accord with nature, in syntax as in soils; high culture, alike in cathedrals and cuisine; diffusion of legacies common to all; and global primacy affirmed by gourmets and connoisseurs worldwide. Though their heritage is steeped in idiosyncrasies baffling to outsiders, the French regard foreign esteem as their rightful due, while their 1996 Heritage Foundation simultaneously protects quintessential French legacies of land and language from foreign incursion.

By contrast, domestic self-esteem suffices the British. An 18th-century patriot held the English "propensity to exalt themselves above others" not quite up to the French, but more candidly expressed.[34]

English sincerity against foreign artifice is still flaunted, from food (honest roast beef) and landscape art (down-to-earth Stubbs and Constable) to, as xenophobes sneer, education (exam scores earned, not bought) and business (upright effort, not Continental "fraud and corruption").

So ingrained is Britain's legacy that it is seldom explicated: "This country has been around for so long that the British simply *feel* rather than think British." Orwell's wartime England featured honesty, privacy, modesty, and unity, but his oft-repeated litany of a land of bitter beer, heavy coins, green grass, and old maids biking to Holy Communion through the morning mist takes such traits for granted. The national identity needs no "mascots, bones, relics, arks of the covenant, princes or presidents, pieces of honorific fluff," says a journalist. "Our ancestors and our descendants, our past and our future, are the nation! We are the nation."[35]

Like the English, many vaunt fixed and stable virtues long gone, if they were ever present. The French cherish myths of eternal glory, shrugging off shameful defeats as aberrations in a triumphal career dating from their Roman inheritance. The magazine *American Heritage*, in the face of mounting violence, poverty, corruption, and loss of national nerve, continued to assert an upbeat triumphalism, "as if a doctor told you that you were suffering from cancer, heart disease, and cirrhosis of the liver, yet assured you at the same time that you were the healthiest person in town."[36] Today's textbooks still hail a progressivist heritage few Americans now find credible.

Some peoples, though, suffer dramatic shifts in their entire heritage corpus, now valuing one set of traits, now their obverse. Thus Hungarians veer between contrary legacies: proudly primitive nomadic origins and civilized but subservient imperial traditions. The former is essentially Eastern (populist, Asian, Magyar, peasant, folkloristic), the latter Western (cosmopolite, European, Hapsburg, high culture). Rival patrons spearhead these polarized self-images. Attila's pagan heir, the warrior-prince Árpád, leads the traditional Magyar cause; the Catholic St. István legitimates the multicultural Western camp.

These versions of Hungarian roots oscillate as national images. "Preserving tradition and protecting . . . ancestral national identity" and "catching up with modernization in Western Europe" are alternative legacies deployed at one or another time. Evading stereotypes of pagan

savagery and Asian impetuosity, Hungarians embrace Catholic universalism and bourgeois thrift; fed up with Western rationality and individualism, they revert to Magyar communal tradition. Popular tribalism
currently elevates the Asian element. Hungarian youth espouses
Buddhist temples and shamanism; pop lyrics dwell on nomadic epics
and steeds from the steppes; Mongolian and Tibetan studies boom
among Budapest academics. Ethnographers trace Hungarian origins
among remnant Ugars in northwest China, whose songs fit the five-
toned Magyar scale.

This dualism spares Hungarians doctrinaire rigidity. Alternative heroes, symbols, and viewpoints interpret folk legacy now as unique (but
archaic), now as generic (but quaint). Flexibility makes heritage a living
crux of Hungarian nationhood. Surveys show most Hungarians know
little of their history, but its legends and heroes infuse daily life and are
rallying points for debates about Hungary's future.[37] Experts at juggling
their heritage, Hungarians move freely between opposing foci of celebration and commemoration.

Others' shifts are impelled by events. Egypt's pharaonic legacy has
within a century moved from marketable commodity, to icon of national freedom, to discredited pagan relic. Under Ottoman and European dominion, the dynastic heritage was mined for sale to conquerors
and tourists, but it had little resonance for most Egyptians. The
pharaohs had left no living memories, only inscrutable stones; history was seen largely through Islamicist lenses. Independence in 1922
renovated pharaonic roots for national identity, with King Tutan-
khamen's newfound tomb made an emblem of cultural continuity. The
pharaohs legitimated modern nationhood; patriots limned a Nile Valley
culture of "everlasting internal independence and permanent civiliza-
tional greatness." Pharaonic in blood, Egyptians owed nothing to later
legacies.

But pharaonic blood soured from blessing to blasphemy. In the
1930s, Islamic and Arabist annalists rejected the dynastic past as pagan
and subversive of Arab unity. The pharaohs now became tyrants, their
relics abhorrent to the faith, as were Hellenistic, Roman, and Byzantine
legacies. Ironically, the new reformers and the old nationalists were one
and the same: Pharaonic spokesmen turned Muslim heritage-mongers.
They said the slave-driving pyramid builders had failed them; "length of

time and mental stagnation have severed our bond with the Pharaonic era"; Islam alone could fuel Egyptian revival. But this heritage threatens to disable the secular state. Dynastic relics are episodically locked away lest they give offense; militant Islamicists target antiquities, crippling Egypt's tourist industry.[38] Egyptians are saddled with a heritage seen first as curse, then blessing, now both at once.

VIRTUOUS VICTIMS

Defeat can be as potent a heritage as victory; misery forges lasting bonds. Some "think that hatred fades. But it does not . . . ; too much French soil has been stolen from us," warned a poet in 1881. "Suffering in common unifies more than joy does," Renan consoled colleagues for France's surrender to Prussia at Sedan in 1870. "Where national memories are concerned, griefs are of more value than triumphs, for they impose duties, and require a common effort." Most of France's legendary heroes have died tragic deaths.[39]

Some are more afflicted than others, but all stress their sorrows; even victors vividly recall having been victims. It is not the erection of the Second Temple that is lamented at Jerusalem's Wailing Wall, but its destruction. "To lose the past in Wales is impossible," asserts a Welsh woman. "It is in the rocks we stand upon and often have to burrow into; in the cries of our dead princes [and] in the tears of our lost poets." Invaded seven times and occupied on four occasions in 140 years, France struck General de Gaulle at the end of the Second World War as singularly beset: "no other state in the universe has been subjected to as much."[40]

Eidetic recall of traumatic events makes the past ever present. Jews remember the fall of the Maccabees, Greeks that of Constantinople; every Serb knows Kosovo as the loss that led to five centuries of Turkish tyranny. A 1903 French monument in Hastings, England, bears the Norman battle cry *Dieux Aie!* "It says something about the English that they permit the record of their greatest defeat in the language of the conqueror," says an English journalist. It says more about the mystique of affliction that the English still term the Battle of Hastings a "defeat."

Stress on loss is age-old. "In Adam's fall we sinnèd all" implies a primordial bequest of mortal weakness. Fabled European origins stem not from haughty Greeks but humbled Trojans, history's quintessential losers. From Hector to Joan of Arc, Masada to the Mount of Olives, Sedan to the Somme, sacrifice sacralizes loss. Bunker Hill, Gallipoli, and Pearl Harbor reinforced losers' bonds more than any subsequent victory. "We were raised in French," blurts a Québécois pop singer, "and I want my children to suffer the same fate—the same beautiful fate." Slavery and genocide traumatize African and Armenian legacies. Seeking in vain for some Armenian "who does not live in a dark room and weep about the past," Michael Arlen hears only the perpetual refrain, "we were murdered, we were innocent, we were slaughtered."[41] Heirs of Albigensian Cathars, Highland Scots, Maori warriors, and the Warsaw Ghetto dwell on last-ditch stands that evoke the tribulations of Troy and Carthage.

Atrocities are invoked as heritage not only to forge internal unity but to enlist external sympathy. "Serbia, the nearly slaughtered nation," is poet Matija Beckovic's slogan for a Belgrade monument encasing the bones of Serbs fallen in myriad battles, intended to show the world the savagery Serbia has suffered. Museums of national struggle in both Turkish and Greek Nicosia show sagas of persecution, the latter's Hall of Heroes depicting Greek Cypriots burnt to death, slaughtered by Turks, hanged by the British, and killed in torture chambers. Saddled with a global legacy of genocidal grief, Israelis complain that "life here is being kept . . . as a museum for Jewish suffering," themselves "tombstones of Jewish history."[42] Yet the Holocaust is integral to Israeli identity, the slain six million mourned as symbolic citizens, reinforcing images of beleaguered Jews as perennial victims.

The heritage of victims takes two forms. One is legacies of loss by erosion, conquest, theft, or folly: a heritage recalled by its absence. The second is legacies of ensuing affliction: traits forged in the crucible of loss. The two at length converge. The lost arcadias of ancient Greece and Ireland, the vanished benisons of precolonial Africa and America, merge with horrific legacies of subjugation and slavery, famine and diasporic flight.

Some thus subdued take pride in their forebears' sheer endurance. "Our culture survives by allowing itself to be overwhelmed," says an Andalusian. "This strategy has defeated every conqueror: the Phoenicians and the Romans, the Vandals and the Visigoths, the Arabs and the kings of Castile. We corrupted the Napoleonic invaders, and we'll deal with tourism as well. Adaptation . . . makes us unconquerable."[43] But ancient injury and injustice still obsess some even after they regain long-lost sovereign legacies. Notably too embedded to forgo are Polish and Irish victimhood.

Most victims point to particular villains; Poles indict everyone. "For as long as we can remember," they say, "our neighbours have always had only one idea: to attack us." The poet Adam Mickiewicz personified Poland as "Christ among nations," crucified for others' sins. Poland has for centuries been stripped of autonomy, scarred by dismemberment, and plundered of cherished heritage. Most losses remain unrecompensed: Poles have scant hope that Russia, Austria, or Germany will return purloined crown jewels, libraries, and other treasures. Polish victimization shows up in defeatism at home and despondency in exile. So ingrained is the legacy of failure that Poles can hardly envision success, which would require them to trust their own leaders. On a 1987 visit I asked what traditions had survived recurrent havoc; a Warsaw academic cited a lasting heritage of opposition to any regime in power. Harking back to a lost ancient Fatherland, Poles keep a calendar of grievous reminders. Polish National Day celebrates not the modern state but the stillborn, quixotic 18th-century constitution.[44]

Rivaling Poles as victims, the Irish cite but a single malefactor—perfidious Albion. Centuries of bards have keened a saga of British iniquity and Irish grief. "Agony the most vivid, the most prolonged, of any recorded on the blotted page of human suffering," as told in A. M. Sullivan's canonical *Story of Ireland* (1867), made Ireland "like no other country in the world . . . in cruelties of oppression endured." Hence the Irish had to strain, in the historian Butterfield's phrase, "to create a 'nationalism' out of the broken fragments of tradition, out of the ruins of a tragic past." Dublin's Easter 1916 Rising became a Yeatsian tragedy to vindicate the past, reducing revolutionaries to vengeful revivalists.[45] The new constitution, more sepulchral lament than triumphal portent, exacted fealty "in the name of God and of the dead generations from whom Ireland received her old tradition of nationhood."

Accumulated animus embitters sovereign Eire seventy-five years later and has left a tragic legacy of violence in Northern Ireland. Hostage to inherited grievances, Ulster folk felt doomed to pay bills run up long before they were born, gunned down because of 1690, 1846, and 1922. A culture of victimhood haunts the classroom: by age 14, says the realm's 1992 cultural heritage guide, pupils should be "aware of the ways in which people have suffered . . . for their beliefs, and have contributed to the suffering of others in times past and present." Suffering and grievance surfeit Irish heritage.

Israeli, Arab, and Jewish youngsters brought face to face in 1994 found common cause in historical grief but vied in lamenting their sufferings. That Jews mourned grandparents lost in the Holocaust amazed Arab children: "You are missing your families from 50 years ago, while my relatives are being killed today." A Jewish boy's tears seemed contrived; how could he weep for an ancestor he had never met, who had died before he was born? Some Christians, too, resent Jews for harping on an ever more distant Holocaust—a strange plaint coming from celebrants of a much more remote crucifixion.

The loudest laments come from folk shorn of ancestral autonomy, who feel their cultural legacies fatally flawed by subjugation. Near-Eastern elites displaced by Greece and Rome looked in vain to retrieve the heritage of ancient Egypt and Babylon. Meso-Americans after the Spanish conquest tried in vain to revive indigenous faith. Post-slavery black Americans in vain sought solace in ancestral Africa. Such legacies are mourned the more for being mere shadows, like the pain of phantom amputated limbs. These dispossessed speak "not in the genuine voice of a surviving tradition still maintained," suggests historian Anthony Grafton, "but in the dilute one of the victim uprooted from a lost tradition still beloved."[46]

Yet among these minorities, as in Poland and Ireland, past deprivations become indelible. So anguished was the black American tradition that one might think, in Richard Wright's words, they "had embedded in their flesh and bones some peculiar propensity toward lamenting and complaining." Occitan autonomists in southern France today excoriate the 13th-century Albigensian crusade as "without doubt the greatest attempt at genocide perpetrated in Europe for a thousand years."[47] Ongoing grievances, actual or fancied, augment legacies of loss among once autonomous peoples the world over; present animus battens on past indignity.

Among many ethnics and indigenes, a legacy of oppression validates present identity: "I have a grievance, therefore I am." At California textbook hearings in 1987, group after group demanded that the curriculum show that its forebears had suffered more than anyone else in history. Bequests of affliction uplift if they do not empower. "Suffering was the big reason why blacks played with more expression in those days," trumpeter Sweets Edison now recalls of the 1930s. "Pain and suffering gave you a certain intensity."

History is still mostly written by the winners. But heritage increasingly belongs to the losers. Even victors now aspire to a legacy of defeat. Like wild wolves, recast from fiendish prey to furry victim and re-stocked in the American West, ex-tyrants co-opt victimhood, begging sympathy as endangered species. To justify keeping out women, the Virginia Military Institute in 1991 claimed to be an imperiled remnant of male sadism deserving "the same protection as the spotted owl and six-legged salamander."

The cult of victims erases victories along with victors from popular history. For example, Portugal portrays its imperial legacy as brief and bloodless. "We weren't brutal and calculating like the others. No, we always abhorred racism, we always wanted only the best for Brazil and Africa and Asia. We were perfect saints," a historian sums up the Portuguese perspective; "we can't quite remember the massacres we carried out." The Spanish, too, in the 168th edition of a first-grade text, stress heroic defeats at Sagantum (Hannibal), Numantia (Scipio), and Saragossa (Napoleon), and the "self-sacrficing spirit unique in history" that led Spanish friars to teach Indians "to read, write, and pray." American textbooks portray slavery without anger, for there is no one to be angry at: "somehow we ended up with four million slaves in America but no owners!"[48] As Chapter 7 details, such selective oblivion is a hallmark of heritage.

New sympathy with the downtrodden signals a broader shift as well—a move away from national allegiance toward smaller and less powerful entities. This shift, to which I now turn, deeply affects how heritage at all levels is seen and used.

LOCAL LOYALTY AND ETHNIC EMPATHY

Two hundred nations, half of them tiny and feeble, today claim birthrights. Only a century ago, the growing might of Britain, France, and the United States and the new unity of Germany and Italy led statesmen to suppose large countries essential to progress: "the day of small nations," declared Joseph Chamberlain in 1904, "has long passed away." Global war and decolonization have turned Chamberlain's tenet on its head. The received view now is that every people, however few, poor, and impotent, have a right to autonomy. Fifty years back viable nationhood meant several million citizens; today a few thousand suffice. "We mark with reverence the feeling of a people that they *are* a people," held a 1977 observer, "however absurd their claims on the definition may seem to others."[49]

The rise of mini-states also reflects disaffection with megapowers too large to command communal loyalty, too remote to respond to their people. National allegiances become less fulfilling than local or ethnic ties. Little legacies supplant greater ones; minority roots matter more than the mainstream. The excesses of national chauvinism lead some to look fondly on less binding, more casual Ottoman and Hapsburg empires; "in Bosnia under Austria-Hungary we had peace," recalled the former crown prince in 1994; "now they kill each other." But most yearn for intimate and apolitical legacies. "We need fewer sovereign states," Lord Menuhin exhorted British peers, "and more autonomous cultures."

It becomes easier to identify with Bavaria or Brandenburg than with Germany, with Picardy or Alsace than France, with Wales or Scotland than Britain.[50] Prehistoric sites proclaim local and regional legacies: Carnac suggests Brittany, not Paris; Stonehenge Wessex, not Westminster. Dialect differences once disdained are now all the rage in arts and media. Local and ethnic legacies seem organic, natural, and communal. Minorities are admired for being intimate and engagé, for tracing roots to tribal pasts—even for minority impotence, for lacking the clout to impose their ways on others.

French heritage exemplifies these trends. The 1980 Year of Patrimony shifted action from Paris to ten thousand local coteries, fêting recipes and rhythms, dialect and folklore. Instead of national unity, Revolutionary commemoratives exalted provincial roots. Vendéean, Occitan, and Huguenot legacies formerly shunned as dissident are now hailed for enriching diversity—more welcome, to be sure, because they are politically toothless. Whereas in 1972 Pompidou saw "no place for regional languages in a France destined to stamp its seal on Europe," by 1990 Breton and Provençal were being taught in primary schools with state aid. Derided by the *ancien régime* as the uncouth tongue of rustic savages and banned by the Revolution as a medium of clerical reaction, Breton is now lauded as a vibrant ingredient of regional rebirth.[51]

Such shifts in heritage allegiance mirrored the 1982 decentralization act that devolved power onto newly elective regional, departmental, and communal forums. Mitterand paid presidential homage to France's past as much in Vimy and St. Tropez as in Paris: once autocratic and centralized heritage agencies became discreetly advisory. Like the cyclists' Tour de France, conceived a century ago to glorify the nation, much French heritage has become intensely local in spirit.[52]

Unlike France, regional and local power in Britain has dwindled. Yet heritage shows a similar decentralizing spirit. The national agencies— SAVE Britain's Heritage, English Heritage, the National Trust, the National Heritage Memorial Fund, the National History Curriculum—have clout and cash. But it is community efforts that spark heritage action, from folk festivals and nature conservation to reenactments and museums. Local initiatives in the 1960s and regional groups in the 1970s transformed heritage from twee nostalgia to major enterprise. Grandeurs of the national saga give way to the palpable immediacy of family and neighborhood roots. Like Raphael Samuel's "little platoons" version of the past, English Heritage extols village legacies from ponds, parks, and piazzas to flagpoles, roundabouts, and millennial bells.[53] Regional languages revive: a campaign to rekindle Cornish, gone since 1800, joins forces with the Breton crusade across the Channel; the cachet of Welsh, Gaelic, and Scots animates politics and popular culture from Aberystwyth to Aberdeen.

Mediterranean regionalists reclaim heritages more lightly veneered with nationalism. The Visigoth mystique of Iberian unity against Moorish incursion never seriously dislodged provincial loyalties. Catalan, Basque, and Andalusian legacies are primary in post-Franco Spain; cultural diversity is the crux of the 1990 education act; even Madrileños now seek separate, noncentrist roots. In Italy, national scandal and Northern and Lombard leagues reanimate regional roots that antedate the Risorgimento, even challenging sports- and media-based unities. Nation-states in eastern Europe fragment along regional and religious fault lines, unleashing ancient legacies of ethnic enmity. Across the Atlantic, ethnic, religious, and regional minority attachments equally spark heritage action.

What features set subnational legacies apart from larger ones? Smallness suggests verities felt lacking in national patrimonies. Such verities are most evident among minorities that deploy heritage not to opt out of nation-states but to achieve gains within them. Resurgent tribalism engages the sympathy of mainstream peoples eager to recover or requite preimperial and preindustrial legacies such as organic wholeness, family warmth, deep-rooted tradition, respect for elders. "Outside the industrialized West," assert Green crusaders, "no one has to be told to respect their elders. It's simply the way society is organized. Which is why the World Wildlife Fund tries to work with older people in the villages of the rainforests."

Technological backwardness thus becomes a bona fide of stewardship. American Indians once damned as irreclaimable savages are now venerated as ecological saviors, endowed with tribal wisdom undimmed over millennia. That "all of nature has to be approached with respect" is seen as a "particularly Indian" legacy, with Indian ways in general set against mainstream "chaos, and people, and traffic, and craziness."[54]

Indeed, heritage in general becomes a strictly minority virtue, with mainstream "progress" its regrettable antithesis. A cradle-board display at New York's National Museum of the American Indian hints that history-impaired Americans could learn from Indian babies' back-facing view, seeing the places their mothers have just left behind, until they are mature enough to walk forward. Cajuns, blacks, Appalachian whites, and other marginalized folk are stereotyped as "creative, coherently and harmoniously ordered into organic communities, subtly in touch with their own feelings and with each other, gentle with their children, respectful of the land, mindful of the value of their cultural traditions, and so on." In the antipodes, too, indigenous insights help "culturally enervated" majorities "recover their sense of locality and historical tradition."[55]

The celebration of ethnic heritage spread in the 1970s and 1980s from marginal indigenes to regional and immigrant groups. Minority heritage became a fount of old-time virtues: devotion to God and country, schooling at any sacrifice, close family ties—even extending, as the cult of the *Godfather* (1969) showed, to the Mafia. By contrast, the mainstream legacy seems cold, barren, mean, and impersonal. Americans especially yearn for the intensity of minority roots—the more ethnic, the more desirable. "I would like to be a member of a group . . . where there is some meat to the culture, . . . like on an American Indian reservation, or a gypsy encampment, or an Italian neighborhood," says a Philadelphian. "They all know their second cousins intimately and they are all involved in each other's lives"; of her own ethnic roots, she would opt for "whichever one is richest."[56]

Majority legacy is now widely traduced. Anyone "merely" French or American lacks real roots. "I used To Be a White American But I Gave It Up In the Interests of Humanity" was a popular banner in the early 1990s. The Smithsonian's 1992 "American Encounters" show portrayed WASPs not only as oppressors, a critic found, but as "a people without tradition or cultural identity" of their own. A Paris-born teacher in Rennes admired the local legacy, "but I cannot speak Breton or Gallo," she grieved, "so I have no language and no culture"; French was not a valid heritage.[57] To include Euro-Americans in a required "American Cultures" course at Berkeley, they were declared an ethnicity on a par with other minorities (as in a sense they were, Asians now being the largest campus group).

Ethnic imperatives commonly impugn national ties. A teacher in Toulouse who used to mock Occitan separatism recently unfurled a banner depicting an Albigensian crucified in flames, with the legend "750 Years of Oppression from Paris." "Françoise, have you joined them?" I asked. "Well, coming from Normandy to the University of Toulouse, I had to." Ohio kindergartners told to bring "their own" foods and flags for an "international Thanksgiving" found that only minority heritage counted. One tearful boy, torn among English, Scottish, Irish, German, and Jewish roots, was grudgingly allowed an American flag and a hamburger.

Minorities deploy similar legacies of subordination in common. At global indigenous-rights conclaves, Maoris, Hawaiians, Amazonians, and Inuits exchange sagas of grievance and strategies for reclaiming sacred sites and symbols, lands and languages. A Welsh farm expert befriended Jamaican peasants by stressing Wales's own saga of vassalage under an English yoke. All-Celtic solidarity against Anglo-French overlords eased a Scots anthropologist's Corsican contacts; as a fellow Celt she was expected to be attuned to "the greatness and tragedy of the Corsican people."[58]

Mainstream heritage agencies now find it hard to limn a national saga without causing ethnic or religious offense. To mollify Indian sensibilities, the American Bureau of Indian Affairs bolted a steel plate with the word Massacre over the previous Battle at Wounded Knee. But correcting earlier biases often simply inverts them. Embarrassed by a 1920s plaque that celebrated the suppression of Canada's rebel Métis at Batoche, the Canadian Sites and Monuments Board went to the opposite extreme, applauding the Métis' survival. Parks Canada brochures used to describe French colonists at Fort Chambly as "needing protection from the terror of the Iroquois"; they now stress that the Iroquois were there from the start until the "white man disturbed their lives in 1609."[59]

Newcomers, too, are urged to cling to ancestral legacies or to create new communal enclaves. Immigrant, like indigenous, heritage denotes authentic living attachments, as against the dead orthodoxies of national patriotism. "The American Revolution was not their revolution, the Civil War was not their war, the women's rights' struggle as commemorated at Seneca Falls was not their struggle," newcomers may reasonably contend. Hence tribal and ethnic Americans may well choose to venerate other places than those the nation now holds canonical.[60] Commitment to diversity, multiculturalists suggest, should override consensual national heritage.

Mainstream mea culpas hallow minority legacies. To admit that the downtrodden have just cause for grievance assuages historical guilt. Heirs of oppressors eagerly admit ancestral cruelty, greed, and genocide. "We took the traditional lands and smashed the traditional way of life. We brought the diseases and the alcohol. We committed the murders. We took the children from their mothers," lamented Australian prime minister Paul Keating, launching the Year of Indigenous Peoples in 1993. "We almost wiped the Indians out," repents a tourist at a Pueblo Indian village.[61] To be sure, these evils are past; "we" no longer do these dreadful things. At a Connecticut tribal site in 1988, local youths chatted with a loinclothed Indian about fire making and the horrors of conquest. Within minutes I watched these outsiders turn insiders. English colonists had wrecked the Indian economy, they agreed, but French cultural genocide was worse; "the French really did us in." *Us!* Hegemonic heirs stay blameless by switching ancestors; back then, they are convinced they would have been Indians—good guys.

Nowadays we all become Indians. As minorities gain favor, more embrace newly prized legacies. Indigenous benefits, heritage roots, and rights to autonomy lead once reluctant tribalists to become Maori or Aborigine, Indian or Inuit. Maori numbers have doubled in a generation, mainly because many New Zealanders who formerly ignored or concealed Maori ancestry now flaunt it. Self-confidence and tribal charisma similarly multiply Sami and Samoyed converts. An estimated 85,000 "hobby Indians" in Germany and Poland nurture Native American religious and cultural heritage as "authentic" as any lineal descendants (Potsdam's "Iroquois" went on the warpath for "native" land rights against a supermarket). All these groups, native and immigrant, aboriginal and imitative, pool their marginal status in a supertribal rhetoric exalting the small, the simple, the savage, and the sincere.[62]

MINORITY HERITAGE AND ITS DISCONTENTS

The new salience of minority heritage exacts costs, however. For one, it tends to smudge or vitiate local distinctiveness. Diverse tribal views of Hopi heritage on different mesas are swamped by all-Hopi needs vis-à-vis Navajos and the Bureau of Indian Affairs. Village differences are forgotten in promoting Basque patriotism. A Pamplona native agrees that Basque dancing in a fiesta is

> good dancing, but what was it doing here in Pamplona? The dances performed came from a fishing village miles [away]. Traditionally it would not have been staged in Pamplona, and certainly not by Pamplonans . . . The annual festival of Basque dance . . . reduces the distinctiveness of regionally based dance routines by making them all assimilable parts of a generalised "Basque culture."[63]

Landscape variables vital to hunters and herders among Yakut shamans in the Siberian taiga give way to generalized abstractions as shamanism becomes a political vehicle of Yakut nationalism.

Diverse ethnic and regional legacies likewise become more alike, as mainstream confrontation erodes distinctiveness. The more minorities negotiate with sovereign powers and exchange views and tactics among themselves, the more all heritage takes on a similar Western tinge. For example, to spearhead demands for autonomy from Russia, the Yakuts turn tribal shamanism into official faith. Soul Consciousness is compulsory in the Yakut curriculum, with the young assigned to seek ethnic wisdom both from rural grandparents and from anthropology texts. Political potency has made shamanism self-consciously Western in style and content.

Shamanism is also Westernized by export. New Age converts adore the sense of community, animism, and above all holism that suffuses tribal legacies. But their appropriation strips the legacy of its holistic character, retooling it into discrete commodities. The lore of Tibetan lamas or of shamanist priests is divested of local elements that do not travel well, such as clan cults and ancestor worship, and reduces holism from the basis of all values to one of many, an option instead of a given.[64] What is more, minorities themselves retool their heritage for export. Native American healing became trendy in England in the early 1990s, but the traditional sacred sweat lodge proved too hot for the English. After "a lot of soul-searching about changing the tradition," the Cherokee in charge "did a gentler sweat lodge with fewer hot stones. You have to adapt," she explained.

Mainstream enthusiasm is bound to debilitate minority legacies. Admiring Indian culture, a white school class mistook empathy for understanding. Responding rhapsodically to anything of Indian origin, they could not move beyond the "everything I read makes me love Native American culture more" syndrome.[65] Indiscriminate adoration is no less demeaning than aversion. And many who claim to admire ethnic legacies betray patronizing contempt in doing so. After his 1991 Florida rape acquittal, the hapless William Kennedy Smith disparaged women and Italian-Americans alike, ending an accolade to trial judge Mary E. Lupo "and I'll bet she makes great lasagna, too." For many, minority heritage is just lasagna.

Turning once-sacred local and tribal legacies into public commodities also divests them of social meaning. From being central to life, minority heritage becomes a frill, an extra, an embellishment. The hominess, *gemütlichkeit*, and *ambiance* that distinguish it from mainstream heritage get debased, in Richard Rodriguez's phrase, into "a tolerance for chili . . . or an eye for the insistent color."[66] Heritage food—lasagna, chicken soup, sauerkraut—is not just tasty; it becomes trivial to and debauched by both minority and mainstream, like the cow skulls that became a home-design fetish of the Western frontier legacy.

Mainstreams trivialize minority legacies by standardizing them. For example, American history texts print a Rita Moreno profile cheek by jowl with a passage on Chinese gold miners, a Kiowa chief's speech, a Puerto Rican nationalist plea, and a Jewish pushcart peddler's letter to his family in Russia. Minority heritage observance follows suit, becoming as formulaic and empty as the mumbo jumbo of outworn national symbols. Ritual observance of African-American legacies gets attenuated to wearing Kente cloth and celebrating Kwanzaa (from Los Angeles, not Lagos), Jewish legacies to a few residual phrases and gestures. "Your more-concerned-than-average Jew doesn't know the name of a single Hebrew or Yiddish poet, let alone a line of his poetry," scolds Martin Peretz. "She thinks Maimonides is the name of a hospital."[67] Ethnic legacies dwindle from living folkways to isolated emblems and events.

Minority heritage wins mainstream praise partly because it *is* seen as trivial, harmless, and personally enriching yet socially retrograde— primitive, in fact. Historical change in traditional cultures is a taint to be eradicated. Efforts to keep minorities authentically primitive are legion. For example, Santa Fe's traditional market protects Indian crafts from outside contamination, but such protection restricts the scope and content of Indian crafts and freezes styles. To appear traditionally primitive, Indians must abandon or hide mechanized skills. One potter complains she cannot now use a pottery wheel without being chastised as inauthentic. Pueblo pottery is now so perfected that many collectors reject it in favor of more unfinished, rustic Navajo and Tarahumara ware seen as less corrupted by mainstream artistic standards.[68]

Shifting mainstream expectations demand continual readjustments. "We have to learn how to be Indian again," said a Pueblo craftswoman. "First the whites came and stripped us. Then, they come again and 'find' us. Now, we are paid to behave the way we did when they tried to get rid of us." Since whites expect Indians to be steeped in tradition simply because they are Indian, Indians must trade on this image. To secure tribal benefits, they exaggerate ancestral continuities and conceal adaptation to Anglo culture. Relating traditional hunting-and-gathering routines, San Tomás Indians omit the fact that they drive to the local Piggly

Wiggly supermarket for most of their food. They speak of traditional dances but not of attending Anglo discos in Anglo clothes.[69]

Other minorities, too, hide from mainstream view impure modern traits incompatible with the unsullied heritage that is their hallmark. Performing for themselves, Yemenite Jews in Israel dance without costumes, choreographed sequences, or stories; but for outsiders they perform in ankle-length caftans and false side-curls and tell how their choreographed sequences hark back to Exodus.[70] Most minority heritage is much less exclusively ethnic than the celebrants feel forced to pretend, or may themselves realize.

These deceptions have practical benefits. They also carry psychic liabilities. One is the difficulty of combining an imputed primitive with an actual modern identity. Another is how to stay "authentic" in a milieu that rewards deceit. A third is coping with a tourist industry that simultaneously consumes and seeks to conserve their heritage. As the *Cannibal Tours* art historian says while buying artifacts, "I for one think it is too bad if they deviate [from their traditions] and work for tourism as such." Australian Aborigines are likewise torn between pressures to retain "unspoiled" primitive traditions, as rare museum pieces in a heritage landscape, and contrariwise to *épater* the mainstream with acrylic postmodernity. Indigenes in general must ceaselessly resist mainstream pressures both to cut them off from their heritage and to bury them within it.[71]

Indigenes who refuse to posture as primitives, instead glorying in being blatantly modern, are punished by mainstream obloquy. For example, many whites construe the new Native American casino enterprises as a sad lapse from traditional tribal virtues. Financial mogul Donald Trump pooh-poohed the wealthy Pequots, whose Connecticut casino had trumped his own, as not looking to him like "real" Indians. They had looked Indian enough, they retorted, when they were poor.[72]

All of us—as individuals, as nations, as ethnic and other entities—adapt the past to our presumed advantage. Such acts undeniably deform history for heritage aims; and heritage is further corrupted by being popularized, commoditized, and politicized. To these presumed heritage crimes I now turn.

Chapter 4

HERITAGE ASSAILED

PROMISING SO MUCH TO SO MANY, heritage is bound to disappoint. Its benefits often come at heavy cost. Hence it generates abuse along with applause. Rancorous criticism is rife. Critics assail heritage as the enemy of truth, lethal to authentic tradition. Popular taste, fickle and readily swayed, is felt to strip hallowed ideas and icons of enduring worth. Instead of deep and durable roots, what we get is instant and ephemeral, even newborn. Detractors find dismaying the very notion of heritage in the making.

Heritage is vilified as selfish and chauvinist, nostalgic and escapist, trivial and sterile, ignorant and anachronistic. Intricacy is simplified, the diverse made uniform, the exotic turned insipid. Shallow and mendacious, heritage spawns avarice and xenophobia. Assuring its possessors of their unique merits, heritage foments vainglory. The roots it reveres are too good to be true: in a heritage home nothing is tawdry or misplaced; in a heritage lineage all ancestors are engaging if not eminent; in a heritage landscape it never rains (except for desert-dwelling Navajo Indians, for whom "back then everything was in harmony and it rained all the time"). Heritage chronicles strew tales of heroism and sacrifice along a tapestry of steady progress.

Heritage is held to fossilize, to preclude ambivalence, to tolerate no doubts. "The true product of the heritage-industry is entropy; history is over, nothing more is to be done." Robert Hewison echoes Nietzsche in warning that fevered nostalgia precludes present action. Turning a blind eye to past turmoil, leaching out past distress and bewilderment, heritage is blamed for stifling enterprise. The penchant for patrimony litters the world with legacies of outworn junk.[1]

False because more commercial than other versions of the past, heritage preserves dross, promotes kitsch, and swamps us in the superficial. The more tawdry a legacy, the more popular it is; when the Duchess of York was snapped in 1992 with an admirer kissing her feet, "Fergie's toe" modeled in Blackpool Rock became England's best-selling sweet. Heritage souvenirs peddled at America's 200th birthday in 1976 were dubbed Bicentennial Schlock.

Five charges lead the litany of complaints: heritage aggravates chauvinist excess; it mushrooms into mindless incoherence; it sells what should be sacred and beyond price; it is run by exclusive elites; and it distorts the true past.

DESTRUCTIVE CHAUVINISM

In asserting our own virtues, we harp on others' vices. The worst fault charged against heritage is that it breeds belligerent antagonism. The abuse of history for chauvinist causes is emphatically censured by the historian Hobsbawm:

> Myth and invention are essential to the politics of identity. As poppies are the raw material for heroin addiction, history is the raw material for nationalist or ethnic or fundamentalist ideologies. [Heritage] is an essential element, perhaps *the* essential element in these ideologies.

But resultant havoc shows it a dreadful use of the past.[2]

"The line between pride in valour and gloating triumphalism should be clear," holds the *Economist*, but it seldom is. Pride in one's past comes to warrant repression; heritage disguised as history becomes a register of rapine. France being the "natural heir" to Greece and Rome justified Napoleon's plunder of papal antiquities; their Teutonic legacy justified Nazi takeover of Slavic lands. The cement of citizenship entombs enemies.

Council of Europe delegates to a 1994 Vienna conference differed about which iniquitous heritage trait most dismayed them, but all condemned heritage for engendering and inflaming chauvinism. East Europeans especially deplored vendettas over heritage possession, primacy, and superiority—an animus that has erased or eroded countless treasured legacies. Mostar and Dubrovnik at once call to mind heritage crimes committed in the name of patriotism.

That such excesses of heritage zeal were on the wane was the sanguine view of J. H. Plumb's *Death of the Past* in 1969. Bygone feats, he predicted, would soon cease to justify tyrannous authority, to affirm self-serving manifest destinies, to incite citizens to voice malign vainglory. In his view, the rise of real history put an end to such misuse of the past.

Plumb's prophecy of the demise of chauvinism seemed to me already passé in 1985. The communist regimes that flagrantly twisted the past have since collapsed. But Orwell's nightmares are no less ominous elsewhere; historians' hegemonic truths are harder to combat in democracies than in state tyrannies, where countercultures can subvert them. Chauvinists everywhere practice the Party slogan in *Nineteen Eighty-Four:* "who controls the past controls the future; who controls the present controls the past."[3] Faith in past beatitude empowers present authority. Partisans of all creeds use heritage to preach their own virtues and incite animus against others. The unhappy results are further appraised in Chapter 10.

ELITISM

Populism notwithstanding, heritage normally goes with privilege: elites usually own it, control access to it, and ordain its public image. That heritage still buttresses elite perquisites strikes some as monstrous. Radical critics fumed that America's Bicentennial lauded not the Revolution but "the takeover of this country by the rich and their traditional exploitation of the poor." Self-styled Historical Terrorists vilified the heritage acclaimed at Australia's 200th birthday as an elite ploy to hoodwink visitors and intimidate locals: "Those who slaughtered the Aborigines, who kept the convicts in conditions of slavery, remain in power to this day," purveying lies of bygone harmony and hiding their crimes in a past "distorted, twisted and ultimately lost in a swirling morass of restoration, pioneer museums and heritage paint schemes." Heritage today, deems a 1990s dissident, "still cedes the upper hand to dominators and oppressors."[4]

Such critics see elite conspiracy wherever they look. Up to a point, they are right: the heritage–elite linkage *is* patent. "Personal ownership of the past has always been a vital strand in the ideology of all ruling classes," asserts Plumb. The very term inheritance echoes privilege and wealth. The rich and the wellborn, far more than the common herd, make wills, devise bequests, hand down property, and empower descendants. Social and economic elites co-opt elites of high taste: coteries of experts set national heritage priorities, choose what buildings to protect, and decide what galleries should buy, ignoring as far as possible the preferences of the public who pay for it all. Heritage experts who come to assess the architecture, notes Graeme Davison of Australia, "do not always consult the locals."[5]

British heritage above all seems an elite domain. Tory grandees hold most of it, decide what to save and display, and instruct others what to venerate. Hereditary gentry own or control the country-house legacy; Establishment values suffuse heritage agencies; the National Trust touts an "ancestralized aesthetic"; Sotheby's and Christie's, the chief purveyors of heritage, vie in aristocratic snobbery (as of 1994, Christie's had five titled directors, Sotheby's four). A lord on the board promises elite contacts and a rich aura of ancient tradition. The National Heritage Memorial Fund used most of its first lottery money to reward the Churchill family for Sir Winston's archives and to refit an exclusive hunting lodge in the Scottish Highlands. This "startling redistribution of wealth from ordinary working people to leading Conservatives," in a national newspaper's words, "is not what most folk expected." Not so, retorted *The Times* arts columnist Richard Morrison; obliging old pals and old school ties was "*exactly* what people expected." If some are galled that "the Great and the Good make a profit out of the past," most assume it is their proper due.[6]

English heritage enshrines a mystique based on inequality and hierarchy. Britons are technically not citizens but "subjects," the Church of England remains officially "established," and half of Parliament is still aristocratic. Palliating misery and arrogance, elites offer a paternalist gloss on gulfs dividing squire and serf, master and servant, propertied and destitute. Heritage centers transmute historical poverty into wholesome, warm, and welcoming frugality.

However defunct, the stately home remains the "heart and centre of the national identity," in Nigel Dennis's epitaph:

A whole world lived in relation to it. Millions knew who they were by reference to it. Hundreds of thousands look back to it, and not only grieve for its passing but still depend on it . . . to tell them who they are. Thousands who never knew it are taught . . . to cherish its memory and to believe that without it no man will be able to tell his whereabouts again.

The descendants of former serfs who now wander in wonder around one-time masters' mansions are said to "feed on a nostalgia for visible social differences. 'The World We Have Lost' is one where people knew where they stood," in Raphael Samuel's words; "classes were classes," yet the British felt themselves a truly unified people.[7]

England's National Trust, whose saga of stewardship I limned in Chapter 3, evokes the poet Peter Levi's credo that this heritage "is and ought to be essentially elitist." In these family-tenanted mansions open to public view, residual elite privilege is mostly respected. If a few peers fear for their heirlooms—at Longleat, spoons are sewn to the table-cloth—most judge that awestruck paying guests are "more likely to pinch the Earl's toothbrush than his Rembrandt."[8]

Lineage is widely felt to entitle stewardship. When environment minister Nicholas Ridley in 1988 told old elites to sell out if they could not keep up the stately homes their ancestors had "bought, stolen or married into," Lord Saye and Sele reacted with hauteur: "Do you think that by removing us and installing a *nouveau riche* family, the heritage would be maintained in the way that we maintain it? Would they want to open their Peter Jones–furnished rooms to the public?" It takes old "families who cherish them and can give them continuity" to husband the heritage. Like other chatelains, Saye and Sele sees himself less an owner than a hereditary national custodian.[9] Breeding is truly all: a variety of cow exclusively owned by Norfolk peers since 1225 is served up as "Chartley Cattle Special" at London's Savoy Grill; an apt end for a noble herd.

Privilege is justified by benefits beyond England alone. Only "a hierarchical society with a large leisure class" has ever had high civilization, holds a *Times* ex-editor. Adducing Augustan Rome (for the odes of Horace), Medici Florence (for Botticelli), Madame Pompadour's Versailles (for Watteau), and Mozart's Vienna—legacies that "still reach out to make us happy"—William Rees-Mogg extols elite virtues alike for high art and for the common weal.

Elite apologists are not confined to Britain. Noble names festoon

Europa Nostra, the Continental historic buildings lobby. The American Heritage Foundation is a bastion of reaction, and America's built legacy still a largely WASP preserve. Most historic houses the world over focus on eminent lives untainted by manual toil. American magnates who amassed European art legacies—Morgan, Frick, Vanderbilt, Carnegie, Huntington—were first famed as robber barons; only immense wealth made them benefactors of national heritage.

Popular nostalgia nowadays sustains elite legacies that long ago lost real power, like British royalty. A cult of nobility flourishes anew in Italy; unlike Old Masters and antiquities, contessas and marchesas cost nothing to conserve and are seldom stolen for collectors abroad. Peoples freed from imposed Soviet leveling dust off legacies of *anciens régimes*, re-embracing not only relics but returning elites. But such retrograde snobberies are exceptions to the general flight of heritage from elite control and concerns.

Even in Britain, Raphael Samuel shows, heritage is not simply or even primarily elite. Much that is marketed as gentrified is actually populist in origin. Edith Holden's nostalgic best-seller, *The Country Diary of an Edwardian Lady* (1977), is the work of a left-wing Birmingham schoolteacher; the very notion of heritage centers was launched as a populist crusade.[10] Radical conspiracy theorists see heritage as a return to feudalism engineered by ruling elites and complain that "patrician cosmopolitan taste" usurps folk tradition. But they ignore the liberal folklorists, steam-engine enthusiasts, and working-class influences that in recent decades have made heritage quotidian, familiar, and open to all.

If elite remnants seem regressive, popular legacies pose their own problems. Populist doctrine justifies the abuse or even the demolition of any heritage damned as exclusive, from Irish Georgian dwellings to West Indian plantation houses. In the supposed public interest, any legacy may be at risk. Timber firms in Tasmania contended that to "preserve our cultural heritage by permitting logging and reforestation [would] serve our future generations" better than creating an "artificial natural heritage by banning it." Promoting mining and timber extraction in federal lands, President Bush's Interior Secretary argued that "land is our heritage to use and not just lock up and put away, where only backpackers can go."[11] Pandering to *lumpenproletariat* anxiety, corporate interests deploy heritage rhetoric to discredit heritage conservers.

Heritage is too complex, various, and widespread to classify by political faith. Left and right, elite and mass spokesmen alike nail heritage to their mastheads—or distance themselves from its follies. "Heritage may be 'people's history' in one manifestation, it may be about New Age travelers or saving old buildings and landscapes from road developments and property barons," Patrick Wright glosses Samuel's view, "but it can also be retrograde arts policy, cowering architectural pastiche, and reactionary polemic recoiling on any progressive development." Yet heritage is also, Samuel suggests, a true rarity in public life today—a realm free from political allegiance where "it is possible to invoke an idea of the common good without provoking suspicion of party interest," and to advance "notions of ancestry and posterity . . . without embarrassment or bad faith."[12]

INCOHERENCE AND INANITION

Heritage today all but defies definition. Overuse reduces the term to cant. So routinely is heritage rated a good thing that few ask what it is good for. In modern Britain "there is no such thing as a bad heritage," charges journalist Neal Ascherson; "everything the government calls heritage is holy." A New Englander groans that "no matter what comes up in this town, somebody fastens the word *heritage* to it. It's a pain in the neck." An Old Englander brands heritage an "invisible, growing, creeping, chintzy monster."

Legacies so protean seem hopelessly amorphous. In Italy, stewards beleaguered by neglect and larceny bewail the lack of a comprehensive inventory; the problem is that "no one really knows what the heritage is." In Britain, scolds *The Times*, "the national heritage is a sacred cow, which everyone wants to milk, but nobody can adequately define." At American jazz and folk festivals the word heritage simply means "different kinds of music." Memorials, monuments, commemorations, and museums merge into muddled incoherence. "Heritage" proving too vague to use in schools, British history curriculum advisers in 1990 replaced it with the narrower term inheritances.

Yet its very *lack* of explicit meaning endears heritage to many custodians. "It's one of those words or concepts which nobody questions," says the British Tourist Authority; hence everyone "tends to want to support" it. Untrammeled by definition, heritage agencies feel free to back whatever they favor at any given moment—an archive, a tithe barn, a snuffbox, an ancient woodland. Since what is valued is always in flux, it is best to let heritage go on redefining itself.[13] This does have some merit, though Britain's National Heritage Memorial Fund deploys it to vindicate, without further ado, its own capricious priorities: yesterday a crumbling castle, today Winston Churchill's papers, tomorrow the mystique of cricket.

Yet, because more accrues than gets discarded, patrimonies grow ever more inchoate. As noted in Chapters 1 and 2, masses of trivia lumber private and public legacies alike. We hang on to empty jars, old phone books, keys to houses long left—all frugally stewarded against unlikely need. Any museum visitor will recognize the Kansan curator who distinguishes fifteen kinds of barbed wire, enumerates three thousand dollars' worth of buttons—"shell buttons, glass buttons, buttons from Europe, all kinds of buttons,"—and lovingly displays "an arrow recovered from the stomach of a cow belonging to James A. Gaumer after the Indian raid, a cigar made by an Oberlin woman who once worked in a cigar factory in New York, [and] a stuffed cobra with electrical tape around it where it broke."

Such outré excess echoes Renaissance cabinets of curiosity that combined ostrich eggs and orangutans with unicorn horns and saucers from the Last Supper. Collectors became targets of 18th-century satire; Addison's Nicholas Gimcrack willed to his wife "a dried cockatrice," to his daughters "my receipt for preserving dead caterpillars and three crocodile's eggs," and to a learned, worthy friend "my rat's testicles." Could even Gimcrack have imagined that lavatory papers and airplane-sickness bags would now be collectors' items?[14]

Pop celebrity endows the most trifling relics with devotional value. Peter Rabbit, the world's oldest licensed character, has spawned 18 million replicas, and Japanese devotees of Beatrix Potter's cuddlesome creatures all but engulf her Hilltop Farm. The crudeness critics deplore in rock 'n' roll memorabilia detracts not a whit from prices paid by avid collectors. Toenail cuttings from John Lennon and Yoko Ono's Amsterdam Hilton "bed-in" are featured in a *Sgt. Pepper* 25th birthday display; devotees circulate liters of Elvis Presley's sweat. Once-quirky foibles become hallowed national legacies. The English National Trust treasures the omnivorous Sir Vauncey Harpur-Crewe's Calke Abbey, crammed with stuffed birds and animals, seashells, rocks, swords, butterflies, baubles and gewgaws as a time capsule, husbanding "the disorder and haphazard arrangement of things" as found.[15]

Heritage not trivialized may be devalued by duplication. Because so many Blue Plaques now mark the homes of Britain's famous, they come to seem less badges of honor than redundant pimples. The Handel House Trust at the composer's London home, 25 Brook Street (1723–59), was peeved by a 1995 application for a commemorative plaque to Jimi Hendrix next door at 23 (late 1960s)—a pique aggravated by the rock guitarist lover's claim that since "Hendrix has sold more records than Handel, he's more relevant to today's society."

Legacies ever less selective and easier to replicate lose the aura of rarity, the vitality of local links, and the verve of actual experience. Gone are the days of "exchanging cigarettes and jeans for an Attic vase in the burnt hills of Greece," grieves an ex-globetrotter; those New Guinea bowls once acquired by arduous travel are no different from the ones you can now get more cheaply at the Pottery Barn. The heritage once cherished by missionaries and anthropologists gives way to tourist kitsch and airport art.

Critics castigate heritage for displacing real industry, with museums breeding like maggots on the graves of enterprise. The sign that once heralded "Chesterfield—Centre of Industrial England" now reads "Chesterfield—Historic Market Town." Loss of skills, prophesy British doomsters, presages "an ill-educated outpost with nothing to sell but our heritage." The advent of a Rock and Roll Hall of Fame in Cleveland, Ohio, struck a fan as rock's death knell, implying the great songs had all been written. Heritage is no substitute for hard labor. "I'm glad I've got a job," says a Welsh coal-museum "miner," "but it isn't real work." Heritage stewardship thwarts farmers' productive zeal; the size of the yield, not the look of the field, makes farming worthwhile.

Much legacy care cripples enterprise. Michael Herzfeld shows conservation bureaucracy stifling local initiatives in Rethemnon, Crete. After a surfeit of heritage in Israel, "a land choked by the clinging vines of its past," Mordecai Richler blessed his native Canada for its absence. But in America, too, heritage shunts aside the present. Made famous by Sinclair Lewis's *Main Street* (1920), Sauk Centre "used to be a town to live in," said its mayor after heritage took over; "now it's Sinclair Lewis's town."[16]

To value everything obsolete as heritage stymies change; yesterday's progress becomes today's tradition and tomorrow's sacrosanct legacy. With a preservation order on a linoleum floor in Newcastle, who can confidently redecorate again? "If lino has come into its inheritance, can limcrusta be far behind?" wonders an observer. "How long will it be before it is an offense to remove a satellite dish?" To save anything and everything old, or to reevoke it in period flavor, seems pathologically regressive, like commemorative ritual in fin-de-siècle France, or the obsessive reliving of childhood memories Freud found in his patients.[17]

COMMERCIAL DEBASEMENT

Heritage is sacred; peddling it affronts decency, and no one should profit from it. Such is the common plaint. What appalls a cathedral librarian about the British Museum buying a rare Bible "is that this transaction should have been made for money. The Tyndale New Testament is part of our national heritage, not an artifact to be sold to raise funds." Heritage should be beyond price. "I could not imagine a sum that would compensate for the ruin of this beautiful countryside," says a foe of a 1994 Bath highway bypass. "Can we call ourselves a civilised society when we can no longer recognise that our rural heritage is priceless?" As a rabbi said of auctioning a treasured Torah scroll given in perpetuity to Jews' College, London, "this is not just a question of Jewish interest, but of heritage interest. To sell is a scandal."

That heritage is an industry at all damns it in critics' eyes. "Save Elgar from marketing!" plead enemies of tourism at the composer's birthplace. So wary of commercial taint are New York's art dealers that they avoid any mention of money; "even when we type our invoices, we don't type a dollar sign," one avowed in 1988. "It's just numbers." Opening Buckingham Palace to paying visitors in 1993 was said to reduce the Royal Family to "ordinary tradesmen." Disney's abortive Historyland evoked images of a Patrick Henry robot declaiming "Give me liberty—or give me a burger with fries."

Heritage customarily bends to market forces. Its vendors confessedly scant history to entertain or, as one put it, "take what's done and give it a little intensification." Few visited an Indiana pioneer village that featured "1836 Prairietown" as a cohesive neighborhood, because, curators found, "the past we presented was boring." So they revamped the Hoosier community as "controversial."[18] Boredom is taboo. A travel brochure purveys such milestones of Connecticut popular culture as the lollipop, the hamburger, the cotton gin, vulcanized rubber, and all-night "I Love Lucy" festivals as "a history lesson without the boring stuff."

Whether hawking medieval squalor or chocolate-box nostalgia, heritage outbids the seemlier pasts of historians, antiquaries, and aesthetes. The 1994 art auction critic who said "history had no price" did not mean it was immoral to mention money, but that historical provenance lured lots of it. "We may not be much good at learning from it," says a lover of England's piquant heritage, "but we daily get better at selling the stuff." Indeed, the price tag on a Picasso attracts more notice than the painting. "To start or expand a collection" you could arduously study paintings and befriend historians and curators, runs a Citibank ad, or—far easier—"you could just talk to your private banker." The heritage market makes philistines of us all.[19]

The luster of lucre dominates heritage tourism. "Wow!" exclaimed an American at the Tower of London's jazzed-up Crown Jewels, "William the Conqueror meets Walt Disney." Launching a 1995 promotion of Hadrian's Wall, Roman Britain's defense against northern barbarians, English Heritage chief Jocelyn Stevens ranked the wall with the Taj Mahal and the Great Wall of China; but his real clincher was that this "awesome construction would cost £3.5 billion to build today."

Legacy peddles everything from cereal to champagne: Moët & Chandon restored two Versailles drawing rooms to celebrate the champagne firm's 250-year union with France's national heritage. Renault advertises cars that echo the refinement of a Gainsborough, the stealth of Henri Rousseau's jungle scenes, the tranquility of a Berthe Morisot. Colt guns, Busch beer, and Wells Fargo Bank sponsor—and vend their wares at—the Gene Autry Western Heritage Museum.[20] Defunct glory has special appeal. "The sun may have set on the Empire, but the legacy lives on," boasts the Bombay Company of its Singapore Raffles Serving Table.

Demand for heritage goods and events is insatiable. The most pious commemorations spawn souvenir kitsch. Any allusion to the bicentenary opened American purses in 1976: Dolly Madison's stars 'n' stripes cupcakes, red-white-and-blue coffins, haircuts with sprayed-on coonskin hats, Uncle Samwiches, and Revolutionary cherry pie made a "buy-centennial" bonanza. D-Day veterans in 1995 stormed Nor mandy beaches strewn with cheap souvenirs. Heritage tourism became travel's fastest growing sector in 1992; tourists may be targeted as victims from Tallahassee to Trebizond, yet they keep on coming.

Heritage *is* entrepreneurial. The reuse of historic buildings in America is pushed "primarily because it can be shown to make money." Tourist profits are the "prime duty" of English Heritage; its chief promised in 1992 to slough off unprofitable sites "to produce more money." Given the art legacy peddled abroad, a parliamentarian surmised that after "selling off the family silver [we] will soon be selling off the cutlery, too."

No wonder the public feels cheated of its birthright. Admission charges at Westminster Abbey and Windsor Castle, inflated to fleece foreign visitors, price heritage out of domestic reach. Plans to conceal Stonehenge from passersby seem aimed to stop "people getting a free look; are they going to screen off all our national monuments," asks a critic, as a "step towards privatizing the nation's heritage?" Degraded by a superhighway, the White Cliffs of Dover are now scavenged for souvenirs. "If the rocks sell well to Americans," fears famed protector Vera Lynn, "that could be the thin end of the wedge as far as the cliffs are concerned."

Heritage artifice sells so well that "meaningful history has all but vanished from public life," Hewison charges; Britain is "a knacker's yard [where] sacrilegious travesty blasphemes [the] real past." A Heritage Trading Company touts red telephone kiosks as national tradition. "Hooligans" at English Heritage become "less and less interested in the past for its own sake," more only "in what they can get out of it." Sales of manorial lordships typify a heritage industry that "taints, falsifies and undermines genuine institutions and traditions . . . for trivial commercial reasons."[21] Hucksters claim they save heritage: were it not for RMS Titanic Inc. stewardship, "unscrupulous treasure hunters with no respect for the past could take over" the shipwreck site.

Such hypocrisy makes heritage a ready target for mockery:

"Get your ancestors here! Get your ancestors here!" The cry came from a raggedy old man, pushing his barrow up the Bayswater Road . . . "Get

your ancestors here! Lovely, fresh ancestors! . . . Cross my palm with traveller's cheques and I'll find you an ancestry you'll be proud of for the rest of
your life."[22]

Antiheritage animus stems partly from doubts that *any* of it remains
authentic. To pass off fake manorial titles, con men copied names from
the 11th-century Domesday Book and got bogus experts to certify their
"Institute of Heraldic Affairs." But how does a real manorial lordship
differ from a pretend one? "What is a 'genuine' title," asks columnist
Matthew Parris, "but a set of ludicrous conventions?" Such legacies are
real only in the mode of the ceremonial stuffed badger in Nigel Dennis's
Cards of Identity—not "the actual, token badger, a clip of artificial fur set
in an osier staff," but just "an emblem of the token."

Heritage is also chided for hallowing the horrific and selling souvenirs of catastrophe and scenes of slaughter. The Kennedy death site is
Dallas's biggest tourist draw. Young visitors to Auschwitz glory in gore,
prize Nazi insignia, and gloat over jackboots. Dubonnet ads cite the
"blood red history [of] the mysterious and ill-fated Cathars" butchered
750 years ago; "no wonder the local drink is blood-red and bitter-
sweet." Heritage tourism touts locales of classic infamy: Paris sewers,
Welsh coal mines, slave auctions, concentration camps. Time-Life
Books invites Americans to bring "the full horror of battle straight into
your living room; relive the horrors of Gettysburg in the comfort of
your own home."

Domesticating horror poses disturbing issues. "Can we learn anything
from history," asks a critic, "when its most sobering lessons are defanged
and turned into vacation amusements?" Slavery and genocide "routinely
depicted as feel-good experiences" make us "morally obtuse to their
shame." A holiday in a converted concentration camp persuades guests
the Nazis weren't really all that bad. Striped pajamas in a 1995 Paris fashion show, suggestive of Auschwitz inmates, typify the banalizing of evil.

Yet victims' heirs often put up with it. To fund its museum, the Anne
Frank Foundation in Amsterdam feels forced to market pens and diaries
with her name but vows to draw the line at crockery, balloons, and T-
shirts. "As a Romanian, I am sorry that Romania's main symbol in the
West is Dracula," said Dan Matei when Coppola's 1992 vampire film hit
the box office, but "as the minister of tourism, I have to take advantage

of this." Lancastrians loathed Orwell's caustic exposé of slum squalor in *The Road to Wigan Pier* (1937), but they welcome the receipts from Wigan's "The Way We Were" heritage theme park. "Orwell used Wigan and got a lot out of it," says a local councillor, and "we've done the same thing back to him."[23]

Marketing corrupts its purveyors along with the heritage; indeed, they are its main victims. Garbed in clogs and shawls, occupying thatched cottages, and mouthing pseudo-Tudor, redundant coal miners and farm laborers keep off the dole by mimicking their forebears. As a miner-father tells his sulky son in Glynn's cartoon, "You'll work down the Heritage Museum, like your mother and me." The Welsh call putting locals into glass cases for tourists to gawp at "cultural prostitution"; Jamaicans bluntly say that "tourism is whorism." The parallel points up our aversion to market a look instead of a product. "Only prostitutes offer themselves, rather than what they make," alleges Yi-Fu Tuan. "In order to prosper, they have to sell themselves—their smile, their accent, their heritage, their grandmother. They are no longer workers but charmers."

Foreigners often get blamed for corrupting our heritage: American preference for a "prettier England" led the BBC to replace *Adam Bede's* harsh Derbyshire scenery with soft Cotswold contours. But the rot spreads; "we ourselves have come to prefer the gussied-up version of our past, allowing foreigners to buy it, tart it up and then sell it back to us." Or replacing our legacy with theirs; much commended for its scenery ("the English countryside never looked so good"), *Cadfael* of medieval Shrewsbury was actually filmed in Hungary. The myth of Britain as a land in love with its past—a past now fatally corrupted by commerce—becomes a reality.

All these laments have hoary pedigrees. To be sure, heritage today peddles a wider range of goods to more buyers than ever before. But it has long been vulgarized, faked, and sold: the medieval relic trade outdid any modern scam. What *is* novel is the mistaken notion that such abuses are new and hence intolerable. Critics seem unaware that heritage has always twisted the past for some present purpose. In damning its distortions, they counterpose a mirage: a past that does not pander to elite and other interests, an unadulterated history that once was and should be ours, a "true" past of archives and artifacts that heritage perverts. From this fallacious contrast flow charges of triviality, vulgarity, bias, mendacity—and above all, of heritage as bad history, history as too precious and fragile to be left to heritage.

"BAD" HISTORY

The crux of most aspersions against heritage is that it undermines "real" history, defiling the pristine record that is our rightful legacy. Critics who idealize this unsullied past view history as true because innate, heritage as false because contrived. History is the past that actually happened, heritage a partisan perversion, the past manipulated for some present aim. Substituting an image of the past for its reality, in the typical plaint, heritage effaces history's intricate coherence with piecemeal and mendacious celebration, tendering comatose tourists a castrated past. English reenactments are alleged to pervert historical fact, American heritage buffs to make history misleading and biased. Inveighing against such fraud, historians claim to be the sole proper guardians of a past they must rescue from shallow heritage semblances. "Do we want historical memory to be managed simply by investors and producers?" asks a leading historian. "Do we want the past remade by people who think they have done their duty when the costumes are taken from the right painting or woodcut?"[24]

Sham accuracy—what Ada Louise Huxtable terms "the studious fudging of facts"—especially vexes historians. Fanatical regard to minutiae is an "authentic" heritage hallmark. Devisers of the Oxford Story exhibit spent "weeks calling experts to find out if the figure of Edmond Halley . . . would have one eye closed when gazing through his telescope. 'Our questions are so thorough that experts sometimes say they are silly, but to do this properly, every detail has to be authentic.'" But as with Disney's "trademark meticulousness" in researching *Pocahontas*, such verisimilitude often cloaks major bias. When television showed the polar explorer Scott as a bungling knave rather than a tragic hero, visual fidelity was felt to verify the calumny. "It wouldn't matter if it wasn't so well done," said Royal Geographical Society director John Hemming. "Scott's ship is magnificent. The dogs are right, the costumes are right. It *looks* like gospel truth—apart from the absence of penguins." But the *history* it told was all wrong.[25]

Historians especially censure heritage's political bents. California's Board of Education fended off minority demands to "delete unhappy events or blemishes" from history texts "in the mistaken interest of fileopietism or children's self-esteem." After all, "the purpose of historical study is not to glorify one's ancestors, nor anyone else's ancestors," as one historian put it, "but to understand what happened in the past" with sober accuracy.[26] As shown in the next chapter, this is an aim most history textbooks reject outright and few historians achieve, though most consider it a worthy ideal.

That ideal was conspicuously absent from Disney's 1994 design for an American Historyland, pandering to a past that would leave a smile on every visitor's face. Disney was "not likely to risk the disquiet good history stirs nor sustain the attention any serious engagement with history requires," feared historians. "What sort of history are we left with if subject matter deemed 'too sensitive' is excised?" Or a Civil War encampment stripped of any connection to underlying social and political issues? Or a small-town America that celebrated middle-American virtues with no mention of local parochialism or coercion by banks and railroads? Any history "that challenge[d] deeply embedded Whiggish notions of progress [was] denied, avoided, or coopted." Typically, sensory overload would preclude all but "the shallowest engagement with historical materials." And simulations that privileged experience over learning would "create a false sense of intimacy with a past" not really understood at all.[27]

Confronting bogus history, historians are bound to "compete with what they believe is the way it really was"—what a leading spokeswoman termed their own "better grounded and less fanciful depictions." Curators of historical museums must likewise "stake their claim to being the best tellers of accurate stories based upon real people and real objects." The historian's past should be potent enough. "It is more exciting to write true history than fictional history," declaims Gertrude Himmelfarb; "to try to rise above our interests and prejudices than to indulge them; . . . to enter the imagination of those remote from us in time and place than to impose our imagination upon them; . . . to get the facts as right as we can than to deny the very idea of facts." For even the most relativist historians "the ability to distinguish between fact and fiction is absolutely fundamental"; it is their sacred obligation to expose heritage-inspired invention.[28]

Too often, critics fear, historians fail to do so. Heritage's mass-marketed deceptions seem more and more to supplant historically objective views of bygone times. The gap left by the scrupulous but often plodding vision of social historians is filled by the "exploitational entertainments" of "rogues and mountebanks." Past events are appraised less by how momentous they *were* than by how much they matter *now*, as measured by the size of the commemorative parade or the television audience.[29]

In sum, those appalled and alarmed by heritage assail three distinct kinds of evil. For one, they see self-praise and xenophobic passion fomenting nationalist and other strife. Abundant evidence substantiates such charges. Chauvinism and narrow insularity are deeply bound up, as Chapters 8 and 9 detail, with notions of heritage priority and innateness. The problems thus posed for global heritage are examined in Chapter 10.

The very popularity of heritage generates the second cluster of complaints. Heritage is said to be too manifold to be meaningful, too trivial and vulgar to be worthwhile, and too sullied by commerce to remain sacred. However populist, heritage is seen by some as still a pawn of powerful elites who bend it to nefarious ends. Such plaints, while not baseless, seem to me exaggerated and self-contradictory.

The third set of grievances is that heritage falsifies the True Past, with real history succumbing to the chauvinist, shallow, vulgar, commercial, and mendacious perversions just noted. Such critiques embody two common assumptions. One is that history does or should retrieve the past in its actual entirety. The other is that heritage subverts this worthy aim.

Both these assumptions are mistaken. History cannot do what such critics imply; heritage seeks other goals than they suppose. Charges that heritage perverts the past, even if true, are pointless. Heritage and history are closely linked, but they serve quite different purposes. To show why such complaints are voiced, and what is wrong with them, Chapter 5 reviews the nature of history, actual and presumed, and Chapters 6 and 7 show why and how heritage agendas differ from those of history.

Chapter 5

THE PURPOSE AND
PRACTICE OF HISTORY

ABUSE OF HISTORY, as just shown, seems the gravest of heritage sins. How just is this charge? We can judge only by clarifying what both history and heritage seek to do. That is my aim in the next three chapters. This chapter surveys history as an enterprise distinct from heritage and explains why their differences render criticisms of heritage as "bad history" null and void.

History is protean. What it is, what people think it should be, and how it is told and heard all depend on perspectives peculiar to particular times and places. An American scholar in 1948 likened Clio, the muse of history, to a career woman (she had once been a social butterfly); in the Soviet Union, Clio was more likely to be a streetwalker or a bureaucrat.[1]

We all screen history through manifold lenses. Carl Becker's 1931 presidential address to American historians described how "Everyman" patterns history out of a thousand largely unremarked and unrelated sources:

> from things learned at home and in school, from knowledge gained in business or profession, from newspapers glanced at, from books (yes, even history books) read or heard of, from remembered scraps of newsreels or educational films or *ex-cathedra* utterances of presidents and kings, from fifteen-minute discourses on the history of civilization broadcast by courtesy . . . of Pepsodent, the Bulova Watch Company, or the Shepard Stores in Boston.

Today you and I chronicle our own impressions out of materials now quite different from, but no less diversified than, those of Becker's Everyman.[2]

Such pastiches of the past are as idiosyncratic in today's Britain as in 1930s America. A journalist's itemized mélange is drawn from

> ill-remembered lessons, what father did in the war, television documentaries with half the instalments missed, bodice-ripper historical novels, fragments of local folklore, . . . what that French man seemed to be saying on the train, what we saw of Edinburgh Castle before the wee boy got sick, several jokes about Henry VIII and that oil painting of the king lying dead on the battle-field with his face all green.[3]

Any deposit the actual teaching of history may leave is overlain and undermined by myriad other modes of apprehension.

This chapter starts from two premises: that meticulous objectivity is history's distinctive noble aim, and that this aim never is—and never can be—achieved. I then examine how the gulf between aspiration and practice affects historians, who are mostly aware of it, and their audiences, who are mostly not. I end by examining how the past as commonly understood (and misunderstood) shapes what devotees and detractors expect both history and heritage to give them. These two routes to the past are intimately linked, often converging or competing; confusing each with the other is a common cause of animus. I acquit heritage of historians' charges not because heritage is guiltless of deforming history, but because its function is to do just that.

History Idealized as True and Impartial

Because the word history means both the past and accounts about the past, these quite different things—the past that was, and the past as chronicled—are continually confused. The exemplary history that critics contrast with the defects of heritage is the authentic actual past, rather than historians' descriptions of that past. But the actual past is beyond retrieval; all we have left are much-eroded traces and partial records filtered through divers eyes and minds. Historical accounts are riddled with most of the same defects that critics think peculiar to heritage.

Prejudice is the most parlous of these flaws. Many who condemn heritage as biased claim for history an objectivity free from special pleading. Believing that the actual past can be retrieved intact and untarnished, they presume it is historians' task to resurrect the past exactly as it was. True history, in this view, is not made but found. No hint of the historian should intrude; to hear an author's voice would taint an account's veracity and erode its authority. To claim omniscience, history must be anonymous.

Past chroniclers, to be sure, are partly to blame for this delusive conviction. Historians from Thucydides on conceived their craft as ideally truthful. They aimed to present the past "exactly as it was," in Leopold von Ranke's famous phrase, without obtruding their own views; historians should efface themselves utterly from what they wrote. Hence the 2nd-century Greek satirist Lucian's metaphor of the mirror: like a perfect looking-glass, the good historian reflects events exactly as witnessed, "in no way distorted, discoloured, or varying" by his own bias or circumstance.[4]

Well into the 18th century, history was viewed as a *speculum vitae humanae*, an impartial mirror of human actions and duties. The recording angel's neutrality was an Enlightenment ideal. "Disengaged from all passions and prejudices," the Abbé Raynal claimed to be so detached that readers would find in his *Histoire philosophique et politique des deux Indes* (1781) no clue to his country, his profession, or his religion. Diderot held aloofness essential to understanding; only an historian "raised above all human concerns" could make sense of the protean past. "History is a science, in which subjective elements have no place," Fustel de Coulanges taught his students: "It is not I who speak, but history which speaks through me." Modern scientific and statistical modes of probing the past further exalt the historian as all-seeing, dispassionate, and unprejudiced.[5]

Historical truth in earlier times, however, meant something quite different from what it does now. Medieval and early modern Europeans set the facts of history against the fictions of poetry. But the facts sought were eternal verities of character; it was historians' task to chronicle deeds and to illustrate motives and processes that faith and moral experience had already established as timeless truths. What Aristotle said of how things happened in the 4th century B.C. was as true of people and events two millennia later.

But these truths deserved continual reinforcement. In line with Cicero's rhetorical precepts, historians strove for elegant narration, omitting "all trifles and common things" and sparing readers tedious detail, the better to convey conviction. Audiences demanded plausibility and eloquence, not literal accuracy; historians used pathos to move and persuade. Few of Froissart's contemporaries expected his invented speeches and selected dialogues to be accurate transcripts or minded that they were not; what mattered was the moral points being made.[6]

Truth also meant adhering to canonical texts. Geoffrey of Monmouth's 12th-century history of Britain was assailed not for fabricating a myth but for failing to back it up with accepted authors like the 8th-century Bede. Holy Scripture sufficed to disprove pagan historical error; thus the ancients' location of the earth's center at Mount Parnassus (because Jupiter's two circumnavigating eagles had met there) was displaced by Jerusalem, which became indisputably central because Jesus had preached and died there.[7]

The great truths of history were in any case received and eternal; the mission of historians was not to discover but to buttress such facts as the existence of God or, later, the inevitability of progress. Examples chosen as illustrative were by definition true, and those rejected false; the end purified the means. A "true" chronicle of Queen Elizabeth was not the facts about her life but an exposition of her virtues. And secular annals were long elided with sacred faith. Even the annals of America evinced divine will. "In listening to the voice of history," declaimed a historian in 1893, "we well recognize the voice of God."[8]

As faith in received truth dwindled, historians were looked to for their own judgments, not just for evidence to bolster preconceived conclusions. Critical comparison of sources made the prejudice of witnesses and chroniclers more apparent and less pardonable; it began to seem wrong to twist history for any purpose. In 1896 Lord Acton exhorted authors in his *Cambridge Modern History* to lofty impartiality: "Our Waterloo must be one that satisfies French and English, Germans and Dutch alike." Americans, too, supposed the disinterested attitude the proper historical one and aimed to replace "factitious [and] spurious patriotism with one that was authentic and sound."[9]

Such impartiality is hard to come by, since any past worth pursuing is bound to arouse historians' passions. "To exclude the subjective involvement of the observer," argues the philosopher Gadamer, the past must be "dead enough to have *only* historical interest." Only by divesting the past of present relevance can the historian "understand . . . what has been handed down, without necessarily agreeing with it or seeing himself in it."[10]

But a past so austerely impersonal may be too arid to bother recounting, let alone reading. No matter how rigorous it is, history must be able to compel our attention. While shunning heritage's "cosy cuteness," it should be no less inspirational than heritage. Historians ever since Herodotus have sought to reconstruct a real past imaginative enough to render embroidery and cosmetics superfluous. To bring the past to life needs rhetoric that is not just "icing on the cake of history," in J. H. Hexter's phrase, but "mixed right into the batter."[11]

Tasty, though, is seldom what history is now thought to be. Deleted from England's 1994 school syllabus as "not serious history" were Guy Fawkes, London's Great Fire, the Plague, and the King James Bible. But "if we take the good stories out of history, we take the blood out of it as well," protested *The Times*'s William Rees-Mogg. Long after "a thoughtful tutorial on Church–State relations in early medieval England has faded completely, the story of Henry II sending his knights to kill Thomas à Becket in Canterbury Cathedral will remain vivid." So memorable is the tale of King John signing Magna Carta that hundreds of thousands a year visit Salisbury Cathedral to see one of the four originals.

Dispassionate precision wins few readers, as famed past historians well knew. Readers today are adjured to give up old history's swashbuckling romp down the centuries for meticulous accounts of the miserable diet of roof thatchers in the 1750s. But this trendy populist fare is indigestible. "The layman turns aside [from scholars] more concerned with trivial truth than with fertile error," a historian parses Pareto, "and seeks interest and enlightenment elsewhere." U.S. National Parks interpreters were once enjoined to bring the heritage alive like "advertisers selling history."[12] But how does history thus brought alive differ from heritage?

The crucial difference lies in their goals. Objectivity remains a holy grail for even the most engagé historian. As vows of chastity constrain priests and Hippocratic oaths obligate doctors, so historians renounce self-interest for truth. A historian caricatures his colleagues as white-coated clinicians who fancy themselves "animated by pure love of truth, [probing] the past with the same objectivity, neutrality, disinterest, the same Olympian superiority to prejudice, as a scientist peering down his microscope."[13]

To strive for impartiality is one thing; to achieve it another. History as actually written was usually as much moral precept as past record. As the historian of antiquity Fustel de Coulanges put it, "the history of the city told the citizen what he must believe and what he must adore." Chroniclers shaped accounts to please patrons, to praise compatriots, and to aggrandize their own reputations. Early annalists unabashedly puffed sponsors; later historians promoted patriotism. Patriotism continues to shape much history writing and inspires most of its teaching to this day, as Marc Ferro has documented from school texts all over the world. "This work is not conceived as a work of scholarship," as Prime Minister Eric Williams prefaced his 1962 *History of the People of Trinidad and Tobago*. Complementing the "National Anthem, National Coat of Arms, National Birds, National Flower and National Flag" that his people already had, their leader saw his National History as "a manifesto of a subjugated people."[14]

Precursors of Eric Williams, European chroniclers exalted their own ancestral peoples to forge 19th-century national identities. "History is above all a science of national self-awareness," in a Russian historian's phrase. Compulsory schooling confirmed this aim. A century ago eight of ten French school-leavers agreed that patriotism was history's main purpose; history teachers in 1919 felt their chief duty was to imbue citizenship; and French history still shows France as the touchstone of civilization. Though three-fourths of England's 1994 primary school history was British, educational authorities deplored the failure to celebrate traditional culture and heroes "who set an example to us."[15]

Just as schoolbooks a generation ago showed the United States both "perfect and yet making progress all the time," American schools now must teach ennobling national history. Texts that "inspire the children with patriotism [must] tell the truth optimistically," insisted the American Legion in 1925; publishers still hew to those precepts, helping children to discover "our common beliefs" and "appreciate our heritage." National fealty remains the prime purpose of historical study. American history, say educators at Williamsburg, "should ultimately be a story about the process of nation making."[16]

Historians, even some who write school texts, think they inhabit a different world, where history is not only honest and impartial but unprescriptive. But they are not so different as they suppose. In vain do ever more rigorous techniques of retrieving ever more of the past heighten hopes of objectivity. Historians who abjure former biases now fancy themselves less prone to bias; recognizing forerunners' flaws, they suppose their own less serious. But this is an illusion common to every generation. We readily spot the now outgrown motives and circumstances that shaped past historians' views; we remain blind to present conditions that only our successors will be able to detect and correct. "Present-mindedness is as prevalent among all camps of historians," judges David Cannadine, as among the earlier scholars "they so zealously disparage for precisely this error."[17]

Professed enemies of patriotic and feel-good history include some who unwittingly practice it. Championing disinterested inquiry, historian Arthur Schlesinger censures those who exploit history to promote social cohesion. But no sooner are these words out of his mouth than he adds that "above all, history can give us a sense of national identity." Historian Ronald Takaki thinks multicultural perspectives give "a more accurate history, as well as a more inclusive view, of who we are as Americans." But civic goals and good scholarship are not always compatible. "'Accurate' history may teach us to get along together, but then again, it may not," responds a critic. Does Takaki's inclusive vision "ineluctably emerge from a cold, dispassionate examination of our checkered . . . past? Is it forced on us by the overwhelming weight of evidence?" No; "it is projected into the past by our current desire to make it true."[18]

Like some historians, much of the public wrongly supposes presentist bias to be an evil now overcome. Queried at a 1984 museum display about colonial impact on Native American life, most visitors thought it "true" that "Thanks to more objective research, the modern picture of Contact is more correct than earlier versions." But the correct answer was "False—Understanding is always based on personal interpretations of historical documents. Like earlier views, contemporary understanding of Contact also reflects cultural bias." Most respondents were outraged; they refused to accept that history did not shed such error. Awareness that history is never complete and ever revised is rare among nonhistorians. Many react to academic uncertainty with the brusque annoyance of a Norwegian delegate at a 1995 Council of Europe colloquy on history teaching. Surely, he insisted, there must be some data bank of fixed historical truths on which we could all entirely rely.

Few historians think *no* progress is being made toward truth, but even history's keenest devotees know objectivity is unattainable. So pervasive does bias feel that historians begin to succumb to postmodern relativism. History used to be considered an accumulation of certainties, but "remembering the past and writing about it no longer seem the innocent activities they were once taken to be," reflects the historian Peter Burke. "Neither memories nor histories seem objective any longer," but rather are the product of "selection, interpretation and distortion."[19] Why is this so?

Why History Cannot Recover the Real Past

Heritage is scolded for swerving from the true past—selecting, altering, inventing. But history also does this. Like heritage, history cannot help but be different from, as well as both less and more than, the actual past. "Composing history," suggests John Updike, "is like packing a suitcase with objects that persist in overflowing or underfilling the space."[20] A huge literature details how historians come to terms with its inescapable mandate, at once menacing and exhilarating, to transcend the mere recording and replication of the past. In what follows I do little more than touch on a few major issues.

Above all, history departs from the past in being an interpretation rather than a replica: it is a view, not a copy, of what happened. Historical chronicles, however thorough and meticulous, are never more than pale surrogates of the past. Lucian's mirror is ever clouded; all accounts are filtered through blinkered eyes and partisan minds. The broad outlines of the well-known past are generally accepted, but most of what has ever happened can be only partly retrieved or is perennially disputed. And everything that is known or surmised about the past gets reinterpreted through each new generation's updated lenses.

History is less than the past because only a fraction of all events have been noted, only a few of all past lives are remembered, and only fragments of flawed records survive in decipherable form. Least accessible are those aspects of past times that historians are apt to find most crucial—the thoughts and feelings of its inhabitants. "The real, central theme of History is not what happened," many would agree with G. M. Young, the chronicler of Victorian England, "but what people felt about it when it was happening." Yet we cannot know how the past was for those who lived it, even if they themselves claim to tell us. They may be telling what is true for them, but they cannot tell the whole truth, or our kind of truth; what they choose to recount is bound to mean something quite different to us than it did to them. "You may multiply the little facts that can be got from pictures and documents, relics and prints as much as you like," as Henry James told Sarah Orne Jewett, explaining why historical fiction could never be faithful to reality. To depict "the old *consciousness*, the soul, the sense, the horizon of individuals in whose minds half the things . . . that make the modern world were non-existent": this was impossible. "You have to *think* with your modern apparatus [people] whose own thinking was intensely otherwise conditioned."21

Even scholars who immerse themselves in bygone times cannot engage with them as natives or re-create their original auras. "The participant understands and knows his culture with an immediacy and spontaneity the [modern] observer does not share," writes Michael Baxandall of 15th-century Italian art.

> He does not, for example, have to list to himself the five requirements of altarpiece paintings: he has internalized an expectation about these [by long] experience of altarpieces. He moves with ease and delicacy and creative flexibility within the rules of his culture . . . learned, informally, since infancy . . . The observer does not have this kind of knowledge of the culture. He has to spell out standards and rules, making them explicit and so making them also coarse, rigid and clumsy.

The historian who seeks to bring Edwardian England to life by marking each page with "some pungent signal—a brand name, song, form of speech, public person or event in the news"—knows this is cheating, notes Peter Dickinson, because "few people living in a period notice such things. Their real sense of their time is as unrecapturable as the momentary pose of a child."[22] The reader who recalls Becker's mention of Pepsodent and Bulova watches at the start of this chapter, unless he or she is a quite elderly American, is apt to have reached for and missed just such a resonance.

Similar constraints cramp retrievals of anything past. We never see a spinning wheel in a museum as those who once used it did. For them it was a tool; for us it is a *former* tool, left stranded in a glass case by the tides of industrial change; it is now an antique in an atavistic setting. For us to see spinning wheels as they were once seen, the whole history of spinning jennies, Crompton mules, and so forth would have to be unknown, could not have happened. But we cannot divest ourselves of such awareness.[23] Instead, the tangible vividness of these remnants tempts us to ignore our own influence on them—to forget that our own acts, reflecting our own changing concerns, continually alter our understanding of their history.

We gauge what is lost not merely by the minuscule fraction of past events of which some trace survives, but also in our lack of any sense of totality. "The quotidian stuff, the living excelsior in which every event is packed, has evaporated," finds a thwarted chronicler, "leaving old bone buttons and yellowing papers nibbled all over by silverfish." The absence cripples our ability to be aware of past events in anything like complete context:

> "Events" have no meaning unless surrounded by the air they breathe at the time. A million little things . . . make up an era, things everyone knows, things most unlikely to be written down, [things missing from] records, however complete, [that] omit what went without saying; yet what is shared, obvious, unspoken, is what gives [any epoch] life and meaning.

Many aspects of past daily life—did apartments in ancient Rome have doors? did medieval towns stink? did 17th-century clothing itch?—are unknown to us, notes Bernard Bailyn, because no one at the time felt such commonplaces worth recording.[24]

History is *more* than the past because it deals not only with what took place back then, but with myriad consequences of events that go on unfolding beyond their participants' lifetimes. History is not just what happened at the time but the thoughts and feelings, hunches and

hypotheses about that time generated by later hindsight. To be sure, historians often try to describe the past by reliving ancient lives, rethinking
Caesar's thoughts about crossing the Rubicon without being influenced
by knowing what happened next. Such retrievals can convey vivid
immediacy. But they are deficient not only because untranslatable, as
noted above, but also because devoid of retrospection. Hindsight makes
history both more dubious yet far better informed than reports by those
who just noted things as they happened.

Lacking our hindsight, people of the past come to be in considerable
part our own creations. Subjects of biographies seemed to Virginia
Woolf "miraculously sealed as in a magic tank . . . They thought when
they were alive that they could go where they liked." But just "look and
listen and soon the little figures . . . will begin to move and to speak,
and . . . we shall arrange them in all sorts of patterns of which they were
ignorant." Our manipulation betrays their impotence. "The past, because it is past, is only malleable where once it was flexible," in Jeanette
Winterson's distinction. "Once it could change its mind, now it can
only undergo change."[25] And the change it undergoes is induced by
ourselves.

In adding to the past, history also makes it seem unlike the chaotic
present. "History never looks like history when you are living through
it," observes Philip Howard. "It always looks trivial and untidy, and it always feels uncomfortable." Historical hindsight tidies chaos into order,
often into predestined sequence, as though things could not have happened otherwise. "Once we know how things have come out," writes a
historian, "we tend to rewrite the past in terms of historical inevitability." Nations, like persons, commonly contrive designs that come to
seem predestined. In sieving bygone events through current nets,
"history is to the past what astrology is to the solar system," in a critic's
simile; "less a serious attempt to chart paths and orbits than a search for
fanciful patterns and pleasing images."[26]

That history cannot avoid being incomplete, biased, and present-
minded is not the fault of its practitioners but the fate of being what it
is—over, yet still influential. In some ways intimately known, in others
so impervious, history is aptly termed "a hard kernel of contemporary
prejudice surrounded by a soft pulp of disputable facts." In history, no
less than in heritage, bias and error infuse our relations with any past.

COMING TO TERMS WITH BIAS

Historians realize that history always attenuates truth, but beyond academe this deficiency is little known or largely denied. Bereaved by the departure of the past, we take comfort in trusting it can be discerned without error or bias—but only by experts. Faithful retrieval is supposedly reserved to objective, dispassionate, infallible historians.

Most historians know they are not such paragons; indeed, they repeatedly disclaim perfection. Newfound evidence, critical revision, stubborn bias, and mere obsolescence remind historians they are inescapably fallible. But their disavowals fail to dispel popular faith that history, and history alone, can unearth and narrate past Truth.

Truth is the daughter of Time; history is famed as truth's ultimate arbiter. Queries typically posed, such as "How will history judge Nixon?" imply that we are all bound, in the end, to get our just due. (Nixon himself believed that "history will treat me fairly," though "historians probably won't."[27]) History is supposed to cut us all down to size, as Reagan recalled Clare Boothe Luce saying at Kennedy's inaugural: "No matter how exalted or great, history will have time to give him no more than one sentence." Laconic and merciless, truth must out.

Historical faith is instilled in school. "Youngsters have been taught history as they were taught math—as a finite subject with definite right or wrong answers," frets a museum director. Most history texts are "written as if their authors did not exist, as if they were simply instruments of a divine intelligence transcribing official truths," like those 18th-century recording angels. Textbooks are not to be questioned. "All the information is written down," students say, "you've just got to find the answers in the book." High marks depend on giving the "correct" gloss to regurgitated facts. Textbook certitude makes it hard for teachers to deal with doubt and controversy; saying "I don't know" violates the authoritarian norm and threatens classroom control. Hence history teachers adopt the omniscient tone of their texts.

Historians know better, even some who write school texts: they are trained to realize "there are no free-floating details—only details tied to witnesses." But their students ignore witnesses' diverse roles and take it for granted that texts and teachers simply report known facts. That children know too little history and get much of it wrong is a plaint reechoed each generation, as Samuel Wineburg shows. But the primary defect is not their lack of a set of canonical facts; it is "that they do not know what history is in the first place."[28]

Most of us learned history as Simone de Beauvoir recalled of her 1920s schooling, "never dreaming there might be more than one view of past events." Today contrary views may be posed, but alternatives are only good or bad, right or wrong; honest differences of opinion are seldom an option. Asked to decide between two versions of a historical event, a student says, "It was cool to hear both sides of the story and choose who you think was telling the truth."[29] Both sides! Truth! History becomes a courtroom: every story has just two sides, and whoever was wrong must have lied.

In most school texts, history remains one-dimensional even where controversy is rampant. For example, the antiquity of Native American settlement is keenly disputed, but textbook readers would never know this; most texts portray either the "early" or the "late" arrival version as undisputed fact. Loose ends are avoided lest they unravel faith. Everything in school history was "presented as if it were the full picture," recalled a student in 1991, "so I never thought to doubt that it was." No wonder historians find it hard to persuade people that there may be more than one "accurate" version of the same event.[30]

To show children "that history and the way we interpret it is not carved in granite, . . . that the past can never be totally reconstructed, that the study of history is always unfinished," the museum director cited above stresses how provisional it really is:

> We're not saying, "This is the past. Believe it!" . . . We're saying, "Given what we know, this is our best interpretation." [Children] find out we're constantly finding out things that change our perception of the past. They'll learn that what we know about the past today is not what we'll know [tomorrow]. They'll also learn that there are some things we can never find out.[31]

But this laudable lesson is seldom learned, for it is hardly ever taught.

Historians often plead for awareness of bias, but they rarely explain how to recognize it. The ability to see texts as slippery, cagey, protean instruments crafted for social ends, reflections of varied contexts and of authors' own concerns, is a skill unheard-of in school and, indeed, in much college history. Those who lack such training and insight think truth a clear-cut goal, view their own prejudices as facts, and decry contrary views as ignorant bias.

Such certitude explains why so many mistake historians' professed ideals for working realities. To avoid doubt about what to accept or reject, most people draw a firm line between storytelling (false) and history (true), "stuffing down the fishiest of fish tales," notes Winterson, "because it is history."[32] Master fabulists swear fealty to historical truth: Reagan's presidential library features a film in which Reagan quotes Roosevelt, without irony, as saying "History can't be rewritten by wishful thinking."

Historians do aim higher than they can reach. They know they cannot retrieve or recount the past in unbiased entirety or shorn of anachronism, yet they strive to do so as far as they can. Aware that such effort is inherently imperfect, they nonetheless cleave to what seems honest. Knowing they cannot be objective, they feel duty-bound to be at least impartial, in Jacques Le Goff's useful distinction. Save for a postmodern solipsist fringe that fancies all history fatally flawed, historians trust that research enlarges what is known of the actual past. Though their own traits and biases shape that knowledge, it retains an integral autonomy; the past as known is bent, but is never wholly broken, to historians' particular views. Hence Novick's "noble dream" of objectivity rightly remains their enduring if unreachable grail.

But objectivity cannot be historians' general practice. Self-interest suffuses history as it does all human enterprise. In theory, "historians are not allowed to use the past for their own ends," reflects a novelist whose fictional historian (like most real ones) has just done so. How then, she asks, do historians differ from "politicians, house agents, antique dealers, autobiographers or any other category of person" that bends the past to private ends "most of the time"?[33] Perhaps historians do so less frequently or at least less blatantly; no doubt they are more conscious of doing so. Certainly, historians are more alert to the gulf between historical precept and practice. Unlike house agents or antique dealers, they usually do rate the truth of the past above its material benefits to themselves. But in choosing and conveying that truth they are bound to alter and update it according to their own lights. That they cannot avoid manipulating the evidence most historians are also well aware.

Pure truth is praiseworthy, but public faith that historians can realize this goal taxes their task with delusive hopes. In debates over history's proper role in museums, historic sites, and textbooks, public insistence that history be immutably true is said to generate more conflict than any other issue. In these realms both heritage and history have publicly acknowledged roles; the public wants to be sure which is which and so exaggerates their differences. But history differs from heritage not, as people generally suppose, in *telling* the truth, but in *trying* to do so despite being aware that truth is a chameleon and its chroniclers fallible beings. The most crucial distinction is that truth in heritage commits us to some present creed; truth in history is a flawed effort to understand the past on its own terms.

Yet historians are also urged to make history "relevant"—in short, to turn it into heritage. Such pressure demotes objectivity to a secret vice: dedication to pure truth seems too bloodless, too aloof, too uncommitted for historians to defend it in public. Like philistines, the politically correct scorn "academic" interest as spineless, selfish, and effete. Ashamed to confess they enjoy the past for its own sake, not for its immediate relevance, historians cloak high-minded scholarship behind some fabricated "useful" motive.[34]

HISTORICAL FACT, HERITAGE FAITH

History as seen by scholars today means open inquiry into any and every past. But this inclusive perspective is quite new, even in the West. Not only were Africans, Asians, and other natives until recently thought to have no history, so were manual workers, criminals, children, and women. And as noted, historians still devote their main efforts to their own peoples. While accepting in principle that history plays a pivotal role in every human realm, most privilege the study of their own pasts to the neglect of others.

Yet the Western concept of history does sanction a comprehensive, collaborative enterprise, open to all—comprehensive in being part of a universal chronology, collaborative in embracing the findings of myriad colleagues, open in permitting any scrutiny. "In recording the common affairs of the inhabited world as though they were those of a single state," wrote Diodorus Siculus in the 1st century B.C., historians made "a single reckoning of past events and a common clearing-house of knowledge concerning them." The common clearing-house remains the accepted ideal.

The idea of history as universal, and universally accessible, is widely endorsed. To be sure, such a history is still alien to many.[35] But within the global community of scholars it is normative. It is such history that I contrast here with heritage. Other kinds of history—tribal, exclusive, patriotic, redemptive, or self-aggrandizing—are, by and large, heritage masquerading as history.

Testable truth is history's chief hallmark. Historians' credibility depends on their sources being open to general scrutiny. The Abbé Raynal notwithstanding, every historical account displays a bias particular to and inseparable from its time and its author; but to be trustworthy a history must conform to evidence accessible to all. It must also be largely consonant with other accepted chronicles. Not even Mr. Everyman's self-made personal history can overstep limits set by his fellows; having "to live in a world of Browns and Smiths" with whose affairs Everyman's are intimately bound up, as Becker put it, "has taught him the expediency of recalling certain events with much exactness."[36]

Historians rely on received knowledge and reasoned estimates of its likelihood. The history we consensually inherit is not all equally certain, but much of it is exceedingly sure and stable: it has survived the test of time and the vicissitudes of rival views. We find it credible not because we ourselves are likely to see documentary proof, but because we also inherit confidence in the repute of those who have checked it out. History is verified as much by collegial trust as by its canonical contents; "we agree to regard each other—at least some others—as bearers of truth," concludes a folklorist, and accept what they tell us as being reasonably close to what must have happened.[37]

Compatibility with the received overall picture lends credence to any account of the past, whereas one discordant with the attested panorama is prima facie incredible. We may be uncertain just who killed Caesar, but for us "to believe that Caesar was not assassinated" at all, we would have to reject "an enormous range of other implicated facts, both about Caesar and about Roman history . . . in general." To jettison all this would soon make it difficult to believe *anything* about the past, Leon Pompa points out. If we seriously doubted so much of accepted history, we would be forced to distrust all extant historical thought.[38]

Since we can accept easily only new histories "compatible with what we have inherited," the historical canon does curtail our ability to learn new things. Advocates of women's or gay or African-American or other alternative pasts justly complain that mainstream historians are slow to heed radically new perspectives. But even these newly emergent histories in the main enlarge rather than falsify the existing canon. And the makeup, not merely the details, of that canon is steadily reshaped as time distances its events, alters their relevance, and demands their reinterpretation.

Heritage is not like this at all. It is not a testable or even a reasonably plausible account of some past, but a *declaration of faith* in that past. Critics castigate heritage as a travesty of history. But heritage is not history, even when it mimics history. It uses historical traces and tells historical tales, but these tales and traces are stitched into fables that are open neither to critical analysis nor to comparative scrutiny.

Heritage and history rely on antithetical modes of persuasion. History seeks to convince by truth and succumbs to falsehood. Heritage exaggerates and omits, candidly invents and frankly forgets, and thrives on ignorance and error. Historians' pasts, too, are always altered by time and hindsight. To be taken seriously by other historians, however, these revisions must conform with accepted tenets of evidence. Heritage is far more flexibly emended. Neither history nor heritage is free to depart altogether from the well-attested past. But historians ignore at professional peril the whole palimpsest of past percepts that heritage casually bypasses.

Heritage is immune to critical reappraisal because it is not erudition but catechism; what counts is not checkable fact but credulous allegiance. Commitment and bonding demand uncritical endorsement and preclude dissenting voices. Deviance from shared views is not tolerated because group success, even sheer survival, depends on everyone pulling together. Thus for Finnish patriots the *Kalevala*, though "a clear counterfeit," is nonetheless a holy book that reflects their deepest being: "if a Finn ridicules the Kalevala, . . . that is a sin against the Holy Ghost." Rooted attachments to *Heimat*, iconic symbols of German village scenes, are likewise antipathetic to rational history. Part and parcel of everyday life, Heimat is enjoyed as an ancestral legacy stressing empathy and identity, not rigorous historical knowledge.[39] Other peoples' heritages, as the next chapters show, similarly scrap historical strictures to embrace spiritual certitudes.

To vilify heritage as biased is thus futile: bias is the main point of heritage. Prejudiced pride in the past is not a sorry consequence of heritage; it is its essential purpose. Heritage thereby attests our identity and affirms our worth. When the patriot upholds "my country, right or wrong," not history but heritage assures him, it is always right. "Monuments, festivals, mottoes, oratory . . . never help history," warned the sociologist William Graham Sumner, "they protect errors and sanctify prejudice." Swamped by bogus tales of wartime heroics, Richard Cobb concluded that to be on the safe side, historians ought to make it a rule "to assume that our country is *always* wrong."[40] Only thus could they begin to question normative national myths.

Heritage diverges from history not in being biased but in its attitude toward bias. Neither enterprise is value-free. But while historians aim to reduce bias, heritage sanctions and strengthens it. Bias is a vice that history struggles to excise; for heritage, bias is a nurturing virtue. Blind allegiance to nation, state, or faith remains the main aim of most school history. A majority of American parents polled in 1977 had grave doubts about history as taught in school, but nonetheless wanted their children to accept it as gospel. "Embarrassed to belong to a country so in love with its legends that it refused to let anybody speculate about them," a British journalist "would be more proud of a country that valued the truth. Even about itself."[41] But no country can afford such bleak transparency.

DEAD HISTORY, VITAL HERITAGE?

History remains remote; personal immediacy is a heritage hallmark. Dealing with distant times and events beyond their own ken, many see history as inaccessibly alien; for them, "historical" events are those before living memory. Thus Burgundian villagers shun written history, which deals with episodes of national scope that are outside their control, remote from everyday life, and menacing to stable routines. Instead they prize an orally recounted local heritage laden with enduring and cyclic events, easy to grasp and comfortingly predictable.[42]

Unless communal memory is sustained as heritage by ritual rehearsal, time soon distances it beyond retention. Even the most striking events fade away as they recede into the distant past, "each succeeding generation losing some . . . significance that once was noted in them," wrote Becker, "some quality of enchantment that once was theirs." The Holocaust, long a part of Israel's school history curriculum, in 1978 became compulsory in citizenship classes and in 1981 a criminally undeniable event—a doctrine anchored in national law. For Israelis, the Holocaust is heritage; elsewhere, the most vigilant memorialists cannot keep it from fading away into history. "For children in schools today," reflects a London journalist,

> the Holocaust ranks along with the Massacre of Glencoe, the Pilgrimage of Grace, and that bloke who got an arrow in his eye and let in William the Conqueror. None of these things has anything to do with us, because they happened a long time ago, and things that have happened a long time ago are "history," and the most obvious thing about history is that it is over.[43]

How far history is over contrasts, for some Britons, with how alive it remains in America. "History really matters to you," Peter Laslett reacted to my book *The Past Is a Foreign Country*. It mattered enormously to every American "that Abraham Lincoln and the North won the Civil War. It is the same with . . . the Founding Fathers: the events, the outcomes of the past are part and parcel of their . . . *being* Americans." For Laslett, "absolutely nothing in British history weighs like this." Cromwell and the Roundheads, Magna Carta, and the Norman Conquest meant little because "nothing whatever in my present life depends upon" them. An odd judgment, coming from the English author of *The World We Have Lost*! But it is a view countless schoolchildren share. Teenagers in northern England, for example, see history as about the rich, the famous, and Home Counties types. Asked if events he himself witnessed might be recorded as "history," a boy responds, "Oh no! not in Castleford; maybe if I lived down South."[44]

Yet across the Atlantic history also feels remote, for reasons both similar and different. "Americans have never been on truly familiar, companionable terms with their history," holds the geographer Wilbur Zelinsky. And despite (or owing to) myriad history theme parks, the past now seems more than ever quaint and atrophied. Surveys show that even college students want to know history only when it impinges directly on self-interest. They otherwise dismiss it as a pointless pot-pourri of puerile strife featuring Columbus, Lincoln, Henry VIII, the Norman Conquest—"the boring stuff from school."[45]

The stuff from school is boring because it is both remote and unrelated to them. "Our country was founded a very long time ago, roughly around 200 B.C.," the cartoon figure Calvin tells his teacher. "200 B.C.?!" "Before Calvin; that's what's important!" He's made to stand in the corner. "For Calvin, as for many others," adds a historian, "the country's history seems to reside in one corner, over there, back then, while *his* life exists in another." So do most dismiss formal history. "I sat through many history classes where I read some of their stuff," said Disney's chief executive of historians who opposed his theme-park plans, "and I didn't learn anything." He had just been bored. "The modern mind has been growing indifferent to history," suggests an eminent historian, "because history, conceived as a continuous nourishing tradition, has become useless to it."[46] Indeed, many get by without ever mentally locating a historical past.

Historical awareness, psychologists since Piaget have noted, may demand more maturity than many adults ever attain. As a child, Annie Dillard "breathed the air of history all unaware, and walked oblivious through its littered layers." Only when she shed her childhood could she "see the setting of her dreaming private life—the nation, the city, the neighborhood, the house where the family lives—[and] locate the actual, historical stream." To apprehend that stream, one must leave the water and survey it from a distant shore.[47]

Few venture so far. An Englishwoman hunting her family roots is amazed "that many of us know far more about Disraeli, Elizabeth I, Florence Nightingale, Tolstoy or Edith Piaf than we do about our own relations." But the majority of Britons, like Americans, have only shadowy mnemonic links with the history they learned in school. For most it is not history, but heritage masked as history, that brings the past to life. "The only strong link we have with the past is to identify with the interests of our predecessors [and] converse with them," judges Frank Kermode. "That still seems a valuable inheritance." But it is valued for its *present* resonance.[48]

It is as heritage that visitors engaged with the statue of St. Patrick at Glasgow's 1992 archdiocesan exhibition—Catholics kissing his foot,

Protestants spitting in his face. Pilgrims used to come to Walter Scott's Kenilworth "not to see a place where the acts of history had really happened long ago," writes a literary historian, "but to see a place where the deeds of fancy were fictionally recurring forever."[49] In Helsinki nurses are on call at many heritage sites lest patriotic ardor overcome visitors; Finns call their heritage "hot."

Active involvement distinguishes heritage from history. "You're pinned down by enemy fire . . . two of your men are badly wounded," runs a British army recruitment appeal. "WHAT USE IS A DEGREE IN ME-DIEVAL HISTORY?" Don't just be a bystander: "Join; instead of reading history, you might be helping to steer its course." The phrase "Barnsley Council will make history today" means that it will do something significant and innovative, not give an historical account or write a text.[50] "Making history" and "steering its course" are quintessential *heritage* activities. As a riveting surrogate, heritage privileges action over books. "Let your children *experience* American history instead of just *reading* about it" runs a phrase from New Jersey's historic sites guide, a Texas museum brochure, and an ad for a Chippendale game table.

Faith in relevance led American schools eighty years ago to scuttle formal history as useless antiquarianism. "A knowledge of the past and its heritage is of great significance when it enters into the present," proclaimed John Dewey, "but not otherwise." Educators jettisoned history for social studies; social studies became civics, a synonym for patriotism. "History," ruled the Kansas Supreme Court in 1927, was no longer a mere record of events but an "inspirational" account "revealing how the past still lives in us; . . . good citizenship is inculcated by giving attention to history as history is now conceived."[51] Note the premise that history was *newly* inspiring.

Historians to this day distinguish *school* history (taught by educators) from the *real* history you get afterward. "Real scholars don't write textbooks," say academics whose careers may actually be hampered by doing so. But those who do, write texts as bland, upbeat, and omniscient as the rest. Like Billy Collins's "History Teacher," they temper harsh reality:[52]

> Trying to protect his students' innocence
> He told them that the Ice Age was really just

> The Chilly Age, a period of a million years
> When everyone had to wear sweaters.
>
> ★ ★ ★ ★ ★
>
> And the Spanish Inquisition was no more
> Than an outbreak of questions such as
> "How far is it from here to Madrid?"
>
> ★ ★ ★ ★ ★
>
> The War of the Roses took place in a garden,
> And the Enola Gay dropped one tiny atom
> On Japan.

A saga of civic pieties to be swallowed on faith, school history is more heritage than history.

Popular usage stresses the contrast. "Designating an event as 'history' means that it is over and done with, that it lacks present and future significance," sums up an American historian; the phrase "he's history" consigns someone to a bygone negligible epoch. In contrast, "heritage" is freighted with sacred import, mandating eternal remembrance. An English scholar limns further contrasts: "History is neutral, just the old things that happened to happen," writes Christopher Chippindale, "which is why history is disappearing from the school curriculum—it is old stuff that has nothing to do with us. Heritage stands for all that is backward-looking *and* alive today *and* good . . . It bears overtones of personal closeness, of identity, and of exclusive possession."[53]

These distinctions go far to explain why complaints of heritage's historical failings generally fall on deaf ears. Most who visit heritage sites, consume heritage goods, and enjoy heritage media take it for granted that the uses of history and heritage, though clearly linked, are unlike and, indeed, often rightly opposed. To the presumed uses of heritage I turn in the next two chapters.

Chapter 6

THE PURPOSE OF HERITAGE

HERITAGE IS KNOWN, as just demonstrated, in ways utterly unlike history. Like medieval relics, heritage is sanctioned not by proof of origins but by present exploits. No one in the 14th century would have thought to test the date of the Turin Shroud, said to have enfolded Christ; what mattered was the shroud's current miraculous efficacy. The worth of heritage is likewise gauged not by critical tests but by current potency.

If historians despise heritage fakery, heritage disdains historians' truth fetishes. "It is our culture and history," say Indian tribal spokesmen, "and we do not have to prove [it] to anyone by footnoting." An Iowa senator was incensed when the state historical society vetoed a bogus memorial to his bailiwick's patron. "All they care about are the historical facts," fumed the senator. "I don't care if he lived in it or not; I just want a memorial. . . . Just put up a plaque, say Ansel Briggs lived here, and who would know the difference?"[1]

Historical films casually dump history: "Getting [things] wrong is quicker, simpler, and usually makes a better story than getting them right." *Pocahontas*, the box office leader as I write, got Indian consultants to OK Disney's detours from the facts. "It's not historically accurate," admits one. "I don't think that's necessarily bad." Producers of *Mutiny on the Bounty* told high-school teachers they portrayed Captain Bligh as a sadist for the sake of "a strong, close-knit, comprehensive" portrayal; the actual story "might have confused the issue."[2]

Britain's National Maritime Museum demoted Sir Francis Drake to a minor slot in its 1988 Armada show in order to "dissolve old myths and prejudices"; this prissy insistence on accuracy outraged Plymouth. Drake *was* the Armada; "what Robin Hood is to Nottingham and

Mickey Mouse to Disneyland, Francis Drake is to Plymouth"—sacred legacy and crux of local tourism. "If you've got something to sell, then package it up and sell it," said Plymouth's Armada spokesman; "What's history if you can't bend it a bit?" The government too was bending history, he charged, Drake being downgraded not for history's sake but to mollify Spain in impending European Community talks.[3]

This chapter details how and why heritage bends history in its creative commingling of fact with fiction.

EXCLUSION AND ERROR ESSENTIAL TO FEALTY

History and heritage transmit different things to different audiences. History tells all who will listen what has happened and how things came to be as they are. Heritage passes on exclusive myths of origin and continuance, endowing a select group with prestige and common purpose. History is enlarged by being disseminated; heritage is diminished and despoiled by export.

History is for all, heritage for ourselves alone. History is not perfectly open—scholars hoard sources, archives get locked away, critics are denied access to records, and misdeeds are expunged. But most historians condemn concealment. In contrast, heritage messages are restricted to an elect. Heritage is the "secret history" that each departing White House press secretary, claimed Reagan spokesman Marlin Fitzwater, has hidden away in a bulletproof waistcoat for his successor's eyes alone: "none has ever divulged their contents."

Heritage reverts to tribal rules that makes each past an exclusive, secret possession. Created to generate and protect group interests, it benefits us only if withheld from others. Sharing or even showing a legacy to outsiders vitiates its virtue and power; like Pawnee Indian "sacred bundles," its value inheres in being opaque to outsiders. White Australian adoption of Aboriginal "dreamtime" bonds with land deprives them of the exclusivity that lent that legacy worth. Being clannish is essential to group survival and well-being.[4]

Heritage keeps outsiders at bay through claims of superiority that are unfathomable or offensive to others. Bonding within and exclusion beyond the group stem from faith, not reason: we exalt our own heritage not because it is demonstrably true but because it *ought* to be. To exclude others, heritage cannot be universally true; to those beyond the pale its tenets must defy reason. Empirical error and irrational argument render our heritage opaque or useless to outsiders, clear and tenable only to us. Heritage resembles the famed Slav soul, hidden and enigmatic, yet irrefutable.

Out of some legendary kernel of truth, each corporate group harvests a crop of delusory faiths—faiths nutritive not despite but owing to their flaws. Heritage actuates a "mountain of false information" that sustains all societies. Like individual beings, Freud posited, "mankind as a whole has developed delusions which are inaccessible to logical criticism and which contradict reality." Such knowledge cannot be exposed to criticism for fear of anarchy. The bad effects of wrong beliefs are more than compensated by the bonding a legacy confers and by the barriers it erects against others. Shared misinformation excludes those whose own legacy encodes different catechisms. "Correct" knowledge could not so serve, because it is open to all, alien and domestic alike; only "false" knowledge can become a gauge of exclusion.[5] Hence heritage mandates *mis*readings of the past.

Such misreadings become cherished myths. Steelworkers in the Italian town of Terni fashioned a coherent heritage in the 1970s by "remembering" things done and said by 1940s anti-fascists that never happened (but should have) and by shifting actual events to more useful times and places. Similarly, "the two absolute facts on which [Londonderry] is built actually didn't happen," says its museum director: it was not founded by St. Columba, and the famed 1689 "siege" of Derry was in truth a mere blockade. But Derry folk dote on these founding fables all the more because they *are* fabulous.[6]

The civic value of "noble lies" is explained in Plato's *Republic*. For the general good, Socrates contrives "a fairy story like those the poets tell, . . . some magnificent myth that would carry conviction to our whole community." He means to persuade the populace that they had been "fashioned and reared in the depths of the earth, and Earth herself, their mother, brought them up into the light of day; so now they must think of the land in which they live as their mother and protect her if she is attacked." Few would believe this myth right away, but Socrates hoped to "succeed with the second and later generations."[7]

Sacred origins sanction like myths today. You are asked if you "believe in the Monroe Doctrine," in Sumner's example. "You do not dare to say that you do not know what it is, because you understand that . . . every good American is bound to believe in" it. "To tamper seriously with America's received story of its past is dangerous," notes a modern historian, because "it disturbs the fixed version of the sanctified past that makes the present bearable."[8]

Heritage thrives on persisting error. "Getting its history wrong is crucial for the creation of a nation," Renan comforted French nationalists. English historians praise their precursors' muddled thinking as a national virtue. "We made our peace with the Middle Ages by misconstructing them; 'wrong' history was one of our assets," exulted Butterfield. "Precisely because they did not know the Middle Ages, the historians of the time gave the 17th century just the type of anachronism that it required"—they mistook England's new constitution for a restoration of ancient liberties. Useful *because* mistaken, this fable became a pillar of the national heritage; "whatever it may have done to our history, it had a wonderful effect on English politics."[9] Unfazed by its exposure as a tissue of errors, the British still revel in Whig unreason. Opposing a 1993 bill in the House of Lords to let daughters inherit noble titles, the historian Hugh Trevor-Roper (Lord Dacre) lauded male primogeniture for its "traditional irrationality."

Swiss heritage, too, sets myth above truth. Since history was "a school of patriotism," warned an educator in 1872, its texts should be corrected with great caution. To destroy faith in traditions that "symbolize liberty, independence, and republican virtues" would corrode public patriotism. Anyway, subtle historical distinctions were "not the concern of the masses." William Tell's defiance of the Hapsburg oppressor is a notorious fiction, but the infallible archer, the apple, and the cap are too pivotal to Swiss identity to give up. A 1994 Lausanne exhibition that debunked Tell and other icons of Swiss virtue as "pseudo-historical" was savagely abused, its authors threatened with death.[10]

The canonical epic of Ireland's quest for freedom is, to heritage champion Brendan Bradshaw, "a beneficent legacy, its wrongness notwithstanding." Puncturing lavishly reinvented Gaelic origin legends would forfeit their "positive dynamic thrust"; depopulating Irish history of heroes of national liberation would "make the modern Irish aliens in their own land." The grand tale of tribulations overcome is crucial to

Irish identity. "They all know it's not true," says an Ulster Catholic of a saga of Protestant infamy, "but that won't stop them believing it. In a few years it will be gospel."[11]

It is a sacrosanct Greek credo that secret schools run by Orthodox monks kept Hellenic culture alive under Turkish oppressors. In fact, Greek schooling was widely tolerated during Ottoman rule, but it is forbidden to say so. A teacher was pilloried in the 1960s for questioning the legend. "Even if the *krypha skholeia* was a myth," explains a prominent Greek, "it should still . . . be propagated, for such myths were an essential element in the national identity."[12]

The stereotype of Indians as nomadic wanderers typifies American legends that are too useful to relinquish. The rare admission that many Indians were settled farmers is forgotten in rationalizing their forced removal. "If the author of [a much-used text] cannot remember from one chapter to the next that the Indians didn't need to settle down" because they already *were* settled, "we can hardly expect his readers to," comments James Loewen. "The story is too powerful an archetype."[13]

Fiction resists fact to persist as heritage. Parson Weems' fables about George Washington have been "shattered again and again," scholars note, "but they live on in the popular mind, and nothing can extirpate them." The saga of Rhondda Valley miners shot down by British troops in 1910 is an outrage the Welsh will never forget, yet "every single man who was there knows that the story is nonsense," in Josephine Tey's words. Nonetheless "it has never been contradicted. It will never be overtaken now."[14] The "ancient" Breton folklore classic *Barzaz-Breiz*, long exposed as a 19th-century pastiche, is still accepted as the authentic voice of the Breton people because six generations have used it to express that voice. "What matter if learned hands have harmonised a few lines in places," writes a defender. "They could not have invented . . . fifteen centuries [of] collective genius." Breton heritage "is not what history bequeathed them," concludes a historian, "but what romantic reconstruction . . . led them to build."[15]

Commending error as heritage is the theme of Joseph Roth's *Radetsky March*, whose protagonist Trotta rescues Emperor Franz Joseph at the battle of Solferino in 1859. Years later, he reads a gushy version of the episode in his son's school text. "It's a pack of lies," he yells. "Captain, you're taking it too seriously," says a friend. "All historical events are modified for consumption in schools. And quite right, too. Children need examples which they can understand, which impress them. They can learn later what actually occurred." The emperor himself rejects literal truth: "It's a bit awkward," he admits, "but neither of us shows up too badly in the story. Forget it."[16]

We routinely purge traits repugnant to national pride. The American Legion faulted 1920s textbooks for "placing before immature pupils the blunders, foibles, and frailties of prominent heroes and patriots." Civic allegiance is still the main aim of most school history. Showing "national heroes in an uncomplimentary fashion [even] though factually accurate [is] offensive" to American school boards today. History lessons that encourage skepticism about British heroes and heroines, sullying the reputations of Florence Nightingale, Lord Nelson, and Alfred the Great, are thought similarly demeaning. "We were taught in history class that the French Empire was all about spreading civilization," a French official reacted to the film *Waterloo*. "We aren't going to make movies to call that into question, even if we know that what really happened was profoundly different." The desire to rewrite the past to conform with group pride is too universal to be dismissed as a conspiracy, historians concede, "nor is it sinister to want to manipulate national history, as we all do with our own lives."[17]

In sum, heritage the world over not only tolerates but thrives on and even requires historical error. Falsified legacies are integral to the exclusive purpose of group identity. Those who seek a past as sound as a bell forget that bells *need* built-in imperfections to bring out their all-important individual resonances.

SLAVE BREEDING: A FALSE AND VALUABLE MYTH

My own research shows how one such myth arose, and why it endures as heritage even when exposed as historically false. It concerns a persisting but mistaken belief that slaves were "bred" on a small West Indian island.[18] Such breeding was not uncommon in the American South, where planters augmented work forces by encouraging slave births. But in the West Indies so few children survived that slave-rearing was seldom a viable option. Planters relied on importing new slaves from Africa.

Only in one Caribbean locale is slave-breeding legendary. This was Barbuda, a small, flat British island long leased to the Codrington family, but too dry and infertile for intensive agriculture. Barbuda's few hundred slaves felled timber and made charcoal, fished and caught lobsters, hunted feral cattle and pigs, and salvaged ships wrecked on the island's perilous reefs. Thanks to the varied local diet and to freedom from onerous plantation regimen, Barbuda was less lethal for slaves than most West Indian locales. From this arose the myth that Barbudan slaves were bred to work on Codrington sugar and cotton plantations in other islands.

Barbuda's slave-breeding role is affirmed in many West Indian histories, including my own. A 1972 travel book limns the supposed scene:

> Christopher Codrington dreamed up the practical idea of developing a race of powerful, king-sized slaves to work his cane fields. The scheme worked and a race of tall, muscular Negroes developed. Today's Barbudans are descendants of the stud farm pioneers, as any visitor to the island may judge for himself.

But the evidence proved elusive. Sources petered out; eyewitnesses evaporated. Barbuda's history remained an enigma until in 1977 Colin Clarke and I found a cache of Codrington letters. Vividly depicting colonial Barbuda, these papers proved conclusively that slave-breeding was a myth.

Struck by the health of his Barbudan slaves, Barbuda's lessee Bethell Codrington hoped in 1790 that young Africans might be "seasoned" there: "I would buy them at the age of 10 or 12 and send them to Barbuda." He never did. But in 1834, when the slaves were freed, Codrington claimed "especial compensation" owing to Barbuda's "extreme fitness for a nursery for Negroes making it a source of much profit to your memorialist and his Ancestors." In pretending Barbuda had supplied other plantations, Codrington hyped his 1790 hope into a settled habit.

This fabrication fomented the slave-breeding fantasy. Later observers read Codrington's gloss on Barbuda as a "nursery for Negroes" as though it had been done: "The Codringtons planned and operated 'slave nurseries' which were filled with little boys and girls bought off the ships." In the retelling, casual surmise becomes *fait accompli*, and nursery gets converted from child care to stud farm. Thus a self-serving fiction later misconstrued became a "truth" unchallenged for over a century.

This unsavory myth had several consequences. Bizarre disrepute left Barbuda shunned and neglected. But the positive effects mattered more. Centuries of being left alone instilled Barbudan pride in their self-reliant legacy. To be seen as descendants of eugenic design bolstered their self-image. Selective breeding during slavery, visitors are still repeatedly told, made Barbudans taller, stronger, and more handsome and intelligent than other West Indians.

Barbudans were fascinated by our disclosure that slave-breeding was a myth. The monthly *Barbuda Voice* (published by Barbudans in New York City) serialized our academic essay with its 134 footnotes. Barbudans did not doubt our historical exposé, but they were only superficially persuaded by it. They neither disputed our evidence *nor* relinquished the slave-breeding myth. The linchpin of their folk history, this tale of unique origins made Barbuda superior to more populous and "progressive" islands. Rather than a shaming saga to be shed with alacrity, the stud-farm past remains a triumphal founding fable—trotted out just now to explain why Princess Diana feels at home in Barbuda "surrounded by beautiful people."[19]

Barbudans thus amalgamate keen interest in newfound ancestral annals with pride in a slave-breeding myth that these annals categorically refute. They welcome the historical details linking them with named ancestors and go on deploying the heritage this data disproves. Barbudans have no difficulty in dealing with the cognitive dissonance these contraries entail; one is history, the other heritage.

Heritage versions differ from those of history, strictly construed, in ways discussed below and in the next chapter.

THE VIRTUES OF VAGUENESS AND IGNORANCE

History strives to know as much of the past as well as possible; heritage is helped by imprecise impression and sketchy surmise. A modicum of knowledge will do, and the less explicit the better. "Heroes and founding fathers . . . must be mythical characters like Romulus and Remus or King Arthur, obscured in the mists of the distant past," argues the historian Gordon Wood; "they cannot be, like Jefferson and the other 'founding fathers,' real human beings about whom an extraordinary amount of historical detail is known."[20] Too much is known of Jefferson as slaveowner not to tarnish his legend.

Ignorance, like distance, protects heritage from harsh scrutiny. Few Finns know the *Kalevala,* the fount of Finnish identity, firsthand; "simply the knowledge of its existence [is] enough to inspire general enthusiasm." The vaguest details of their Hebridean heritage suffice Canada's Prince Edward Islanders. When their plight is likened to the Scottish Highlands after the Clearances, or Glencoe after the Massacre, it does not matter that few know what these mean; "the mere sound of the words arouses a homing instinct, a feeling of belonging to something tragic but durable."[21] The Islanders belong to the Hebrides in a way that explicit knowledge would only weaken.

The past is more admirable as a realm of faith than of fact. "We have a history here, you know," say Greek villagers content to leave its details to scholars and intellectuals. For the villagers what counts is the certitude that "here a history existed," that Greece had a history when no one else did. In America, the past's precise content is often beside the point: "We don't know what *sort* of history Adamsville has had," a Rhode Island village's roadside heritage display implies, "but we feel certain *that* it had a history." Faith in having had a lot of history matters more than being able to recall any specific historical events.[22]

That few Americans know their Constitution augments their awe of it; its "sacredness is enhanced rather than lessened," judges Wilbur Zelinsky, by "being vested in archaic, even incomprehensible tongues." Never having read the Constitution, McCarthyites mistook its precepts for communist propaganda, all the while insisting that everything in it was sacrosanct; to this day, half of those shown Marx's 1875 maxim "From each according to his abilities, to each according to his needs" believe that it comes from the Constitution.[23]

Distance adds stature to personal as well as national legacies. "A great man never draws so near his public as when it has become unnecessary to read his books," observed Edith Wharton. Known "only through a crayon portrait and a dozen yellowing tomes on freewill and intuition," her own fictional philosopher was "at least secure from the belittling effects of intimacy." His demise some years back had luckily left "no little personal traits—such as the great man's manner of helping himself to salt, or the guttural click that started the wheels of speech—to distract the eye of young veneration from the central fact of his divinity."[24]

Great men themselves often hide all-too-human dithering from posterity. Until the recent vogue for rough drawings and first drafts as authentically revealing, and hence lucrative, most painters and writers preferred to keep their raw early creations from public view. Michelangelo in old age effaced signs of his early stumbling steps, burning many drawings, sketches, and cartoons "so that no one would be witness to his struggle to express his genius," in Vasari's account, "lest he should appear less than perfect." Similarly, U.S. Supreme Court judges fear losing mystique if they are seen as less than authoritative. Hence their anguish over the Library of Congress's early opening of Justice Thurgood Marshall's papers, which revealed shifts and hesitations that undermined the Supreme Court's proper image as surefooted and definitive. A French colonial educator a century ago found "something objectionable about revealing, through history, the mistakes we made before arriving at the stage of civilization we have attained."[25]

The more casual the history, the more engrossing the heritage. "Play with history—in the ancient hills of Judea . . . pursued by a Philistine who is trying to kill you!" ran a 1985 video-game lure; "NO PRIOR KNOWLEDGE OF THE BIBLE IS REQUIRED." Stressing a "playful approach to history," heritage fashions in clothing and jewelry shun too-specific roots. Ancient concepts of design may be "somewhat recognizable," so long as customers are "never sure exactly where they are from." The virtues of vagueness are clear at Disney World, where theme-park "Canada" elicits more interest than "France" because it is far less recognizable; the aura of a place or a time is best tapped by generalized myth.[26]

Exotic enigmas enrich heritage more than drab details. Academic research on Easter Island statues and alpine Stone Age ice men serves only to "diminish the world's mysteries and replace them by lifeless certainties," rebukes a critic. "Why do we have to know everything? Where is reverence? belief? feeling?" Noting the exotic attraction to many English of dance and art from India, an Indian surmises that "the fact they can't understand it is part of the mystique."

THE INDISCRIMINATE PAST

Heritage lumps together all the past, commingling epochs without re-gard to continuity or context. Largely indifferent to linear chronology, heritage like popular memory assigns events to generalized good old days (or bad old days) or to the storyteller's "once upon a time." Living history favors period crafts over particular events, as if, in Chris-tina Cameron's phrase, one were at a Bread-Baking or Barrel-Making National Historic Site. The heritage realm is not a sequence of events but a timeless fabric, conjoining distinct places as cavalierly as periods. Thus specific kibbutz histories are storified into a generic kibbutz tale. "Well, it may not have happened in Ein Shemer, perhaps it was in Ein Harod," says the guide, "but it did happen someplace, so what differ-ence does it make?"[27]

Alternatively, patrimonial focus singles out a particular epoch from the stream of time. To see the French court as *history* requires reviewing the origins of royal routines and centuries of regal stability and change; to see the court as *heritage* is encapsulated by recalling one monarch, Louis XIV. Colonial Williamsburg staff admit that the 1770 Botetourt inventory of the Governor's Palace was "only a brief moment out of the long sequence of Time's perfection" but base the Palace restoration on that inventory as "indisputable evidence [of] the fullest and most com-plete moment we have."[28]

Iconic fatherland images never stem solely from original history; they derive in large measure from later findings and fabulations of patriot-scholars. Fiji and Maori origin myths have accreted insights (and errors) from belated conquerors, missionaries, and ethnographers.[29] Conflating ancient with recent, endemic with exotic, versions of local culture pro-duced for outside consumption swiftly become traditional. Thus the an-thropologist Ernest Beaglehole, visiting a Polynesian atoll in 1935, found Christianized Pukapukan islanders about to stage their annual biblical play. "Why not play for a change old Pukapukan stories, the story of Malotini for example, or the Eight Men of Ngake, or the Slaughter of the Yayake people?" he asked them. "The acting of them would help us to remember them more vividly when we came to write them down." Village elders gladly jettisoned David and Goliath for native legends. Sixty years on, these are performed in tandem with the biblical tales on Cook Islands' Gospel Day.[30]

Tourism and the media amalgamate medieval, Renaissance, and recent times into an indiscriminate, prototypical past. Hampton Court Palace and the Tower of London merge as Tudorbethan bastions of tragic queens and bloody axes. Heritage centers and history museums guide visitors down the centuries from B.C. to A.D., these pasts ending up much the same to most viewers. Nostalgic fashion denotes no particular period but anything fancied from any bygone time, like the general aura of pastness in old photo reproductions. When *The Times* in 1994 can refer to South African ostrich feathers decorating "Hollywood costumes, chorus-line outfits, [and] flapper boas . . . *in Queen Victoria's day*," we see how even recent pasts soon coalesce in public memory.

In popular recall the Gauls come close to de Gaulle, Elizabeth I joins Elizabeth II, Salem witches and Watergate twisters tread the same American stage. Tradition conflates Greek culture to a single entity embracing all periods from Homer on. For most Americans, "there's the present and then there's this dumpster of undifferentiated synchronic trivia called 'history.' Ask a kid which happened first, the Peloponnesian Wars or the Korean War—no clue."[31] An English boy asks, "When you were young, Mummy, was that . . . the Olden Days?" To be sure, Olden Days also jumbled epochs, as with historical paintings showing Dante holding hands with Virgil and Charlemagne chatting with Napoleon. But these implied affinity *across* epochs, not time-travel coexistence as in Stanley Kubrick's *Spartacus*, dubbing in the dead and the unborn to get as many famous Romans as possible into one film.

Such conjunctions violate historians' deepest instincts. Heritage may twin Washington with Lincoln—the Father of His Country, with its Savior—but should not do so "to the point of anachronism," chides a historian, by casually "fading out one figure and supplanting him with the other." But this is what heritage is *meant* to do: post–Civil War Lincolnization transformed the aloof aristocratic Washington into the folksy rail-splitter then needed; a First World War painting showed "The American Cincinnatus" as a blacksmith wearing the apron of a slave he is relieving at the forge.[32] It was in this spirit that Plymouth, long after the initial landing, installed a suitable Rock on which *Mayflower* pilgrims ought to have stepped ashore.

Plymouth is manifestly mythic. This is clear from common tourist queries at the site's bizarre classical canopy: "Why doesn't the rock say '1492'?" some wonder; others ask "Where is the sword?" The nearby *Mayflower* replica reinforces the spurious Columbus connection. "Where are the Nina and the Pinta?" ask visitors. And best of all: "How did he get all those animals on that little boat?"[33] All the past is made one, the Planting of New England merged not merely with the Discovery of America but with medieval legend and biblical lore. As history this is absurd; but as heritage it is hugely symbolic. The Rock and the *Mayflower* come to stand for all beginnings, all voyages to new worlds, all paths to new ways.

CONFLATING PAST WITH PRESENT

Collapsing the entire past into a single frame is one common heritage aim, as just shown; stressing the likeness of past and present is another. The purpose is different: the generalized past is set off as a legacy distinct from the present; coalescing past with present creates a living heritage that is relevant because it highlights ancestral traits and values felt to accord with our own. The chief purpose of our "material and moral inheritance," alleged an eminent American in 1874, was "to quicken the sense of connection" between then and now.[34]

History, opined an eminent Victorian, is the view of one age taken by another. In contrast, heritage when conflated treats the past as our own age. Viewed as history, the past is a foreign country; viewed as heritage, it is highly familiar. Were the Victorians really like that? asks Virginia Woolf's Isa. "I don't believe that there ever were such people," replies old Mrs. Swithin, "only you and me and William dressed differently." As William rightly retorts, "You don't believe in history."[35] What she does believe in is heritage.

One way of likening past to present is to play down grand historical events and focus on ongoing usages of everyday life. A wooden darning egg, a needle holder, a detachable pocket, and an old comb are displayed at Minute Man National Park with the legend: "Life was a daily thing. Battles only temporary. But both went on while colonists waited out the war." This display domesticates the Revolution, but it shows no past events—only familiar tools. Valley Forge, Washington's

1777–78 headquarters, offers timeless values in modern cliché; the soldiers encamped there "demonstrated the universal desire of the human spirit in its pursuit for freedom and self-determination."[36] Unlike period-crafts sites, Minute Man and Valley Forge stress everyday legacies valued for *resembling* the present.

Vaunted timeless traits are more usually national than universal. Community of English descent "preserved our national character throughout the ages," held Eton's historian and royal tutor in 1905. "The medieval, the Elizabethan, and, we hope, the modern Englishman all show the same individuality . . . , the same initiative . . . , the same independence . . . , the same practical sagacity."[37] American history museums and texts likewise liken past and present. Indiana's Prairie Pioneer museum wanted visitors to "know that the problems of the people in 1880 are still very much the same problems of the people in 1980" (farm prices and energy). "People in all our communities today have serious problems, just as slaves had problems before the Civil War," asserts a schoolbook. To see all problems as alike makes slavery less alien and unspeakable. Struck by the seeming "innateness, depth, and historical rootedness of modern American problems," many historians look to some immemorial strain "that has always led to these kinds of problems."[38]

Perceived parallels enable "people of today to make contact with people of the past," avers an American museum head. "The stage is different, the stakes are different, but the story is that of the human condition." The presumption that deep down we are or should be one with our forebears infuses heritage perspective; since people then had the same desires, foibles, and strengths as ours, our own viewpoints become congruent with national character or human nature. Folk rituals seem living proof of unchanging emotion; as a Morris dancer put it, "Our dances are what they were and what they'll always be." Like the celebrant who claims Padstow's Hobby-Horse festival "still means the same to us as a thousand years ago," he voices heritage feeling, not historical fact.[39]

In linking past with present, many feel they are sustaining a hoary, unbroken tradition—a heritage goal examined in Chapter 8. Continuity is the hallmark of heritage in Harrow, my own English home. "Under the watchful gaze of St Mary's Church," runs a house agent's blurb, "groundsmen lovingly tend Harrow School's cricket pitch, living figures in a scene which could have been plucked out of any decade in

Harrow's history." The scene spells legacy because presumed to be long unaltered. Britain's tourist board touts the monarchy as heritage-worthy not just because it is ancient but because it still endures: it is a thrill "to visit the home of the Queen—not that of some monarch of the distant past, as in other countries, but of the present occupant of the throne."

Enduring heritage icons accrue multiple resonances. Thus the Pantheon in Paris, viewed in successive epochs as a shrine of Christian faith, a symbol of secular Enlightenment, a monument of national unity, and a Temple of Humanity, embodies mutually anachronistic French virtues.[40] At Genesis Farm in New Jersey, Dominican sisters raise organic crops in a setting variously evocative of the First Creation, of seven millennia of Native American husbandry, and of medieval pilgrimage.

Resonance across a temporal gulf, like Renaissance veneration of classical learning or Henry Adams's devotion to the Virgin of Chartres, forges bonds more potent for seeming reborn after a long hiatus. Such legacies likewise justify current acts. Identifying with the remains of imperial Rome, Mussolini demolished later buildings in order to point up the parallel grandeur of antiquity and modern fascism—though he did not hesitate to get rid of antiquity, too, when it stood in the way of his own imperial megalomania. The present is not just the past's inheritor but its active partner, reanimating the sleeping, excavating the buried, and reworking a legacy in line with present needs.

Scripture provides untold parallels for later use. In early medieval France, biblical personae and scenes were held to prefigure Frankish figures and events; identifying a ruler with Joshua or a battle with Jericho made the 8th century a rerun of biblical history. The Old Testament's legacy led to the consecration of Pépin and Charlemagne by priestly anointment; as heir to the Israelite sources of Merovingian royal blood, Charlemagne was regularly referred to as "David." A millennium later, Americans harnessed their own ideals to the Old Testament and their independence to the ancient covenant, seeing the New World as a New Israel. England and George III were equated with Egypt and the Pharaoh, the Founding Fathers with Hebrew leaders. "The American Moses," Washington gave up domestic ease for a sacred mission; both liberated their people from enemies external and internal. Washington's Farewell Address was likened to the Mosaic legacy, his death on the verge of the move to a new capitol to Moses succumbing en route to Canaan.[41] (The 1880s obelisk in Fredericksburg, Virginia, honoring "Mary the Mother of Washington" implies an equally exalted congruence with the Virgin Mary.) More than analogy, this was identity reincarnate.

Such parallels are integral to heritage. Photo captions assure *National Geographic* readers that "though kingdoms rise and fall, these Kurdish fishermen carry on" (1938) and that "across the gulf of countless generations, the Minoan love of dance still finds expression in Crete" (1978). Galilee fishermen are posed in postures evoking Jesus as fisher of men. For the bicentennial of the American Revolution, National Parks guides dressed as Founding Fathers held colloquies with the late 20th century; in a traveling show called "We've Come Back for a Little Look Around," Ben Franklin and Abraham Lincoln inquire into the fate of their own legacies (Franklin being reassured about scientific advance, Lincoln left uncertain about national unity).[42]

Heritage stewards stress that only a past reanimated through present efforts can remain relevant today. It is thanks to modern care that classical splendor still suffuses Greece, patriots proudly assert. "When you are born, they talk to you about the Parthenon, the Acropolis," said Melina Mercouri in 1988. "Everyone in Greece thinks they have built it with their own hands." A living legacy needs constant nourishment; to show themselves worthy of their ancestors, Greeks build open-air-theaters, launch replica triremes, copy classical facades, and decry "Turkish" cultural revolution.[43] Faith that "if you spoke like Plato you might also begin to think like him" fuels attachment to the ancient tongue.

Meaningful legacies are not passively learned but actively felt. "The force of 4,000 years of history is great if it is alive in our hearts, but if it is merely written in books, then it has no value," said Israel's education minister in 1954. "If we want to be heirs of the people of Israel, then we must instill those 4,000 years into the heart of every person." Washington's Holocaust Museum heightens empathy by making the horrific legacy intensely personal: each visitor wears the identity tag of a specific victim, a ghostly companion whose persona the visitor adopts and whose fate is disclosed, with haunting impact, at the tour's end.[44]

Heritage is sometimes equated with reliving the past; more often, it improves the past to suit present needs. For such purposes, as I have shown, we contrive a heritage exclusive to and biased in favor of our-selves. Exclusion and bias are supported by error and by mystification. We dwell on mythic fables rather than specifics, consolidate history into a generalized past, and revamp a legacy in line with what we think the present is or want it to be.

HERITAGE AND LIFE HISTORY

The creative contrivance of heritage has revealing parallels in the free reconstruction of personal histories. Ever refashioned for present needs, heritage and autobiography are similarly possessive, self-serving, and cavalier in their use of evidence. Those who chronicle their own pasts alter facts and tolerate fictions in ways that would ban historians from academe. Mistrusting memories that can neither be verified nor falsi-fied, historians take a jaundiced view of what psychology calls narrative truth—accounts based solely on unsupported recollection.[45]

As with heritage, life histories become coherent and credible only by continual invention and revision, often in defiance of known fact. They are validated not by being explicitly true but by being compellingly plausible. When ex-hostage Jackie Mann disavowed an anecdote in his memoir, *Yours Till the End* (1992), his wife retorted: "But darling, it's autobiography. You've got to give them a good story. They don't want truth." Nor does the writer himself. "You do not even think of your own past as quite real," John Fowles muses, "you dress it up, you gild it or blacken it, censor it, tinker with it . . . fictionalize it, in a word . . . —your book, your romanced autobiography."[46]

The need to romance our own past is evident to every autobiogra-pher and analyst. While the historian strives to subdue subjectivity, the memorialist exults in privileged self-perception. Like medieval annalists limning exemplary lives, today's memoirists aim to impose their own moral versions of the past as a drama in which they were the leading player. "We often choose to remember mistakenly what we *need* to remember," comments a historian, "to preserve our individual and col-lective identities." As we saw for national heritage, the benefits of these mistakes more than compensate their costs.[47]

Such revisions of truth vary with author and audience. Black Amer-icans, notes Richard Wright, were *expected* to lie about themselves; if they told the truth, whites disbelieved them. Wright's own life story continually dissembles to underscore this point. As every child and parent knows, school and home events are often alien and incommunicable. The teacher who set Richard Rodriguez an essay on life at home expected and got a fictional account: "I never thought that nun *really* wanted me to write about my family life," nor could he. To depict family life for any outsider is to falsify. "Even when I quote them accurately, I profoundly distort my parents' words," adds Rodriguez, because "I change what was said only to me" into something for public consumption.[48]

What may be essential in one narrative form is false or deplorable in another. Karen Fields's grandmother told wonderful stories about church life that propriety demanded not be printed. At the same time, she insisted on amplifying tedious detail as a matter of record. The book "needed to mention Mrs. So-and-So, of Such-and-Such Streets. It could not possibly be published without remembering Pastor This-and-That. Why, these are the people I have worked with for decades." But what she felt obliged to remember, her editor-granddaughter felt obliged to forget. Anecdote clashed with archival truth in the grandmother's story of John C. Calhoun, the pro-slavery leader so hated by Charleston blacks that they habitually defaced his statue—"scratch up the coat, break the watch chain, try to knock off the nose." Calhoun finally had to be rescued by being raised so high no one could make out his features. As Fields says, her grandmother's tale proved to be splendidly "true but not veridical."[49]

Life stories reshape legacies imposed even before birth. Children weave self-accounts within an inherited web, little aware of its constraints. Time makes liars of us all. A famed analyst cites the 25-year-old who said he'd been third in his class; at 50 he recalled being second; at 75 he was sure he'd been first. To see themselves as heroes of "a life worth remembering, a drama worth having lived for," oldsters recast memories to accredit their exploits. Since "the goal of their recollection is justification rather than insight and responsibility," the elderly readily mythicize their pasts.[50]

However inconsistent our recall, we rely on it as our very own. Even if we cannot wholly expunge what once shamed or vexed us or fails to fit what we now want to have happened, we feel we can tell our tale better than anyone else. "It's an excellent biography of someone else," said Robertson Davies of Judith Skelton Grant's new life of him. "But I've really lived inside myself, and she can't get in there." A line in the song "Killing Me Softly" runs "Telling my whole life in his words," but we really want to tell our life in our *own* words. The classic case is Thomas Hardy, who spent years ghost-writing his own official biography and had it passed off as his wife's memoir—an impersonation deserving to be called "*The Life and Work of Thomas Hardy by Florence Hardy*, by Thomas Hardy."

Would-be biographers are often thwarted and deceived; not being us, they are bound to get things wrong. Like stewards who keep heritage impenetrable to outsiders, subjects may even strive to ensure biographers *do* get things wrong—impugning their motives like Freud, evading them altogether like Pynchon and Salinger, like James crafting a canny memoir precluding alternative views of his early years, presenting partial and conflicting insights like Beckett and Nabokov, or, like Compton-Burnett, setting rival biographers at one another's throats.[51]

Since self-chronicles rely on recall to which others lack access, they are not really open to correction. A sole survivor is a uniquely privileged witness. Chided for omitting parts of a letter by his brother William from *Notes of a Son and Brother* (1914) Henry James explains that he "instinctively regard[ed] it at last as all *my* truth, to do what I would with." The brothers' letters were of "*our* old world, mine and his alone together," for James not "mere merciless transcript" but "*imaginative* record."

Equally possessive of her past, Mamie Fields was outraged to learn that her grandaughter had checked her stories in the local archives—going behind her back, violating her trust. Even aspects of our lives we cannot possibly remember, such as our birth, are not subject to question. Autobiographers give the impression "that their birth is like a piece of property that they would own in the country, or like a diploma," holds Philippe Lejeune. "This grounds their entire narrative on an irrefutable beginning."[52] Heritage is similarly possessive and, as shown in Chapter 8, origin-obsessed.

Salman Rushdie's "clear memory of having been in India during the China War" in 1962, contrary to the facts, shows the tenacity of delusive recall:

I "remember" how frightened we all were, I "recall" people making nervy little jokes about needing to buy themselves a Chinese phrase book . . . I also know that I could not have been in India at that time. Yet *even after I found out that my memory was playing tricks* my brain simply refused to unscramble itself. It clung to the false memory, preferring it to . . . literal happenstance.

So Rushdie's protagonist in *Midnight's Children* clings to known error. "It is memory's truth, he insists, and only a madman would prefer someone else's version to his own."[53]

Heritage shares with life history this immunity to correction even by ourselves. Once we have consigned our childhood to print it is hard to remember it in any other way; the act of transcription fixes that account as our only memory and condemns us, like John Dean after Watergate, to formulaic repetition. "After you've written, you can no longer remember anything but the writing," notes Annie Dillard. "My memories—those elusive, fragmentary patches of color and feeling—are gone; they've been replaced by the work."[54] So with heritage: what gets recorded and celebrated becomes all but immune to deliberate revision.

Collective heritage draws from sources that range far beyond personal recall, but these sources too resist correction by others. Since we alone understand the legacy that is ours, we are free, or even bound, to construe it as we feel it ought to be. Those who share a communal legacy must accept some mutual notion of its nature. But each sharer treats that corporate bequest as his own; like personal memory, it remains barred to outsiders. In paying homage to that legacy, we resemble those who validate memories by ever recounting them. "By acting in a traditional way," writes an anthropologist, societies behave "as if the past might be 'proved true' if commemorated assiduously enough."[55]

Fiction is thus not the opposite of fact but its complement, giving our lives a more lasting shape. To "locate our own private stories within a larger collective narrative," notes a historian, we embrace "true" lies, credible falsehoods. That myths are batty and irrational does not spoil their worth. Camelot and the Grail lack historical credibility but convey psychological authority; like the Mayflower saga, these rooted mythologies lend cosmic meaning to our own lifetime quests. As the presenter of Alex Haley's flagrantly anachronistic *Roots* said, "There you have it, some of it true, and some of it fiction, but all of it true, in the true meaning of the word."[56]

The heritage past just described may seem unseemly. It is a jumbled, malleable amalgam ever reshaped by this or that partisan interest. Flying in the face of known fact, it is opaque or perverse to those who do not share its faith. Those who do share it, though, find heritage far more serviceable than the stubborn and unpredictable past revealed by history. Such an unrevised past is too remote to comprehend, too strange to be exemplary, too regrettable to admire, or too dreadful to recall. It may also be too dead to care much about. Hence heritage radically restructures historical domains. The next chapter delineates the most frequent modes of heritage intervention: imposing present images and aims on past events and actors, stressing what is praiseworthy, and bowdlerizing or consigning to oblivion what is not.

Chapter 7

THE PRACTICE OF HERITAGE

THE LAST CHAPTER SHOWED *why* heritage alters history; *how* it does so is the subject of this chapter. Three modes of revision stand out. One is to update the past by garbing its scenes and actors in present-day guise. A second is to highlight and enhance aspects of the past now felt admirable. A third is to expunge what seems shameful or harmful by consigning it to ridicule or oblivion. These processes repay separate scrutiny, yet they are often concurrent: a present-minded view of the past is bound to celebrate and forget selectively. Selective bias in heritage is, I show, as widely acceptable to the public as the autobiographical fictions just discussed.

UPDATING

History and heritage both refashion the past in present garb. But the former does so to make the past comprehensible, the latter to make it congenial, as shown in Chapters 5 and 6. For historians, presentist reshaping is unavoidable, a translation needed to convey things past to modern audiences. For heritage, as we saw in the last chapter, updating is not just a necessity but a virtue that fructifies links with the past. In this section I show how such linkages are contrived.

Where tradition is orally transmitted, updating is a matter of course, because no past witnesses—books or other records—survive to gainsay it. "The notion of the past as a charter for the present carries more relevance" in oral societies, declares Jack Goody, noting how Tiv tribesmen in Nigeria disowned genealogies British administrators had written down for them fifty years before because these no longer accorded with the ancestors the Tiv *now* felt they needed. Historical films, suggests Robert Rosenstone, are postmodern equivalents of oral narratives. Like epic sagas and griots' tales, cinema persuades by emotional force and immediacy, implanting truths more through the heart than the mind.[1]

Remolding old idols and ideals in later guise is common among all peoples. Like memories retrieved by analysis, notes a psychiatrist, public history is a record of present beliefs and wishes, not a replica of the past. Patrick Geary shows how medieval monastic memories changed when founders' dynasties crumbled. To ensure their own survival, monastic orders altered benefactors' names and rewrote the histories of their foundations. For example, the origin of the Camargue monastery of Montmajour, founded in 949 to perpetuate the memory of King Hugo of Italy, was reattributed to a fictional victory by Charlemagne over the Saracens. When new Provençal ducal alliances required a Carolingian ancestry, Hugo's founding role became an embarrassment that had to be effaced.

> The memory of Hugo . . . meant nothing. What mattered was the counts' relationship to a new family. . . . The expulsion of the Saracens by Charlemagne and his subsequent support of the monastery as a burial place for his fallen warriors is the archetype for the role the new counts played. That this memory did not correspond with the "facts" of the past is much less important than that it corresponded to the circumstances of the present.[2]

Religious orders were not the only such revisers. Early chroniclers had Charlemagne attacked by Basques at Roncevaux in 778; Crusaders later aided their own cause by turning Basques into Saracens. After the Capetians ousted Charles the Simple in the early 10th century, chroniclers expunged his reign's achievements, made him out an archetype of weakness and folly, and shifted his benefactions to his grandfather Charles the Bald or to his grandson Charles of Lorraine.[3]

Updating likewise conformed New World legacies to later needs. The Mayflower Compact of 1620 was originally designed to ensure Pilgrim control of the new colony. Later heritage promoters recycled the Compact into an emblem of Revolutionary freedom, a fin-de-siècle symbol of Anglo-Saxon democracy and social cohesion, a WASP genealogical bona fide, and, most recently, a hallmark of community self-help.[4]

The text of Abraham Lincoln's "Letter to the Working-Men of Manchester," commending their refusal to manufacture Southern cotton during the American Civil War, was inscribed on the plinth of the Lincoln statue Americans gave Manchester in 1920. The statue was refurbished in 1986, with Lincoln's letter re-incised to laud not the working-*men* but "the working *people* of Manchester." City councilors expunged the "sexist" wording of Lincoln's message as unbearably discordant with his stand against slavery. Feminist diktat similarly gives the Calvert family maxim and Maryland state motto, *Fatti maschii, parole femine* (manly deeds, womanly words), a gender-free translation: "Strong deeds, gentle words."

Presentism is often politically motivated. The history of royal rogues limned by Sweden's 16th-century archbishop Johannes Magnus stressed for readers the evils of the current king, Gustavus Vasa. The heroic traits Margaret Thatcher saw in the 16th-century crew of the *Mary Rose* mirrored her Falklands forces against Argentina. "Just as the recovery of the *Mary Rose* was presented as giving 'us' something back," remarks Patrick Wright, so "the Falklands war proved that 'we' are still powerful, still capable of rallying to one flag with confidence and moral righteousness, still, above all, capable of action."[5]

Only in the 5th century B.C. did Jewishness, formerly patterned on biblical patriarchs, come to be defined by maternal descent. But if Jewishness were strictly matrilineal, the sons of biblical heroes by foreign wives could not be Jewish; these legendary "sons" became Jews once again only by being retitled "grandsons."[6]

Pasts that are more recent and better documented may, Gordon Wood suggested, be harder to update. But current pieties, as seen in Chapter 3, are notoriously read back into minority heritage. The nonpareil anachronism is Chief Seattle, whose 1854 letter to President Franklin Pierce, "Brother Eagle, Sister Sky," is recited at many an Earth Day powwow:

> The earth is our mother. I have seen a thousand rotting buffaloes on the prairies left by the white man who shot them from a passing train. What will happen when the buffalo are all slaughtered? The wild horses tamed? ... when the secret corners of the forest are heavy with the scent of many men and the view of the ripe hills is blotted by talking wires?

But no buffalo had roamed within six hundred miles of Chief Seattle's Puget Sound; the railroad first crossed the Plains only in 1869, three years after he died; the famous buffalo slaughter happened a decade later; and the prose is pure Pretend Indian.

Chief Seattle *did* write to the president, but not about nature. The letter that made him an ecological guru was penned in 1971 by Ted Perry, a Texan scriptwriter. "The environmental awareness was based on my own feelings," Perry admitted in 1992; he hadn't "the slightest knowledge of Indian views on the environment." Rueful, Perry now finds the episode "typical of the way we want to patronize and idealize Indians." But for Susan Jeffers, whose children's book of the speech has sold 250,000 copies, Chief Seattle incarnates the Native American creed that "every creature and part of the earth was sacred . . . Basically, I don't know what he said—but I do know that the Native American people lived this philosophy, and that's what is important."[7] She "knows" this because modern rhetoric has made it a heritage virtue, much as Amazon rain-forest defenders give ecological maxims a tribal imprimatur.

Today's rectitudes likewise explain prehistory. The abandonment of an Isle of Jersey megalithic temple five millennia ago is said to denote democracy toppling religious tyranny. Captions on Native American artifacts in a Connecticut museum declare that "There never was oppression and colonization without native resistance." A preponderance of female figurines in Shantok Indian pottery is held to show that women were "leaders in a movement to reject the values, desires, and laws of the [English] colonists." Scholars who ascribe today's Indianist and feminist credos to early indigenes update as blatantly as Hollywood's *Last of the Mohicans* or Disney's *Pocahontas*.[8] The past thus becomes not just familiar and comprehensible but also an accountable, coercible legacy.

Presentism is deemed integral to England's national legacy. Long accretion proves this heritage was "formed with a wish to deal with Englishmen as they are," not just as they were, historian-cleric Mandell Creighton assured readers. What endears the heritage is not its finished form but the long process of forging it. Its potency derives from being both ancient *and* responsive to present needs. Stressing the *process* of heritage formation, Creighton's Englishmen alike secure its continuance and ensure its openness to ongoing change.[9]

Much updating, though, is unconscious. Summoning up a past that now suits us, we come to believe in its independent existence and imagine our faithful adherence validates its truth. Into Magna Carta later generations "read back whatever political maxim or precedent they required," taking for granted it was in the original. An American jurist in 1845 marveled at "how easily men satisfy themselves that the Constitution is exactly what they wish it should be."[10] Since then it has become an epitome of timeless Americana, its 18th-century authors reborn as modern saints or sinners.

Heritage pathways are potholed with unrecognized anachronisms. Early music today often unwittingly substitutes modern for "authentic" modes of performance. "Recreating the music of Bach or Handel as the composer himself might have heard it" is a promise that has launched a thousand disks but is never fulfilled; instead, performers "are actually recreating it in the high-tech, precise, pristine style that chimes with modern taste."[11] Old Master paintings are "restored" to a sumptuous radiance less in line with their original appearance, as restorers often claim, than with expectations based on Impressionist art. We see what we see through modern eyes and biases, which is why many prefer a Michelangelo to look like a Matisse.

Critics rail in vain against presentism. "Would you like to see machine guns inserted into Uccello's 'Battle of San Romano'?" asks a historical purist. "Or a reference to AIDS into Shakespeare's famous sonnet about lust? Or a psychoanalyst into *Oedipus Rex*?" Yet art is ever updated in just such ways. Chastised in 1826 for playing *King Lear* with the happy ending substituted by Nahum Tate in 1681, Edmund Kean explained he could not restore the original, for "a large majority of the public—whom we like to please, and must please to be popular—like Tate, better than Shakespeare, [so] I fell back upon his corruption." Morality served to justify Tate's update; whereas Shakespeare killed Lear and Cordelia "without reason [or] fault," Tate's revision rewarded their virtue. Conversely, creative anachronisms like the Cokes, Marlboros, and Mercedes in Alex Cox's *Walker* (1987), a film about American freebooters in 19th-century Nicaragua, defy chronology to stress how present vantage points permeate all perception of past scenes.[12]

The media routinely update while boasting fidelity to the past. An "authentic period recipe" for Plimoth Rock Ale (The Taste to Give

Thanks For) "is slightly updated for today's tastes." A 1990s authentic facsimile of the 1942 *Rupert Annual* unblushingly owns that "certain terminology [then] acceptable has been changed or deleted [in] line with present day sensibility." Such changes cater not just to the squeamish; the BBC made Edith Wharton's *The Buccaneers* (1938) "accessible" in 1995 by adding a rape and a homosexual encounter. Almost *anything* that makes the past seriously different is now apt to be axed as too hard for audiences to digest.

Presentism seems most egregious when perpetrators claim to be truly authentic. But we are bound to update the past whenever we engage with it; no matter how much we may feel we owe to or empathize with earlier epochs, we remain people of our own time. Historians justly deplore making things past uncannily like (or wholly unlike) things present. Yet most inheritors, much of the time, must see the past in such an anachronistic fashion. We cannot avoid misconstruing other times and earlier ways in terms similar or opposite to our own. The issue is not whether presentism is deliberate or unwitting. It is how to cope with the seemingly unpalatable fact that heritage, given its aims, always updates the past.

UPGRADING

Updating almost always means upgrading. We improve our heritage, as just shown, by endowing the past with today's exemplary perspectives. We also endow the present with idealized traits of earlier times. Both acts annex heritage to the angels. Chiding the Cassandras who defame "our heritage and our past," Prime Minister Thatcher in 1983 found Britain's history wholly laudable and vowed to "keep the best of the past." The Government's curriculum adviser in 1996 bade British schools transmit "a commitment to the best of the culture we have inherited." President Reagan admired American history as the triumphal saga of "why the Pilgrims came here, who Jimmy Doolittle was, and what those 30 seconds over Tokyo meant." In the lines of a popular 1960s school song, "Take a look in your history book, / And you'll see why we should be proud."[13]

Past worthies are remade to reflect current pieties. The plantation homes of American founding fathers—Washington's Mount Vernon, Jefferson's Monticello, Monroe's Ash Lawn—are models of social propriety, suggesting that slavery was benignly paternalistic. Visitors are reassured that these presidents were reluctant owners, morally opposed to slavery. Washington's vows to buy no more slaves and to manumit those he held are stressed; his later slave purchases and his failure to free them are shrouded in silence.

Critics decry such coverups. "Why do we need to purify our heroes when they do not meet with contemporary standards?" asks a historian. "The apologies offered for slavery at these sites suggest a shallow faith in the greatness of these men . . . if we are interested in history more than enshrinement."[14] But these sites *are* patriotic shrines. It is their custodians' function to regret slavery yet salvage owners' reputations, like the Alabaman who assured Jonathan Raban that her Civil War hero "did not *believe* in slavery. He had a *very* few, only about 16 or 20, something like that." Painting heroes as reluctant accessories helps to mitigate what are now, but were not then, irreconcilable stances. Even that apostle of liberty Patrick Henry confessedly kept slaves, owing to "the general inconvenience of living here without them."[15] Seeing slaves (and women) as less than men was not then discordant with professing liberty and equality. But because it is now, we feel forced to improve on history in our heritage.

The black American presence in general is a heritage minefield because that presence was long slighted, because its relics and records are relatively scanty, and because the African-American legacy is so highly politicized. To make Colonial Williamsburg credible, say black interpreters, half the staff must be black; only with a black moiety of costumed personnel will visitors truly realize that half the 1770 community *was* black. Other aspects of history bow to present agendas. In replica slave huts, rumpled facsimile blankets once suggested slaves stumbling out to labor at dawn had no time to tidy up. But this pandered to stereotypes of blacks as slovenly and slothful, so the blankets are now neatly folded. And despite crop records, watermelon rinds and plantings are banned as stereotypical, as they were symbolically slashed in Edward Zwick's 1989 Civil War film *Glory*.[16] Whatever the aim, current pieties weigh heavily on heritage.

At odds with such pieties is the curatorial vogue for a warts-and-all past. Seeking early-American design stimulus, Colonial Williamsburg's customary clientele were distressed by the dreary realism of garbage-strewn walkways and dung-laden streets, mandated by 1980s authenticity: "We can see all the dust and lint balls we want without ever leaving home."[17] Nor will a newfound homely photo of Charlotte Brontë oust the flattering George Richmond portrait in the Brontë Parsonage souvenir shop. "People would rather buy a pretty Charlotte," the director explains. "We've always known she wasn't very attractive," commented a Brontë scholar in 1994. "We just don't want to believe it." Seemly nicety outbids naked truth.

Indeed, heritage is habitually fig-leafed. The Council of Trent ordered garments painted over torsos in Michelangelo's *Last Judgment*; the Vatican still refuses to erase them, lest prurient eyes focus on parts newly unveiled. "Ee!" said a young museum visitor of a painted Canovaesque maiden with her hand demurely hiding her crotch, "If I'd felt like that about it, I'd've kept me knickers on." A clearly phallic Greek pot in Oxford's Ashmolean Museum long passed genteel muster by being labeled "vase with a peculiar foot." On rare occasion, heritage adds genitals: a sculptor set Mexican War commander Winfield Scott astride the old mare the aging general actually rode; his grandchildren remade it a stallion suited to a hero. Genitals of the *Hercules* carved for London's Great Exhibition of 1851, sawn off in 1883, were reattached in 1977 in conformity to shifting mores.

Health fetishes also get backdated. Today's antismoking crusade excises tobacco from mementos. Cigarettes are brushed out of portraits of bluesman Robert Johnson on U.S. stamps, of Enver Hoxha when dictator of Albania, of Stalin shown with Ribbentrop, and of Mao, though Mao's visible shadow still puffs away. Only Churchill's dogged cigar and Roosevelt's debonair cigarette remain marginally acceptable. Whether Roosevelt's new Washington memorial should show FDR crippled (as the disabled demand) or conceal his crutches and wheelchair (as he himself usually did) is now hotly contested. But animal rightists won out in getting Eleanor Roosevelt's famous fox fur "corrected" to a cloth coat.

Upgrading the past may stress the seedy as well as the seemly. Underscoring a sordid or shaming legacy suggests a laudable regard for truth at any cost, a frank avowal of guilt, a humble wish to make amends. Hence the myriad Holocaust memorials, the Irish Famine museum, the American exhibit on wartime Nisei internment camps. But warts-and-all displays often show only warts, defaming the past to conform with modern views of misery. Helsinki's Tenement Museum shows life among the working poor over a 150-year period; one room, home to a turn-of-this-century family of twelve, holds little but beds. "This doesn't look how it should—it isn't bad enough!" exclaimed a journalist at the 1991 opening. He wanted squalid disarray, smashed toys and dishes all over the floor, and shit-smeared walls. That toys were then rare and tidiness a fetish does not fit today's image of a downtrodden legacy.

In sum, we use heritage to improve the past, making it better (or worse) by modern lights. We do so by hyping its glories (like Thatcher and Reagan), by divesting its exemplars of current anathemas (slaveholders, smokers), by banning demeaning clichés (watermelons), by fig-leafing (everywhere), and by improvising former splendor or squalor.

EXCLUDING

What heritage does not highlight it often hides.[18] We are bound to forget much of the past, but heritage leaves out far more than history, and for other reasons. Historians presume that nothing should be forgotten but deploy selective memory simply to make sense; heritage is enhanced by erasure. Because the Armada hero Sir John Hawkins's pioneering role in the slave trade today makes him a pariah, the city of Plymouth ignored the 400th anniversary of his death in 1995. Unlike Lincoln, whose male-chauvinist letter was so easily corrected, or smokers made statesmenlike by deleting their cigarettes, Hawkins is for now simply irredeemable.

Hence we practice oblivion. For the national good, Carlyle urged Britons wisely to forget as well as remember. Devotion to heroes is strengthened "by seeing in them deeper and deeper virtues," held an American educator in 1927, "and by mercifully forgetting those weaknesses . . . which seem irrelevant to their fame."[19] Those who forget the past may be doomed to repeat it, but those who remember it too well get stuck with it. "Come back, my boy," the Alzheimer-ridden father tells his prodigal son, "all is forgotten."

In nations as in families, to forget can be to forgive. Amnesty conveys both meanings. As Hobbes put it, forgetting is the basis of a just state, amnesia the cornerstone of the social contract. Offenses should be pardoned, not punished, evils forgotten, not avenged. Remedial oblivion became an explicit tool of 17th-century English statecraft: to heal Civil War hatreds, antagonists were adjured to forget past animus; "the oblivion of injuries [was] an Act in every way as noble as revenge." General pardons, expressly termed "Acts of Oblivion," in 1660 exempted from punishment men who had borne arms against Charles II and in 1690 those who had opposed William III. Suppressing memories of wrongs spared England from being crippled by inherited resentments.[20]

The French Revolution decreed oblivion an adjunct to freedom; *écrasez l'infâme* in its widest sense exhorted reformers to expunge any trace of a base past. After the Terror of 1794 citizens were told to "forget the misfortunes inseparable from a great revolution." Competing loyalties must be swept aside. "I beg you to forget that you are Bretons," Léon Gambetta urged provincial troops recruited against Germany in 1870, "and to remember only that you are French." Amnesia was integral to the national heritage, preached Renan in 1882. "Every French citizen has to have forgotten the massacre of St. Bartholomew, the massacres in the 13th century Midi." Only consigning such crimes to oblivion ensured undivided loyalty to *la patrie une et indivisible*. "Are we going to keep open the bleedings wounds of our national discords forever?" exclaimed Pompidou in pardoning Paul Touvier for murdering Jews in 1944; it was time "to forget those times when the French didn't like each other."[21] At Fort Louisbourg, Canada, "consecrated by the blood of your forefathers, the English, and my forefathers, the French," Prime Minister Laurier in 1900 urged with less success that "the memory of those conflicts of the last century be forever forgotten."[22]

Oblivion has been extolled by American leaders from Lincoln on. President Bush's inaugural address aimed to bind past wounds: "the final lesson of Vietnam is that no great nation can long afford to be sundered by a memory." Indeed, oblivion is central to the American Dream. Immigrant offspring eagerly forget the Old World to embrace the New. "We had to try to obliterate centuries' worth of memory," says an Italian-American, "in just two or three generations."

Amnesiac motives are diverse. Some destroy others' memories so as to immortalize themselves: Herostratus torched the temple of Diana at Ephesus to make posterity forget her name and remember his own. Medieval excommunication punished the accursed with *damnatio memoriae* that forbade intoning the names of the wicked at the altar. Victors conceal legacies of the vanquished lest they rekindle flames: Austro-Hungarians quelled nascent Bosnian nationalism by hiding or minimizing Bogomil royal graves, and American forces in Japan after 1945 deconsecrated scores of imperial sacred sites to quash the emperor worship blamed for Japanese aggression.[23]

Out of sight, out of mind: iconoclasts down the ages obliterate detested reminders. Against the infection of idolatry, Reformation Protestants sought to wipe out every trace of icons, to make "utterly extinct and destroy all shrines," in the 1547 Tudor injunction, "so that there remain no memory of the same."[24] The missionary founder of Berea College, Kentucky, Dr. William Fee, so loathed slavery that he literally knifed out every Scriptural reference to servitude; the excised Bible, on display in Berea's library, attests Fee's faith that evil can be undone by being unwritten.

Some would tear down anything built in a bad cause, which would eliminate most of the world's best-known monuments. Happily for the survival of our global legacy, few recall or care that the pyramids reek of incest and slavery, the Arch of Titus of imperial arrogance, Versailles of absolutism, or the civic splendors of Victorian Britain of elite privilege.

History texts are even more ruthlessly truncated, lest exposure to the untoward nip patriotism in the bud. If children learned what really went on, they might lose respect for authority; hence "anything damaging to the image of an American president should be suppressed to protect the younger generation," ruled a judge in 1964. We are exhorted, observed Lord Acton, "to judge Pope and King unlike other men, with a favourable presumption that they did no wrong"—a doctrine detestable to that Catholic historian, for whom "great men are almost always bad men; [there was] no worse heresy than that the office sanctifies the holder of it."[25]

Profit if not piety sways publishers to expunge the infamous, the awkward, even the debatable. "Are you going to tell kids that Thomas Jefferson didn't believe in Jesus?" a textbook editor asked a history teacher. "Not me!" "If there's something that is controversial, it's better to take it out." One publisher would omit such "controversial" past notables as Roosevelt and Nixon, along with any "living people who might possibly become infamous."[26] The dubious future is ditched along with the suspect past.

Even fictional echoes may be too loud; until George III died in 1820, *King Lear* was banned from the London stage for analogies too near the royal bone. "Aunt Jemima," the ex-slave cook whose secret recipe and ubiquitous smile made Quaker Oats famous, has vanished even from Disneyland, where her semblance once signed autographs all day long; gone too are Redskins, Mexicans, frontier dentists, and others of whom any portrayal might now be deemed offensive.[27] Many traditional mascots are consigned to oblivion. Some years back Amherst College lost its long-familiar "Redman"; today his musket-carrying "Minuteman" successor is censured as a white, male, racist armed thug. It is a common delusion that to retain any memory of a past iniquity serves to justify it.

Remembering great evil is hard for any people saddled with ancestral guilt. Fifty years on, Germans veer between having forcibly to remember and wishing fervently to forget Nazi atrocity. The Berlin bunker found in 1994, with murals depicting the SS routing the British with the aid of Zeus, typified such angst: should the bunker be kept as a legacy of iniquity, or sealed off? (It was sealed off.) "Negative-form" memorials (*Gegendenkmal*) to Nazi victims in Hamburg and Kassel, obelisks slowly submerged underground to leave no trace but memory, imply hopes that myriad monuments to German shame will hurry up and disappear. Because Holocaust recall still looms large, other tragic events remain unsung. The 150,000 German dead at Stalingrad lie in oblivion, a legacy Germans cannot yet confront. The East German historical museum on Unter den Linden was swiftly closed in 1990 for "forty years of lying about history"—as if the objects, not those who made them, had been doing the lying.[28]

Other legacies require sporadic concealment. For Pompidou's visit to the House of Lords, the huge canvases of French defeats at Trafalgar and Waterloo in the anteroom were said to have been draped in muslin. In like spirit, Lord St John of Fawsley in 1994 concealed the portrait of Oliver Cromwell above the high table at Sidney Sussex College, Cambridge, to spare Princess Margaret having to dine under the gaze of the "executor" of her forebear Charles I.

Blanket oblivion is indefensible. But there is a vital difference between remembering and celebrating. "Fear of a past that might not fit into the self-portrait [Swedes] would like to draw" is held to explain the two-century hiatus in Stockholm's historical museum; after the Vasas, approved historical memory seems to start again only with the 1870s, omitting the saga of Swedish imperialism. Chiding Swedes for this "liquidation of their own history," a Norwegian asks, "How can such an old nation know what it's doing if it doesn't know what it has inherited?"[29] In fact, Swedes *know* what they inherited; it is in their history books. But it is not a legacy they wish to *commemorate*.

Unlike historical writings, museums are meant to show only sanctified or sometimes scandalous bits of the past. Hence museums in Brazil (unlike Stockholm) celebrate largely an imperial and religious heritage (c. 1700–1920), omitting primitive Indians, slavery, and post-colonial decline. Hence New York's Museum of Immigration on Ellis Island makes no reference to the immigrant underworld of Sicilian mafiosi and Jewish prostitutes. Hence a Vietnam memorial would wrongly hallow the war, argued a veteran: "Let's not perpetuate the memory of such dishonorable events by erecting monuments to them." Hence animal rightists damned a proposed museum of British hunting as glorifying "part of our heritage we ought to eradicate altogether from our minds." They did not mean to delete hunting from *history*; its evils had to be chronicled. But to museumize hunting implied approving it as *heritage*. Conversely, a British Peoples Museum is now said to deserve a central London showcase, for "we have a history as proud as the French or the Americans." *Pride*—tribal, local, or national—is what most museums are for.[30]

Confusion between remembering and celebrating provoked the Smithsonian 1994–95 Enola Gay quarrel ("The Atomic Bomb and the End of World War II"). The conflict went deeper than disputed versions of why the bomb was dropped (to shorten the war, to save American lives, to preclude Soviet involvement): some wanted to celebrate the defeat of Japan, others to dispel "feel-good national myths" by showing history in all its agonizing complexity. At last Congress vetoed what it saw as wallowing in a "bath of American guilt" based on hindsight. In trying to help Americans decide "how we want to think about dropping the bomb," the Smithsonian Secretary had failed to foresee "the intense feelings such analysis could evoke," especially among veterans who "weren't looking for analysis anyway," but rather for admiration. "I don't want 16-year-olds walking out of there thinking badly of the United States," declared a Massachusetts congressman. Representative

Sam Johnson, a new Smithsonian Regent, was more explicit: "We've got to get patriotism back into the Smithsonian. We want the Smithsonian to reflect real America and not something that a historian dreamed up." As the whole affair showed, the commemorative urge is profoundly anti-historical.[31]

The natural oblivion of time soon liquidates much that is collectively shameful. Washington tour guides still point out where the Watergate scandal began, but that ignoble episode now survives mainly as a suffix for any sleazy fix (Irangate, Whitewatergate). "Where are the preservationists who usually rally to the salvation of historic bars and battlefields?" wondered a columnist when the Watergate plumbers' headquarters literally vanished. Heritage fanciers had no use for this infamous shrine now "metaphysically denied."[32]

Forgetting what displeases us is not only normal but necessary; heritage decorum rightly demands concealing the unspeakable, the unpalatable, and the outdated. To sanitize a seamy past may aid understanding more than laying it bare. Modern sensitivity mandates many suppressions; performers must bowdlerize old lyrics that would now grossly offend. Consider the second verse of Stephen Foster's legendary "Oh Susannah":

> I jump'd aboard de telegraph
> And trabbled down de ribber
> De lecktric fluid magnified,
> And killed five hundred Nigga.

No wonder this icon of American heritage is now never sung in its entirety. These lines would utterly dismay modern hearers, just as a functioning privy in a restored village prevents visitors from taking in any other aspects of the past.

"Should we censor *Birth of a Nation* or *Jud Süss* because of their racist messages?" rhetorically asks historian Alon Confino. "The answer is, of course, no." But in fact the answer depends on the audience. *The Birth of a Nation*, D. W. Griffith's rabidly racist 1915 movie of the Civil War and Reconstruction (lauded by President Woodrow Wilson as "all so terribly true"), became a cinematic classic. But it was left out of the Library of Congress's 1993 film centenary because Griffith's depiction of blacks as eye-rolling Uncle Toms and leering defilers of white womanhood would, for most viewers today, have drowned out the film's historical and aesthetic merits.[33]

Loss of familiarity dooms many legacies. Since their classical motifs no longer convey their allegorical intent, some public statuary becomes too obnoxious to display. Frederick MacMonnies's 1922 *Civic Virtue* triumphant over the Siren of Temptation is now banished from New York's City Hall to the boondocks because so many viewers ignorant of mythology took offense at a male chauvinist trampling a woman.[34] Language change, too, can consign a work to oblivion. Well into the 18th century the stomach, not the heart, was the seat of emotions. We still "stomach" things and speak of "gut feelings," but Wesley's great hymn, "How blest the man whose bowels move," is today quite unsingable.

Oblivion and memory alike thus distinguish heritage from history. Those who knowingly tamper with the past, as in Orwell's doublethink, must then forget they have done so. But needing to forget implies a present concern akin to commemoration. Those who deny the Holocaust, no less than those who memorialize it, show its efficacy as legacy. That may be the main reason the deniers feel compelled to make others forget it. One horrific coda to the Holocaust is that the Nazis, far from expunging its memory, planned a museum of former Jewish life to celebrate the Final Solution. "The Jews were not to be annihilated and then forgotten, but annihilated and then remembered forever," with Germans absolute masters not just of Jewish lives but afterlives; their "eternal death was not to be oblivion," historians now see, "but the torture of being eternally remembered by the[ir] persecutors."[35]

PUBLIC ENDORSEMENT

Celebrating some bits and forgetting others, heritage shapes an embraceable past. Some such revisions are overt, others unconscious; most are unashamedly advanced and readily welcomed. Heritage departures from history distress only a handful of highbrows. If Oliver Goldsmith was appalled by the "ecclesiastical beggars" who rattled off lies and legends as facts at Westminster Abbey's Poets' Corner, most viewers neither seek objective veracity nor mind if it is absent. Echoing Washington Irving's indulgence of spurious Shakespeare relics at Stratford in 1815, they are "ever willing to be deceived, where the deceit is pleasant, and costs nothing. What is it to us, whether these stories be true or false, so long as we can persuade ourselves into the belief of them?"[36] Irving himself was a practiced spinner of false historical yarns, but neither he nor his readers minded such deceptions—rather, they relished them.

Many consumers, to be sure, are readily duped; and heritage producers happily connive at gulling them. Like the surrealists Magritte and Dali, embroiderers of legacies exult in the acceptance of their concoctions. The Hampshire hobbyist who built for himself a full-scale "Hursley" railway station, complete with tarnish and soot, was delighted by a visitor's accolade: "Do you know, my grandfather used to work in that very signal-box?" An autobiographer invents a tale about her brother saving her from childhood bullies and is elated by his reaction: "I'm so glad you put that in, I'd forgotten all about it. Now I remember it perfectly."[37]

Legacy promoters feel obliged to cater to popular error. "Medieval" performers play late-Renaissance melodies on 16th-century shawms and regals because these later sounds and instruments exemplify what audiences mistake for medieval. Adolph Zukor's 1934 film of Catherine the Great, *The Scarlet Empress*, replaced St. Petersburg's elegant classical palaces with neo-Gothic monstrosities and the delicacies of Baroque harpsichord and strings with lush Wagner and Tchaikovsky, because these were what palaces and Russia conjured up in the popular mind.[38]

Audience expectation countenances many such fictions. A BBC play shows Vita Sackville-West dining alone with her mother at Knole, the family seat, in 1910.

> They were both in full evening dress, sitting at opposite ends of a long table. Their meal was finished, but two footmen in livery and a butler in tails still stood impassively along one side of the table while Vita and her mother discussed sex.

But "in 1910 mothers did not discuss sex with their daughters, let alone in front of the servants," objected Vita's son Nigel Nicolson; "they would not be wearing evening dress, nor the footmen livery; they would be sitting side by side at a much smaller table." The director was unregenerate: "The scene needed highlighting in a way that the audience expected. It was more truthful than actuality."[39]

Consumers countenance blatant departures from actuality. An adviser who disputed invented episodes in the 1970 film *Cromwell* was "told that most people wouldn't know that such events hadn't happened, so it wouldn't matter." It wouldn't have mattered if they had known; most willingly suspend disbelief for vivid impression. "Do you prefer your history on TV (a) straight, (b) fictionalized?" asks an interviewer only half in jest. "If fictionalized, do you balk at (a) invented speech, (b) invented characters, (c) invented incidents?" Few care that television history so casually commingles fact and fancy.

Finding that revered tradition is recent invention leaves most people unfazed. From the Donation of Constantine to the Protocols of the Elders of Zion, biases that induced fakes in the first place sustain faith in them long after their exposure. Indeed, dubious origins enhance many a tradition. Exposing the poems of Ossian as James Macpherson's forgery rather than discovery inflamed the Scottish nationalism it had ignited. Merely querying the authenticity of "medieval" manuscripts found in Bohemia in 1817–18 kindled Czech nationalism; philologist Václav Hanka was even more acclaimed as their forger than their finder.[40]

Israel continues to deploy Masada as a prime symbol of national identity, though literary and material evidence totally discredit the myth of 1st-century mass suicide ("rather than be taken as slaves, 967 zealots committed suicide; only one family survived to tell the tale"). Masada became an Israeli ritual mecca; scouts gathered around camp fires, intoning Yitzhak Lamdan's "Masada Shall Not Fall Again," while guides read aloud the speech Josephus invented for the last Jewish survivor. Just as the Donation of Constantine lost little potency after being shown false, so Masada's fabulous history leaves it no less gripping than if it were true. Visitors come to Masada today not for tangible evidence of the ancient legend but to experience a modern passion play of national rebirth.[41]

Sites willfully contrived often serve heritage better than those faithfully preserved. Knowing that "authentic Old Tucson" was actually built in 1939 as the film set for *Arizona* increases rather than impairs visitors' enjoyment. Tourists find no fault with heritage kitsch at Liverpool's Albert Dock; they have come for a good time, not for a history lesson. A visitor to Beatrix Potter's Hilltop Farm in the Lake District exclaims, "This is how I always imagined it!"[42] That Scotland, rather than the Lake District, had inspired Peter Rabbit is beside the point; hers was the fulfillment not of fact but of fancy. We ask of heritage an imagined past, not an actual one.

Heritage fabricated by the media often seems more real because more familiar than the original. Visitors thronged the Alamo when its memorial mural replaced the actual heroes with Hollywood actors from the 1960 film; Davy Crockett was easier to recognize as John Wayne than with his own face. The "Spirit of St. Louis" that Lindbergh flew across the Atlantic, enshrined at the Smithsonian in Washington, awes fewer than the plane in Dearborn's Ford Museum that Jimmy Stewart "flew" in the movie; it was the Hollywood plane that people "*saw* crossing the ocean."[43] The legacy of Mark Twain's boyhood Hannibal, Missouri, attests the force of fictive truth. When the home of Twain's old sweetheart Laura Hawkins became "Becky Thatcher's" house, the elderly Laura "embraced this fictional identity" and had "BT" inscribed on her headstone.[44]

Faked heritage is often highly felicitous. In 1993 six missing Haydn sonatas were unearthed—and then exposed as modern fakes. The Haydn expert who had vouched for their authenticity was unrepentant. "If it's a fraud it's the most brilliant fraud I've ever heard of," said H. C. Robbins Landon. "I don't mind being taken in by music this good— what Haydn would have written at this time."

Two generations ago Evelyn Waugh told of a little girl at Cana peddling wine jars as true relics of the miracle; if he preferred smaller models, she assured him these too were authentic. Waugh stressed the girl's ignorance and cupidity. Today, such tales spell sophistication. The guide who tells tourists, "This is a piece of Noah's Ark; or maybe it's just a symbol," and "Here is the spear that pierced Christ's side. Though maybe it's a copy, who knows?" would once have been rebuked for libeling sacred history; nowadays he is lauded for deconstructing it. Leading a group of nuns in Christ's footsteps, a tour conductor says, "This isn't the way He actually came. But it's a more interesting route"; the guide is not mocking the sacred past but offering a more accessible Via Dolorosa.[45]

The modern guide is also following the lead of Henry James's Bardic "Birthplace" curator. A true Shakespeare devotee, the curator initially refuses to lard the fragmentary facts, thus discouraging visitors—and reducing receipts. Warned to improve his pitch or lose his job, the curator veers in despair to the opposite hyperbolic extreme:

> Across that threshold He habitually passed; through those low windows, in childhood, He peered out into the world that He was to make so much happier by the gift to it of His genius; over the boards of this floor—that is over *some* of them, for we mustn't be carried away!—his little feet often pattered. . . . In this old chimney corner—just there [is the very] angle, where His little stool was placed, and where, I dare say, if we could look close enough, we should find the hearth-stone scraped with His little feet.

Far from such subversive nonsense getting him sacked, visitors lap it up. "Don't they want then *any* truth?—none even for the mere look of it?" asks an appalled crony. "The look of it," says the curator, "is what I give!" The look of it equally suffices modern film audiences. "If historical accuracy were the thing people went to the movies for," says director John Sayles, "historians would be the vice presidents of studios."[46]

Yet the public and producers alike do require a *semblance* of accuracy; historical films must be touted as "based on a true story." As with heritage generally, the problem is that many producers still share D. W. Griffith's faith that they are contriving true history—and are dismayed that customers who claim to care in fact seem quite blasé. Unaware how radically they reshape history, heritage mongers themselves swear fidelity to truth.[47]

Fifty years' experience at Colonial Williamsburg illustrates the point. "Authenticity has been virtually [our] religion," avowed its director in 1941; "sacrifices have been offered before its altar. Personal preferences, architectural design, time, expense, . . . even the demands of beauty have given way to the exacting requirements of authenticity." Fifty years on Williamsburg staff can see it was all wrong back then—and express confidence that they are *now* getting it right. The toll-free telephone number, 1-800-HISTORY, suggests that Williamsburg deals not in heritage but in history. Staff take pride in purveying real history, as opposed to Disneyland fiction. Worried about a prospective Disney history theme park in their backyard, they were shocked to find the public saw little difference. When ten discussants were asked if they thought Williamsburg authentic, all agreed that it was.

"And Disneyland?" and without a pause, every one of them said, "Oh yes, yes, Disneyland is authentic too." [The moderator] asked "How can this be? We all know that Disney's America . . . is going to be totally made up. It isn't even a real historical site. Everything will be artificial. And you all know that Colonial Williamsburg is a real place, even if much restored." "Sure," they said, but . . . "Disney always does things first-class, and if they set out to do American history, they'll hire the best historians money can buy . . . to create a completely plausible, completely believable appearance of American history."[48]

In the public view, plausibility is as good as truth, and historians are worthy of their heritage hire.

Salutary deceit is the raison d'être of *Lettice and Lovage*. Peter Shaffer's eponymous tour guide thrills historic-house visitors with flights of fancy that bring Fustian Hall to life as bald facts signally failed to do. "Enlarge—enliven—enlighten" is her maxim; "fantasy floods in where fact leaves a vacuum." Such tales not only delight in heritage hype, they suggest a *need* for fantasy. Gluttons for false facts, we bring to the most improbable past an "immense assumption of veracities and sanctities, of the general soundness of the legend," noted Henry James; like Washington Irving at Stratford, we swallow the reliquary shell's "preposterous stuffing" almost whole. But not *quite* whole, for we know we are being fed this legacy by partisans. As playwright Alan Bennett says, "Scepticism about one's heritage [is an] essential part of that heritage."[49]

HOW HERITAGE AND HISTORY COMBINE

That history and heritage are profoundly at odds these last four chapters have made abundantly clear. This section shows how the two enterprises collaborate as well as compete. Heritage and history are not so much disparate species as opposite sexes, ever contesting roles and domains, yet mutually dependent and with more in common than they like to realize.

Heritage departs from history in what it sees, what it stresses, and what it changes. From the same past, history and heritage carve out unlike and often competing insights. "We are not here to teach history, to do the teachers' work," says a guide at an Israeli settlement museum. "Let them learn history at school. We are here for the experience."[50]

The aim of the experience is to show heritage, unlike history, alive and kicking. Many Americans, says the head of the new National Museum of the American Indian, "believe Indians, along with our culture, to be dead, gone, relegated to history." Hence we "must show Indian culture as the vital, breathing, changing phenomenon that it is. This gem of a museum attests that we are neither dead nor primitive." The "experience" experience, in a British observer's term, makes today's museums among "the most exciting and dangerous places on earth."[51]

By dangerous, he means marvelously misleading. Dynamic heritage yields dubious history. But this is both natural and, as I have shown, harmless, if we bear in mind their utterly unlike aims: history to explain through critical inquiry, heritage to celebrate and congratulate. "Experiencing" the past is not learning about the past, as the Israeli guide just cited well knew. Empathetic role-play and reenactment feed the illusion that heritage experience suffices to know the past. We need history's reminder that we never really get into its denizens' shoes or simulate their souls.

But to harp on the contrasts slights the convergences. History and heritage are less dissenting ventures than disparate viewpoints. Each aims to show things "as they were"—bring the dead to life with imaginative empathy, make the past more knowable, tie up loose ends, remove unsightly excrescences, offer images clearer than reality. And their ways of seeing and using the past fructify one another; many enterprises share features of both. Public history, folk history, collective memory, building restoration, battle reenactment, historical fiction, and docudramas combine heritage aims with historical research, history's lofty universality with heritage's possessive intimacy. Most would agree there is more to history than heritage alone, but "the *whole* of history," observes historian Michael Kammen, "is heritage."[52]

Moreover, events keep shifting from one realm to the other. Much that commences as heritage in time becomes history; much that first passed for impartial history is later seen as partisan heritage. Gibbon's *Decline and Fall of the Roman Empire* is now read less as history than as a literary legacy. After a solid documentary start, 19th-century Scottish history became religious and political polemic. Personal papers passing from family heritors to archival holdings get used first as historical sources and later are venerated as collective heritage. Heritage is seen to merge with history in Colonial Williamsburg's "cheerful conspiracy with the past."

The shifting repute of Israel's legendary Tel Hai shows history discarding heritage grown passé. A Zionist frontier settlement in northern Galilee, Tel Hai was the site of an heroic stand against Arab assault in 1920, costing the life of the one-armed ex-Czarist officer Yoseph Trumpeldor. Tel Hai and Trumpeldor became role models for Palestinian Jews. Unlike the submissive, landless Jew of the Diaspora, the Zionist warrior/settler's credo was symbolized by the twin icons of the plough and gun carried by Trumpeldor. His fabled last words, "It is good to die for our country," festooned countless classrooms and were endlessly intoned at commemoratives. Tel Hai was for decades an Israeli founding legacy.

But not any more. Tel Hai is contrary to current verities. The militant settler has given way to the angst-ridden skeptic; the moral certitudes of Zionist pioneers seem smug platitudes in a post-Holocaust world. To jettison Tel Hai, it was historically debunked, mocked as a risible myth. The one-armed hero bearing gun and plough became a blatant sham: "any person in his condition would have had difficulty performing either of these tasks, [yet Trumpeldor] excelled in performing both." Since Trumpeldor knew no Hebrew, his famous dying words must be bogus too—misheard, cynics suggest, for the Russian "fuck your mother." From essential founding fable, Tel Hai has in a half century become a cautionary tale about the misuse of history.[53]

Yet historians too conspire with the past, bending facts in battling heritage-mongers. "Protect Historic America" damned a Disney desecration of Civil War sites as "a crime against the national heritage" in a locale that, historians said, had "bred more founding fathers, inspired more soaring hopes and ideals and witnessed more triumphs and failures" than any other. But historians have mounted no comparable crusade to preserve other sites—such as Pennsylvania's coal fields or South Chicago's riot scenes—where, John Bodnar notes, battles were "also fought to sustain American democracy and economic justice." History texts, marketed as tools to help students "appreciate our heritage," favor celebration over scholarship: "No publisher tries to sell a textbook with the claim that it is more accurate than its competitors."[54]

Yet history is the bedrock of communal heritage; heritage zeal draws attention to history and nurtures its sources. Finland owes its invaluable folk-life archives to the labors of patriot-scholars. Notable research has personal roots; fascination with his own family legacy inspired Philippe Ariès's histories of childhood and old age. Something of the antiquarian's engrossment with the old and the genealogist's with lineage stokes the most detached historian's quest; every effort to fathom the past is fueled by some such feeling.[55]

History also needs heritage to carry conviction. If the historian's task is to "promote social understanding of how the community has got to be where it is," writes Brendan Bradshaw of Irish chroniclers, the Olympian detachment of revisionist history lamentably fails. A public steeped in memories of the past "as it really was" cannot credit such bloodless chronicles.[56]

To contend that heritage precludes good history is to see the public singularly blinkered, as if infection by Disney destroyed historical curiosity. "That a child who takes one look at Mickey Mouse dressed as Abraham Lincoln will never be interested in the Gettysburg Address defies logic," held a columnist; it might more likely have the opposite effect. Previous historians have peddled popular, schmaltzy, or silly history without lasting harm. As the *Civil War* television series spurred academic book sales, so might Disney's Historyland generate interest in actual historic places and themes.

Envy may help explain historians' hostility toward what many see as the cuckoo in their nest; competing for the same terrain, heritage often comes out ahead. The latter is popular, Raphael Samuel suggests, because in many ways it outshines history—in visual skills, in alertness to public mood, in access to popular memory, in regard to environmental issues, sense of place, and "public history" of all kinds. Unlike history proper, heritage is backed by myriad volunteers, enjoys state support, and commands corporate patronage. It is also popular because, like Hollywood, it combines a historical imprimatur—"based on a true story," say all the ads—with the emotional credibility of being "so morally unambiguous, so devoid of tedious complexity, so *perfect*."[57]

No historian could match heritage's most awesome feats. "The most successful archaeologist in history," said Israel's Yigael Yadin, was the 4th-century Queen (Saint) Helena. "Whatever she looked for she promptly found hundreds of years after the event: the stable where Mary had given birth, . . . the twelve stations of the cross, Calvary, the true cross, the nails, the lancet, the Holy Sepulchre and so on and on."[58] By comparison, the exploits of Clio, muse of history, seem plodding and prosaic.

Yet history and heritage both offer astounding leaps into realms that now exist thanks only to imagination. However treated, the past is generously biddable; since few from yesteryear can answer back, it harbors scope for invention denied to the present. Take E. L. Doctorow's rejoinder to the elderly Texan who challenged his novel *Welcome to Hard Times*, set in 19th-century Dakota Territory:

> "Young man," she wrote, "when you said that Jenks enjoyed for his dinner the roasted haunch of a prairie dog, I knew you'd never been west of the Hudson. Because the haunch of a prairie dog wouldn't fill a teaspoon." She had me. I'd never seen a prairie dog. So I did the only thing I could. I wrote back and I said, "That's true of prairie dogs today, Madam, but in the 1870s . . ."[59]

To be a living force the past must be ever remade. Heritage is not to be stored away in a vault or an attic; the true steward adds his own stamp to those of his predecessors. A museum curator is sure that "we wish to influence how our lives and times are perceived by future generations"; she assumes a *duty* to augment what we bequeath. To receive and transmit a legacy is not enough; it must be refurbished and given new resonance while in our care. Heritage must feel durable, yet be pliable. It is more vital to reshape than just to preserve. "Societies which cannot combine reverence to their symbols with freedom of revision," warned the philosopher Whitehead, "must ultimately decay either from anarchy, or from the slow atrophy of a life stifled by useless shadows." As Orwell bluntly warned those English he saw mired in compliant reaction, "we must add to our heritage or lose it."[60] Like all forgers of identity, we add by fabricating.

Yet, while altering and enlarging earlier legacies, we never wholly supplant them. Doctorow's prairie dog remains a recognizable prairie dog. New-minted memories coexist with inherited ones; the present retains as well as reconstructs the past. Though Washington and Lincoln become radically transformed in the public eye, they are not mistaken for each other or for other men; the coherence in each image, Barry Schwartz shows, survives the conversions.[61] Indeed, a prime function of heritage is to sustain traditional perspectives in the face of each generation's autonomy and unlikeness. So we conflate as we create, keeping menacing breaches at bay by making the new seem old and the old feel new.

In securing us these benefits, two traits fundamental to heritage assume crucial roles: virtues linked to precedence or priority, discussed in Chapter 8; and to what is innate or rooted, surveyed in Chapter 9.

Chapter 8

BEING FIRST

CLAIMS OF PRIORITY suffuse every realm of heritage. Everyone eagerly insists their lineages, languages, fossils, even rocks are previous to those of others. But *why* do we care? What makes priority crucial? This chapter shows why being first seems so fundamental, and why it is so ardently claimed, and when needed invented, for so many of our legacies.

"First come, first served" expresses impartial justness. It is also a law of nature: like early birds, first-comers feed best. In heritage, maxim becomes precept. Precedence is legendarily preferred. Double portions were allotted to Old Testament firstborn sons; in primogeniture, a mode of succession long common, the eldest took all.

Not every firstborn legacy is enviable. Old Testament readiness to sacrifice eldest sons won those sons a reward in heaven, but here on earth the second-born took over. The first on line have been at gravest risk since Jehovah smote the eldest sons of Egypt and took unto himself all the firstborn of Israel. But precedence normally implies superiority and confers supremacy. Matthew's "the first shall be last, and the last shall be first" piously inverts the mundane reality. The firstborn's double portion, for some still obligatory, for many retains a primordial resonance.

The virtues of priority color every use of first. First fruits, first class, first prize, first violin, first of all, first and foremost, primate, prime minister are phrases so customary we forget their ordinal implications. The first blow is half the battle, the most important if not the only thing that counts. Caesar made no scruple "that he had rather be first in a village, than second at Rome."[1] Guinness books of firsts show precedence to be a potent spur. The first to find a cure or a continent, to detect hidden treasure, to walk on the moon, or to cry "Bingo!" inherit fame or fortune; no one remembers who came next. As Alfred Russel Wallace and next-at-the-patent-office pioneers of the telephone and the auto assembly line found to their cost, first-comers Darwin, Bell, and Ford alone got the kudos.

Metaphors of priority pervade patriotic maxims. "First in war, first in peace, first in the hearts of his countrymen" was Washington's archetypal accolade. Where you originally come from, says Oliver Goldsmith's *The Traveller* (1764), is what finally counts:

> The patriot's boast, where'er we roam,
> His first best country ever is, at home.

Firstness comes in the various guises explored below. What is prior confers prestige and title; primordial origins connote divine aims and attributes; things indigenous are deeply rooted; long persistence betokens stability; great antiquity is a bona fide of civilized progress. These values intertwine (the primordial may be divine or natural) or at times conflict (persistence and progress both imply antiquity), but each mode must be understood in its own right. Those who reject remote for ready-made heritage are seen to be rare exceptions.

PRIORITY

Precedence evokes pride and proves title. To be first in a place warrants possession; to antedate others' origins or exploits shows superiority. "The most important point about English history," held Bishop Creighton, "is that the English were the first people who formed for themselves a national character at all."[2] Descent from "first peoples" validates tribal rights in America and the Antipodes. Ethnic French in Manitoba demand a rich legacy because "we were here as a nation before there was a Manitoba." Mohawk Indians in Quebec stake an analogous claim: "Why do the people of Quebec have this right to self-determination if people who've lived here many more hundreds of years don't have that right?" And the Mohawks scold separatists who blamed "newly arrived immigrants" for the 1995 referendum loss as themselves only newly arrived.

Priority can enshrine even a relatively recent heritage. While America is often disparaged as "new," its historians note with pride that the United States is the oldest extant republic and democracy and has the oldest written constitution. Monuments and memorial albums in American prairie towns only fifty years old commemorated the first couple to marry there, the first child locally born, the first funeral. Australian goldfield museums feature panning tools and billy-cans of the earliest settlers.

Claims to priority commonly derogate rivals. Pre-Trojan origins, held Alfonso de Cartagena at the Council of Basle in 1434, entitled the Spanish monarch to ceremonial precedence over England's king. East European students in Vienna scoured medieval charters to prove "their own culture was much older than" that of others, a historian recalls; "no nation within the [Hapsburg] monarchy wanted to have a younger history than its neighbour."[3] Scions of New York's "original" Dutch settlers shunned a 1921 commemorative parade that denied them the lead role they felt entitled to. Ulster Protestants vie with Irish Catholic antiquity claims; "British Israelites" contend that the prophet Jeremiah and the daughters of Zedekiah carried the Ark of the Covenant to County Antrim and liken the siege of Derry to Jericho. Orangemen term Ireland's 17th-century British conquerors the rightful heirs of original Britons, exiled to Scotland by Gaelic intruders in the remote past.[4]

The more previous the past, the more compelling the claim. "What are you talking about?" retorted Prime Minister Ben-Gurion when the Vatican in 1950 rebuked Israel for making Jerusalem its capital. "Jerusalem *was* Israel's capital a thousand years before the birth of Christianity." When told that African rock art dated back thirty to forty thousand years, Tanzanian children joyfully hugged the archaeologist for finding them a culture older than the British.[5]

Professions of priority extend to fossil traces and rock layers. Ancient strata became British national emblems; in 1835 the oldest rocks known were named Silurian, after a tribe famed for resisting Roman invaders. Parallels drawn in 1849 between a British fossil crocodile and a petrified creature from conquered Sind implied, for British imperialists, "a prior claim to the territory justifying the occupation" of that Indian province.[6] The 1995 Chinese quarry fossil find of *Eosimias sinensis*, the "first" proto-human, launched a Peking claim to primate primacy antedating Africa's "Lucy" by 45 million years.

The charisma of precedence lures many to fabricate it. Britons in 1912 eagerly embraced the Piltdown forgery as a find that trumped French Cro-Magnon primacy. Since national prestige depends on priority, prehistoric expertise is widely coerced. To buttress Nordic mystique, Nazi archaeologists found sites and artifacts "proving" a Germanic family tree antedating Romans, Celts, and Slavs. To chauvinists, only their own antiquity counts. The French repudiate Lucy, the world's oldest found humanoid, as an alien African. Greeks besotted by any trace of Philip of Macedon dismiss English prehistory as irrelevant. So what if Stonehenge is older than the Acropolis; Greeks all "know" *their* history goes back two and half millennia, while England had no "real" history before 1066.[7]

PRIMORDIAL BEGINNINGS

Being ancient makes things precious by their proximity to the dawn of time, to the earliest beginnings. "Antique is above ancient, and ancient above old," judged an 18th-century French scholar; he put the antique as over a thousand, the ancient as two hundred, the old as one hundred years back. The more ancient a lineage the more highly venerated it is.

The length that glorifies genealogies also aggrandizes group prestige and privilege. Tracing forebears back to Troy not only ennobled feudal families but lent whole peoples collective glory. The cult of Gaulish ancestral antiquity centered on Vercingetorix echoes today not only in Asterix but in the modern historian who exalts France as "the oldest of the mature European nations." The English preen themselves on royal antiquity: other countries have "Mickey Mouse leaders, whilst 'our' monarchs have biological lines stretching back in their purity to the dawn of history." Whereas "some guy" in Spain just "set himself up as King, ours can look right back to Ethelred the Unready."[8]

The remote antiquity of specific heritage icons is often invoked. That Dutch was *the* primordial tongue an early scholar held obvious from the very word *Duits*—*de* (the) plus *oudste* (eldest); ancient biblical names like Adam, Babel, and Noah also made sense only in Dutch.[9] Similar claims long came from Sweden, and even today the writer Franz Stark vaunts German as "the oldest of the living cultural languages on the continent." Geological and Aboriginal legacies dating from the dawn of time console Australians for the felt brevity, vis-à-vis Europe, of their national saga. The 1994 find of living Jurassic-era pine trees boosted Aussie pride in native antiquity, as had the 1968 discovery at Kow Swamp of the world's oldest-known cremation, edge-ground axes, and millstones.

Ancestral antecedents inspire patriotic rites in lands as diverse as Iceland and Ireland, Indonesia and Iraq, and most markedly in Israel. Finding papyri missives from Bar Kokhba, fabled leader of the Jewish uprising against the Romans in A.D. 120, in a Judean desert cave in 1960, General Yigael Yadin told President Ben Zvi before the assembled cabinet: "Mr. President of the State of Israel, I have the honor to present to you letters dispatched by the last president of the State of Israel 1800 years ago."[10]

Reborn nations typically lay claim to ancient paragons: revolutionary France, the American republic, 19th-century Germany, Mussolini's Italy harked back to classical prototypes to stress devotion to time-tested perfection. Bygone autonomy is antiquated to justify its rebirth; feats admired as primordial authorize freedom crusades. As Finnish patriots in 1910 said of the *Kalevala*, "a nation able in early times to create such a work of genius cannot succumb."

Great age of origins and achievements or lasting endurance is usually requisite to group glory; when absent, antiquity is fabricated. Early Christian conversion and ancient Erse freedom braced the Irish quest for liberty; pride in being Europe's oldest sovereign state underpins modern Basque separatism. Pakistan was invented within living memory, but a book on the Indus Valley is called *Five Thousand Years of Pakistan*; five thousand is more impressive than fifty. President Sukarno used to harp on the 350 years of colonialism endured by Indonesia, though most of Indonesia was under Dutch rule for less than a century.[11]

Relying on antique precedent has drawbacks. It can immure life in outworn shibboleths, like a recent rabbinical annulment of a marriage on the ground that twenty-five centuries back, the wife's priestly ancestor might unlawfully have wed a divorcee. Invoking precedent may backfire: reminded of Exodus in 1960 when Israel withdrew from Sinai, Prime Minister Ben-Gurion was censured by Orthodox zealots for saying 600 families, not 600,000 adults as in Holy Scripture, had left Egypt. Allusions in 1992 to King David's homosexuality and in 1994 to his womanizing outraged the Knesset. But other Israelis voiced pride that "there exists no other state where events of three thousand years ago can cause such a heated controversy."[12]

Sheer inaccessibility adds to the mystique of the very ancient. Wordsworth's "secrets older than the Flood" and Shelley's "thrilling secrets of the birth of time" evoke awe of events ineffably mysterious because remote. The primordial still promises transcendent understanding. Alex Haley's *Roots* set slavery's origins in a mythicized Gambian village because, he explained, "We need a place called Eden. I wanted to portray our original culture in its pristine state."[13]

Yearnings for the primordial similarly inspired English folk-life revivalists. Viewing only the most ancient elements as authentic, folklorists exhorted villagers to strip away subsequent corruptions and restore original verities. And though few villagers had heard of the ancient fertility rituals the professionals exalted, they deferred to the experts and changed things accordingly. The annual "Souling play" at Antrobus adopted Arnold Boyd's theory that characters reincarnated the Halloween ghosts of their ancestors; Violet Alford in the 1930s revived the Marshfield Mummers' perambulation as a pagan "magic circle"; while the ascription of Castleton's 17th-century Garland ceremony to Celtic sacrificial rites stems from the 1977 visit of a persuasive Celticist. To understand present-day British folklore, one must retrace the routes of recent folklorists who "purified" it. Locals, however, are conned into thinking their revised rites are truly archaic.[14]

People everywhere antiquate newborn heritage in ways of which they soon become unaware, as with now immemorial royal rituals invented for Edward VII's coronation in 1902, or the House of Lords life-peerage pageantry that seems to stem from the mists of time but actually dates from 1958. For the annual church festival in the Italian village of Ripacandida, impoverished peasants used to dress children as abstemious monks in honor of St. Anthony of Padua. In the 1950s they began arraying them in richer garments, emulating the martyred local bishop St. Donatus; the switch from humble monk to splendid bishop was fueled by a bonanza from pensions and emigrant remittances. The villagers now insist their children have dressed as St. Donatus since the 4th century.[15] Only a killjoy anthropologist would query a claim so crucial to pride in heritage.

The earliest sources of self, of society, or of the species promise to reveal our place in the scheme of things. In psychology a cult of origins long exalted the deep truths of archaic experience; psychoanalysis sought clues to present behavior in primal scenes. A vogue for beginnings and remote prefigurations until lately dominated historical inquiry as well. But it is heritage partisans who are most eager to show that "here is where it all began," as Israeli settlement museums proclaim, or "here it was all born," as Prague's Mozart Foundation says of Central Europe's musical culture: "This is who we are because this is how and where we began." North America's initial (1979) World Heritage sites stressed the primordial: Mesa Verde as the earliest Indian settlement, Canada's L'Anse aux Meadows as the first-known European site.

DIVINE ANTIQUITY

"All that was ancient was venerable and sacred," said Fustel de Coulanges of the Greeks and Romans. Sacred is the key word here. European elites that hark back to Hector or Noah ultimately revert to "Adam, son of God"; such descent implied heavenly favor. Divine lineage became a prime requisite of royal rule. Louis VII of France's long-awaited son, "scion of a sacred race," born 1165, was named Philippe Dieudonné in gratitude for divine intercession. "God so loved the most Christian nation of France," declared Gilles de Paris, "that he would never leave it without an heir."[16] Other monarchs claimed similarly divine aid and ancestry. "Kings are not only God's lieutenants upon the earth," asserted James I in 1609, "but even by God himself, they are called Gods."

Royal origins the world over are rooted in the dawn of time when mythic kings were scions of the gods. Citing a 14th-century text, a Japanese academic acclaims imperial divinity:

> Is it not a glorious tradition for a nation, that its emperor should be descended directly from th[e] grandson of "the great heaven-illuminating goddess"? What other nation can point to an Imperial family of one unbroken lineage reigning over the land for twenty-five centuries?[17]

Shinto rites affirming the emperor's divinity imply that the nation, too, is sacred. In the 1980s when excavation finds pointed to a Korean ancestry for the imperial family, the ancient tombs were swiftly sealed to safeguard the legend of unbroken descent from the sun goddess.

Since in the mists of time men had been ruled by the gods themselves, ancient priority signaled divine intercession. A 15th-century papal nuncio assured the French they were "the first to be planted on earth by God." Divine attributes passed on from royal inheritors promised entire peoples they were God's "elect nation." Puritans saw England as a second Israel succored by Jehovah against its foes; that God first revealed His new great age to "his English-men" was the message of Foxe's *Martyrs* (1563) and of Milton's *Areopagitica* (1644).[18]

In divine primordial nature 19th-century Americans found traits morally superior to degenerate human history. Yankee encomiasts contrasted Europe's temples built by Roman robbers and towers of feudal oppression with their own "deep forests which the eye of God has alone pervaded. What is the echo of roofs that a few centuries since rung with barbaric revels . . . to the silence which has reigned in these dim groves since the first Creation?" Deifying nature, Americans positioned themselves nearest the deity.[19]

Deserved proximity to God is exemplified in the golden telephone tale. One version has Prime Minister Thatcher at a papal audience; she sees a golden telephone on the Pope's desk. Told it is a direct line to God, she asks to use it, does so, and pays £50. Soon after at Ian Paisley's office in Ulster she sees an identical phone, speaks for the same length of time, and is asked to pay ten pence. Recalling what heaven cost in Rome, she wonders why it is so cheap in Belfast. "Ah," explains Paisley, "you see, from here 'tis only a local call."

In lauding our heritage, we extol our ancestors and obey the deity who enjoined them—and us—to exalt it. Ancient Israel prevailed through God's favor, attesting both His right and Israelite merit.[20] America's Manifest Destiny devolved from a national longing inspired by the deity's own design. Previous to secular history, the primordial sacred heritage is thereby exempt from the erosions of time or accident; France is lauded as a land that has always been. Primordial origins even presage future fortune: as there has always been an England, so there always will be one.

Edward Said distinguishes beginnings, as history, from origins, which are divine; he suggests that "beginning is *making* or *producing difference*."

Making and lauding difference is the very essence of heritage, an enterprise half historical, half divine.[21]

INDIGENOUS ROOTEDNESS

Uniquely acclaimed are the legacies of those still rooted where their ancestors began it all. Tribal indigenes range from fragmented clusters in, say, the United States (where Native Americans are less than 1 percent of the whole), to substantial minorities in China and India, Mexico and New Zealand and large majorities in Guatemala and the Andes. Some indigenes (Ainu in Japan, Sami in Scandinavia, Berbers in North Africa) were until recently too few, too subjugated, or too divided to assert forceful heritage claims. But most native peoples now insist that prior habitation entitles them to possession.

European invaders who swore by sedentary cultivation and private property long rejected such claims; in their view, lands held in common or by nomadic tribes were unappropriated, empty, *terra nullius* in legal terms. Indigenous property claims nowadays meet more receptive ears. An imprimatur of rectitude attaches to ancient occupance; tribal peoples regain more and more land usurped from their forebears. Australia's repudiation of *terra nullius* in 1992 heralds extensive reversion of Crown Lands to Aborigines; ancestral rights of Maoris, Native Americans, Inuits, Hawaiians, and other "First Nation" peoples are increasingly endorsed.

In times past, terms denoting priority were seldom complimentary; they traduced inferior and backward "natives." "Primordial" implied simple savages doomed by civilization. "Aboriginal" and "indigenous" linked prior with primitive, implying that folk who had stuck around so long lacked the brains or the energy to move on and better themselves. These stereotypes still poison such words. Though the United Nations made 1993 the "Year of the Indigenous Person," many shunned the term as invidious. Some Australian tribes want to replace "Aborigines" with "original owners," even if this suggests that they are owners no longer. A category proposed for the U.S. census is "Original Peoples of the Western Hemisphere."

The Canadian term "First Nation" has caught on globally by avoiding any negative nuance. Acknowledging Indians and Inuits as Canada's original occupants, it also links their legacies with pre-conquest peoples the world over. Just as no Canadian politician dares ignore First Nations, so nativist slurs in America or Australia reap swift revenge, and Maori mystique becomes mandatory in New Zealand. As shown in Chapter 3, indigenous heritage that once evoked mainstream fear or disgust, and then aroused avarice or voyeurism, is now prized as a precious global legacy.

First-comer claims, however, are no less anachronistic than other heritages; the identities they compel are newly constructed. The pre-Columbian America to which "first peoples" migrated millennia ago had no such meaning for ancestral Inuits or Indians; their horizons were as circumscribed as those of medieval Europeans. Among Aborigines today Australia is a significant concept, but for their ancient forebears, disjoined by diverse tongues and folkways, Australia by any name had no consensual character. Aborigines became one people, consciously identified with their island continent, only when it ceased to be theirs, as an aftermath of British invasion and settlement.

All ancestral roots are ultimately of equal age; each of us harks back to Lucy and her ilk. But the charisma of prehistoric occupance attaches only to locales with tribal denizens. Modern Hopis and Navajos are held to deserve the Four Corners country, ancestral knowledge of this harsh terrain making them its natural managers. To be sure, this idealized stability ignores the actual annals of European innovation, tribal upheaval, and environmental change that have utterly transformed the Southwest and its peoples. Mistaken for unchanged ancestors, Hopis and Navajos are venerated as hoary traditionals.

Nativist virtues long antedate the New World natives who now mostly incarnate them. Arcadia was a Classical realm of innocence and purity. Convinced that sophistication cheapened and corrupted, 18th-century *primitifs* abjured architecture after the Doric, literature later than Homer, sculpture beyond Phidias. Pre-Raphaelites reverted to quattrocento "primitive" and "natural honesty." Archaic art become a modernist touchstone; ancient artifacts validated contemporary art's archetypal appeal. Cults of the primordial lent worthy mystique to European folk legacies.

To fend off strangers and newcomers, natives insist they have always been there. Welsh and French, Polish and Romanian heritage hark back to Celtic and Gaulish, Sarmatian and Dacian "first nations." The phrase "our ancestors the Gauls" transmutes the dross of primitive ethnicity into a French dream of communal legend. Green nostalgia in England conjures up a warm, wooded, well-watered land of Neolithic harmony seven millennia back.

Indigenous antiquity, once a stigma of backwardness, now redeems European recency in New Worlds. Dreamtime legacies deepen white Australian roots. Traces of extinct Arawaks become heritage emblems for West Indian states. Americans who grope for a usable past today locate it less in Old World reminders than in Indian relict landscapes—"the earth from which we sprang," in the words of National Park director Roger Kennedy. This one-time chronicler of America's classical revival now stresses America's indigenous antiquity. Folk in the Midwest should "walk out along Main Street and look about and say, 'Oh, that's two thousand years old. That's as old as the Emperor Augustus.'"[22] No matter that few midwesterners could date Augustus; they should enjoy being aware that their own indigenous America is just as augustly ancient.

The mystique of native antiquity is no longer confined simply to those who have stayed put; as we saw in Chapter 1, many migrants cling to—and magnify—legendary origins via a portable heritage. Yemenites are relative newcomers to modern Israel, but they claim and are conceded autochthonous ancestral status. Patronized on their arrival a half century ago as exotic primitives, they gained acceptance as custodians of ancient Jewish culture, notably dress and dance. Here could be seen "the source, the fountain of one of our basic steps," Israeli folk-dance revivalists enthused; these biblical echoes might be "directly descended from the most ancient prayer movements." "Israel is a Biblical land, so . . . its dance company should be Yemenite," argued a dancer. "The Yemenites are a Biblical people. We even dressed Biblically in Yemen."[23]

The vital import of priority claims is evident in South Africa. Boer settlers a century ago justified their expansion by arguing that they had moved into empty land after the Bushmen, South Africa's first inhabitants, became extinct. Far from being robbed of an ancestral heritage, Bantus and Hottentots were later intruders. Not even the end of apartheid has dented this claim; Cecil Rhodes's statue in Cape Town still imperiously beckons northward and white South Africans still cleave to the legend of prior white arrival.[24]

TIME-HONORED STABILITY

The worth of many legacies is weighed by their durability. "If it's lasted that long," as Prince Philip says of Britain's monarchy, "it can't be all that bad." Long endurance shows a heritage is no ephemeral fancy but a rooted verity. Defending his choice of the Maison Carré in Nîmes as the model for Virginia's Capitol in Richmond, Jefferson argued that "it has obtained the approbation of fifteen or sixteen centuries, and is therefore preferable to any design which might be newly contrived." Better still is a long-sustained original. "The most noticeable thing about our history is that we have more of it than any other country," says an English columnist. "Rome is older, but Italy is a nineteenth-century upstart. The length of time, the depth and richness of our island story, gives us a claim to pre-eminence."[25]

Heritage pride inheres no less in precedence than in perpetuity—unbroken connections, permanent traits and institutions. Maintaining or restoring such links confirms that the groups we belong to are not ephemeral but enduring organisms. It was the perpetuation, as much as the purity, of French royal blood from the Franks to the Valois that gave that monarchy its prestige.

Since any breach in a lineage might jeopardize heritage transmission, stewards exalt continuity. Lauding apostolic tradition as seamless, a 16th-century ecclesiastic aimed to demonstrate "the visible monarchy of the Catholic Church . . . founded upon Peter and his true and legitimate successors . . . preserved inviolate, neither broken nor interrupted but continuous, for ever." Duty to founders "whose principles we inherit" required 19th-century Americans to ensure "there are no gaps in the record" to be left to their own heirs.[26] Proof of continuity is crucial to today's Native Americans: to secure federal benefits and reclaim ancestral property, tribes may have to show an identity unbroken since European contact.

Longevity and continuity combine in boasts that Germany is a two-thousand-year-old being sustained by eighty-seven generations of collective experience. The French feel uniquely unabridged; "all other history is mutilated, ours alone complete," held Michelet. "Italy lacks the last centuries, the Germans and the English lack the first." French continuity survived the break from *ancien régime* to republic; a 1989 history text exhorts pupils "to thank God for having allowed our people, led by its kings, to give the world a model of moderation, of progress, of civilization." The Revolution was no breach but a bridge: regal protector of Christendom or champion of liberty and reason, France remains, in Mitterand's words, ever culturally supreme.[27] A Lascaux cave painting in a 1995 France Telecom ad adds persistence to priority: "20,000 years ago we were on the cutting edge of communications. And we've been there ever since." The French got there first and are still the best.

Great antiquity may palliate or exonerate a breach. Turning a blind eye to long Byzantine and Ottoman hiatuses, Greeks claim to continue to speak the same language as their classical ancient forebears. Church chroniclers directed by Ferdinando Ughelli in the mid-17th century sought to list bishops over the entire span of each Italian diocese, but certain gaps spelled great antiquity—the very absence of names attested the parlous plight of early Christianity. English Whig historians avid for "enduring" Anglo-Saxon virtues resurgent in the 17th century treated intervening epochs as a sad but reparable lapse in continuity. Since marks of any breach might imperil habitual loyalties, states like churches pretend to be bastions of tradition even in the midst of turbulent upheaval.[28]

Britons especially laud malleable steadiness, the English virtue of an ever-evolving, never-broken palimpsest. "Almost uniquely among European nations, we are at ease with our past," bragged a Tory Cabinet member in 1994.

> We have not had to tear down our royal palaces or convert them to soulless museums. We have not had to bulldoze our great churches or convert them into warehouses. We have not had some great constitutional rupture in our affairs [like] the French, Germans and Italians. . . . Here is a nation proud of its past.

Perpetual linkage is the ritual refrain. "No existing institution or right or claim can be explained without going back a long way," Bishop Creighton averred, "no [other] nation has carried its whole past so completely into its present." Such continuity struck the historian Butterfield as a unique source of strength. "Many English institutions have century upon century of the past, lying fold upon fold within them. . . .

Because we in England have maintained the threads between past and present we do not, like some younger states, have to go hunting for our own personalities." English Heritage today reaffirms this "sense of entity and continuity, of evolution as a nation over more than ten centuries."[29]

English stability is notably enshrined in landscapes that bear the stamp, as its champions fondly say, of centuries of countrymen and women—even of surviving aboriginal cattle. An environment chief lauds stewardship that leaves much of rural England "as she was: changeless in our fast-changing world." Reassurance that "some things remain stable, permanent and enduring" is, a scholar concludes, the countryside's main value. Rurality sanctions the status quo. Exalting his rural roots, Prime Minister Baldwin in 1926 termed himself not "the man in the street . . . but a man in a field-path, a much simpler person steeped in tradition and impervious to new ideas."[30] To brag of being immune to change is true heritage hubris.

English devotion to precedent is immortalized in Francis Cornford's satire of Cambridge academic life, making the past a rock on which all reform would founder. Any proposed change could be rejected as having once been tried and found wanting, needing revisions for which the time was not yet ripe, or inciting demands for further reform. From this it followed that "Every public action which is not customary, either is wrong, or, if it is right, is a dangerous precedent. It follows that nothing should ever be done for the first time."[31]

The English still cleave to Cornford's precept. To keep the House of Lords just as it is, an ex-Tory MP in 1996 hailed the hoary dictum that "if it is not necessary to change, it is necessary not to change." A few years ago, in the Codrington Library of All Souls College, Oxford, I was shown the will of Sir Christopher Codrington. Soon afterward the librarian came back, perturbed. "By the by," he asked, "you've used our library before, haven't you?" "No," I said, "I haven't." "Oh, then I'm afraid you can't use it now." (An All Souls Fellow was torn away from tea to vouch for me.)

Those with shallower roots are apt to envy Old World permanence. A Philadelphia journal in 1837 held it useless to preserve American relics because "our *antiquities* are too *modern* to excite veneration." English patina still humbles Americans. "Is this college pre-war?" asks a tourist. "Ma'am," says the Cambridge porter, "it's pre-American." Europe's "older vision" remains authoritative in American heritage. When a British journalist on American television called his monarchy obsolete, a shocked Barbara Walters asked, "Mr. Hitchens, how can you say such an awful thing in that lovely old English accent?" The American who tells his aide, "I'm off to Britain on Friday; remind me to turn my watch back 500 years," envies British fealty to the past as "a virtually genetic trait."[32] The felt absence of such fealty in Australia animated a Slovene migrant to guide me around neo-Gothic Victorian Melbourne. "I'm from Europe," she explained. "The Australians are new. Only we old Europeans *appreciate* heritage."

BONA FIDES OF PROGRESS

Persistence may also spell progress, attesting a heritage made laudable by time's fruition. Schoolbooks narrate tales of achievement, limning past triumphs and tragedies as preludes to a better present. The image of England as "rooted in the past [and] sticking to old ways" is deceptive, in historian A. L. Rowse's panegyric, for "no country has had a more dynamic history, for ever changing and developing, while retaining the outward forms and institutions that were still useful." Eschewing revolutionary rhetoric and Napoleonic hubris, "the English were inventing the Industrial Revolution, the whole basis of modern civilisation. [They] made progress all right—nobody more so—but cautiously, moderately, and all the more solid, lasting and continuous for being so."[33]

Long cumulation accretes riches, every generation adding to the legacy. Hawthorne's American visitor admired an English estate because "the life of each successive dweller there was eked out with the lives of all who had hitherto lived there." Being around for a long time suggests accrued wisdom—a civilized maturity, even in the forms of nature. "These trees are older than I am," writes a chronicler of England's New Forest, "and I can't help feeling that makes them wiser."[34] Jews under the Palestine Mandate (1923–48) derided British rulers as uncouth newcomers: "A thousand years before your forebears came down from the trees our ancestors were writing the Old Testament." In Russia "all was darkness," held a German historian; Russians were "a people without government, living like the beasts" until the coming of Nordic Varangians in the 10th century. Perfected by their own long history, Germans could help belated savages realize lesser destinies.[35]

Those defamed as recent never dream of questioning the virtue of priority. Instead, they recite their own bona fides of antiquity. While Europe was still the haunt of heathen savages, Marcus Garvey assured his United Negro Improvement Association, Africa had long been peopled by black masters in art, science, and literature. Inverting Eurocentric bias that confined the heritage of progress to whites alone, Afrocentric priority claims today suffuse black rhetoric. To requite later degradation, diaspora Africans ever stress that their culture, their exploits, their very existence antedate all others. They seldom go on to wonder, with the Greek villager, why "two-and-a-half thousand years ago a Greek discovered electricity. We got it four years ago. What happened?"[36]

Few, black, white, or other, query the assumption that those whose ancestors were first on the scene are thereby superior. "Old" peoples revel in progress perfected over centuries, if not millennia. To be sure, a contrary prejudice damns ancientness as enfeebling and regressive, even a reversion to savagery. This was the view of fin-de-siècle apostles of gloom and doom like Spengler, who likened ancient states to worn-out organisms. But it is now rarely advocated, even by devotees of recency like those to whom I now turn.

DEVOTION TO RECENCY

Persuasive as priority is, it is far from universally admired. Not everyone hunts hoary antecedents or hallows the tests of time. Rebels against an established order may revel in being newborn, owing nothing to ancient property or precept.

To expunge reminders of age-old evils, French Jacobins inaugurated a new epoch expressly severed from the strictures of outworn custom and ecclesiastical error. The first years of Liberty (1789) and Equality (1792), and then Year I of Republican France (1793) inaugurated a decimal calendar. Based on rational arithmetic and natural seasons, the revolutionary calendar was stripped of the saints and superstitions that structured its Gregorian and Julian precursors. To be sure, classical precedents shared the young republic's stage with decimal innovation. And just as the archival and reliquary *auto-da-fé* gave way to a zeal to conserve, so the new rational calendar failed to supplant the old religious one.[37] Yet the new broom made a unique revolutionary sweep, signifying reason's decisive rupture with the legacy of hoary reaction.

Revolutionary Americans likewise exulted in new-made heritage, even when professing to revert to Anglo-Saxon roots. Recency, not remoteness, validated inheritance from Founding Fathers. While Europeans mused on distant dark ages, Americans honored bright deeds within living memory: "their *fathers* did great things," exclaimed a German visitor, "not their *great-great-grandfathers!*" A Vermont encomiast felt that "our early history, though modern in date," had ample claim to esteem. "The youngest father is old and reverend in the eyes of his child; and to the true American, the hoariest antiquity has no memories more venerable" than the Pilgrim landing, barely the day before yesterday in the annals of mankind.[38]

Future visions were better suited to America's heritage than past memories. "It is for other nations to boast of what they have been," a patriot put it in 1815; "the history of their youthful exploits only renders [their present] decrepitude more conspicuous." Emerson excoriated English ancestral pride:

> Twenty thousand thieves landed at Hastings. These founders of the House of Lords . . . took everything they could carry, they burned, harried, violated, tortured and killed until every thing English was brought to the verge of ruin. Such however is the illusion of antiquity and wealth, that decent and dignified men now existing boast their descent from these filthy thieves.

For Americans to look back was retrograde. "Did we live amidst ruins and . . . present decay," said a canal builder in 1825, "we might be as little inclined as others, to look forward. But we delight in the promised sunshine of the future, and leave to those who . . . have passed their grand climacteric to console themselves with the splendors of the past."[39]

Esteeming antiquity struck Americans as a sinister embrace of evil precedents—like falling in love with your own grandmother, in one critic's phrase. "Whatever is old is corrupt, and the past turns to snakes," warned Emerson. "Reverence for the deeds of our ancestors is a treacherous sentiment."[40]

As the 19th century wore on, others joined Americans in disowning antiquity. Fin-de-siècle Nietzscheans, Futurists, and modernists decried ancient legacies as brakes on creative energy. Social scientists condemned hidebound tradition; just as evolution doomed primitive peoples, so old practices and rituals too were fated to die out. To many, perhaps most, people of olden times still seem inherently inferior. Ancient Egyptians stuck to bizarre and hapless remedies because, a 15-year-old student put it, "they were closer to the monkeys in them days."[41] Remote and even proximate forebears are not to be emulated but eclipsed.

When not aligning us with ancestors or exhorting us to copy their virtues, heritage-mongers, too, denigrate what is old as barbarous, filthy, or stupid. A warts-and-all past displays historic sites as primitive precursors of our times, rather than nostalgic retreats from it. Precedence as a bona fide of progress is derided. "Europeans are always bragging how their pedigrees go back to cavemen, as if this entitled them to still think like cavemen," notes an Updike character. To travel ads that urge "Come to the old country, see where your ancestors came from," an American historian ripostes, "Come to the new country, see what your descendants have created."[42]

Lacking indigenes, some new states eschew any heritage of ancient vintage. Caribbean Creoles, amalgams of many Old World diaspora, seldom refer to ancestral Africa, Mother India, or, nowadays, to European origins; they mainly hark back to more recent Caribbean legacies. Polyethnic and multifaith Mauritians share no remote past in common; their collective identity dates only from independence in 1950. Eschewing ancestral cults and customs, they stress becoming rather than having been.[43]

For most, though, becoming requires awareness of having been. Zionist pioneers in Palestine eager to shed marginalized European roots shunned the humiliating legacy of the *shtetl*. Nor had the biblical past much meaning for these secular settlers. Hence their children had access to a family heritage only one generation deep. "Before our parents," said some, "there was the dark. History begins with Father. Perhaps there was something Father knew and loved, but all we know about is the negation of the Diaspora."[44] The new nation erased that negation by forging a retrospective historical consciousness. What had been felt as a rupture now became a grand Zionist narrative of temporal endurance. The dispersed Jews had "never ceased to pray and hope for their return," affirmed the historian and education minister Ben Zion Dinur, and "strove in every successive generation to re-establish themselves in their ancient homeland."[45] Ruptured roots were reattached to nourish a sacred secular continuity.

Attachment to ever more recent heritage, as detailed in Chapter 1, seems at odds with reverence for remote priority. Conserving 1970s building legacies, collecting 1980s pop memorabilia, stressing contemporary history, celebrating twentieth and twenty-fifth anniversaries—this focus on living memory suggests only disdain for the first and the early. In America, Vietnam and Watergate make 1776 passé; in Britain, 1940 replaces 1066 and 1688 as the national turning point. Recency rules; the latest in Guinness's records series is a *Book of Lasts*. Stress on the recent clearly devalues priority as a bona fide, making the latest legacy as desirable as the earliest. Instead of privileging ancient occupance and original creation, devotees of recency view heritage as self-generating.

Yet there are also parallels. Cults of times just past mirror new fascination with the ineffably ancient, a concern both ecological and occult. Recent and remote pasts alike rely on sources and insights that are more visual than written, less print- than artifact-oriented, wide open to surmise and conjecture, imbued with mystery and mystique. Both very old and very new heritage is accessible to a broader public than are the epochs in between—those to which historians, by contrast, devote most of their attention.

Recent and remote share a stage on which legacies are largely inherent, a heritage fundamental to which I now turn.

Chapter 9

BEING INNATE

IN TIMES PAST, LINEAGE AND KINSHIP were vital to heritage, if not synonymous with it. As shown in Chapters 2 and 3, power, property, prestige, and identity itself derived from forebears and were sustained by family. Today inheritance comes less freighted with either privilege or obligation, and lineage becomes a faint, even unseemly, echo.

Yet in other ways biological ties have more profound import than ever. Bloodlines are valued for a host of virtues, including fixed personality traits, adhesion to tradition, and unswerving fealty. Millions seek family roots; nations and minorities trumpet ancestral ties. To be a Breton, a Hawaiian, a Cherokee, a Maori, an Amish, or a Hutterite means first and foremost to be born of such stock. One does not inherit Basqueness simply by wanting to; it comes with birth. The stress on descent is reminiscent of dynastic Europe. This chapter shows how and why determinism is rife and discusses its fearsome consequences.

Popular notions of nation and race, purity and mixing mirror determinisms based on blood and genes. Despite lip service to free will and cultural change, what we inherit is increasingly felt to be imparted at birth, innate and immutable. Pseudoscientific fatalism promotes the resurgence of racism and eugenic bias. Stress on biological causation finds ready allies among heritage champions, fostering partisan chauvinism and passive compliance with the status quo. Few know or want to know that, far from being innate and fixed, heritage is ever devised and reshaped by new needs.

The next section below shows how traditional concern with elite descent diffused to entire peoples. Nations became organic entities owing unique traits to ancestral "germ-plasms." With imperial conquest, differences between civilized and primitive peoples came to seem inherent and ineradicable. Science affirmed these differences and decreed eugenic control, setting the stage for Nazi racial hygiene and modern stress on genetic inheritance.

Bygone Ancestral Roles

In the past, descent secured property and ordered most affairs. Procreation and filiation were feudal foci of memory and power. Family was all. Annalists recited personal deeds as exemplary of a lineage; personal features bespoke family traits; inherent virtues or vices surfaced in offspring. Genealogists in 16th-century France traced twenty thousand elite pedigrees to gauge rights to fiscal boons, court favor, and royal schooling for their sons; some entitlements needed seven generations of undiluted nobility. Descent distanced nobles from others: aristocrats enjoyed ancestry from Abel, peasants were the progeny of Ham or Cain. Merit was exclusive to an unsullied elite.[1]

The fall of feudal regimes and the rise of middle classes by no means effaced the efficacy of lineage. Indeed, French bourgeois aspirants hired more genealogists to upgrade their pedigrees than old elites had employed to ensure exclusivity. The cult of ancestry not only outlasted the *ancien régime* but diffused among the peasantry. It still props up lineage pride in much of the Western world.

In England, male descent was crucial to transmit estates and titles; failing sons, subterfuge kept patrilineage alive—taking wives' family names as forenames, title adoption by sons-in-law, and accumulating hyphens (like Sir Ranulph Twistleton-Wykeham-Fiennes or Lady Anne Howell-Thurlow-Cumming-Bruce today).[2] It is no coincidence that the lineage of British social anthropology, a kinship-obsessed field, stems from such men as Lane-Fox Pitt-Rivers (today shorn of hyphens spurned as ostentatious), Radcliffe-Brown, and Evans-Pritchard.

The mystique of lineage infected even scions of New World pioneers proud of shedding Old World roots. Cults of ancestry may seem strange preoccupations for ostensible democrats, but "Sons of" and "Daughters of" this or that have long littered the American scene. Many who scorned European antecedents cherished native forebears. A Vermonter thankful in 1844 that his veins were "tainted by no drop of royal or of noble blood" vaunted the "nobler genealogy" of the Mayflower Compact. Like the snobs Mark Twain limned in *An American Claimant* (1892), the grandee diplomat John Jay II bought bogus European titles and gained ever grander ancestors the more he paid genealogists.[3]

Genealogy lost consequence as democracy and citizens' rights curtailed inherited privilege. Noble descent went on conferring wealth and office, but such perks dwindled during the 19th century, and the 20th saw their virtual extinction. Legacies of lineage remain social cachets but no longer suffuse everyday awareness as they once did.

If lineage mattered less to individuals, it gained potency as a manifest of group merit. To Herder and romantic nationalists, folk traits spelled collective spirit. To be French, German, Czech, or Polish meant inheriting the germ-plasm of a primordial organism. The identity of sovereign state or ethnic entity was thought to inhere in the soil and soul of a people defined by descent. Milieu and tradition, culture and consciousness were organic, natural, and genetically transmitted.

Descent-based national feeling diffused from the Old World to the New. Descendants of American Puritans claimed origins in a millennial seed; Teutonic devotees traced democracy to early German tribes. These legacies were prized as lasting and immutable. An American scientist valued his 1936 Heidelberg honorary degree all the more for coming "from a nation which for many centuries nurtured the human seed-stock" of America's founders.[4]

Nationalist fervor cost racial groups the pliancy given them by the Enlightenment. Peoples formerly thought improvable by teaching and example became wholly determined by descent. Gobineau's classic *Essay on the Inequality of Human Races* (1854) made races primordial (patent since time immemorial), immutable (inborn and unalterable), and unequal (innately superior or inferior). In America, subjugated Indians and enslaved Africans lent sanction to Aryan and Anglo-Saxon precepts. Historians like Bancroft and Motley narrated the past in terms of innate racial traits. Emerson saw most peoples unaltered from archetypes: "the Arabs of to-day are the Arabs of Pharaoh."

The genie of progress was thought to grace the higher races alone, notably Anglo-Saxons, freed from stagnant fixity by civilized enterprise. Incapable of improvement, other races were fated to be underlings. The Irish, once thought backward because deprived, now became doomed because depraved. Africans were incorrigibly "subhuman." Earlier thought tameable, Indians were by the 1850s as irredeemable as Negroes; "you might as well attempt to change the nature of a buffalo" was a typical aspersion. As shown below, genetic slurs are still routinely leveled at Native Americans.[5]

Civilized encounter fated lower races to death or servitude. For Indians, Aborigines, and South African Bushmen, who lacked the will or skill to be fruitful and multiply, the end was imminent. The "Indian race is run," judged an American in 1851; they were "disappearing, to give place to a higher order of human beings." Since Australian Aborigines were moving "hopelessly on towards the gulf of extinction," the sooner they shuffled off the better. American blacks no longer "protected" by slavery and unable to compete with superior whites would soon succumb to inherent defects.[6] To survive, inferior races must forever be childlike dependents.

Biology bolstered racist precept. Skull shape, brain size, and schooling "proved" nonwhites incapable of reason. Rare exceptions were discounted as mimics or, like Booker T. Washington and W. E. B. Du Bois, as largely white. A Harvard geneticist dismissed the achievements cited in Alain Locke's *The New Negro* (1925) as not really black, for most of their authors' "germ-plasm is nine-tenths white at least." The archaeologist V. Gordon Childe, though famed for underdog sympathies, believed Aryans had bequeathed conquered colonials "a more excellent language and the mentality it generated."[7]

Racial fixity was avowed as much by foes as by friends of slavery. Harriet Beecher Stowe's *Uncle Tom's Cabin* (1852), America's prime anti-slavery tract, ascribed black Christian ardor to racial innateness. Unlike cool, practical Anglo-Saxons, an ingrained aptitude for feeling left Africans uniquely open to God's word. Stowe's black hero George Harris yearns for his own Africa; in her view, two centuries in America left the essential African legacy intact. Blacks, too, were racial determinists. Applauding Disraeli's maxim that "all is race," the black activist Alexander Crummell held that "races, like families, are the organisms and the ordinances of God; and race feeling, like family feeling, is of divine origin." Ethnic traits, like racial traits, were innate and ineradicable, asserted the educator Horace Kallen in 1915; he foretold (and welcomed) widening cleavages in American society based on ancestral and immutable Irish, Jewish, Polish, Norwegian differences. "Men may change their clothes, their politics, their wives . . . : they cannot change their grandfathers."[8]

Biological innateness in class, like race, gained credence through Francis Galton's eugenic work. The eight male geniuses in Coleridge's family, the natural history bent among Darwin's kin (himself included), the nine painters among Titian's, and forty musical Bachs in five generations led Galton to proclaim the sway of genetics in *Hereditary Genius* (1869). Cesare Lombroso's criminological studies fed fears of degeneracy if breeding were uncontrolled. .Across the Atlantic, landmark accounts of the feckless Jukeses and Kallikaks empowered eugenicists eager to eradicate idiocy by sterilization. Citing Harvey Jordan's *Eugenics: The Rearing of the Human Thoroughbred* (1912) and William Stokes's *The Right to Be Well-Born, or, Horse-Breeding in Its Relation to Eugenics* (1917), devotees rebuked those "so careful for the pedigree of our pigs and chickens and cattle" but who left "the *ancestry of our children* to chance or blind sentiment."[9]

Thus within a few centuries the focus of Western heritage moved from family lineages to entire peoples determined by inherent traits. As heritage expanded from familial to national and imperial arenas, biological transmission gained new credence. With the role of culture sharply reduced or erased, heritage came to seem forever fixed.

ENDURING LINEAGE MYSTIQUE

Eugenics is now passé, racial science having been discredited by Nazism. But the world was only briefly weaned from supposing heritage innate. Stress on genetic explanation resurged in the 1970s and, with the Human Genome Project, dominates the 1990s. Heritage seems ever more biologically fixed, less amenable to social and cultural reform. In David Schneider's terms, we attribute what we are to *being*, which cannot be changed, rather than *doing*, which can.

So deeply embedded are such views that many are unaware they hold them. Even avowed foes of determinism worship at the altar of inherited traits. Assailing genetic fatalism, a journalist then echoes Galton's emphasis on Dryden, Swift, and Walpole being cousins, and "putting this together with the Mozart and Bach families, who can doubt that genes matter?"[10] That all these cousins were equally swayed by family training, emulation, and environment is ignored; they are made geniuses, as others are idiots, by genetic inheritance alone.

Popular parlance ascribes every trait to racial or ethnic inheritance. Like past scholars, people today see personality engendered by group features as simple and stable as eye or skin color. "If I cleaned my room," says an Italian-Irish-American, her mother would say, "'Oh, look, you are a Rosio,' which was the Italian. So I thought all the Irish were hotheads and all the Italians had clean houses and good food."[11]

Unaltered over time, such traits legendarily crop up ages later. A Pole who loathed Jewish traits ("the set of their eyes, the shape of their ears, their oriental impetuosity") claimed she could "detect the traces of these features to the third or fourth generation and beyond." That the remotest touch of African parentage may produce a coal-black child is firm folk belief. Genetic forces are perverse popular deities. "There must be a faulty gene which has crisscrossed on to him, a mean streak in his genotypes which surfaces," says the owner of the tiger that killed a keeper in 1994; inherited traits were "known" to come out eight generations on.[12] To be sure, it is undesirable traits—Jewishness, blackness, tiger violence—that are usually said to show up; Polishness, whiteness, and tiger docility get ignored.

Minority heritage is especially linked with immutable traits. Like Third World folk in the *National Geographic*, indigenes are viewed as unchanged and unchangeable. Whites assume Native American poverty and alcoholism are genetic, hence ineradicable. But all Indian heritage is seen as ingrained. When the Mexican-American writer Richard Rodriguez taught at Berkeley, a student approached him "cautiously, as if I were a stone totem, to say with no discernable trace of irony, 'God, it must be cool to be related to Aztecs.'"[13] Rodriguez's exotic Aztec connection had living validity; the student's own descent from, say, Celts or Vikings went unnoted because not innately bound up with her modern self.

Primitives once deemed inferior are now exalted, but on precisely the same racial basis: they are wonderful, as they were dreadful, because born like that, traits ingrained at conception. Today's visitors at Plimoth Plantation's Wampanoag Indian camp accredit Native American interpreters with such inherited skills as slithering silently through the forest.

The stereotype is pervasive. "You know what they do with the Indians?" a Choctaw soldier in a Vietnam War novel writes his brother. "They put us on point. The stupid bastards think Indians can see at night, that we don't make any noise, that kind of shit." The least trace elicits the cliché. "It doesn't matter if you're a half-breed or full or whatever. They call you chief and put you out in the fucking jungle at night." Indians themselves trade on such virtues: city Lumbees aspiring to be army scouts asserted, "we Indians have special abilities to move silently through the forest"; Sioux claim "a timeless culture that was, is, and will be," its values ever the same.[14] Similarly fixed are the patience, eyesight, and instinctual "awareness of danger, so quickly born in all wild things, and the aboriginal race so closely allied to them," of Upfield's half-Aboriginal detective. All these cases imply a primitive, even animal, talent akin to indigenes' instinctive ecological empathy.[15]

Supposedly innate virtues are usually vices in disguise. Television commentator Jimmy "The Greek" Snyder in 1988 imputed black American success in major-league baseball, football, and basketball to selective breeding and survival during slavery. But unlike the Barbudans of Chapter 6, African-Americans resented prowess assigned to birth rather than effort, implying that black talent lay in brawn, not brains.

National legacies are similarly seen to be innate and inescapable. Their bonds transcend reason—blood is thicker than water; my country, right or wrong. "Old race memories twang, ancient loyalties stir" on behalf of Britain's royal heritage, for example. "Heredity happens to be how Britain chooses its head of state," a former *Times* editor refuted critics of the monarchy in 1994. "Nobody has suggested a better way nor does public opinion want one." Regretting that "the British peerage stopped breeding for brains at least 150 years ago, and started to breed for looks," another ex-*Times* editor took comfort in the belief that "the hereditary principle is very strong in the cognitive élite," too.[16]

Half a century after Hitler, an ideology of *Blut und Boden* (blood and soil) remains embedded in German minds; all that really matters, insisted an official spokeswoman in 1993, are "aspects of culture you are born with." What you are born with, and never lose, is folk culture reified as race. Hence Germans settled eight centuries in Transylvania or beyond the Volga—even if devoid of German speech—at once become citizens, whereas the most acculturated Jew (or today Turk) could never become truly German. *Blut und Boden* is not just about citizenship; it is, in Jane Kramer's phrase, a German "ethnic exaltation" advanced from Herder to Hitler, as germane to today's Green crusade as to Wagner's *Parsifal*.[17]

Blood and soil are heritages routinely linked. "The love of plants and of landscape breaks forth from our blood," held Germany's rural planning guru before, during, and even after Nazism; "the feeling for harmonious landscape . . . belongs to biological laws within ourselves." Similar laws were invoked by Norwegians to explain why German occupation troops got helplessly lost in the "real" Norway of "snow and stone and ice, the land [our] ancestors [gave] us as a heritage." Likewise, British rural ties must stem from a "mystical, atavistic . . . sense of having been exiled from the countryside where all Englishmen and Englishwomen belong," an arcadia still enduring "in our genetic memory bank." Japan's prized cultural homogeneity is also in essence racially determined, and the postwar influx of aliens intensified the cult of purity.[18]

Ironically, the only state besides Germany to predicate citizenship wholly on remote origins is Israel, where any child of a Jewish-born mother has an automatic right of return. So rigidly biological is Israeli law that it disfranchises even someone adopted by Jews at birth, whose natal mother is later shown to have been Gentile. The 1970 broadening of the right of return to spouses and offspring of converts has roused fears of being flooded by immigrants not "really" Jewish.

Greeks, too, deploy race in deciding who belongs; biology buttresses the classical heritage. To oust Ottoman overlords, philhellenes promoted 19th-century Greeks as direct heirs of ancient Athens and Sparta, the pure essence of Hellas prior to Oriental corruption. Patriots gained roots by descent from classical heroes like Miltiades, Themistocles, and Leonidas. Hellenic descent enabled modern Greeks to claim they were the same as ancient Hellenes. Diaspora Greeks, too, vaunted Greekness. "Many of them speak only Turkish or Russian, but their hearts speak Greek fanatically," wrote Kazantzakis in 1961. "They are of our race. Just to look at them—the way their eyes flash, . . . the way they have managed to become bosses . . .—it's quite enough to convince you that they are the descendants of your beloved Odysseus."[19]

Such descent became crucial to refute the German scholar Jakob

Fallmerayer's notorious 1835 aspersions that modern Greeks were not true Hellenes but mere ethnic Slavs or Albanians. Others, too, deplored the gulf between what "the Greeks had been, and what . . . they are no longer." The "barbarian antics [of] the dusky garrulous" boys who guided Virginia Woolf and her brothers at Mt. Penteli in 1906 proved them spurious interlopers "who had parodied the speech and pilfered the name of the great"; true Greeks would have been silent and picturesque like the figures on vase paintings, or spoken Greek "as Plato would have spoken it had Plato learned Greek at Harrow."[20]

Fallmerayer's slur and Woolf's sardonic dismay still echo among Britons bent on keeping the Elgin Marbles from the "illiterate, resigned, enfeebled race," in journalists' gibes, "that now breeds amid the ruins of an ancient civilization." When Melina Mercouri (as culture minister) in 1992 noted her own classical origins, a British foreign-affairs spokesman scoffed that "if Miss Mercouri is descended from Plato, then Omar Sharif is descended from Rameses II." Since its present inhabitants "are not descended from the race of Pericles," holds Gavin Stamp, "modern Greece has very little in common with the nation and the people who carved the Marbles."[21]

Where the Elgin Marbles rightfully belong is not at issue here; my point is that *both* camps equate heritage with lineage—all depends on modern Greeks being pedigreed Hellenes. This racist rationale is routine; descent is the ultimate criterion of loyalty and legacy. If they had to choose between Chinese Hong Kong and British South African refugees, the English, too, would favor their patrials. Only "unambiguously English" cricketers should play for England, argues a 1995 columnist in cricket's canonical journal; those of alien stock are bound to lack British ardor. Cultural identity is racial, "cricket patriotism [an] *instinctive* matter of biology." As Enoch Powell put it in a 1995 interview, "racism is the basis of nationality. Nations are united [by] similarities which we regard as racial."[22]

Hereditarian bias not only excludes aliens, it backs selective culling and breeding. Like Sweden up to 1971, Singapore today exhorts educated elites to improve the national stock. Echoing exiled nobles who fled Lenin, Russians blame current bungling on the loss of elites under Stalin, who slew or expelled the nation's best birth stock. The view that talent is inherent led Germans and Soviets to extirpate Polish elites in the 1940s to ensure a genetically stunted Poland's lasting subjugation.

It is now proper to disavow lineage as snobbish and exclusive, yet it still confers prestige and privilege. In Britain many callings besides the monarchy—journalism, television, theatre, diplomacy, stockbroking, property development, and, above all, heritage stewardship—are riddled with blood ties. "Genetics may be hard to defend as a basis for personal advancement," writes a *Times* editor, but it is ubiquitous; "leaf through the pages of . . . any magazine and count the bylines of the children of the famous." Some will contend that talent is often "in the blood."[23] But whether nepotism or eugenics is the driving force, kinship seems no less compelling today than when Galton stressed the family talents of the Bachs and the Darwins. Hereditary peers are "brought up with a sense of responsibility to govern," the Marquess of Reading defended their role in the House of Lords; others hold "self-selection by birth" and "genetically accumulated political skills" essential to probity and patriotism.

In American life, too, kinship looms larger than is usually tactful to admit. Mayflowerites still feel more "American" than later arrivals. Blood ties feature more and more family-dominated corporate boards. Old-boy fealty more than fortunes explains why Ivy League colleges signally favor alumni offspring. A 1990 inquiry turned up Harvard admission referee comments like "Lineage is main thing," "Without lineage there would be little case," "Double lineage but lots of problems," and "Lineage tips it, I guess." Harvard took 43 percent of these "legacy" applicants against only 16 percent of all who sought entry to the Class of 1993. Such nepotism, termed by Michael Lind "by far the biggest affirmative action program in the United States," harks back to President A. Lawrence Lowell's 1920s efforts to keep Harvard a haven for "people of our culture"—meaning Boston Brahmins, not Jews. In Lind's view, inherited wealth and professional entrée now make America an all but "semihereditary aristocracy."[24]

In short, legacies linked to birth and breeding remain potent the world over. Even where equality is axiomatic, preferment is based on kinship. Heredity is prized among minorities as among major states and elites. Heritage thus defined by ancestry everywhere aggravates chauvinism and animus.

BLOOD

Blood will out. Lineage is commonly reified in some bodily secretion—semen, saliva, bile, even bone, which people of Madagascar believed gradually ossified within individuals as collective ancestral coral. Collective legacies, too, comments a historian, are "passed on in blood and bone, as real and relevant as DNA or chromosomes." In saying "blood is thicker than water," we stress relationships made for us rather than by us. Blood bonds are independent of choice or behavior.[25]

In Western culture blood, consecrated in the ritual of the Eucharist, is the founding archetype of descent. We say that our ancestors "have shed it in a certain way," writes Paul Connerton, that we ourselves are "of the same blood." Status stems from forebears "whose achievements and merits were held to have endured in the blood." The French conflated the blood of Capetian kings with that of Christ, sanctified like His after the Resurrection; "blood rights" licensed power among "princes of the blood." The Corsican blood feud is termed an atavism that enters the bloodstream before birth. Bloodstock phrases suffuse aristocracies. "Nothing like blood, sir," says Thackeray's James Crawley, "in hosses, dawgs, *and* men." *Burke's Peerage* ranks royalty by blood; thanks to his echt-English mother, Prince William's 58.8 percent "British blood" promises to make him the most "native" sovereign since James I.[26]

Hue denotes rank. Royal blood is red; aristocrats are blue-blooded, like blue-veined Castilian nobles uncontaminated by Moors or Jews. Blood mystique imported from the Old World to the New found parallels in sanguinary Indian ritual. In the United States the best "native" blood was Anglo-Saxon—a Cape Cod man in 1887 boasted he had no drop of "foreign blood," since all his ancestors had come on the *Mayflower*. Sociologist E. A. Ross in 1913 bemoaned the "sub-common blood being injected into the veins of our people [by] hirsute, low-browed, big-faced" East European immigrants of "obviously low mentality." Isolated Appalachian folk were credited with "the purest and best Anglo-Saxon blood." One drop of African blood, in the received view, made one black (a definition upheld by the Supreme Court as late as 1986).[27]

Blood is held to harbor its distinctive traits however dispersed or combined, as with the Lumbees' white, black, and Indian "blood and inclinations." To an 1844 essayist, "Gaelic blood" explained why the French were as hopeless as the Irish. Blood is a common trope for what is unalterably superior or inferior. "What alchemy will change the oriental quality of their blood," asked an American senator-historian opposing Filipino autonomy in 1900, "and set the self-governing current of the American pouring through their Malay veins?"[28]

Blood is still widely held to determine not only pigment and physique but character and fate. In Japan, blood type—A, O, B, or AB—is all-important: baseball managers and soft drink manufacturers rely on them, millions plan careers and love-lives by them (As are worried, Bs curious, Os sympathetic, ABs hyperactive). Like unto like is the customary rule. Being raised by converts rather than blood relatives "explains" an Amish youth's 1994 murder: "All the boy's bloodline is from the outside world," a neighbor says. "If you're not raised by Amish blood, you have an awful hard time being an Amish."

Nordic blood held high iconic worth for Germans long before Hitler; early nationalists acclaimed an *Urvolk* free from foreign blood and ready to sacrifice its own for the Fatherland. For Nazis, blood was no mere symbol but the very substance of race. Race-specific maladies—sickle-cell anaemia in blacks, Jewish "accumulative diseases"—were ailments of blood, and marriage prohibitions were entitled "Blood Protection Acts." As Americans had reputedly gauged Negro blood by the half-moon at the base of fingernails, so Nazis did with Jews. Citing a Russian claim of 90 percent success in telling Jewish blood, a Württemberg doctor hoped to "identify non-Aryans in the test-tube! Then neither deception, nor baptism, nor name change, nor citizenship, and not even nasal surgery" would let Jews escape detection, for "one cannot change one's blood."[29]

Hence blood banks kept Jewish and Aryan blood separated. When an SS officer hit by a car near a Jewish hospital in 1935 got a transfusion of Jewish blood, his racial purity was at risk; he was reinstated when the donor, though Jewish, "proved" to be a First World War hero. Blood apartheid was not solely Nazi: "colored" blood, at first banned from American Red Cross banks, was sequestered from white blood from 1942 until the 1950s, though doctors agreed there was no difference between the two.[30] Small wonder some African-Americans today mistrust blood transfusion as a white genocidal plot.

Blood pooling still connotes contamination. The French 1985 blood scandal that infected 1,250 hemophiliacs with AIDS (of whom more than 400 have died), arose from chauvinist confidence in the blood donated by patriotic *benevolés*. Faith that all the French were pure forbade scrutiny of donors' identity or medical history. In the miraculous blood of France, AIDS was simply unimaginable; infection must have come from abroad, secreted in African sweat or carried by alien mosquitoes.[31] How emotive a marker of identity blood remains emerged in Israel in January 1996, when Ethiopian Jews rioted over the disclosure that their donated blood was being secretly dumped for fear of AIDS contamination.

Broken Blood, a recent Tennant family memoir, illustrates the endurance of the sanguinary metaphor. Old gentry found Tennant "blood not settled enough to be dependable for marriage; . . . it was blood of which to be wary." Wealth at length ennobled it, but in the 20th century the "effete blue blood" of the Wyndham family tainted the Tennant legacy "by genetic frailty," to vary the image.[32] To that new image I now turn.

GENES

Determinisms once based on blood now stress genes—or combine the two. "The disease they have is in their blood, in the structure of their chromosomes," says Toni Morrison's black protagonist about whites. But while blood is mostly a metaphor, genes are the real thing. Molecular science stamps genetic transmission with a simplistic sheen; genes explain everything from everyday behavior to the final secret of life. "Infallible" DNA tests echo the magical power of sacred relics. Scientific text and moral guide, the Human Genome Project is both Scripture and Holy Grail; finding DNA in *E. T.*'s dying hero was likened to finding the King James Bible in a Martian spaceship. The "germ-plasm" of the 1920s was but a pale precursor of today's deified gene.[33]

Genes accrue the awe once accorded immortal souls, their worth beyond price. An invisible yet real substance with an immortal aura, the genome—like the True Cross—can replicate without being depleted, yet is too sacred (or risky) to tamper with.[34] Though our genetic makeup is copied in every cell, we hoard it like rare gems. "Don't kill it!" shouts a man whose wife is set to swat a mosquito. "That mosquito is carrying my DNA!"

Genes and DNA are said to explain every trait and talent, vice and virtue. "There are selfish genes, pleasure-seeking genes, violence genes, celebrity genes, gay genes, couch-potato genes, depression genes, genes for genius, genes for saving, and even genes for sinning," notes a surveyor. "The genes or chromosomes for leaders come forward whether it's kings or presidents," observed the editor of *Burke's Peerage* in 1988, noting George Bush's manifold royal connections. That one in three American presidents are related to royalty shows "you can not hold back the genes." When Colin Powell's candidacy seemed imminent in 1995 he, too, proved related to most of Britain's ancient great families, another "example of the royalty and leadership gene in action."[35] Powell's descent from Edward I spurred British genealogists to trace sixteen members of the Tory government with a "Plantagenet gene."

Genes also justify what might appear weird, irrational, racist, or reactionary. Americans who grossly exaggerate what Washington spends on foreign aid (1 percent of the budget, not the 15 percent they think), and when corrected still feel it too much, have a misanthropic gene, fancies pollster Andrew Kohut: "it's ingrained in the DNA code of Americans when they're born." Genetic stereotypes coerce some to give up at the start, like the Hispanic student told she was likely to fail because "you don't have that 'thought gene.'" A Reagan appointee in 1992 termed black Americans "conditioned by 10,000 years of selective breeding for personal combat and the anti-work ethic of jungle freedoms"; Afrocentrist Leonard Jefferies riposted that lack of melanin in white DNA fatally flawed white brains and spinal columns. To promote national "biological fitness," China launched research in 1993 to locate quintessentially "Chinese genes" in the DNA code.

Sperm-donor profiles giving details of studs' favorite colors, songs, and hobbies imply such traits are heritable. Stewards of religious legacies cleave to genetic barriers: sperm banks may not use Muslim semen for Hindus, or vice versa; Jewish women specify Jewish sperm donors. A Minnesota aspirant for governor in 1994, backed by Christian fundamentalists, declared that men were genetically tooled to be heads of households.[36]

Genetic transmission enhances product ads, as in "Thanks for the genes, Dad." The BMW sedan has a "heritage" that comes from its "genealogy"; the Subaru is a "genetic superstar." Genes similarly saturate marketing: "DNA: the reason you have your mother's eyes, your father's smile . . . and Bijan's perfume" in a double-helix bottle, "a family value" inspired by "the stuff of life." *The New Yorker* boasts an "unchanged and enduring underlying character, a DNA-like set of fingerprints."[37] DNA is itself a collectible; fans compare rock stars' gene sequences on souvenir clone cards sold by 1993 Nobel Prize winner Kary Mullis. Privacy is not yet a problem, though Mullis fears celebrities may veto mass scrutiny of their genetic signatures once science "can figure out from DNA who is a creep and who isn't."

The cult of genes, like that of blood, is overwhelmingly deterministic. Preaching biological fatalism, it promises predictable certainty. We are what we are because blood and DNA make us that way; to try to remake ourselves is futile. For all the real benefits of DNA research, the lessons drawn from it are bleak indeed. It was ominous to be told, early in 1996, that researchers had found a "novelty-seeking" gene, suggesting that the penchant for being unpredictable is itself predictable. Hereditarians glorify a heritage of which we are hapless captives rather than inspired creators.

PURITY

Whether blood or genes are at issue, purity is the customary ideal. Purity breeds thoroughbreds; mixing spawns bastard monsters. What is impure is corrupt, defective, diseased. "Thou shalt not let thy cattle gender with a diverse kind; thou shalt not sow thy field with mingled seed," God told Moses (Leviticus 19:19). Mixed-race names all disparage: a mongrel is an ill-bred dog, mulatto is Spanish for mule, half-breed and half-caste imply half-made—part white, part worse. Unsullied nature remains the norm a century and a half after Darwin reproved British breeders who "cling with superstitious tenacity to the doctrine of purity of blood." In the grounds at Kenwood, London, English Heritage boasts of using native plant seed "to protect ancient genetic lineage"; an English gardener sees imported flowers "jeopardising the purity of the native flora; ecofascists persist in preaching; "native good, alien bad."[38] All fears of admixture—degeneracy, blood poisoning, atavistic throwbacks—

betoken faith in inbred superiority; if our own genes are best, commingling is bound to sully their virtues.

Purity's merits are rooted in Old Testament tirades against filth, taint, abomination, and defilement, culminating with Ezra's (9:12; 10) command to the Israelites to put away alien wives and children. Fear of attrition by intermarriage still suffuses *halakhik* (religious) rules of conduct. Ancient Jewish concern for purity was not unique; Pericles proved harsher than his contemporary Ezra in not only stripping Athenian citizenship from five thousand offspring of mixed unions but selling them into slavery. American racial purists in the 19th century supposed hybrids to be spawned by Cain and believed God had sent the Flood to exterminate them, as He would all amalgamationists.[39]

European royal lineage demanded descent undefiled by commoners. "The blood of France [is] perpetual to the thousandth degree," puffed a 14th-century panegyrist; "the sacred blood has known no bastard in 48 kings since Priam." Only base folk mixed; Defoe mocked the "Het'-rogeneous" English as "Barb'rous Offspring" of the "Dregs [of] all Mankind." After forcing mass conversions, Portugal was accused of being impure and so expelled former Jews, Moors, and mixed races. So pervasive was the mystique of purity that a mid-Victorian found "few educated Englishmen" who had not from "infancy been taught that [theirs] is a nation of almost pure Teutonic blood."[40]

Subjugating "inferior" others augmented aversion toward amalgamation. A freed Roman slave of the same race "might mix with, without staining the blood of his master," held Thomas Jefferson, but a freed black had "to be removed beyond the reach of mixture" with white Americans. "Impurity of races is against the laws of nature" declared a Southerner in 1854; "mulattoes are monsters." Abolitionists shared that view. Crusading to end slavery, John Quincy Adams in the 1830s took as *Othello's* "great moral lesson . . . that black and white blood cannot be intermingled in marriage without a gross outrage upon the law of Nature." To preclude a "community of mongrels," Australia excluded half-castes from its Aboriginal Protection Act in the 1880s.[41]

Emancipation aggravated animus, rousing white fears of black incursion; most American state laws forbidding mixed-race marriages were enacted after the Civil War. The very term "miscegenation," censuring mixed unions with an invidious scientific ring, was coined after emancipation. But abhorrence of race mixing was by no means solely American. A retired British colonial nabob's "instinctive certainty that sexual relations between white women and coloured men revolts our very nature" echoed bias still routine after the First World War. For white men to couple with colored women (a far more common event) was thought less heinous than the reverse. White men had put much white blood in black veins, admitted Senator Theodore Bilbo of Mississippi in 1947, but since mixed-race offspring were defined as black this hardly mattered; what *did* matter was that white women had kept the *white* race pure. Bilbo "would rather see his race and his civilization blotted out with the atomic bomb than . . . destroyed in the maelstrom of miscegenation."[42]

Blacks as well as whites spurned mixing. The pan-African crusader E. W. Blyden sought in the 1850s to ban marriage between "genuine Negroes" and "half-castes"; to recolonize Sierra Leone and Liberia required "unimpaired race instincts," not "weak, immoral, decadent" mulatto hybrids. Fifty years later Marcus Garvey condemned miscegenation as race suicide, made common cause on racial purity with the Ku Klux Klan, and reviled Du Bois as "a lazy dependent mulatto . . . monstrosity" who "bewail[ed] the drop of Negro blood in his veins." Yet Du Bois himself, presaging the *négritude* of Aimé Césaire and Léopold Senghor, venerated pure black blood and soul.[43]

Aversion to mixing remains the global norm. Belying the very existence of two million Cape Coloureds, South Africa's 1949 Mixed Marriages Act declared miscegenation detested by all. Caribbean offspring of East Indians and Creoles were viewed askance by each; Canada's Métis were looked down on by whites and Indians alike; Anglo-Indians are patronized by the British and shunned by Hindus; and Korean- and Vietnamese-American children are virtual outcastes in both parental societies. Ethnic cleansing is a worldwide "cure" for impurity.

Indians who prized racial purity set white Americans a salutary example. Spurning immigrants who would sully Anglo-Saxon stock, turn-of-the-century nativists stressed newfound affinity with red men as true, untainted Americans. This espousal was not of the flesh but the spirit; absorbing the archetypal savage soul, whites became, as the psychiatrist Jung averred, true heirs to the New World. Chaste embrace of Indian ways beat mixing with European newcomers. (On the same chaste basis Aborigines offered white Australians an admirable heritage—"brothers" in Christianity, but not in blood.) For WASP Americans, "biological laws show," Vice President Calvin Coolidge attested in 1921, "that Nordics deteriorate when mixed with other races."[44]

Biologists indeed argued that hybrids inherited the vices of both parents and the virtues of neither; race mixture was a disaster. A 1924 visit persuaded Julian Huxley that "the American negro is making trouble because of the American white blood that is in him." The much-touted *Race Crossing in Jamaica* (1929) "documented" such inherited mulatto disharmonies as long black arms combined with short white legs, and mental tests showing Browns "exceptionally befuddled." South African geneticists noted hybrid discords like "large native teeth in small European mouths."[45] Critics took it for granted that white and black were pure and homogeneous races, whereas any mixture was deplorably heterogeneous and unstable.

Citing such sources, Nazis abhorred hybrids even more than inferior races, Hitler himself ascribing every calamity since the fall of Rome to race mixing. Pure gypsies were at first thought harmless; only half-breeds caused problems. The French were "irredeemable" because they had too much Negro and Jewish blood to strain out. To avert a like threat, Germany in 1937 forcibly sterilized five hundred "Rhineland bastards" (offspring of black French occupation troops and German women). Jews were African-Oriental hybrids, defective owing to the discordant life spans of their internal organs.[46] In simplifying all inheritance to single-cell mechanisms, Nazis merely echoed widely held Western genetic misconceptions.

The evils of Nazi racial hygiene by no means ended anti-hybrid animus. Well into the 1950s, mixing was authoritatively held to produce infertile and degenerate offspring; the British-American Pioneer Fund, founded in 1954 to protect Anglo-Saxon purity, continues to promote racial homogeneity. Ending apartheid has not yet expunged the "sin of blood mixture" from South African textbooks. Everywhere, tirades against "imminent mongrelization" persist.[47]

However mixed a people may have become, heritage demands homogeneity. In Australia's Northern Territory it was set policy to "breed out the colour" by inducing half-caste women to marry European men and bear "legitimate, fair-skinned babies"; "breeding Aborigines white" was termed an "opportunity to outgrow their heredity." Racial purity in Brittany is an evident chimera, yet Breton nationalists urged British and Irish women to breed there, replacing "Latin and Saxon dross [with] Celts like our illustrious ancestors." The Basque elite long fancied itself free from Castilian and French riffraff, as well as Jews and Moors; modern nationalism made racial purity socially imperative. As immigrants poured in, Basques shunned intermarriage. "The more Basque surnames a person has, the prouder he is," noted a local lawyer in 1974. "You marry a Basque so that you can transmit undiluted Basque blood to your children."[48]

Purity is a resurgent faith, though ever less a fact, among American minorities. Native Americans mourn the passing of "full-blooded" leaders. African-Americans whose forebears boasted Indian blood ("I am the only Negro in the United States," quipped Zora Neale Hurston, "whose grandfather on the mother's side was *not* an Indian chief") or elite white kin (mulattos unequaled for "aptness in tracing their ancestry to the times of William the Silent") now venerate exclusive African descent and stigmatize the mixed as a shaming legacy of white rapine.

To be less than fully black is for some African-Americans disconcerting, even polluting. "My mother said that a lot of her own relatives did not want to eat her cooking because her skin was light," one woman recalls. "A lot of people think that light people . . . are not clean cooks," she explained. "The black, black woman is our essential mother—the blacker she is the more us she is," declares Alice Walker, herself brown (and long married to a white). It was always a tonic to see one "very, very black" friend, "for she was 'pure.' Genes untampered with. Totally 'unimproved' by infusions of white or Indian blood."[49] Boasts the hero of Spike Lee's 1990 film *Mo' Better Blues*, "No white blood in me. My stock is 100 percent pure."

Yet, as most American blacks are at least partly and often largely "white" in ancestry, their group identity demands a different genetic gloss. It requires cohesion among all with *any* African ancestry—a unity forged by slavery and enduring discrimination. Their diverse ancestry makes those unified by self-protection and collective concerns all the more fiercely reprove *present* miscegenation. Hence black and white purists preach the same segregated dogma. After a white Alabama principal banned interracial couples from the 1994 school prom, he told a biracial girl, who asked whom *she* could bring, that she was a "mistake" not to be repeated. The same week, a Howard University law student leader warned, "Brothers, don't let us ever catch you out there with a white woman." Whether condemned as racist or condoned as racial pride, segregation is invoked to protect a mythic politicized purity.

Such purity flies in the face of both history and biology, yet it suffuses popular culture. Media depiction demands simon-pure ancestry in defiance of known fact. Light-skinned American actresses like Jane White and Lena Horne were barred as blacks from white roles, and barred as too light from black roles. The half-caste Maori Rena Owen could not get film parts in 1980s New Zealand: "If I went for European roles they said I was too dark, and if I tried for Maori parts they said I was too European."[50]

Mestizo rhetoric officially exalts admixture, but it too hides enduring Iberian and Indian biases, each ancestry valued as "pure." The mestizo medley lauded in Mexico is seen, deep down, as a tainted amalgam of two authentic components. The allure of Hispanic purity is matched by zeal "to recapture their lost Indian heritage," declares a mestizo, a "need to know that part of them that is genuine Native American." Only racially unmixed legatees are held to "deserve" the indigenous heritage. "Few true descendants of the ancient artisans are in control of their patrimony," grumbles an American, of Mexican heritage management. "Mestizos and politicians . . . use the ancient material as a political football."[51]

Even its champions see race mixture as conflict-ridden. "Ever the inherited influences of the two races warred for the soul" of Upfield's detective hero. "A full blood would have acted with resolution, but the white man's impetuosity" and compassion "brought reason to clash with instinct [and] primitive intuition." Mixed origins confused rather than fused, making him irresolute. "He is *not in harmony with himself*," said a South African of the half-caste who "despises his own blood." Another found "the flaw in the blood of the half-caste an instinct for death and chaos. . . . Mixed blood is a harbinger of doom." "Yalla" Jardine in Morrison's *Tar Baby* (1981) suffers a tug-of-war between her white and black blood.[52]

The confusion of biracial consciousness stems, however, not from biology but from culture, not from divergent genetic strains but from social stigmas against mixture. To be "a little of everything" is to be "wholly nothing" for a Californian of African-Mexican-Asian-European descent. "Why can't I just be black or why can't I just be white?" exclaims a young woman. "Why do I have to be mixed up?" Many want to be one or the other, not both. "There's a strong sense that if you're a full race then you're better," says a mother. "You're not full-blooded. You're this, that, and the other, so you're not as good as we are."[53]

Being mixed, or at least *too* mixed, demeans white ethnic Americans as well, interviewer Mary Waters shows. A man who is three-fourths Irish complains that his French-German grandmother "messes up the line." A self-styled "Polish-German" is irked when told she also has an English ancestor: "I am already this mishmash, don't tell me that I am anything else too."[54] For individuals as for groups, the least complex birth legacy often seems the most secure and gratifying.

Ancestral purity is a traditional token of national strength, lack of it felt a fatal flaw. Horror of hybrids mounts when a racial legacy seems threatened. In Greece, when the menace of Macedonia required citizens to reaffirm their Hellenic roots, a student was jailed in 1993 for asserting that "there are no races. We are all of mixed descent." An ethnographer received death threats for depicting Macedonians of northern Greece as Slavic and Slavonic-speaking, and in 1995 Cambridge University Press aborted her book for fear of reprisals against staff in Athens. Revulsion against mixture goes beyond simple xenophobia: miscegenation is linked with violence and evil. Sanctity is violated by marrying out of one's own kind. Dread of foul impurity from his own mixed union impels the Old Man in Yeats's *Purgatory* to kill his young son, lest the lad should in time "beget, and pass pollution on."[55] An abiding abhorrence of deviance burdens resurgent heritage with demands for purity proven by descent.

HYBRIDS

Race mixing is so widely censured that it is almost a surprise to find it ever championed. Yet cross-breeding has a career of advocacy. Royal prestige in ancient Asia and premodern Europe demanded a broad blend of ancestries; Enlightenment pundits saw communal benefits in hybridizing; and a few reformers hoped massive mixing might dispel America's and South Africa's racial polarities. Hybrid vigor is still commended against endogamous ills. "The Jews and the British and Saudi royal families, as well as the Labrador dog," noted the biologist R. T. D. Oliver in 1994, "have all learnt to their cost the damaging effects produced by in-breeding."

Until the 19th century, mingling was almost as much praised as deplored. It was to *mixed* ethnic origins that many ascribed Britain's unique strengths. An 18th-century antiquary lauded Britons for augmenting native heritage with that of sundry invaders. "By the admixture of nations, Asiatic hordes formed that race to which it is our pride to belong," wrote Anthony Trollope in 1860. "No Anglo-Saxon could be what he is now but for that portion of wild and savage energy which has come to him from his Vandal forefathers." Only after the 1860s did writers like George Eliot, following Disraeli's purism, abandon ideals of racial fusion. Mixture was healthful, purity a chimera. "We flatter the self-love of men and nations by the legend of pure races," noted Emerson, but we experience only mixture and gradation. Staunch patriot as he was, Renan disavowed race purity: "The noblest countries, England, France, and Italy, are those where the blood is most mixed."[56]

American advocates of mixing echoed Enlightenment faith that racial traits were malleable and improvable. Virginians promoted white–Indian union. Once tribes settled and adopted private property, Jefferson told them, "you will mix with us by marriage, and form one people with us." Even blacks might join the amalgam—at least black women. Black seed tainted, but white seed "improved" the black ovum, held apologists for white rapine, "eras[ing] all traces of the black race not capable of advantageous mixture with the white."[57]

Merging Celts with Saxons, Danes, and Normans was said to have invigorated imperial Britain. "The noblest race," future Prime Minister Rosebery praised fellow Scots, "is a generous mixture of great races." In East Anglia an academic found a "glorious amalgam" of Norse and Saxon: "Where there is most mixed blood, the greatest ethnic complexity, genius or ability most frequently appears. The hybrids have it." Britain's hybrid legacy served as a salutary riposte to Nazi Nordic monomania.[58] The Commonwealth still mandates a rhetoric of mixing; when some deplored a 1993 ad depicting the Queen as black, *Burke's*

Peerage said she was "proud she has the blood of the world in her veins, including Jewish and Muslim."

The British were not the only partisans of mixing. Even Germans once extolled *some* hybrids. Lauding variety as a recipe for fitness, biologist Alfred Ploetz in 1895 saw in the Japanese a fruitful Mongol-Malay mix. As late as 1933 the Nazi eugenicist Eugen Fischer, hailing hybrids in German South-West Africa, judged Nordic-Alpine and Nordic-Mediterranean amalgams superior to pure Nordics. In 1920s California the high IQs of Japanese-white children seemed proof of hybrid vigor.[59]

Melting-pot devotees long looked to diverse immigrant legacies to fructify America, albeit culturally rather than genetically. Jacksonians hoped frontier mingling would breed out English patronage and snobbery; romantic racialists trusted that "simple-hearted and forgiving" freed Negroes would shame and soften the "harsh and grasping" Anglo-Saxon spirit; later populists hoped European newcomers would compensate the dour aridity of Puritan tradition. To enliven the Anglo-Saxon legacy, fin-de-siècle Americans sought immigrant gusto. "We old Americans need . . . to learn to laugh and dance and not be afraid of our feelings," held an educator; Italians and Slavs could show them how. WASP mental and moral virtues leavened by southern and eastern European joie de vivre promised a grand amalgam.[60]

Whether purity or mixture is normative depends on history and circumstance. Unlike the American South, economic and social need in the colonial Caribbean set racial purists at naught. Trollope termed mixing there destined and desirable: "Providence has sent white and black men to these regions in order that from them may spring a race fitted by intellect for civilization, and . . . by physical organization for tropical labour." Just as Vandals and Anglo-Saxons had bred the versatile English, so "a race will inhabit these lovely islands, in whose blood shall be mixed . . . northern energy . . . and African physical powers."[61] A hybrid legacy was essential to West Indian well-being.

Trollope's conclusion was right but his rationale wrong. Mixing became customary in the Caribbean not for biological but for social reasons. Despite a parallel legacy of white rule and black slavery, regimes radically unlike the slave South led to a mixed-race norm. In the West Indies the value of slave-grown sugar doomed white yeoman settlement early on; by the 18th century black slaves were the great majority, white planters and officials a small minority. White women were few; white men *openly* cohabited with black women. Between black and white emerged the "free colored": freed slaves, in the first instance planters' own offspring. In the absence of white yeomen, the free colored occupied a vital niche as artisans and tradesmen.

Caribbean whites generally welcomed the mixed-race presence for buttressing a social hierarchy graded by color. Among the planter class purity still counted, but whites needed a mixed element—attached to them by family and by free but not equal status—to control the mass of black slaves. To stave off slave revolt in 18th-century St. Domingue, for example, whites urged suffrage for light free-colored men who were their close kin.

Social and sexual dynamics spurred the free-colored advance. In small islands where everyone's lineage was known none could, as in the United States, move away to pass for white; but the wealthy and well-connected could be made legally white. For this favor, a white Jamaican in 1782 promised to "bestow such fortunes" on his offspring "as to raise them above the common level of people of colour." All over the Caribbean free-colored people amassed property and gained privileges that generally aligned them with whites.

The benefits of light skin and European kin accrued to free-colored descendants after slavery ended. Erosion of white fortunes and numbers enhanced mixed-race influence; a "Mulatto Ascendancy" governed the British island of Dominica from 1838 to 1898. Browns ruled every realm—even black pride. "I was a black man," recalled Marcus Garvey in 1914, "and therefore had absolutely no right to lead. Leadership should have been in the hands of a yellow or a very light man."[62] Even when sovereign statehood came a half century later, blacks were few in Caribbean cabinets. Wealth and influence throughout the Caribbean still go with mixed race.

Yet few West Indians found black pride credible. To be sure, 1970s black-power advocates warned browns to "repudiate the mulatto heritage," and some leaders stressed blackness; Premier Bradshaw of St. Kitts bragged of being a full-blooded Ashanti. But black power was mainly dismissed as a brown academic conceit. A light-skinned Afrocentrist aroused derision in his native Dominica: "Rosie Douglas black power? But he's a *brown* man. Everybody knows that."

Though white planters, foreign eugenicists, and black-power leaders variously preached purity, mingling remained the norm. Indeed, mixed Creoles are often termed the truest West Indians: pure races came from elsewhere, mixing took place after they got to the Caribbean. Many West Indians boast of being "a real mix-up"—blacks claiming European forebears, whites claiming African ancestry—in a ritual rhetoric of applause for the tolerance implied in commingling.

The West Indian hybrid ideal finds fertile soil where mingling gains acceptance. Bosnia and Rwanda notwithstanding, more and more people worldwide marry outside their supposed race or ethnic group. And despite purist crusaders, awareness grows that purity is a chimera, that biological bequests have always been mixed, that so-called racial legacies are really malleable social artifacts. Many now relish manifold ancestral roots.

Yet acclaim for mixed heritage, no less than for axiomatic purity, is often rooted in determinist premises. Purists fear mixing will pollute and fray social control; hybridizers fear endogamy will hamper diversity and assimilation. But each camp traces desired traits to an *inherent* legacy. Far from contesting purists' basic premises, hybrid devotees simply invert their biases—for example, hailing gifted half-castes (Pushkin, Tolstoy, Gorky) as "proof" of hybrid vigor. While purists' and hybridists' differences are real and important, they share the common delusion that cultural legacies stem from birth and lineage and see group traits as biologically transmitted.

The very effort to disown racism paradoxically rekindles biological bona fides. As minority identity gains kudos, ancestry resurfaces as a safeguard against a surfeit of claimants. For example, while the number of self-identified American Indians has tripled since 1970, more than two in three now marry non-Indians. To remain viable, tribes relax lineage rules; one Indian grandparent may now suffice. But competition for benefits renews stress on pedigrees. The 1990 Indian Arts and Crafts Act requires vendors to show a federal "Certificate with Degree of Indian Blood." Exclusion serves worthy aims: Indians do not want non-Indians peddling their cultural heritage. But resurgent apartheid is regressive all the same. "No other racial group in the United States," complains a Cherokee academic, has "ever had to prove their ethnic heritage . . . to sell their art." Yet even close kinship fails to earn the five hundred Eastern Pequots shares in the Mashantuck Pequot casino. "We share a legacy, a history and a culture," says a self-styled Pequot genealogist. "We just don't share the casino."[63]

Similar conundrums affect Australia, where descent is no longer a legal criterion of Aboriginality: to be an Aborigine, one only has to be accepted by existing tribal groups. Since tribal rules vary from state to state, someone denied Aboriginality in Victoria may achieve it in Queensland. New Age folk devoid of Aboriginal descent lately arrived in Tasmania are said to have claimed and gained Aboriginal status because no locals could deny it, the last having died out in the 1880s. The new-made Aborigines then sued for the "return" of "ancestral" bones and relics. Elsewhere, as Aboriginal heritage wins more adherents, racial descent regains clout as a bona fide. Australian government funds and other benefits spawn a "trace-back-a-black" racket. In like fashion, white ethnic Americans seek to climb aboard the minority benefits bandwagon; in 1988 the Boston fire department sacked Philip and Paul Malone for job applications falsely claiming a black great-grandmother.[64]

Among long-polarized Americans—supposedly pure whites, seemingly mixed blacks—multiracial trends begin to blur identities. After eighty years, the Census Bureau gave up graded color categories in 1920, judging so many blacks to be mixed that soon all would be. Some 85 percent of black Americans are partly white or Indian, millions of "whites" partly black. But until lately only blacks acknowledged this. "Look at us," said a black reporter of the varied hues at a 1992 Virginia symposium; "we got to be that way because people were miscegenating at all hours of the day and night."[65]

Many still shun all mention of *that* legacy. Blacks are now a major presence at Colonial Williamsburg, but guides who deal with slavery and family life do not mention the sexual unions that profoundly affected both blacks and whites. Only when drunk, recalls black writer James McPherson, might older Southern whites blurt out, "We're all cousins; most people don't understand just how we're related." An assertion at the 1992 Virginia symposium that every black and many whites in the room were "mongrels" stunned participants.[66] But only a generation ago, mayhem might have ensued.

Earlier, fewer had repressed the reality of mixing. At the end of the Civil War black leader Frederick Douglass joined abolitionist Wendell Phillips in predicting the absorption of black Americans into "a blended race," and dismissed racial purity as "the merest affectation." Opposing an anti-miscegenation bill in the South Carolina legislature in 1879, George Tillman "asserted as a scientific fact that there was not a full-blooded Caucasian on the floor of the convention."[67]

It may be too soon to appraise Douglass's prophecy—Bilbo's nightmare. But more and more Americans of mixed race, once stigmatized as "tragic mulattoes," now speak openly of and find pride in both black and white forebears. "I'm composed of two different races and I choose to value each," says a typical young respondent. Alex Haley's *Roots* not only inspired blacks to seek out African legacies but led Haley himself on a parallel quest for his Ulster forebears. Many of Shirlee Haizlip's "pass-for-white" cousins, previously unaware of black ancestry, claimed to be thrilled by their newly disclosed biracial identity; what would once have been a traumatic stigma is now seen, at least by some, as exotic enrichment.[68]

Racial redefinition is now a heritage battlefield. Many proud of multiracial roots spurned the 1990 U.S. census's exclusive options. "I don't want to check just one box," they said; "I don't want to deny part of my heritage. . . . Human beings are sometimes two things." Or more; those not content to be "Other" added 300 "races," 600 "tribes," 70 Hispanic groups, and 75 new blends to census forms. Half those polled in 1995 wanted to be multiracial—or to expunge race entirely as a divisive social fiction. "People are already talking about giving us a heritage, . . . making us a census box," says a biracial woman. "I want to see the day when there are no boxes." More and more aim to identify with the totality of their diverse heritage.[69]

Such a step faces other obstacles besides ingrained assumptions that racial legacies are decreed by God or genetics. To scuttle customary criteria threatens many to whom race is both stigma *and* refuge, focus of indignity *and* fount of identity. Consider the "one-drop" rule, forged to keep blacks subjugated and now forcing many to deny white links. What gives "African Americans the audacity to say that they own people because they have one drop of African blood?" asks a mixed-race Californian.[70] One answer is racial politics: black leaders justifiably fear a multiracial census option will erode hard-won minority benefits. If one in ten took that option, black legislative districts would be lost and rights programs slashed. It is ironic that multiracialism jeopardizes black benefits just when "race" had begun to be of help.

Pragmatism is not the only reason black Americans cleave to the one-drop rule. The antebellum white ancestors of many blacks are too remote to be reliably identified. Others spurn that ancestry anyway for its usual abominable origin—the violation of a slave. "What can be the destiny of a people that . . . cherishes the blood of the white slaveholder who maimed and degraded their female ancestor?" asks a black woman. Who can bear to acknowledge such men as progenitors? Malcolm X's mother "was glad that she had never seen" her father: "Of this white father of hers, I know nothing except her shame about it." Malcolm, too, "learned to hate every drop of that white rapist's blood that is in me."

Solidarity is another disincentive to mixed heritage. Many are reluctant to avow white origins lest they be thought to forsake the black community in all its catholicity. "One hundred percent Negroes and even one percent Negroes will stand together as one mighty whole," thundered Garvey. "One can only have one heritage," insists the Africanist Molefi Kete Asante; "we inherit a unified field of culture, not [useless] bits and pieces."71

Black unity is not just an American goal, though its rationale and rhetoric are New World. In Britain, where "black" usually denotes Asians, Arabs, and others along with Afro-Caribbeans, many reify a generic black culture. Any who acknowledge a "mixed" identity are accused of race betrayal.72 That the American one-drop rule so alien to West Indian culture should now shape a polarized black-or-white ideology among some British Afro-Caribbeans seems sadly retrograde.

Most who are embroiled over racial identity share simplistic assumptions that make heritage a matter of inborn pedigree. Advocates of mixing and apostles of purity have utterly opposed views of what collective roots ought to be, but they are alike deterministic in ascribing heritage to some racial lineage. Likening cultural legacies to biological traits, hybridizers see heritage in terms as innate as the most fervid blood-stock purists. Both camps reflect the rampant tendency, contrary to fact, to see heritage as little more than biology.

INNATENESS IN BIRTH AND ADOPTION

Child adoption trends exemplify views of heritage as biologically innate. Lineal descent is the norm, and only birth legacies are considered natural. The true mother of Solomon's judgment was the birth mother who would give up her baby rather than see it perish. Kinship and race are felt primary in transmitting cultural legacies, too. Science is seen to endorse this bias, privileging blood relationships as natural and normative.[73]

Yet the notion that blood is thicker than water is no universal truth; it is an ideal sanctified in certain cultures, especially those of European origin. And ideal and practice commonly diverge. The prevalence of adoption all through Western history does not gainsay the primacy of natal ties but shows them chronically breached. Countless abandoned children owed their upbringing to "the kindness of strangers," in John Boswell's phrase. Yet until recent times, total severance from natal parents was rare. Most people lived in small communities; an unwanted child would be taken in by someone nearby. And birth parents were lauded for reclaiming offspring and restoring their natal heritage to them.[74]

Many circumstances led Europeans to privilege birth over adoption. One was inheritance, which canon and civil law confined to legitimate offspring; lacking such children, a family legacy might be engorged by church or state. A second was the onus attached to foundlings, perhaps abandoned because of lowly origins or for defects of mind or body. A third was a fear lest unknown origins unwittingly end in incest. Above all, inherited traits seemed bound to surface, even in children cut off from natal families at birth. Folklore and fiction are replete with genteel, well-spoken foundlings who, like Oliver Twist, prove paragons thanks to "good" ancestry.[75]

Natal ties remain normative in modern parenting. Interwar adoption agencies aimed to match both looks and culture, the latter assumed to be inherited like the former. Adoptees should pass as natural offspring not only in others' eyes but in their own; to absorb the legacy, they must simulate the pedigree. To turn legal fiction into living fact, birth records were sealed, knowledge of and contact with birth parents banned. For a few decades the virtues of adoption outweighed the bonds of kinship, but only by feigning them.

Birth parents regained status in the 1960s, when the cult of roots glorified genetic bonds; by the 1980s psychic health, even physical well-being, came to depend on knowing one's engendered origins. The most loving adoption could not compensate the "cosmic loneliness" and "genealogical bewilderment" of losing one's place on an ancestral chain of being, let alone being deprived of perhaps critical genetic data. "Knowledge of one's biological parents and hereditary history is crucial in ordering one's affairs and making life's decisions," ruled a California judge in 1989. Despite a huge rise in adoptions, parenting is more than ever equated with procreation. Children are said to truly belong only to progenitors. "How does your *own* child feel about them?" many adoptive parents are asked. Adoption is ersatz, birth parents the model to which adopters can never quite live up.[76]

Like genetic advances, reproductive technology bolsters the primacy of blood ties. In the past, a woman who gave birth was indisputably the mother; gestation made the maternal bond more natural than the father's, which was based on seed alone. But now that bearing can be detached from engendering, the latter is "natural"; genetic is privileged over gestational motherhood, pregnancy derogated as imperfect evidence of parentage. A surrogate mother's suit to keep the in-vitro fertilized baby she had borne was denied on the ground of her being a "genetic hereditary stranger"; she was likened to a foster mother who becomes redundant when the "real" parent resumes parenting. Like hired wombs in soap operas, her claim to have bonded with the baby was seen as outré, her motive mainly mercenary.

Genetic fatherhood, too, gains status. A father refutes a charge of buying his child from the surrogate mother, for "it is his own biological, genetically related child. He cannot purchase what is already his." What is his, and the genetic mother's, is theirs because kinship is innate. Innateness rules even when genetic primacy is denied, as a rare exception shows. In 1984 a rabbi held that nine months in a Jewish womb was enough to overcome the taint of an egg's Gentile origins and so ruled the child Jewish.[77] Gestation here won out over genetic determinism; but Jewishness still depended on the *biological* bona fide of the womb.

Bonds sanctified as innate extended beyond near kin to whole communities in the 1970s and 1980s. Stressing collective ancestral roots, color coding in adoption became mandatory in America, Britain, Australia, and New Zealand. Transracial placements that had been common (many black children were homeless, many whites eager to adopt) ended abruptly. Racial self-esteem was said to require same-race placements; transracial adoption was rejected as "miscegenation." To conform with same-race criteria, the New York Foundling Hospital in the

1970s sent abandoned orphans to the Museum of Natural History for biometricians to assess their "color."[78]

Indian adoption in America followed the same separatist path. Through the 1960s Indian children were still "rescued" from parental "neglect" and placed with white families, much as Australian Aborigines were until 1961 detribalized in urban homes. But child removal came to be seen more a cause than a consequence of Indian family woes, and a 1978 act empowered Native Americans to recover orphans of tribal origin.[79] For them as for African-Americans, presumed heritage innateness made child placement a "tribal birthright."

Three determinist views fueled race-matching. One was pragmatic: whites could neither fully accept black children nor help them cope with pervasive racism; they would become pariahs in both black and white worlds. "Mixed-race children are cemented into their blackness," warned a black British sociologist; white adopters want to make them "culturally assimilated colourless Europeans," but bias doomed them to a blackness made endurable only by black family self-esteem. To help adoptees feel truly black, Hindu, or whatever, was deemed beyond white families' ability. Indeed, telling a child to "go down to the Sikh temple because that's your background" struck one white adopter as "artificial." Sheer mixture stymied others. "To give this child some kind of racial heritage," an adoptive mother said of a Kenyan Asian–Creole West Indian girl, "you just don't know where to start."[80]

A second ground was ideological: whites were stealing blacks' most precious heritage, their survival as a race. "Black children in white homes are cut off from the healthy development of themselves as black people," declared social workers. Children must from birth "identify with all black people in a black community; we need our own to build a strong nation." Evidence that blacks raised by whites fared well was slated as racially disparaging: "having white families raise our children to be white is the ultimate gesture of disrespect for us as African people." The success of transracial adoptions thus became an argument for terminating them. That race was a minimal factor in these adoptees' sense of heritage distressed survey takers as adaptive but wrong; lack of explicit racial pride "proved" critics right.[81]

Underlying both these arguments was a third assumption that cultural heritage was biological in essence. Culture and color were one and the same, race or ethnicity immutably given. Officials sought total "match of heritage"—that is, race. Whites who fostered a black boy were denied adoption as they could not "teach him his culture"; a mixed-race British child was removed from a foster family whose interest in opera showed them to be too "white-oriented." English social workers praise young Asians who reject assimilation for "identifying with authentic roots." A London borough disallows the adoption of abandoned Chinese girls, since they would not be able to maintain links with China's "rich culture."[82]

Racial criteria of heritage dominate all these judgments. Whether pure or mixed, a biologically defined legacy is presumed crucial. Stereotypes stemming from white bias are repeated to sanction a new apartheid to protect the oppressed.

Racial bias does endure. But in positing race as a fixed essence, minorities and mainstream agencies alike fall prey to biological determinism. They reify heritage as an unalterable state of being rather than the fluid social artifice it is.

HERITAGE CHOSEN OR DETERMINED

Recent years have seen racial apartheid proscribed and ascribed status distinctions progressively outlawed. Yet the view that heritage is biologically innate has at the same time intensified. Engendering offspring takes legal precedence over gestation, nursing, fostering, and educating. Adoption laws mandate placing children by racially defined criteria. Birth origins become sacred bona fides; what men say of women, or whites of blacks, or Swedes of the Swiss, is alleged to have no merit because it is not bred in the bone. "Do reporters have to mail out copies of their family trees," asks one whose racial legacy was suspect, "before they can presume to write about African Americans?"[83] And every genetic advance is construed as proof of biological fixity, confirming views of heritage as innate and immutable.

Multicultural trends at once resist and reinforce these determinisms. Heritage seems both inherent *and* a matter of choice—a genetically ordained market commodity. Thus white Americans stress roots that are self-chosen rather than inborn. Comfortable with connections from several ethnicities, they opt now for one heritage, now for another. "No belief is more cherished by Americans," holds Rodriguez, than "that one can choose to be free of American culture. One can pick and choose. Learn Spanish. Study Buddhism. . . . My Mexican father was never so American as when he wished his children might cultivate Chinese friends."[84] Being Jewish, once a caste-like legacy that could not be shed even by conversion, now seems as optional as any other heritage in America.

All minorities in theory enjoy the freedom of choice the historian Diane Ravitch extols: "America has provided a haven for many different groups, and has allowed them to maintain their cultural heritage, or to assimilate . . . or both; the choice is theirs." But in fact that choice is limited to some; racial and ethnic ascription still force others to endure legacies that whites like to fancy being freely chosen.

> Many of the Hopis have college diplomas, [yet] they live in a very simple way, and choose to do that . . . I've met traditional [Lakota] college graduates. They've traveled all over the world, and they've chosen traditional lifestyles . . . They fit in beautifully, and they decide to be a traditional person.[85]

These Indians are admired not for *being* innately traditional but for *electing* to be traditional—not hanging on to a heritage acquired by birth but, like the rest of us, buying it in the heritage hypermarket. But by the same token, blacks and others still stymied by birth legacies are aspersed as innately inferior, even by white ethnics who celebrate their own roots by borrowing, consciously or otherwise, from blacks. In this view, minorities who fail to make it in mainstream America display some racially inherent defect. Thus whites simultaneously deny racial constraints and blame persisting inequality on immutable legacies of race.[86]

Genetic science, racial politics, and social pessimism converge in positing individuals as impotent in the face of fixed inheritance. The huge sales of Charles Murray and Richard Herrnstein's *The Bell Curve* (1994), a tome unmasked as mendaciously racist and statistically absurd, suggests how eager we are to hear it is not our fault, that others cannot be improved, that to worry about the poor or the deprived is futile—they were born to fail. Even confirmed egalitarians succumb to innateness rhetoric, as with Rutgers president Francis Lawrence, who in 1994 linked low black test scores with a certain "genetic hereditary background." Like eugenicists sixty years ago, genetic fatalists today ignore environment and history to stress inborn cognitive defects that nullify meliorist effort.

Genetic research brings undoubted benefits. DNA scrutiny lends forensic inquiry new precision, fixes the fate of the last Russian czar's family, exposes impersonators, and proves innocence or guilt beyond a likely shadow of doubt. Above all, knowledge of lineage helps to predict and so avoid passing on inherited diseases like Huntington's chorea and early-onset Alzheimer's disease, releasing many at risk from ancestral onus.[87]

Yet new genetic knowledge also resurrects old ancestral specters. Biological determinism is again a weapon against the unwanted, with eugenic culling widely practiced. Rural Chinese abort girls as genetic defects. The miracle of modern Japan is credited to fifteen generations of samurai who purged the nation's gene pool of "assertive and egalitarian DNA, with the same impunity that a breeder culls his flocks of undesired traits." The Nobel Sperm Bank, censured as dehumanizing when founded in 1980, had by 1995 produced 156 children; dozens of sperm banks now win praise for promoting high-IQ births.[88]

Genetic advances feed fallacies that reduce heritage to biology. A typical genetic heritage text implies that sperm and egg make us "an inevitable reflection of the genes." The Human Genome Project lends credence to the vulgar error that human beings are nothing but the product of their genes. Genetic omnipotence relieves society of responsibility and exonerates criminals who claim, "It wasn't me; it was my genes." DNA-hereditarians ignore evidence that animals and humans alike transmit features not simply via chromosomes but by training offspring.[89] The genome project in fact shows that traditional races are irrelevant to most genetic differences; yet in the media and the public eye, the project confirms racial distinctions as momentous and immutable.

Metaphors of kinship and home show innateness to be deeply embedded in collective heritage. Terms like motherland, fatherland, and *Heimat* imply things to which one is naturally tied. What is natural is never a matter of choice but only of birth and blind indifference, as Italo Calvino prefigured the genome project:

> What my parents programmed me to be in the beginning is what I am: that
> and nothing else. And in my parents' instructions are contained the instructions

of my parents' parents handed down in turn from parent to parent in an endless chain of obedience. . . . All a genetic heritage has to do is to transmit whatever was transmitted to it for transmitting, not giving a damn about how it's received. I continue carrying my parents within me in all my cells, and I'll never be able to free myself of this burden.[90]

Heritage in all its guises thus risks being swallowed up in features felt to be predetermined. Growing reliance on innateness and determinism leaves us more and more at the mercy of doomsters, fatalists, and fundamentalists.

An upsurge of popular feeling has intensified long-standing biases that discern heritage as innate and unalterable. This trend, rampant in realms ranging from medical research to child adoption, leaves heritage prey to divisive chauvinism and racism. The regressive drift can be curbed only by recalling that heritage, far from being fatally predetermined or God-given, is in large measure our own marvelously malleable creation.

Chapter 10

RIVALRY AND RESTITUTION

WE CLING TO OUR OWN HERITAGE and hold sacred its unique merits. Ardent advocacy affirms the worth of every legacy—but at the same time incites others to beleaguer or belittle it. Here I show how heritage foments conflict between rival claimants, rival visions of past and present, and rival views of truth and error. Its very sanctity needs belligerent defense. That heritage now serves as a panacea for so many ills and evils aggravates the acrimony noted in Chapter 4. Conflict over cultural relics and rights to ancestral emblems embroils rival claimants. Rhetorical bombast inflames animus, and myopia blinds partisan rivals to their underlying affinities.

Too much is now asked of heritage. In the same breath we commend national patrimony, regional and ethnic legacies, and a global heritage shared and sheltered in common. We forget that these aims are usually incompatible. Heritage more and more addresses similar goals with similar strategies. But possessive passions largely fuel these goals and direct these strategies; heritage is normally cherished not as common but as private property. Ownership gives it essential worth: though heritage is now more convergent and like-mindedly cherished, it remains inherently exclusive. "You never Enjoy the World aright, till you Perceiv yourself to be the Sole Heir of the whole World," observed a moralist three centuries ago; but we need to remember that other "Men are in it who are evry one Sole Heirs, as well as you."[1]

GLOBAL LEGACIES

World heritage is an ideal today ritually proclaimed by global agencies and national states. "Cultural property belonging to any people," held

227

the Hague Convention in 1954, is also "the cultural heritage of all mankind." American leaders hail universal heritage as mutually enriching. Patrimony is now "primarily seen in a global context, as part of the common heritage of humanity," in a typical phrase; Canadians accept as a duty the protection of foreign heritage as well as their own. Though "natural and cultural resources belong to the people of a given country," world heritage spokesmen hold each country answerable to the global community for legacies in its own care.[2]

That the natural heritage is global is now beyond dispute. Fresh water and fossil fuels, rain forests and gene pools are legacies common to us all and need all our care. Cultural resources likewise form part of the universal human heritage. Remains of ancient Egypt and China, relics of Greece and Rome, echoes of Europe's Renaissance and Enlightenment, and the rich diversities of a thousand tribal traditions embellish and animate the whole world. Classical names, biblical prose, and Confucian precepts suffuse global culture.

Archetypal national icons are also global legacies. The loss of Stonehenge or the Sphinx, Angkor Wat or the Acropolis would impoverish not just their homelands but all of us. The designation of 440 World Heritage sites in 142 countries enhances their fame, enables their care, and sways national stewards to share them with folk the world over. "I hope they get it right," says a Swedish visitor of English Heritage plans for Stonehenge. "Stonehenge belongs to all of us, you know. You Brits are just its lucky custodians."[3]

The primacy of global heritage is invoked when national folly threatens—against a Portuguese dam that would flood the Côa Valley's Ice Age rock art or industrial pollution at Agra that imperils the Taj Mahal. Greenpeace protests forced Shell in 1995 to ditch plans to deep-six the Brent Spar oil rig; as the Law of the Sea declares, the oceans truly are "the common heritage of mankind."

Global accolades deter despoliation and lend sanctuary to rare legacies. The World Heritage Convention has helped secure Cambodian temples, Celtic megaliths, and czarist palaces against neglect and plunder. Only global listing at the eleventh hour saved Tasmania's temperate rain forest from hydroelectric rapine. Global aid and expertise alone avert the ruination of Angkor Wat. World Heritage designation spared Avebury's neolithic stone ring an unseemly hotel and helped Hadrian's Wall to avert open-cast coal mining and erosion by hikers.

Heritage is justly lauded as the legacy of all mankind. We have come some way since Napoleon amassed antiquities from every land his armies conquered, and rich Americans "would carry away all England if it was possible"; J. P. Morgan's bequests of European heritage, including entire ancient abbeys, to New York's Metropolitan Museum of Art were held to do "more to put the old world and the new upon an equality than all the trade balances that ever were written."[4] But national rivalries are still potent, global action rare and often grudging. When in 1994 Israel readily relinquished to Egypt all relics excavated in Sinai since the 1967 conquest, the cession was commended as unprecedented. Priam's golden hoard—the Trojan treasure Schliemann smuggled out of Turkey, kept in Greece, and gave to Berlin, where Soviet forces seized it—is claimed by four nations as their rightful sole legacy. The Kohinoor diamond might by rights be Indian, Pakistani, Iranian, or Afghan. African-Americans feud with Ghanians over how to restore and display the legacy of Gold Coast dungeons from which millions of slaves were shipped to the New World.

Heritage provokes internal as well as international rivalry. National, regional, local, and in situ museums contest its allocation. Great museums claim visibility for national icons and the benefits of comparative study, those on the spot stress the fusion of heritage with habitat: tangible relics in their own locale. Shetland local pride demands more than mere replicas of the locally found relics of St. Ninian. Seeking to regain their fabled 12th-century chessmen, Lewis Islanders warn the British Museum that "people have died horribly in the seizure of these pieces." Would-be stewards ceaselessly dispute where heritage is best displayed.

Russia was widely praised for sharing "appreciation of a magnificent common heritage" when art taken from Germany in the Second World War was put on public view in 1994. But Russia is far from ready to give up that heritage. "It was a sin not to show the works," says Mikhail Piotrovsky, director of the Hermitage. "It was not a sin to take them out of Germany." Asked to return books and art central to German heritage, Russians retorted that the French never gave back Napoleonic loot, that the Germans burned millions of Russian books, that Nazis had seized much from Jewish owners, that return would undermine Russian claims to czarist treasures, and that wartime booty was just reparation for past slurs. "The Germans said the Slavs have no cultural heritage and that all must be destroyed," as St. Petersburg palaces and Novgorod frescoes bore tragic witness. "We have a right to compensation."

Our global common heritage gets more than lip service. But it faces huge, often insuperable, obstacles in the possessive jealousies of particular claimants. The heritage crusade is mounted not just against destroyers and forsakers—the developers, vandals, iconoclasts, and erosive forces discussed in Chapter 1. Rather, its chief targets are rival claimants to its custody and benefits. Our severest animus is directed against those who crave our heritage or contest its claims. Indeed, the very notion of a universal legacy is self-contradictory; as we saw in Chapter 6, confining possession to some while excluding others is the raison d'être of heritage.

EXCLUSIVE LEGACIES

Each of us inherits multiple and overlapping legacies, as discussed in Chapter 3. But zealous patriots are intolerant of partial allegiance and demand our exclusive loyalty. Since we cannot cleave to nation, locality, faith, vocation, and family all at once, we mute our ties to competing legacies. In being true to *one* self, we play false to our other collective selves.

Nationhood above all demands sole fealty. To serve as identity, Europeans aver, "nationalism has to fill one's life." Non-Magyar minorities were "ulcers on the body of the motherland" for Hungary's poet-patriot Sándor Petöfi. "A man who thinks of himself as belonging to a particular national group in America has not yet become an American," President Wilson harangued foreign-born citizens in 1915. "We can have no 'fifty-fifty' allegiance," agreed Theodore Roosevelt. "Either a man is an American and nothing else, or he is not an American at all."[5]

Each group's heritage is by definition domestic. The past we prize is our own; foreigners' pasts are alien and incompatible. Chroniclers treat their own legacies as possessions jealously *un*shared. "Professional historians in almost every country," in Novick's resumé of traditional practice, dwelt on the history of their own nation "and frequently disparaged the capacity of outsiders to penetrate its *Geist* or *génie*."[6] They still do. And by the same token, we cannot know the heritage of others. Mutual exclusion leaves us ignorant of their legacy and them of ours.

Outsiders' judgments are discredited on principle. UNESCO's listing of Durham as a World Heritage site was for Auberon Waugh no tribute but an insult: why should *foreigners* choose which English cathedral city rated this accolade? He felt it "impertinent for an international organisation—especially one largely dominated by Afro-Asian militants—to express a preference." (Waugh was unaware that the choice was actually British and only rubber-stamped in Paris.) Foreign acclaim demeans domestic heritage even when echoing national sentiment. Students at an English university accepted my views on English landscape tastes, a colleague told me, but felt it offensive that an *outsider* had publicly delineated them.[7]

Heritage exclusivity, as noted in Chapter 6, is rooted in tribal needs for cohesion with like-minded kith and kin and for solidarity against outsiders. In Genesis, God punishes men for aspiring to divinity by scattering them among incommunicable tribes. Gibberish is still divinely ordained: "If everyone could understand everyone else," runs the fundamentalist creed, "American Christians might be contaminated with foreign ideas and religions. Even worse, global unity might result": unbridgeable difference is God's mandate.[8]

True insight is seen to need native upbringing—life histories however ancestrally diverse stitched into a common collective legacy. Stable and persisting, that legacy comprises a shared national grammar of gesture and social relations, temperament and topical references. In America, for example, an enduring impress of biblical and pop music, derived from centuries of preachers, teachers, lawyers, and entertainers, turned the offspring of immigrants first into reincarnated 17th-century Englishmen, in Michael Lind's phrase, then into cultural legatees of both George Washington and his slaves.

Such an inheritance can be acquired only through protracted experience. Newcomers unfamiliar with the homely minutiae of baseball, high-school proms, and Rotary clubs can never, nativists insist, grasp the essence of the American spirit. Aliens remain alien by nurture if not nature. Hence we hold on to what we inherit as ours alone. And the usual view, limned in Chapter 9, is that only our own flesh and blood can cherish heritage intact; newcomers and colonials erode or debase it. "Nobody who did not look exactly like them," as a West Indian says of her island's colonial overlords, "would ever be English."[9]

In protecting the West Indian archive referred to in Chapter 6, I myself fell afoul of English exclusivity. When I decried the impending dispersal of this legacy at auction, I earned rebuke for trespassing on a Codrington family preserve. "I gather from your name," wrote one titled lady, "that your people have not been in England very long. One must be here as many generations as the Codringtons to say anything about English property." Again, lecturing on the pros and cons of heritage restitution, I alluded to the Elgin Marbles and the Sphinx's beard in the British Museum. My talk was academic and my attitude neutral, yet I was told it was wrong for me, as an alien, even to discuss British property.

Ranks close when heritage seems at risk. Hence ex-Master of the Rolls Lord Denning censured Leon Brittan for ceding sovereignty to the European Parliament—"a German Jew, telling us what to do with our English law." (Of Lithuanian parentage, Brittan was in fact born and raised in England.) A national newspaper concurred: Since someone "of foreign origin is unlikely to have the same feeling for our history and institutions as we have", his views "should be appropriately discounted."[10] As with the "unambiguously English" players vital for cricket loyalty, how far back a "foreign origin" might disqualify was unclear; but Englishness is unshareable.

Thus English remains for the English *their* language, torn or tarnished by usage abroad. Poet-laureate Robert Bridges, founder of the Society for Pure English, saw English dissipated by imperial diffusion, defiled by the "blundering corruptions [of] other-speaking races [who] learn yet enough of ours to mutilate it." Skill availed nought; the foreigner who parades impeccable English is more suspect than the mongrel who mangles it. Heritage mystique needs its native context. To the English, London Bridge in Arizona is a tawdry joke, Turner paintings at the Getty Museum pale in the Pacific glare, and Shakespeare in Bengal—even on Broadway—is shorn of rooted resonance. Pride in the Bard's global appeal is swamped by "xenophobic suspicion at the sheer unEnglishness" of a Japanese *Hamlet*.[11]

Not even to kith and kin are legacies securely exported. After a century and a half of Caribbean commingling, variants of Hindu and Muslim ritual in Trinidad strike visitors from India and Pakistan as "parodic, even degenerate," notes Derek Walcott. "These purists look on such ceremonies as grammarians look at a dialect, or as empires on their colonies—illegitimate, rootless, mongrelized."[12]

Content with our own heritage, we know little and care less about others. Tracing English insularity to 13th-century purges of foreign influence, the historian Buckle lauded his country's "long standing . . . condescension towards foreigners." Visiting in 1847, Emerson judged the English "provokingly incurious about other nations." They remain aloof from those beyond their shores. Europeans eager to emulate England's National Trust are derided by the Trust's chairman as folk with "funny names [from] silly countries. A French observer holds "no country more consistently bent upon differing from others."[13]

Dismissive ignorance extends to recent incomers. Britons of Indian and West Indian descent seek in vain to add their own legacies to school curricula. "If people feel proud of their identity and rich in their cultural inheritance," in a common survey response, why bother "to spend time learning about those of others?" Nativists everywhere shun foreign heritage. "I can relate to my own culture," says a Texan college student, so "why study others?"

Lauding native traits means denigrating others. East Europeans came to Vienna University a century ago not to broaden outlooks but to burnish local legacies. "Refus[ing] particularly to study the history of their neighbours, whom they invariably disliked," relates a chronicler, they perused their own "to be better equipped for their controversies with those neighbours." In "all histories of the Serbian people," noted a critic in 1905,

> the Serbs are always angels, whereas the neighbouring peoples are the progeny of hell. The Serbian historian reviles and belittles all that is foreign and praises all that is ours. . . . We were always good and intelligent and brave and judicious and tender and kind and fair, whereas we always were and today still are, surrounded by wily and dishonest and cowardly and uncivilized peoples.[14]

Such vainglory often has dire effects. Today's Bosnian bloodbaths stem inexorably from ingrained Serbian stereotypes.

Yet few can avoid feeling their own heritage incomparable and imbuing heirs with the same conceit. "The belief that one's own culture and tradition are the norm and superior to anyone else's," notes a specialist, comes "from the earliest stages of learning." So each country "clings to the memory of its glorious past," in Luigi Barzini's phrase, "and mounts guard, jealously and suspiciously, over its unique heritage."[15]

Indeed, uniqueness was the crux of the new national creed. "Every [nationality] carries within itself the seeds of its own perfection, which can in no way be compared with those of others," preached Herder in 1794. "The most natural state is *one* people with *one* national character." Since people treasure most what distinguishes them from others, each nation vaunts a special legacy based on its own unique origins. Distinctiveness not only begets nations but is seen essential to their survival. Hence Israel stresses Jewish singularity: "if the Jews were to become 'like all other nations,'" fears a patriot, "that would be the end of the Jewish people."[16]

Glorying in uniqueness, we shun seeing any likeness with others' legacies. Striving to be different, we often define our heritage by opposition. Many a patrimony is described by what it is *not*; what matters most is being unlike some rival or oppressor. The bedrock of Canadianness is widely seen as being *not* the United States. Legacies are forged by inverting odious others. German, Jewish, Polish, and American vices led 19th-century Russian Slavophiles to trumpet opposing virtues. Ukrainians and Balts define their heritage as "not Russian." Irish legacy is archetypally anti-English. "Anything recognisably of English origin must automatically be non-Irish; . . . anything Irish must be devoid of the imprint of England," sums up an Irish scholar. "The Irish people were so busy being not-English," concludes a Dubliner, "that they had scarcely time to think of what it might mean to be Irish."[17]

Minorities construe their heritage by negating the mainstream. "All we know is what we are not," say Bretons: "We are not French!" Orkney and Shetland know little of their Norwegian roots but know well they are *not* Scots, *not* Gaelic, *not* Highland chieftains' churls. Aruba islanders dismiss Curaçaoans as "not like us" because the latter are descendants of slaves. Cajuns distance themselves from Louisiana Creoles by stressing that they are "not black"; to avoid any hint of Africa, some Cajuns disown the blackened food that is their culinary hallmark ("they even throw away their burnt toast!").[18]

CONFLICT AND RHETORIC

Conflict is thus endemic to heritage. Victors and victims proclaim disparate and divisive versions of common pasts. Claims of ownership, uniqueness, and priority engender strife over every facet of collective legacies. Clashes ensue when rivals press entitlements to being first, being distinctive, or being sublimely endowed. Archaeological legacies become pawns of personal feuds and nationalist goals, ruins and refuse sites fashioned into metaphors of identity. What gets excavated and how reflects heritage needs more than scholarly aims. Of Schliemann's obsession with finding Homer's Troy and his wholesale removal of layers that did not fit his Trojan needs, a chronicler concludes that "archaeology was not the handmaiden of history. It was the delivery boy of myth." Commandeering the past for his people, an Israeli antiquities chief retitled the Iron Age the Israelite Period, the Hellenistic the Hasmonean, the Roman the Mishnaic, and the Byzantine the Talmudic epoch.[19] Archaeologists are incessantly importuned to certify national and tribal sagas, testifying that this or that people came first and kept tribal faith.

Opposing versions of Indian history exacerbate Hindu–Muslim conflict. To Pakistanis, Nehru is a shallow playboy, Gandhi a religious hypocrite; Indians depict a Pakistan spawned by feudal lords and greedy merchants, its founder, Jinnah, a Westernized opportunist and British stooge. Earlier epochs get yet more polarized portrayals. Indians vilify Mughals as destroyers of their ancient civilization; Pakistanis begin their history with Islam, ignoring ancient Mohenjo-Daro, Harrapa, and Taxila and obliterating the Hindu past.

Monuments become hostages of these disputed annals. Sindhi separatists tax Pakistan with neglecting pre-Islamic sites to suppress Sind heritage. Pakistan spokesmen retort that Mohenjo-Daro anciently fell because Allah destroyed Sindhi ancestors who defied His commands; moreover, Mughal monuments matter more for tourism. Belittling the talents of Muslim conquerors, Hindus reclaim Islamic shrines as Hindu-inspired. In Delhi they hawk a popular guidebook that contradicts the official plaque at Qutub Minar and recounts a Hindu origin and subsequent perversion into a mosque. At the Taj Mahal, Sanskrit chanters sell plastic replicas with a *trishul*, the Hindu trident of divinity, replacing the crescent on the Taj dome.[20]

Rivalries intensify as more and more comes under the rubric of heritage and becomes sacralized in some national or ethnic legacy. Lawsuits to recover or retain fragments of patrimony mount each decade by orders of magnitude and now account for more international disputes than any other cause. "Memories are a larger and larger component of politics," says a historian, with heritage grievance its chief currency.[21]

Exempting sacred legacies from customary commercial codes is a notable source of strife, exemplified in a 1987 Quebec case annulling a 1962 sale of articles from a parish church. L'Ange-Gardien's parish priest had sold off some old chalices and statuary for what later proved much less than their "heritage" value. In the mid-1970s the archdiocese claimed back these objects as not formally deconsecrated and hence still sacred. The judge agreed: as "sacred things are excluded from being objects of commerce," the church should repossess its heritage. If other dioceses followed suit, a Quebec curator feared, "our museums would be emptied of a very important part of their collections."[22] The l'Ange-Gardien ruling affects heritage stewardship everywhere. Multicultural equity could hardly deny like sanctity to any sacred legacy, whether Islam or Inuit, Sikh or Scientologist.

Australia faced a similar dilemma after deciding not to honor Aboriginal claims for *all* sites but only sacred ones. In Aboriginal terms, it then emerged, many if not most sites were sacred. The U.S. Navy learned the same lesson when forced by Native Hawaiian religious protests to give up Kaho'olawe Island as a bombing range. Indigenes accused of inventing sacredness at will retort that they do not categorize separately, making Western distinctions among religious, economic, and other uses, nor value sites in piecemeal fashion. And if others were unaware these sites are sacred, it is because such matters are not generally divulged to outsiders.[23]

Fervent advocacy makes heritage a byword for acrimony. Communal quarrels mirror personal feuds: states dispute sovereign icons and ethnic factions demand equal deference, much as siblings squabble over parental bequests. Newly sovereign Macedonia's name and flag enrage Greeks, who assert exclusive rights to both. Washington's Columbus quincentenary had to allot the same amount of exhibit space to European, Oriental, and Native American perceptions. A 1994 display of Protestant and Catholic views on Londonderry's legacy had to be sure, noted heritage director Brian Lacey, "not to have a single millimetre more material on one side than the other." Princess Diana was likened in New York to Helen of Troy—"another war might occur before we handed her back to her own people."

Bellicose xenophobia is a heritage hallmark. It was not enough for Finns to see Russia as their hereditary foe; they must "know how to *hate* it." Polish historians in the 1960s aimed to "arouse sentiments of hatred towards the [German] enemy." Gory, saber-rattling national anthems are lauded for making it "easier to cheat, fight, and kill outsiders."[24] Hence heritage disputes are impervious to reason or compromise. "If you want a war, nourish a doctrine," wrote the sociologist Sumner in 1903. "Civilized men have done their fiercest fighting for doctrines." Only shifting their dispute from the realm of heritage to that of defensible terrain secured the 1993 Israeli-Palestinian peace treaty. "Rabin is not talking about *ideology* and he is not talking about a land that is *promised* to his people by *God*," noted a Palestinian delegate. "He is talking about needing land for security reasons. Security we can discuss."[25] Credos and sacred covenants, the stuff of heritage, are beyond discussion.

Heritage causes are supremely self-righteous. Seizing land or commodities is censured as criminal; seizing heritage is condoned as self-respect. A Mexican journalist in 1982 stole an Aztec codex from the Bibliothèque Nationale in Paris; the codex was then given to (and kept by) the Mexican state. This patriotic theft was widely hailed, the heritage end sanctioning the illicit means. Such acts echo the medieval "translations" of saints' bodies and relics, as with the supposed Magi cited in my introduction. Priests and others who stole such relics from churches justified these "kidnappings" as vital for the security and reputation of the saints themselves, who acquiesced in being taken to new communities where they would receive proper honor and devotion; the thefts were sanctioned as acts of true Christian virtue. In like spirit today, to claim anything as cultural patrimony elicits sympathy for its retention or return.[26]

Hyperbolic cant suffuses heritage causes. Gettysburg gets hallowed as "the most important battlefield in the Western Hemisphere," the English Civil War's Naseby as "the place parliamentary democracy was narrowly preserved." Disney's Historyland was "a crime against the national heritage." A duke who first installed and then removed two antique fireplaces "has raped our heritage." The 1992 Windsor Castle fire left most of its ancient fabric intact, yet was "the greatest heritage loss of the century." Selling stately-home art abroad is likened to Cromwell's dispersal of Charles I's great collection. Nearly bankrupt Dulwich Art Gallery is "a gem in the cultural ecology of our world to be preserved at all costs." A television-franchise takeover means "the destruction of a vital part of our heritage." Such knee-jerk excess at length leads many to ignore threats to heritage, like the boy who too often cries wolf.

Yet rhetorical bombast can be its own reward, with honor satisfied by ardent petition. It may better aid the Greek cause to go on asking for the Elgin Marbles than to get them back. Nothing sustains fervor like a grievance unassuaged: to gain Québécois sovereignty or Scottish home rule would cost separatists their best weapon. Black slave-reparation demands aim less to raise cash than to arouse consciousness. Calls for the return of Britain's crown jewels and Egyptian antiquities to their "rightful home" in Africa and India, eliciting Westminster bluster about "inalienable national heritage," serve purely rhetorical ends. Identity is succored more by a quest for lost heritage than by its nurture when regained. Basque extremism ebbed into aimless petulance once autonomy was conceded. "Before, we had answers to our problems," said a spokesman in 1986; "self-government, *conciertos económicos*, the restoration of our Basque culture. All that has been achieved . . . Now our problems seem to have no answers at all and what we have achieved doesn't seem that important."[27]

Obsession with righting a grievance or recovering a loss raises delusive dreams for regained heritage. The long saga of the Iroquois to retrieve wampum purloined from them in the 1890s "built up the hopes of some who expected something more spectacular and miraculous" than what tribal leaders could do when they got back the wampum. And inflated rhetoric leads some to query claimants' good faith. The wampum case aroused suspicion that repatriation patrons "only want to enhance their political power."[28] Heritage haves and have-nots trade charges that aggravate animus.

Disconcerting gulfs sunder rhetoric from result. Quixotic claimants rely too much on moral justice to regain lost legacies; to keep what they have, impoverished heirs strive in vain to stem market forces. Greece, Turkey, Italy, Peru strictly forbid antiquities exports that go on all the time; outraged protests show up the lack of effective controls. British rhetoric reflects aggrieved impotence about "family silver" sold off "to foreigners at bargain-basement prices."

The gulf between insistent concern and utter negligence breeds cynical apathy. Curators, archaeologists, and police stewards of Etrurian heritage exchange histrionic abuse with tomb robbers—then they all meet in the village café. A militant champion of Greek patrimony is brought two antique sculptures by her brother. "I found these at the bottom of the garden," he says; "can you get them valued at Sotheby's?" She is appalled: "How can you ask? It's Greek heritage, and against all I stand for." "But Marina, it's for the *family!*" At that moment, she told me, "I knew I had lost." Heritage devotees who take their own inflated advocacy at face value are doomed to disappoint themselves—and others.

National Exemplars

Myopic rivalry is, I have shown, endemic to the very nature of heritage. To insist we were the first or the best, to celebrate what is ours and exclude others, is what heritage is all about. But we are not condemned to be forever driven by tribal demons. As noted above, contrary impulses gather force, defining heritage as a global good. In the last century heritage became an ideal increasingly shared among each nation's peoples. Now it begins to belong, as of right, to all the world together.

This globalizing trend is recent, because only lately have all the world's peoples begun to be seen as similarly entitled to and jointly accountable for a global heritage. And global agendas are still viewed with intense suspicion, because they are recognizably rooted in chauvinist and imperial self-regard. These ideas stem above all from Europeans who rate their own national heritage as so superior it *ought* to be global. Indeed, many peoples prize their own legacies for uniquely embodying universal merits. "Each historian regards his own nation as the torchbearer of civilization," noted Sumner ninety years ago. He cited virtually identical passages about the "civilizing mission" of Russians, English, French, and Germans. Such hubris is now more muted but no less pervasive. "Some nations are prouder and more jealously attached to their past grandeur than others," but each, concludes Barzini, "is persuaded it has contributed in a decisive manner to . . . the world's civilization."[29]

As we saw in Chapter 3, France routinely equates its own with global heritage. As "the pilot of the vessel of humanity," France would remake the world in its image, promised Michelet in 1831. French language and literature had long been global paragons; "today it is our laws, our liberty, so strong and so pure, that we are going to share with the world." France was "much more than a nation," he added in 1846; it was "the saviour of the human race." The *mission civilisatrice* echoes yet: "to be a patriot in France," in Tony Judt's words, "is to be a patriot for nations and peoples everywhere."[30]

The same arrogance long marked German global claims. Unlike "egoistic, narrow and hostile" folk, Germany's legacy embraced the aspirations of all mankind. As the "most perfect nation," Germany would refine the "imperfect individualities" of others. The coming "confederation of European nations will wear German colors," prophesied Adam Müller two centuries ago, "for everything great, thorough and lasting in all European institutions is German." And German happiness lay "not in the suppression but in the highest flowering of the civilization" of inferior peoples. In keeping their heritage intact, Germans in the New World would similarly fulfill their world-historical mission to "elevate" American culture.[31] Hitler's Reich was a true exemplar of a national legacy of universal uplift.

In American eyes, God imposed a global mission on the New World called into being to redress the errors of the Old. "He has marked the American people," held an eminent turn-of-this-century scholar and senator, "as His chosen nation to finally lead in the redemption of the world." British ambassador Lord Bryce remarked on Americans' faith that "the rest of civilized mankind" was bound "as by a law of fate" to copy their institutions.[32] From Washington to Clinton, presidents portray the United States as disinterested peacekeeper to feckless others. Wilson termed America "the only idealistic nation in the world"; Kennedy held that while "other countries look to their own interests," the United States alone assumed global obligations. A Liberty Bell replica that would peal out decisive dates in *world* history was held unneeded; America's bell already rang for all.[33] Americans who fantasize their global generosity naturally assume the world should be grateful for their heritage.

EUROCENTRIC EXEMPLARS

In the course of dispensing global benefits, Western powers also acquired global heritage and then came to construe their spoils of conquest as global stewardship. European mandates to plunder stemmed from the common view that their Christian and scientific legacy was immeasurably superior to the barbarous customs of others. Though each nation's patriots had to puff their own land, "a philosopher [must] consider Europe as one great republic," thought Gibbon, at a level of "arts, and laws, and manners above the rest of mankind."[34]

"The rest" were deemed incapable of creating, let alone conserving, the legacies they lived among. The ancient mounds of mid-America must have been built by biblical tribes, while Great Zimbabwe was clearly an Aryan achievement. Only lately have African and American indigenes been credited with a heritage earlier thought too impressive not to be Indo-European.

Indeed, until lately the West alone *had* a self-conscious heritage; save in the Orient, other peoples were presumed to lack historical awareness. This was assumed by scholars of every stamp. Marx regarded non-Europeans as unreachable by revolutionary change because outside the stream of history. Up to 1950, a canonical architectural text dismissed non-Western buildings as "non-historical." In 1965 the historian Trevor-Roper famously concurred:

> Perhaps, in the future, there will be some African history . . . But at present, there is none, or very little . . . The history of the world, for the last five centuries, in so far as it has significance, has been European history.

Eurocentric bias is not confined to Europeans. White and black California eighth-graders all agreed that "if Africa had had a history worth learning about, we would have had it last year in Western Civ." The historian Arthur Schlesinger even now terms Europe "the *unique* source of those liberating ideas of individual liberty, political democracy, the rule of law, human rights, and cultural freedom that constitute our most precious legacy."[35]

In this view, civilized progress ensured the global sway of Western heritage. Other customs were bound to succumb; the Western legacy alone had durable worth. The relics of remnant primitives would be collected and studied as vignettes of early mankind, yardsticks of progress, and stimuli to art and travel. The urge to compare was held uniquely European. Just as Old World antiquities had moved from royal and private into state collections, so exotic relics acquired as trophies came to adorn national museums and enlighten Western scholars. Like "high" art, tribal art was deemed to "belong to the world." But that world was Western; Westerners alone cared about and were competent to cherish the globe's diverse cultures.[36]

"Openness to the outsider's world is the underlying dynamic of Western history," say two Harvard scholars.[37] But openness first and foremost took the form of acquisition; Europeans viewed the world as theirs. Explorers, traders, and missionaries over four centuries amassed the world's heritage *in* the West, where it largely remains. To this day, the material legacy of Asia and Africa, indigenous America and Oceania is centered in the museums and galleries of London and Paris, Berlin and New York. Beyond Europe and North America no major global repository exists.

The concept of global patrimony thus derives from an era of conquest that leaves much of it in a few privileged hands. The legacy of mankind ends up in the Louvre and the British Museum but is absent from Samoa and Somalia. Universalism endows the haves at others' expense. Few British connoisseurs, dismayed by the 1986 sale to Japan of Newcastle University's collection of Pacific tribal art, spared a moment's thought for Micronesians who could not afford to buy back any of the items fashioned by their own forebears.[38]

Interest and expertise commonly justify Western custody of other legacies. A century ago, safekeeping was the excuse for procuring Egyptian antiquities: "Once a mummy . . . is lodged in the British Museum, it has a far better chance of being preserved there than it could possibly have in any tomb . . . in Egypt." Removing such legacies was really doing them a favor, like the "sinister regalia and trophies" the British took away from the "bloodthirsty and vengeful" Ashanti in 1874.[39]

The same logic vindicates tomb-robbing today. Arkansas looters of prehistoric graves are "protecting" a heritage to whose beauty Indians are blind. A New York importer claims to be the savior of smuggled Eastern art that would otherwise end up as road-building rubble. "These things are not appreciated in those countries," says a dealer. "They're brought here and given a home. Now cultured people can see them." A Yoruba "expert" holds it "better that these important pieces should be preserved [by] sometimes irregular methods of acquisition, than be left to rot on neglected shrines" or willfully destroyed by Yorubans "blind to their patrimony."[40]

Those not blind to their tribal legacies may now need to be helped to see them properly, in one current rationale justifying Western possession. At the New South Wales Art Gallery, a visitor sees

> sullen and totally unresponsive Aboriginals . . . being reintroduced to their confiscated property, washed and ironed. "We know this is your religion and we *love* the fact that it's so important to your wonderful culture, . . . but we just thought we could look after it better in our air-conditioned gallery. Doesn't it look nice here? Why don't we all enjoy it together?"

Small wonder that Aborigines mistrust "world heritage" ideals that threaten to arrogate both their prehistory and their present culture.[41]

Global demand sanctions the removal of other indigenous legacies—genetic property in plants, animals, and human beings marketed for medicinal and other uses by multinational firms. Human genes, too, as we have seen, are now part of the heritage industry. Despite previous indigenous protests from Brazil, in 1995 the U.S. government patented the DNA of a Papua New Guinea tribesman seemingly resistant to leukemia. Yet again, global interests justify "sharing" Third World legacies, even "the bloody issues of life," in Donna Haraway's censure, by submitting them to Western technological exploitation.[42]

THE GREEK AND GLOBAL CLASSICAL LEGACY

Heritage blindness was imputed not only to savages but to civilized Europe's archetypal heirs, the Greeks. Debased 18th-century Athenians strolling "with supine indifference among the glorious ruins of antiquity" struck Gibbon as "incapable of admiring the genius of their predecessors." As classicism gained devotees, more and more of them found modern Greeks unfit guardians. The "rightful inheritors" of Hellenic legacy, in Woolf's words, were in London, Paris, and Berlin. They were truer heirs not only because they cared and knew more about it, but because in their hands it became truly universal—a legacy inspiring philosophers and statesmen, poets and architects everywhere. "We are all Greeks," Shelley declared; "our laws, our religion, our arts have their root in Greece." The genius of Hellas was "a gift of Greece to the modern world." For Wilhelm von Humboldt, the Greeks alone, "step[ping] out of the circle of history," embodied ideals suited to all mankind. Though time eroded the Athenian originals, "the permanence and vitality of the *spirit* and *intelligence* which produced these works was immortal," exulted Harrow's classicist, Christopher Wordsworth. "Here is the heart; the spirit is every where."[43]

Being everywhere made that heritage uniquely problematic. Taste for things Greek led to the gutting of classical riches. Pottery, sculpture, and architecture fell prey to foreigners from Roman times on, above all in the 19th century. The finest relics of ancient Greece adorn museums abroad: the Parthenon frieze in London, the Aphaian pediments in Munich, the Winged Victory of Samothrace in Paris. As with Greek literature, the diffusion of its art and architecture made classical antiquity a global patrimony. "Every one of these treasures," says Mary Lefkowitz, "have for more than two millennia been representing ancient Greek civilization to the rest of us."

Hence the modern Greek dilemma. Global admiration has forced them to share their heritage more than any other people. Prolonged dispersal of antiquities and diffusion of classical texts leave Greeks at the same time the source of a global heritage, bereft heirs of a legacy in others' hands, and embittered custodians of remnant glories.

Current Greek efforts to claw back heritage stem, to be sure, from a philhellenism that itself is largely imported. So eager were Western allies to restore ancient Hellas that Greeks felt bound to exalt the classical legacy, the Acropolis coming to symbolize national rebirth. But debts to foreign neoclassical genius—Corfu's Doric temple of St. George by a British architect, the University, the Academy, and the National Library of Athens by Bavarians and Danes—do not negate the sense that the world has gained at Greek expense.

Greece is the archetype of stress between local and global heritage. Proud of their forebears' fame, Greeks at the same time feel deprived by sharing it. The Elgin Marbles exemplify the problem of a legacy that is both Greek *and* global. As noted in Chapter 6, all Greek children learn that the Acropolis belongs to them. But as "art ancestral to us all," the Elgin Marbles also belong to a world heritage of which the British Museum is a preeminent custodian.

Greek admission to the European Community was termed by a

British diplomat a "fitting repayment by the Europe of today to the cultural and political debt that we all owe to a Greek heritage almost three thousand years old." Alas, Greeks take formulaic tribute at face value. Yes, they invented democracy, Plato and Socrates did found Western philosophy, Herodotus and Thucydides were the first true historians, Greek tragedians do outnumber if not outshine Racine, Cervantes, and Shakespeare. Every Greek prizes Hellenic primacy in the Western canon, but few realize how little the West heeds that canon. Hurt that his fabled ancestral legacy reflects so little glory on himself, as Richard Clogg puts it, the modern Greek fails to see "that playing up the Classical merely reinforces a stereotypical image of Greeks as poor relations of their ancient forebears." Greece itself is "a cut-price theme park of broken marble," in Paul Theroux's dismissal, where the visitor is "harangued in a high-minded way about Ancient Greek culture, while some swarthy little person picks your pocket."[44] Global celebration inflates local pride in Greek heritage but makes it less their own legacy.

REPATRIATION AGAINST WESTERN GLOBALISM

"Thank you for admiring our heritage," say the Greeks; "now please give it back." Others even more despoiled voice sterner demands for repatriation, internationally through the aegis of UNESCO, internally through ethnic and tribal pressure. Often angrier than the Greeks, aggrieved claimants see their purloined heritage less admired than desecrated as global commodities in others' hands. And because their plaints seem morally just, legal rights to own heritage tend more and more to be reserved to national or ethnic heirs.[45]

Tribalist sanctions frustrate cosmopolite zeal for shared legacies. Global pieties seen rooted in acquisitive avarice cut no ice with the disinherited eager to recoup their own. Against collaborative heritage concerns, vengeful victims turn fiercely exclusive. Abetting native protectionism, academics and museum curators stress the overriding importance of context, forbidding the removal of heritage objects from sites of origin and provenance.

Restitution is a key issue in ex-colonial states. A drumbeat of demands for ancestral relics—the Benin bronzes in London, Sri Lanka's seal of Kandy in Amsterdam, Tahitian treasures in Paris—signal sweeping change in heritage attitudes. In the 19th century heirlooms became emblems of European nationhood; in the late 20th century relics betoken sovereign pride the world over. A rich and representative patrimony is deemed essential to citizenship, creativity, and sheer national survival.

In times past, to the victor belonged the spoils; losers' legacies were routinely purloined. Only at the turn of this century did heritage rights gain even lip service. Third World retrieval was orchestrated in the 1970s, ethnic and minority claims in the 1980s. Skulls and grave goods are withdrawn from public display; museums and academies yield sacred relics to tribal heirs; a spate of rulings mandates repatriating smuggled antiquities. Legacies illicitly dispersed are ever less acceptable to reputable museums and galleries.

Chronic victims of rapine are most apt to curtail outside involvement in their heritage. Even though (or because) they have trained and equipped locals, Western archaeologists are often banned from Third World digs. American fossil hunters charged in 1995 with invading an Ethiopian site were warned that Ethiopia would not tolerate "neocolonialist" academics. Persisting mistrust obstructs cooperative care for legacies that are nonetheless ever more globally appreciated.

Collectors of other people's heritage once assumed they thereby served global welfare. Some still make such claims, but foreign acquisition—by excavation, by theft, even by purchase—offends morality more and more. In the past, universal heritage meant all the world's legacies gathered into Western collections. Today it means global aid for all cultures to retain and retrieve essential legacies.

Mutual respect for the heritages of others is a byword in agencies like UNESCO, ICOM (International Council of Museums), and ICOMOS (International Council on Monuments and Sites). But international conventions like Unidroit, aiming to curb an illicit art and antiquities trade now allegedly second only to drug trafficking, focus mainly on keeping heritage inside national borders. These efforts mirror the dualism that makes heritage a dilemma for all its devotees. Every collaborative advance confronts new pressures to reaffirm the sovereign primacy of heritage as exclusive to one particular possessor. Every effort to legitimize antiquities commerce for global ends inflames cultural nationalism, confirming zeal among nations rich in heritage to retain all they hold. Just as sects and ethnic minorities claim sole rights to perform or attend certain rituals, so each state sees itself the exclusively ordained guardian of the relics, institutions, legal codes, and art objects that reify its sacred traditions. Yet, as with martyrs' bodies and saints' relics in medieval times, every effort to hoard such legacies at home by prohibiting their export inflates market demand and multiplies looting, theft, and contraband trade.[46]

CONCLUSION

Visions of a heritage transcending our own domain are age-old. They reflect diverse aims: to convert others to our faith, to improve the common lot by sharing our superior bequest, to reunify a fractious world. The missionary zeal of Catholic orders was universal in focus. And the secular legacies of science, capitalism, and communism have been as ardently avowed as the sacred.

In the main, heritage inevitably voices private, even selfish, interests but is no longer just parochial and self-centered. Global agencies lead the way in conserving and celebrating national and local legacies. Global codes of practice ally heritage-rich and heritage-greedy lands. Major powers concede the heritage rights of small states and nonsovereign minorities. We begin to appreciate that our global village requires a unified natural and cultural legacy.

Accelerating global diffusion of ideas and technologies makes heritage sharing easier and more customary. To be sure, the Church long ago promoted the dispersion of sacred relics as tribute and as a token of its global sway over the hearts and minds of men. Israeli readiness to sell or make gifts of antiquities follows this example. Every Israeli relic in foreign hands, like the Canaanite scimitar and Iron Age oil jar given Prime Minister Thatcher, highlights for outside consumption Israel's identity and raison-d'être.[47] Enhanced public access makes it easier to perceive heritage export not as a tragic attrition of one's own legacy, but a happy growth of its meaning to global neighbors—not diminishing but augmenting each group's legacy. Asserting that "almost all great art belongs to the whole world," the London *Times* in 1994 welcomed the dispersal of heritage hidden away in stately homes to wherever it could best be seen.

It helps to recall that no heritage is wholly homegrown. "We ourselves

largely took it away from somewhere, didn't we?" expostulates Henry
James's Englishman. "We didn't *grow* it all." The classical legacy is everywhere a composite accretion, stemming from imperial Rome, Byzan-
tium, the Renaissance, Palladianism, and 19th-century romanticism as
well as ancient Athens.[48] Though some scoff at "foreign" bunk, most
regard the Elgin Marbles, Leonardo drawings, and Rembrandt paintings
as part of British heritage. Like Canova's *Three Graces,* they are judged to
have "been here so long, we have now assimilated them as memorable
friends." To become fixated on what is purely endemic hardens instincts
to hoard, thwarts efforts to share. Likewise futile, though, is the frequent
impulse to keep everything regardless of provenance. Incensed that "national heritage" was being sold abroad, a reporter at a recent Sotheby
auction had to be reminded that the art works in question had arrived in
Britain only a fortnight before.

Diversity is desirable; we rightly admire what is distinctive in our
legacy. But to savor and sustain diversity calls for comparative insight. To
prize what is unique in our own heritage we must see how it is like, as
well as unlike, that of others. Insularity sours both sameness and difference. Avowing our ineffable uniqueness, we dissipate fealty in fretful acrimony over what belongs to us. Group solidarity is, as I have shown,
innate to forming and fostering a heritage. But as legacies coalesce,
tribal jealousies must be curbed. After all, each collective heritage attracts the allegiance of heirs whose makeup and motives are themselves
in perpetual flux.

"The history we study is never our own," writes one historian; "it is
always the history of a people who were in some respects like us and in
other respects different."[49] The heritage we admire, in contrast, is usually our own, but never only our own; we share it with others who are
in some respects like us, in others very different. We can never wholly
know a heritage not our own. But we can now appreciate its alien traits
as more cognate, in many ways, to our own domestic legacy than we
ever before realized.

The growing worth of heritage aggravates conflicts over whose it is,
what it means, and how to use it. Heritage builds collective pride and
purpose, but in so doing stresses distinctions between good guys (us)
and bad guys (them). Heritage faith, heritage commodities, and heritage rhetoric inflame enmity, notably when our unique legacy seems at

risk. Entrenched myopia foments strife; ignorance inhibits reciprocity. Besotted by our heritage, blind to that of others, we not only eschew comparison but forfeit its benefits.

As every legacy's virtues are incomparable, so seem its vexations. All suppose their problems unexampled elsewhere. In Australian eyes the attrition of heritage by populist mockery is a problem solely their own. Italians imagine that they alone have a heritage too burdensome to live with. Greeks feel uniquely bereaved by the classical legacy's global dispersal; none but Israelis suffer a suicidal Masada complex; Egyptians uniquely lack empathy with ancient roots. Only Americans parade their past with patriotic hype, debase it with Disney, and feel guilt on both counts. Or so they all think. But they are wrong; most of these heritage ailments are pandemic.

Every legacy is distinctive, to be sure. But realizing our heritage problems are *not* unique makes them more bearable, even soluble, if we see how time or effort resolved them elsewhere. Swedish and Danish curators came with me to a 1987 Smithsonian exhibit, "A More Perfect Union," on Second World War Nisei internment camps. They were stunned to see American infamy self-revealed—and wondered what hidden aspects of their own histories it might be salutary to display. Israelis who mourn the passing of pioneer Zionist founders and voice dismay at current moral decline might take heart from patristic annals that record the filial distress of Church Fathers too late to have known the Apostles, or from the self-abasement of "degenerate offspring" of American Founding Fathers.[50] Few inheritors avoid the angst of falling short of godlike precursors.

Another anxiety common to many heritages is doubt about authenticity. Chapters 4 through 7 showed that attachment to heritage depends on feeling and faith, as opposed to history's ascertained truths. Lack of hard evidence seldom distresses the public at large, who are mostly credulous, undemanding, accustomed to heritage mystique, and often laud the distortions, omissions, and fabrications central to heritage reconstruction.

Heritage producers and stewards, however, seem increasingly concerned to ground their goods and stories in verifiable evidence. As heritage suffuses more and more of everyday life, and claims to property and pride hinge on rival versions of the same experienced past, heritage-mongers feel compelled to cloak wares in historical authenticity. Material relics are scrutinized, memories retrieved, archives examined, monuments restored, reenactments performed, and historic sites interpreted with painstaking precision. Heritage apes scholarship with factoids and footnotes to persuade us that our legacy is grounded in irrefutable evidence.

It is all in vain, for two reasons: first, heritage by its very nature *must* depart from verifiable truth; second, adherents of rival heritages simultaneously construct versions that are equally well-grounded (and equally spurious). Because they are bound to fail, heritage claims so bolstered are hugely counterproductive. Invoking scientific history to underwrite heritage fictions, they bring science, history, and heritage all into disrepute, adding to rather than alleviating inheritors' anxieties.

At the start of this book I showed how heritage had become a quasi-religious cult. Sacredness secures fealty, enhances community, and exalts purpose as long as heritage is a creed not to be queried. But to bolster heritage faith with historical scholarship, as is now the fashion, smudges the line between faith and fact. It deprives adherents of rational scrutiny and choice, mires them in fatalism, and leaves them at the mercy of simplistic chauvinists. To embrace heritage *as history*, disguising authority as authenticity, cedes it a credence it neither asks nor deserves.[51]

Facing up to what distinguishes heritage from history lets us live more fruitfully with both. We need not fear or feel shame for imposing mutations on heritage, for they are innate to it. As I have shown, such manipulation and invention please and benefit the public. Heritage is popular because *we* make it so, while all along remaking it.

Awareness that heritage is not fixed but changes in response to our own needs is no less integral to our creative involvement with history. In realizing how we variously affect these linked realms, we learn to relish, rather than resent, our own interventions and even to tolerate those of others. And we come to feel that history and heritage are not simply imposed on us by the dead hand of remote ancestors or the diktat of bygone autocrats but are our very own. Salvaging the spoils of history, heritage crusaders are amazed to find history itself still in splendid health.

References

Abbreviations

AASLH   American Association for State and Local History
AHA   American Historical Association
AHR   American Historical Review
AQ   American Quarterly
H & M   History & Memory
IHT   International Herald Tribune
IJCP   International Journal of Cultural Property
JRSA   Royal Society of Arts Journal
LM   *Lieux de mémoire* (Pierre Nora)
NYRB   New York Review of Books
Times   The Times (London)
TLS   Times Literary Supplement

Cambridge means Cambridge, England, unless otherwise stated.
References exclude ephemeral material from recent newspapers and weekly magazines, except in the case of lengthy or crucial quotations.

Introduction

1. Graeme Davison, "The meanings of 'heritage,'" in Graeme Davison and Chris McConville, eds., *A Heritage Handbook* (North Sydney, 1991), 12; Bernard Smith, "Art objects and historical usage," in Isabel McBryde, ed., *Who Owns the Past?* (Melbourne, 1985), 81–3.
2. Patrick J. Geary, *Living with the Dead in the Middle Ages* (Ithaca, NY, 1994), 251–5; Timothy Raison, "The Magi in Legend," in *We Three Kings: The Magi in Art and Legend*, exhibition catalog, Buckinghamshire County Museum (Aylesbury, England, 1995), 7–10.

Chapter 1

1. James Lees-Milne, *People and Places: Country House Donors and the National Trust* (London, 1992), 5; Adam Nicolson, "Tidiness and the Trust," *National Trust Mag.*,

no. 58 (Autumn 1989), 37–9; Les A. Murray, *Persistence in Folly* (London, 1984), 114, 26.

2. Carl Schorske, *Fin-de-Siècle Vienna* (New York, 1981), xvii.

3. Edmund Burke, *Reflections on the French Revolution* [1790] (London, 1940), 29; Alain Bourdin, *La patrimoine reinventé* (Paris, 1984), 18; Pierre Nora, "L'ère de la commémoration," in his *LM*, III. 3:995.

4. *Museum*, 33 (1981), 117–23; John Henry Merryman, "The nation and the object," *IJCP*, 3 (1994), 68–9; Jean-Phillippe Lecat quoted in Dominique Poulot, "The birth of heritage," *Oxford Art Journal* 11:2 (1988), 41; UNESCO, *Conventions and Recommendations . . . Concerning the Protection of Cultural Heritage* (Paris, 1985).

5. Françoise Choay, *L'Allegorie du patrimoine* (Paris, 1992), 10–12.

6. Kevin T. Walsh, *The Representation of the Past: Museums and Heritage in the Post-Modern World* (London, 1992), 52; James Marston Fitch, *Historic Preservation: Curatorial Management of the Built World* (New York, 1982); Alfred Grosser, *Le crime et la mémoire* (Paris, 1989); Murray, *Persistence in Folly*, 109–29; Graeme Davison, "The meanings of 'heritage,'" in Davison and Chris McConville, eds., *A Heritage Handbook* (North Sydney, 1991), 4–5.

7. Peter Spurrier quoted in "Europe's genealogy craze," *Newsweek*, 7 Mar. 1988, 58–9; National Genealogical Society president quoted in Michael Kammen, *Mystic Chords of Memory* (New York, 1991), 642.

8. C. H. Warren (1943) quoted in Malcolm Chase, "This is no claptrap, this is our heritage," in Christopher Shaw and Malcolm Chase, eds., *The Imagined Past* (Manchester, 1989), 131; Herbert Butterfield, *The Englishman and His History* (Cambridge, 1944), 2; Reg Gammon, "Our country, all earthly things above, as always," *The Field*, 282 (May 1990), 82–3.

9. Harold Nicolson (1944) quoted in John Henry Merryman, "Two ways of thinking about cultural property," *American Journal of International Law*, 80 (1986), 840.

10. François Furet, "L'Ancien Régime et la Révolution," in Nora, *LM*, III. 1:107–39; Roy Pascal, *Design and Truth in Autobiography* (London, 1960), 57; Richard Terdiman, "The mnemonics of Musset's *Confession*," *Representations*, 26 (Spring 1989), 26–48.

11. Mervyn Jones quoted in Daniel Bell, "Technology, nature and society," *American Scholar*, 42 (1972–73), 385–404, ref. p. 396; Yi-Fu Tuan, *Landscapes of Fear* (Oxford, 1979), 215; John Clive, "The use of the past in Victorian England," *Salmagundi*, 68–9 (1985–86), 58–9.

12. Jonathan Raban, *Coasting* (London, 1987), 172.

13. William Maxwell, "The man in the moon," in his *Billie Dyer and Other Stories* (New York, 1993), 57.

14. Pierre-Jakez Hélias, *The Horse of Pride: Life in a Breton Village* (New Haven, 1978), 343.

15. William B. Wood, "Forced migration: Local conflicts and international dilemmas," *Annals Association of American Geographers*, 84 (1994), 607–34; Penelope Lively, *Oleander, Jacaranda: A Childhood Perceived* (London, 1994), 175.

16. Marc Guillaume, *La politique du patrimoine* (Paris, 1980), 143; Michel de Certeau, "Les revenants de la ville," *Traverses*, 40 (1987), 74–85; Simon Jenkins, "Dead and dismembered on the Nile," *Times*, 9 Jan. 1993, 12.

17. Ruth Ellen Gruber, *Jewish Heritage Travel: A Guide to East-Central Europe* (New

York, 1994); Ulf Björklund, "Armenia remembered and remade: Evolving Issues in a diaspora," *Ethnos*, 58 (1993), 335–60.

18. Ron Crocombe, "The continuing creation of identities in the Pacific islands," in David Hooson, ed., *Geography and National Identity* (Oxford, 1994), 317; Brazilian quoted in Michael Kepp, "Rebels who stay true to Dixie," *Observer on Sunday*, 2 Aug. 1992, 11.

19. André Chastel, "La notion du patrimoine," in Nora, *LM*, II.2:446; Guillaume, *Politique du patrimoine*, 149; Bernard Smith, "Art objects and historical usage," in Isabel McBryde, ed., *Who Owns the Past?* (Melbourne, 1985), 83–4.

20. Thomas F. King, "Beneath the American mosaic: The place of archaeology," in Robert E. Stipe and Antoinette J. Lee, eds., *The American Mosaic* (Washington, 1987), 260.

21. Nora, "Entre mémoire et histoire," in his *LM*, I:xxv–xxviii (my translation; see Marc Roudebush's in *Representations*, 26 [Spring 1989], 7–24); Lisa B. Weber, ed., *Documenting America: Assessing the Conditions of Historical Records in the States* (Albany, NY, 1983), notably essays by Richard J. Cox (19–36) and William L. Joyce (37–46); Barry James, "Archivists raise the alarm: France's collective memory is in danger," *IHT*, 17 Oct. 1995.

22. Nathaniel Hawthorne, 29 Sept. 1855, *The English Notebooks*, ed. Randall Stewart (New York, 1941), 242.

23. Christopher Gordon, *National Cultural Policy in Italy*, interim report, Council of Europe (Strasbourg, 1995).

24. Roberto Weiss, *The Renaissance Discovery of Classical Antiquity* (Oxford, 1959), 65–70, 98–104; Guillaume, *Politique du patrimoine*, 99–100.

25. Eric Gable and Richard Handler, "Deep dirt: Messing up the past at Colonial Williamsburg," *Social Analysis*, 34 (1993), 3–16.

26. Kammen, *Mystic Chords of Memory*, 681–2; Peppino Ortoleva, "Tradition and abundance: Reflections on Italian-American foodways," *Altreitalie*, 7 (June–July 1992), 54.

27. Catherine Milner, "The last Straws," *Times Mag.*, 3 April 1993, p. 38.

28. Pierre Nora, "L'ére de la commémoration," in his *LM*, III.3:1000–5.

29. David Lowenthal, "Uses of the past in Australia," in Brian Hocking, ed., *Australia Towards 2000* (London, 1990), 46–54 (Malouf on p. 46); Alistair Thomson, *Anzac Memories: Living with the Legend* (Melbourne, 1994).

30. Robert Taylor, Jr., and Ralph J. Crandall, "Historians and genealogists," in their (eds.) *Generations and Change* (Macon, GA, 1986), 14–15; survey in "Europe's genealogy craze," *Newsweek*, 7 March 1988, 58–9; André Burguière, "La généalogie," in Nora, *LM*, III.3:20.

31. Raban, *Coasting*, 152, 172.

32. Graeme Davison, "The broken lineage of Australian family history," in Donna Merwick, ed., *Essays on Honour of Greg Dening* (Melbourne, 1994), 335; Norma Tuck quoted in Seth Mydans, "Those convict fathers? Not so bad," *New York Times*, 3 Feb. 1988, p. 4; Carol Shields, *The Stone Diaries* (London, 1993), 166.

33. Raphael Samuel, *Theatres of Memory* (London, 1995), 243–59.

34. John Young and Paul Wilkinson, "Radar 'golf balls' are finally sunk," *Times*, 12 Aug. 1992, p. 5; Tom Griffiths, *Hunters and Collectors* (Melbourne, 1996), 240–2.

35. James Lane Allen (1911) in *Munsey's Magazine*, quoted in Kammen, *Mystic Chords of Memory*, 256–7.
36. Olgierd Czerner, "Communal cultural heritage in a unified Europe," *ICOMOS News*, 1:1 (March 1991), 25.
37. Wang Gungwu, "Loving the ancient in China," in McBryde, *Who Owns the Past?* 175–95; Pierre Ryckmans, *The Chinese Attitude towards the Past* (Canberra, 1986), 2–4, 7–11.
38. F. W. Mote, "A millennium of Chinese urban history: Form, time, and space concepts in Soochow," *Rice University Studies*, 59:4 (1973), 49–53.
39. Michael Ann Williams, "The realm of the tangible," in Burt Feintuch, ed., *The Conservation of Culture* (Lexington, KY, 1988), 199–200.
40. U.S. National Trust vice president Peter Brink, in *Historic Preservation News*, Dec. 1992, 27; Antoinette J. Lee, "Discovering old cultures in the New World," in Stipe and Lee, *American Mosaic*, 179–205; idem, "Cultural diversity in historic preservation," *Historic Preservation Forum*, 6:4 (1992), 28–41.
41. Jan Morris, "Barchester lives on," in Ronald Blythe, *Places: An Anthology of Britain* (London, 1981), 146–55, ref. p. 146.
42. R. Poujade (1980) quoted in Guillaume, *Politique du patrimoine*, 167–70; Emory Campbell (1984) quoted in Dale Rosengarten, " 'Sweetgrass is gold': Natural resources, conservation policy, and African-American basketry," in Mary Hufford, ed., *Conserving Culture: A New Discourse on Heritage* (Urbana, IL, 1994), 152–63, ref. p. 153.
43. Archaeologist Walter Alva quoted in Sidney D. Kirkpatrick, *Lords of Sipán* (New York, 1992), 139–42; Mary Dempsey, "Protectors of Peru's shining past," *New Scientist*, 20 Aug. 1994, 23–5; "Stones of their ancestors," *Newsweek*, 11 Sept. 1989, 57.
44. Ki Hadjar Dewantara [Suwardi Surjaningrat] (1929) quoted in Denys Lombard, "Indonesia: Pulling together the strands of time," *UNESCO Courier*, April 1990, 26–8; Fernanda Eberstadt, "The palace and the city," *New Yorker*, 23 Dec. 1991, 41–84, ref. p. 72.
45. Giuliana Luna (1976) quoted in John Henry Merryman, "A licit international trade in cultural objects," *IJCP*, 4 (1995), 36; Diura Thoden van Velzen, "The world of Tuscan tomb robbers," *IJCP*, 5 (1996), 111–26.
46. Roger D. Abrahams quoted in Jack Rosenthal, "Yogi-isms and pop philosophy," *IHT*, 8 Sept. 1991, p. 14; V. S. Naipaul, *A Bend in the River* (London, 1979), 152–3.
47. Jamaica Kincaid, *A Small Place* (New York, 1988), 31, 36–7; Orvar Löfgren, "Materializing the nation in Sweden and America," *Ethnos*, 58 (1993), 164–5; Jacques Darras, "Should we go on growing roses in Picardy? The future for our cultural heritages in Europe," *JRSA*, 138 (1990), 526.
48. Neil MacGregor, "Scholarship and the public," *JRSA*, 139 (1991), 191–4.
49. Yigael Yadin (1963) quoted in Amos Elon, *The Israelis: Founders and Sons* (New York, 1971), 288 (my emphasis); Michel-Rolph Trouillot, *Silencing the Past: Power and the Production of History* (Boston, 1995), 142.
50. *New York Times* (1910) quoted in Neil Harris, "Collective possession: J. Pierpont Morgan and the American imagination," in his *Cultural Excursions* (Chicago, 1990); other material from my *The Past Is a Foreign Country* (Cambridge, 1985), 394.
51. Edward Gibbon, *The Decline and Fall of the Roman Empire* [1781–88], ch. 62, 7 vols.

(London, 1896–1900), 6:486; Lord Durham (1839) quoted in Richard Handler, "On having a culture: Nationalism and the preservation of Quebec's *patrimoine*," in George W. Stocking, Jr., ed., *Objects and Others* (Madison, WI, 1985), 211.

52. James Lees-Milne, *Another Self* (London, 1970), 93–5; idem, *People and Places*, 1.

53. Henry James, *The Outcry* [1911] (New York, 1982), 43–5.

54. David Ely, *Time Out* (London, 1968), 90–1, 101.

55. Vitaly Komar quoted in Lawrence Weschsler, "Slight modifications," *New Yorker*, 12 July 1993, 59–65.

56. Donald Hall, "Scenic View" [1983], in his *The Happy Man: Poems* (London, 1986), 8.

57. Robert Townson (1799) quoted in Christopher Chippindale, *Stonehenge Complete* (London, 1994), 91.

58. English Heritage chairman Jocelyn Stevens quoted in Alexander Frater, "The lasting lure of the stones," *Observer on Sunday*, 20 June 1993, 49–50.

59. Christopher Chippindale et al., *Who Owns Stonehenge?* (London, 1990); English Heritage *Conservation Bull.*, Nov. 1994; Christopher Chippindale, "Putting the 'H' in Stonehenge," *History Today*, 43 (April 1993), 6–7; Barbara Bender, "Stonehenge—contested landscape," in her (ed.) *Landscape: Politics and Perspectives* (Providence, RI, 1993), 245–79.

60. D. J. Mulvaney, "A question of values: Museums and cultural property," in McBryde, *Who Owns the Past?* 87–8; idem, "Past regained, future lost: The Kow Swamp Pleistocene burials," *Antiquity*, 65 (1991), 12–21.

61. Australian Aborigine quoted in Griffiths, *Hunters and Collectors*, 226; Carolyn Gilman to the author, 29 June 1995, recalling a 1989 symposium.

Chapter 2

1. Walter Annenberg quoted in *IHT*, 13 March 1991, 2; Henry James, *The Outcry* [1911] (New York, 1982), 72; Carol MacCormack, "Nature, culture and gender," in MacCormack and Marilyn Strathern, eds., *Nature, Culture and Gender* (Cambridge, 1980), 1–24, ref. p. 16.

2. Hugo Williams, "Freelance," *TLS*, 11 Feb. 1994, 14.

3. Ivy Compton-Burnett, *A Heritage and Its History* (London, 1959); Jean Besson, "Family land and Caribbean society," in Elizabeth M. Thomas-Hope, ed., *Perspectives on Caribbean Regional Identity* (Liverpool, 1983), 67; Jean Besson and Janet Momsen, eds., *Land and Development in the Caribbean* (London, 1987); Cicely Howell, "Peasant inheritance customs in the Midlands, 1280–1700," in Jack Goody et al., eds., *Family and Inheritance* (Cambridge, 1976), 113.

4. Margaret R. Somers, "The 'misteries' of property," in John Brewer and Susan Staves, eds., *Early Modern Conceptions of Property* (London, 1995), 78, 83.

5. Alisdair MacIntyre, *After Virtue* (Notre Dame, IN, 1984), 221; Mamie Garvin Fields with Karen Fields, *Lemon Swamp and Other Places* (New York, 1983), xv.

6. Seamus Heaney, "Past, pastness, poems," *Salmagundi*, 68–69 (1985-86), 32; Norwegian quoted in Bjarne Rogan, "Things with a history—and other possessions," in *The Global and the Local: Consumption and European Identity* (Amsterdam, 1993), 103, 109.

7. Robert Starer, "Continuo," *New Yorker*, 6 Jan. 1986, 23–7.

8. Gordon S. Wood, *The Radicalism of the American Revolution* (New York, 1992), 149; Cynthia Jordan, "'Old words' in 'new circumstances': Language and leadership in post-revolutionary America," *AQ*, 40 (1988), 509–10; James W. Loewen, *Lies My Teacher Told Me* (New York, 1995), 87.

9. Eruera Stirling (1980) quoted in Anne Salmond, "Self and other in contemporary anthropology," in Richard Fardon, ed., *Counterworks: Managing the Diversity of Knowledge* (London, 1995), 43–4.

10. Khalid Abdul Muhammed, speech at Kean College, Union, NJ, 29 Nov. 1993; William Piersen, *Black Legacy: America's Hidden Heritage* (Amherst, MA, 1993), 74–5.

11. Donna Morganstern, unpublished survey of General Society of Mayflower Descendants and Spouses, September 1990.

12. Quotes from Betty Jean Lifton, *Journey of the Adopted Self* (New York, 1994), 120, 220; David M. Brodzinsky et al., *Being Adopted: The Lifelong Search for Self* (New York, 1992), 99, 131–4, 145; Katrina Maxtone-Graham, *An Adopted Woman* (New York, 1983), 10; Lucinda Franks, "The war for Baby Clausen," *New Yorker*, 22 March 1993, 56–73, ref. p. 59.

13. Eric L. Santner, *Stranded Objects: Mourning, Memory, and Film in Postwar Germany* (Ithaca, NY, 1990), 39–40; Daniel Bar-On, *The Dark Side of the Mind: Encounters with Children of the Third Reich* (Cambridge, MA, 1989), 328–30; adoptees' search tales in *Independent on Sunday* (London), 26 Sept. 1993, 23, and *Observer* (London), 25 Oct. 1992, 56.

14. Randolph W. Severson quoted in Lifton, *Journey of the Adopted Self*, 190.

15. Wendy W. Fairey, *One of the Family* (New York, 1993), 230–3, 260, 287; Germaine Greer, *Daddy, We Hardly Knew You* (New York, 1990).

16. Peter Marris, *Loss and Change* (London, 1974), ch. 2; Graeme Davison, "The broken lineage of Australian family history," in Donna Merwick, ed., *Essays in Honour of Greg Dening* (Melbourne, 1994), 336.

17. Gillian E. M. Bridge, "Report on a Visit to Jamaica: Children with Disabilities" (London School of Economics, June 1992).

18. Sally Morgan, *My Place* (Fremantle, Australia, 1987); Patsy Cohen and Margaret Somerville, *Ingelba and the Five Black Matriarchs* (Sydney, 1990), 1–8.

19. Thomas A. Bass, "The gene detective," *Observer Mag.*, 17 Oct. 1993, 31–4; Estela Barnes de Carlotto and Dr. Juan Carlos Volnovich quoted in Nathaniel C. Smith, "Children of the 'Disappeared' emerge from darkness," *IHT*, 12 May 1993, 2.

20. John Kotre, *Outliving the Self* (Baltimore, 1984).

21. Elizabeth Bartholet, *Family Bonds: Adoption and the Politics of Parenting* (Boston, 1993), xviii, 198–9.

22. Matthew Parris, *Times*, 7 Dec. 1992, 14.

23. Lifton, *Journey of the Adopted Self*, 204–5; David M. Schneider, *A Critique of the Study of Kinship* (Ann Arbor, MI, 1984).

24. Lifton, *Journey*, 128, 44 (quoting Jerome Bruner).

25. William Fleetwood quoted in Susan Staves, "Resentment or resignation? Dividing the spoils among daughters and younger sons," in Brewer and Staves, *Early Modern Conceptions of Property*, 194–218, ref. p. 204.

26. Thomas Jefferson (1786) quoted in T. H. Breen, *Tobacco Culture* (Princeton, 1985), 141.

27. Grant McCracken, *Culture and Consumption* (Bloomington, IN, 1988), 46–53.

28. Alan Coren, "The last word on last wills," *Sunday Times*, 8 April 1990, 50; Pierre-Jakez Hélias, *The Horse of Pride* (New Haven, 1978), 140, 152.

29. Charles Dickens, *Bleak House* [1852–3] (Norton, 1977), xvi, 196; Anny Sadrin, *Parentage and Inheritance in the Novels of Charles Dickens* (Cambridge, 1994), 137; Paul Thompson, "Believe it or not," in Jaclyn Jeffrey and Glenace Edwall, eds., *Memory and History* (Lanham, MD, 1994), 12; Tom Griffiths, *Hunters and Collectors* (Melbourne, 1996), 115–16, 187.

30. Charles Dickens, *Martin Chuzzlewit* [1843–4] (Oxford, 1982), viii, 121; Sadrin, *Parentage and Inheritance*, 14.

31. Carole Shammas et al., eds., *Inheritance in America from Colonial Times to the Present* (New Brunswick, NJ, 1987), 149; Harold James, *A German Identity 1770–1990* (London, 1989), 50; Libby Purves, "When we are all heirs to a fortune," *Times*, 17 Mar. 1992.

32. Michel de Montaigne, "On the affection of fathers for their children," *Complete Essays* [c. 1580–88] (London, 1991), 446; David R. Unruh, "Death and personal history: Strategies of identity preservation," *Social Problems*, 30 (1983), 340–51; Alan Radley, "Artefacts, memory and a sense of the past," in David Middleton and Derek Edwards, eds., *Collective Remembering* (London, 1990), 46–59.

33. Christopher Milne, *The Enchanted Places* (London, 1974), 165, 58; A. O. J. Cockshut, *The Art of Autobiography in 19th and 20th Century England* (New Haven, 1984), 73–6.

34. Gunnhild O. Hagestad, "Dimensions of time and the family," *American Behavioral Scientist*, 29 (1986), 679–94; Salman Rushdie, "The Courter," in his *East, West* (London, 1994), 202; Dan Jacobson, *Time and Time Again* (London, 1985), 209.

35. Mervyn Jones, "Learning to be a father," in Sean French, ed., *Fatherhood* (London, 1992), 26; Stephen Owen, *Mi-Lou: Poetry and the Labyrinth of Desire* (Cambridge, MA, 1989), 114.

36. Gillian Beer, *Arguing with the Past* (London, 1989), 140; T. S. Eliot, "Tradition and the individual talent" [1917], in his *Selected Essays* (London, 1934), 16; Olaf Stapledon, *Last and First Men* (London, 1937), 320.

37. Rogan, "Things with a history," 105; James Clifford, "Objects and selves—an afterword," in George W. Stocking, Jr., ed., *Objects and Others* (Madison, WI, 1985), 236–46.

38. John Boswell, *The Kindness of Strangers: The Abandonment of Children* (London, 1988), 27–8, 58–9, 430.

39. Arthur Riss, "Racial essentialism and family values in *Uncle Tom's Cabin*," *AQ*, 46 (1994), 531–3; *Historical Memoirs of the Duc de Saint-Simon*, trans. Lucy Norton, 3 vols. (London, 1974), I:ch. 2, III:107, 115–17; Liah Greenfeld, *Nationalism: Five Roads to Modernity* (Cambridge, MA, 1992), 137–8.

40. Boswell, *Kindness of Strangers*, 303.

41. Charles Dickens, *Dombey and Son* [1846–8] (London, 1982), 2, 77; Sadrin, *Parentage and Inheritance*, 45; John Fuller, *Look Twice* (London, 1992), 164; Pierre Nora, "La génération," in his *LM*, III.1:950–1.

42. Susan Ertz, *The Proselyte* (1933), and Herbert Quick, *Vandermark's Folly* (1922), quoted in Nicholas J. Karolides, *The Pioneer in the American Novel 1900–1950* (Norman, OK, 1967), 205, 77; Leo Cullum cartoon, *New Yorker*, 14 Aug. 1995, 34.

43. Montaigne, "On the affections of fathers," 435; Susanna Centlivres, *A Bold Stroke for a Wife* (1718) quoted in Staves, "Resentment or resignation?" 205.
44. *Symposium*, 208b–209c, trans. Michael Joyce, *Collected Dialogues of Plato* (London, 1991), 560–1; Montaigne, "On the affection of fathers," 449–51.
45. Petrarch quoted in Samuel K. Cohn, Jr., *The Cult of Remembrance and the Black Death* (Baltimore, 1992), 19.
46. Jack Goody, *The Development of the Family and Marriage in Europe* (Cambridge, 1983), 81–107, 121–7, 212.
47. G. C. Brodrick (1881) quoted in V. G. Kiernan, "Private property in history," in Goody et al., *Family and Inheritance*, 377; see also J. P. Cooper, "Patterns of inheritance and settlement by great landowners," in Goody et al., *Family and Inheritance*, 196.
48. Cohn, *Cult of Remembrance*, 178–83.
49. Montaigne, "On the affection of fathers," 446; Alex Shoumatoff, *The Mountain of Names* (New York, 1990), 282–3.
50. Amanda Filipacchi, *Nude Men* (London, 1993), 333–8; Helen Fraser, "The Time Capsule," AASLH Technical Leaflet No. 182 (1992); Brian Durrans, "Posterity and paradox: Some uses of time capsules," in Sandra Wallman, ed., *Contemporary Futures* (London, 1992), 51–67; Selby Whittingham, "Breach of trust over gifts of collections," *IJCP*, 4 (1995), 255–309.
51. Johann G. von Herder [1790s] quoted in Robert R. Ergang, *Herder and the Foundations of German Nationalism* [1931] (New York, 1966), 122; William James, *The Principles of Psychology* [1890], 2 vols. (Cambridge, MA, 1981), 1:279–81.
52. David Sugarman and Ronnie Warrington, "Land law, citizenship, and the invention of 'Englishness': The strange world of the equity of redemption," in Brewer and Staves, *Early Modern Conceptions of Property*, 111–43, ref. p. 130; Eileen Spring, *Law, Land, & Family* (Chapel Hill, NC, 1993), 9–65 (Samuel Johnson quoted pp. 18–19).
53. Carol Blum, "Of women and the law: Legitimizing husbandry," in Brewer and Staves, *Early Modern Conceptions of Property*, 162–6.
54. Henrietta L. Moore, *Feminism and Anthropology* (Cambridge, 1988), 29; Bronislaw Malinowski, *The Father in Primitive Society* (London, 1927); Johs Pedersen, *Israel: Its Life and Culture* (London, 1926), 257–9; André Burguière, "La généalogie," in Nora, *LM*, III.3:18–51; Jenny M. Jochens, "The politics of reproduction," *AHR*, 92 (1987), 327–49; Nancy Jay, *Throughout Your Generations Forever: Sacrifice, Religion, and Paternity* (Chicago, 1992); Ludmilla Jordanova, "Gender, generation and science," in W. F. Bynum and Roy Porter, eds., *William Hunter and the 18th-Century Medical World* (Cambridge, 1985), 405–6.
55. Sean French, "Introduction," in his *Fatherhood*, 3–4; Sigmund Freud, *Moses and Monotheism* [1939], and "Family romances" [1909], *Collected Works*, 23:114, 9:235–41; 1990 U.S. census ruling quoted in Lawrence Wright, "One drop of blood," *New Yorker*, 25 July 1994, 46–55, ref. p. 47.
56. Schneider, *Critique of the Study of Kinship*, 168–9; doctor quoted in Brodzinski et al., *Being Adopted*, 152; Woolf to Vanessa Bell, 2 June 1926, in *The Letters of Virginia Woolf*, III (London, 1977), 270; Elizabeth Tonkin, *Narrating Our Pasts* (Cambridge, 1992), 118; MacCormack, "Nature, culture and gender," 16; Sherry B. Ortner, "Is female to male as nature is to culture?" in Michelle Z. Rosaldo and Louise

Lamphere, eds., *Woman, Culture, and Society* (Stanford, CA, 1977), 67–88; Barbara Babcock, "Taking liberties, writing from the margins and doing it with a difference," *Journal of American Folklore*, 100 (1987), 394.

57. Billie Melman, "Gender, history and memory," *H & M*, 5:1 (1993), 5–41; Bonnie G. Smith, "Gender and the practices of scientific history: The seminar and archival research in the nineteenth century,'" *AHR*, 100 (1995), 1150–76, ref. pp. 1162–4; Natalie Zemon Davis (1983) quoted in Peter Novick, *That Noble Dream: The "Objectivity Question" and the American Historical Profession* (Cambridge, 1988), 495.

58. Amanda Vickery, "Women and the world of goods: A Lancashire consumer and her possessions 1751–81," in John Brewer and Roy Porter, eds., *Consumption and the World of Goods* (London, 1993), 274–301, ref. pp. 293–4; Shammas et al., *Inheritance in America*, 12–21; Cohen and Somerville, *Ingelba and the Five Black Matriarchs*; Griffiths, *Hunters and Collectors*, 233–4, 179.

59. Patrick Geary, *Phantoms of Remembrance: Memory and Oblivion at the End of the First Millennium* (Princeton, 1995), 52, 63, 69–71; Enoch Powell (1981) quoted in R. C. Lewontin et al., *Not in Our Genes* (New York, 1984), 135; Shoumatoff, *Mountain of Names*, 31, 37; Babcock, "Taking liberties," 395.

60. Caroline Sparks quoted in "For women, no room in a dome," *IHT*, 21 Aug. 1995, p. 3.

61. Loewen, *Lies My Teacher Told Me*, 263.

62. McCracken, *Culture and Consumption*, 42–3, 50; Shammas et al., *Inheritance in America*, 211–12; Kiernan, "Private property," 397.

63. Morton Schatzman, "Cold comfort at death's door," *New Scientist*, 26 Sept. 1992, 36–9; but see Phil Bagnall, "Cold comfort for Christmas," *New Scientist*, 23 Dec. 1995, p. 74.

64. Sadrin, *Parentage and Inheritance*, 24–5, 148; Alfred, Lord Tennyson, *Ulysses* [1833], ll.33–4.

Chapter 3

1. David A. Hollinger, "How wide the circle of 'we'?" *AHR*, 98 (1993), 330.

2. Alexis de Tocqueville, *Democracy in America* [1835], trans. Henry Reeve, 2 vols. (New York, 1945), 2:104–6; Benjamin Franklin, 1789 codicil to will, quoted in Gordon S. Wood, *The Radicalism of the American Revolution* (New York, 1992), 182, also 342; Quentin Anderson, *The Imperial Self* (New York, 1971), 228–9; R. W. B. Lewis, *The American Adam* (Chicago, 1955), 5–7. See my "Past in the American landscape," in Lowenthal and Martyn J. Bowden, eds., *Geographies of the Mind* (New York, 1976), 91–3.

3. David Lowenthal, "The bicentennial landscape," *Geographical Review*, 67 (1977), 265.

4. Charles Dickens, *Bleak House* [1852–3] (Norton, 1977), xli, 511; Virginia Woolf, *Orlando* [1928] (New York, 1960), 69; Nathaniel Hawthorne, "About Warwick" [1862], in his *Works*, 14 vols. (Columbus, OH, 1962–80), 5:65–89.

5. Alfred Greenwood "Smiler" Hales quoted in John Eddy, "Australia," in Eddy and Deryck Schreuder, eds., *The Rise of Colonial Nationalism* (Sydney, 1988), 153; Jean-Marie Le Pen, *Les Français d'abord* (1984) quoted in Robert Gildea, *The Past in French History* (New Haven, 1994), 338. On bellicose ardor as a mark of British

allegiance, see Linda Colley, *Britons: Forging the Nation 1707–1837* (London, 1992), 9, 291–300.

6. Harold R. Isaacs, *Idols of the Tribe* (New York, 1973), 116; Alisdair MacIntyre, *After Virtue* (Notre Dame, IN, 1984), 220–1.

7. Michael Arlen, *Passage to Ararat* [1975] (Harmondsworth, England, 1982), 136.

8. Conrad Russell, in Juliet Gardiner, ed., *The History Debate* (London, 1990), 45.

9. Annette B. Weiner, *Women of Value, Men of Renown* (1976), cited in Marilyn Strathern, *After Nature: English Kinship in the Late Twentieth Century* (Cambridge, 1992), 59, 64–5.

10. Marc Guillaume, *La politique du patrimoine* (Paris, 1980), 97–8; Verlyn Klinkenborg, "Family stories," *New Yorker*, 17 Feb. 1992, 89–92.

11. E. B. Browning to G. Barrett, 2 Feb. 1852, quoted in Michael Millgate, *Testamentary Acts* (Oxford, 1992), 17; Edith Wharton, "The touchstone" [1900], in her *Madame de Treymes and Others* (London, 1984), 38.

12. Chicago journalist and Rev. George Hepworth (1865) in Barry Schwartz, "Mourning and the making of a sacred symbol: Durkheim and the Lincoln assassination," *Social Forces*, 70 (1991–92), 356, 352. See Merrill D. Peterson, *Lincoln in American Memory* (New York, 1994), 14–27.

13. Liah Greenfeld, *Nationalism* (Cambridge, MA, 1992), 170, 217; Jerzy Tomaszewski, "The national question in Poland," in Mikulas Teich and Roy Porter, eds., *The National Question in Europe in Historical Context* (Cambridge, 1993), 295–300; Keiichi Takeuchi, "Nationalism and geography in modern Japan," in David Hooson, ed., *Geography and National Identity* (Oxford, 1994), 104; Eugen Weber, *Peasants into Frenchmen* (London, 1979), 110; Maurice Agulhon, "Le centre et la périphérie," in Nora, *LM*, III.1:826–7; Carlo Levi, *Christ Stopped at Eboli* [1947] (London, 1982), 89–90. Colley, *Britons*, 272–3, cites similarly intense and persisting localism.

14. Paul Connerton, *How Societies Remember* (Cambridge, 1989), 87.

15. Patrick J. Geary, *Living with the Dead in the Middle Ages* (Ithaca, NY, 1994), 2.

16. Neil McKendrick et al., *The Birth of a Consumer Society* (London, 1982), 1–2; Grant McCracken, *Culture and Consumption* (Bloomington, IN, 1988), 50.

17. Honoré de Balzac, *Le Sarassine* (1830), quoted in Anny Sadrin, *Parentage and Inheritance in the Novels of Charles Dickens* (Cambridge, 1994), 126.

18. E. J. Hobsbawm, *Nations and Nationalism since 1780* (Cambridge, 1990); Thomas de Zengotita, "Speakers of being," in G. W. Stocking, Jr., ed., *Romantic Motives: Essays on Anthropological Sensibility* (Madison, WI, 1989), 88–89; Cecil Sharp on folksong (1907) cited in Dave Harker, *Fakesong* (Milton Keynes, England, 1985), 185; Kristian Kristiansen, "A social history of Danish archaeology (1805–1975)," in Glyn Daniel, ed., *Towards a History of Archaeology* (London, 1981), 20–44; James J. Sheehan, "From princely collections to public museums," in Michael S. Roth, ed., *Rediscovering History* (Stanford, CA, 1994), 169–82; Orvar Löfgren, "The nationalization of culture," *Ethnologia Europaea*, 19 (1989), 5–25.

19. J. B. Jackson, *The Necessity for Ruins* (Amherst, MA, 1980), 93–6; Eric Hobsbawm, "Mass-producing traditions: Europe, 1870–1914," in Hobsbawm and Terence Ranger, eds., *The Invention of Tradition* (Cambridge, 1983), 271–3; Daniel J. Sherman, "Art, commerce, and the production of memory in France after World War I," in John R. Gillis, ed., *Commemorations* (Princeton, 1994), 186–211; K. S. Inglis, "Entombing unknown soldiers," *H & M*, 5:2 (1993), 7–31.

20. Krzysztof Pomian, "Les archives: du Trésor des chartes au Caran," in Nora, *LM*, III.3:181–91; Henri Grégoire (1974) quoted in Guillaume, *Politique du patrimoine*, 119–21, 126–8.

21. John Stuart Mill, *Representative Government* [1861], in his *Utilitarianism, Liberty and Representative Government* (London, 1972), 175–393, ref. 363–4; Gérard de Puymège, "Chauvin and chauvinism," *H & M*, 6:1 (1994), 35–72.

22. Weber, *Peasants into Frenchmen*, 333–7; Pierre Nora, "Lavisse, instituteur national" and "L'*Histoire de France* de Lavisse," in his *LM*, I:247–89, II.1:317–75 (I use the Lavisse translation in Jacques Le Goff, *History and Memory* [New York, 1992], 152).

23. Colley, *Britons*, 284–7, 368–71; Bernard Cracroft (1867) quoted in Jeanne C. Fawtier Stone and Lawrence Stone, *An Open Elite? England 1540–1880* (Oxford, 1984), 422.

24. Colley, *Britons*, 177 (her emphasis); Henry James, *The Outcry* [1911] (New York, 1982), 83, 171, 21.

25. Simon Jenkins, *The Selling of Mary Davies* (London, 1993), 99–103 (*Times*, 24 Oct. 1992); Paula Weidiger, *Gilding the Acorn: Behind the Façade of the National Trust* (London, 1994), 100; Adam Nicolson, "When an Englishman's home is the nation's castle," *Times Mag.*, 22 Oct. 1994, 16–23.

26. Peter Levi, "Knowing a place," in Richard Mabey, ed., *Second Nature* (London, 1984), 41.

27. Shirley Hazzard, *The Transit of Venus* (London, 1981), 189; Grey Gowrie quoted in Andrew Billen, "The whole world in his hands," *Observer Rev.*, 29 Jan. 1989, 16–21.

28. Ralph Waldo Emerson, "English traits" [1856], *The Portable Emerson* (New York, 1946), 454; John Martin Robinson, "The ruin of historic English collections," *Connoisseur*, 200 (March 1979), 162–9.

29. John Ruskin, *The Seven Lamps of Architecture* [1849] (New York, 1961), "The Lamp of Memory," XX, 186.

30. Henri Krop, "The antiquity of the Dutch language," *Geschiedenis van de Wijsbegeerte in Nederland*, 5 (1994), 1–8; Marie Tanner, *The Last Descendant of Aeneas* (New Haven, 1993), 72; Greenfeld, *Nationalism*, 69–70, 98, 244–5, 376.

31. Marc Fumaroli, "La génie de la langue française" and "La conversation," in Nora, *LM*, III.3:911–93, III.2:679–743; Jean-Claude Chevalier, "L'*Histoire de la langue française* de Ferdinand Brunot," in Nora, *LM*, III.2:436, 449–50; Antoine Compagnon, "La *Recherche du temps perdu*, de Marcel Proust," in Nora, *LM*, III.2:959.

32. Peter Bichsel, *La Suisse du Suisse* (Lausanne, 1970), 9–19, 26–35. See André Retzler, *Mythes et identité de la Suisse* (Geneva, 1986); Catherine Santschi, *La mémoire des Suisses: Histoire des fêtes nationales du XIIIe au XXe siècle* (Geneva, 1991); and Bernard Crettaz, Hans Ulrich Jost, and Rémy Pithon, *Peuples inanimés, avez-vous donc une âme?: Images et identités suisses au XXe siècle*, Université de Lausanne, *Etudes et mémoires de la section d'histoire*, 6 (1987).

33. André Vauchez, "Le cathédrale," Pascal Ory, "La gastronomie," Georges Durand, "La vigne et le vin," in Nora, *LM*, III.2, 91–127, 822–53 (Brillat-Savarin p. 824), 784–821.

34. John Andrews, *A Comparative View of the French and English Nations, in Their Manners, Politics, and Literature* (London, 1785), 442–3.

35. George Orwell, *The Lion and the Unicorn* [1941], in his *Collected Essays, Journalism*

and Letters (London, 1968), 2:57; other quotes in my "British national identity and the English landscape," *Rural History*, 2 (1991), 211–12.

36. Gildea, *Past in French History*, 112–15; Roy Rosenzweig, "Marketing the past," in Susan Porter Benson et al., eds., *Presenting the Past* (Philadelphia, 1986), 45.
37. Tomás Hofer, ed., *Hungarians between "East" and "West": Three Essays on National Myths and Symbols* (Budapest, 1994).
38. Israel Gershoni, "Imagining and reimagining the past: The use of history by Egyptian nationalist writers, 1919–1952," *H & M*, 4:2 (1992), 5–37 (Tawfiq al-Mar'ashli [1929] and Muhammad Husayn Haykal [1937] quoted pp. 18, 28). See Jack A. Crabbs, Jr., *The Writing of History in Nineteenth-Century Egypt* (Cairo, 1984).
39. Paul Déroulède (1881) quoted in Le Goff, *History and Memory*, 87; Ernest Renan, "What is a nation?" (1882), in Homi K. Bhabha, ed., *Nation and Narration* (London, 1990), 19; Ronald Koven, "National memory: The duty to remember, the need to forget," *Society*, 32:6 (1995), 52–8.
40. Charles de Gaulle (1945) quoted in Gildea, *Past in French History*, 130.
41. Scot McKendrick, "'La vraye histoire de Troye la grant,'" in Mark Jones, ed., *Why Fakes Matter* (London, 1992), 71–80; René Simard quoted in Mordecai Richler, "Inside/Outside," *New Yorker*, 23 Sept. 1991, 65; Arlen, *Passage to Ararat*, 24, 126.
42. Svetlana Slapsak, "The savage words that kill came from genteel Balkan desks," *IHT*, 27 May 1993; Yiannis Papadakis, "The national struggle museums of Nicosia," *Ethnic and Racial Studies*, 17 (1994), 400–19; Yitzhak Laor, "Unfaithful to Wagner," *NYRB*, 22 April 1993, 41–2.
42. Andalusian quoted in Hans Magnus Enzensberger, *Europe, Europe* (London, 1990), 255.
44. Ladis K. D. Kristof, "The image and the vision of the Fatherland: The case of Poland," in Hooson, *Geography and National Identity*, 221–32; Norman Davies, "Poland's dreams of past glories," *History Today*, 32 (Nov. 1982), 23–30; Enzensberger, *Europe, Europe*, 190, 228.
45. A. M. Sullivan quoted in Roy Foster, *The Story of Ireland*, inaugural lecture (Oxford, 1994), 11; Herbert Butterfield, *The Englishman and His History* (Cambridge, 1944), 114; Declan Kiberd, "The war against the past," in Audrey S. Eyler and Robert E. Garratt, eds., *The Uses of the Past: Essays in Irish Culture* (Newark, DE, 1988), 24–54.
46. Anthony Grafton, *Forgers and Critics* (Princeton, 1990), 41.
47. Richard Wright, *White Man, Listen!* [1957] (Westport, CT, 1978), 118; François Fontan (1970) quoted in Gildea, *Past in French History*, 213.
48. Portuguese historian quoted in Enzensberger, *Europe, Europe*, 159–60; Antonio Álvarez Perez, *Enciclopedía primer grado* (1965), quoted in Marc Ferro, *The Use and Abuse of History or How the Past Is Taught* (New York, 1984), 96; James W. Loewen, *Lies My Teacher Told Me* (New York, 1995), 138.
49. David Lowenthal, "Social features," in Colin Clarke and Tony Payne, eds., *Politics, Security and Development in Small States* (London, 1987), 26–49, quotes pp. 27–8.
50. Christopher Harvie, *The Rise of a Regional Europe* (London, 1994).
51. Maryon McDonald, *"We are not French!": Language, Culture and Identity in Brittany* (London, 1989), 32, 45–6, 88, 110–11; Gildea, *Past in French History*, 190, 199–208.
52. Agulhon, "Le centre et le périphérie," III.1:824–49; Thierry Gasnier, "Le local,"

III.2: 477, 492; Nora, "L'ère de la commémoration," III.3:977, 995–6; all in Nora, *LM*; Alain Bourdin, *La patrimoine reinventé* (Paris, 1984), 168–9, 221–3.

53. Raphael Samuel, *Theatres of Memory* (London, 1995), 158, 237–8.
54. Joan D. Laxson, "How 'we' see 'them': Tourism and Native Americans," *Annals of Tourism Research*, 18 (1991), 374–5.
55. David E. Whisnant, "Public sector folklore as intervention," in Bert Feintuch, ed., *The Conservation of Culture* (Lexington, KY, 1988), 236; Gary Gerstle, "The limits of American universalism," *AQ*, 45 (1993), 230–6; Graeme Davison, "Cities and ceremonies: Nationalism and civic ritual in three new lands," *New Zealand Journal of History*, 24 (1990), 116.
56. Micaela di Leonardo, "Habits of the cumbered heart: Ethnic community and women's culture as American invented traditions," in Jay O'Brien and William Rosebery, eds., *Golden Ages, Dark Ages* (Berkeley, 1992), 238–43; Thomas J. Ferraro, "Blood in the marketplace: The business of family in the *Godfather* narratives," in Werner Sollors, ed., *The Invention of Ethnicity* (New York, 1989), 176–208; Philadelphian quoted in Mary C. Waters, *Ethnic Options* (Berkeley, 1990), 152. See *AQ*, issue on "Multiculturalism," 45:2 (June 1993), 195–308.
57. Leah Dilworth, "Object lessons," *AQ*, 45 (1993), 275; McDonald, *"We Are Not French!"* 143.
58. Anya Peterson Royce, *Ethnic Identity* (Bloomington, IN, 1982), 191–220; Rosemary McKechnie, "Becoming Celtic in Corsica," in Sharon Macdonald, ed., *Inside European Identities* (Providence, RI, 1993), 125.
59. On Thanksgiving, Kay Sunstein Hymowitz, "Babar the racist," *New Republic*, 19/26 Aug. 1991, 12–14; on Wounded Knee, Eddie Nickens, "Somewhere in the Black Hills," *Historic Preservation* (Nov.–Dec. 1994), 16–20, 84; on Canada, Christina Cameron, "Commemoration: A moving target?" Place of History symposium, Hull, Canada, Nov. 1994, citing research by Claudette Lacelle.
60. Robin W. Winks, "The nature of the terrain," *National Parks*, 65:5–6 (1991), 32–4.
61. Paul Keating (1992) quoted in Paula Hamilton, "The knife edge: Debates about memory and history," in Kate Darian-Smith and Paula Hamilton, eds., *Memory and History in Twentieth-Century Australia* (Melbourne, 1994), 14; Laxson, "How 'we' see 'them,'" 380.
62. Signe Howell, "Whose knowledge and whose power? A new perspective on cultural diffusion," in Richard Fardon, ed., *Counterworks: Managing the Diversity of Knowledge* (London, 1995), 164–81; Pierre L. van den Berghe, *The Ethnic Phenomenon* (New York, 1981), 254–6.
63. Ken Yellis, "Mesa scenes: Notes from a journey to the 4th world," and Lydia Wyckoff, "Field work, pottery, and friends: Hopi pottery from the 3rd mesa," *Discovery*, 24:2 (1993), 4–8 and 9–13; Jeremy MacClancy, "At play with identity in the Basque arena," in Macdonald, *Inside European Identities*, 92.
64. Piers Vitebsky, "From cosmology to environmentalism: Shamanism as local knowledge in a global setting," in Fardon, *Counterworks*, 182–203.
65. Robin Riley Fast, "Outside looking in: Nonnatives and American Indian literature," *AQ*, 46 (1994), 62–76.
66. Richard Rodriguez, "An American writer," in Sollors, *Invention of Ethnicity*, 10.
67. Martin Peretz, "Identity, history, nostalgia," *New Republic*, 6 Feb. 1989, 43.
68. Edwin L. Wade, "The ethnic art market in the American Southwest, 1880–1980,"

in George W. Stocking, Jr., ed., *Objects and Others* (Madison, WI, 1985), 167–91; Deirdre Evans-Pritchard, "The Portal case: Authenticity, tourism, traditions, and the law," *Journal of American Folklore*, 100 (1987), 287–92; idem, *Tradition on Trial* (Ann Arbor, MI, 1991); David M. Brugge, "Cultural use and meaning of artifacts," *CRM Bulletin*, 10:1 (Feb. 1987), 9.

69. M. Estellie Smith, "The process of sociocultural continuity," *Current Anthropology*, 23 (1982), 127–35.

70. Shalom Staub, "Folklore and authenticity," in Feintuch, *Conservation of Culture*, 176.

71. *Cannibal Tours* quoted in Dean MacCannell, *Empty Meeting Grounds: The Tourist Papers* (London, 1992), 46; Deirdre Evans-Pritchard, "How 'they' see 'us': Native American images of tourists," *Annals of Tourism Research,* 16 (1989), 89–105; Jeremy R. Beckett, "The past in the present," 212, and Deirdre F. Jordan, "Aboriginal identity," 109–30, ref. p. 120, in Beckett, ed., *Past and Present: The Construction of Aboriginality* (Canberra, 1988); Tom Griffiths, *Hunters and Collectors* (Melbourne, 1996), 181–6.

72. See Paul Pasquaretta, "On the 'Indianness' of bingo-gambling and the Native American community," *Critical Inquiry*, 20 (1994), 694–714.

Chapter 4

1. Patrick Wright, *On Living in an Old Country* (London, 1985); Robert Hewison, *The Heritage Industry* (London, 1987); Richard H. Kohn, "The future of the historical profession," AHA *Perspectives*, 27:8 (Nov. 1989), 8–12; Charles S. Maier, "A surfeit of memory?" *H & M*, 5:2 (1994), 136–54; Gertrude Himmelfarb, *The New History and the Old* (Cambridge, MA, 1987); André Chastel, "La notion du patrimoine," in Nora, *LM*, II.2:434ff; Andreas Huyssen, "Monument and memory in a postmodern age," *Yale Journal of Criticism*, 6 (1993), 249–61.

2. Eric Hobsbawm, "The new threat to history," *NYRB*, 16 Dec. 1993, 62–4.

3. "Not a foreign country," *Economist*, 30 April 1994, 16; David Lowenthal, "Heritages for Europe," *IJCP*, 2 (1995), 377–81; J. H. Plumb, *The Death of the Past* [1969] (London, 1973), 36–7; David Lowenthal, *The Past Is a Foreign Country* (Cambridge, 1985), xxv; Baruch Kimmerling, "Academic history caught in the cross-fire: The case of Israeli-Jewish historiography," *H & M*, 7:1 (1995), 41–65; Michael Schudson, *Watergate and American Memory* (New York, 1992), 205; George Orwell, *Nineteen Eighty-Four* (London, 1954), 31.

4. People's Bicentennial Commission quoted in my "Bicentennial landscape," *Geographical Review*, 67 (1977), 266; Historical Terrorists of Tasmania quoted in my "Uses of the past in Australia," in Brian Hocking, ed., *Australia Towards 2000* (London 1990), 46–54, ref. p. 47; Kenneth L. Ames, "Background history and social responsibility," *Museum News*, Sept.–Oct. 1994, 33–5, 59.

5. Plumb, *Death of the Past*, 26n; Alan Peacock, "A future for the past: The political economy of heritage," 1994 Keynes Lecture, *Proceedings of the British Academy*, 87 (1996), 189–243; Graeme Davison, "The meanings of 'heritage,'" in Davison and Chris McConville, eds., *A Heritage Handbook* (North Sydney, 1991), 11.

6. Luke FitzHerbert, *Winners and Losers: The Impact of the National Lottery* (York, Joseph Rowntree Foundation, 1995).

7. Nigel Dennis, *Cards of Identity* [1955] (London, 1974), 119; Michael Billig, "Collective memory, ideology and the British royal family," in David Middleton and Derek Edwards, eds., *Collective Remembering* (London, 1990), 76; Raphael Samuel, *Patriotism.* I. *History and Politics* (London, 1989), xlix. "The World We Have Lost" refers to Peter Laslett's book so titled (London, 1965; 3d ed., 1983).

8. Peter Levi, "We built on absolute trust," *Spectator*, 24 Oct. 1992, 34–5; James Lees-Milne, *People and Places* (London, 1992), 199; Nigel Nicolson, "Open to the public," *Spectator*, 4 April 1992, 42–3.

9. The Ridley–Saye and Sele exchange is in my "British national identity and the English landscape," *Rural History*, 2 (1991), 220.

10. Raphael Samuel, *Theatres of Memory* (London, 1995), 160–3, 238–59, 262–6, 296–302.

11. Gunns Kilndried Timber Industries submission to Commission of Inquiry into the Lemonthyme and Southern Forests, Launceston 1987, quoted in Tom Griffiths, *Hunters and Collectors* (Melbourne, 1996), 275; Manuel Lujan quoted in Keith Schneider, "Bush environmental policy: Opening up the land," *IHT*, 21 May 1992, 3.

12. Patrick Wright, "Heritage clubs slug it out," *Guardian*, 4 Feb. 1995, 29; Samuel, *Theatres of Memory*, 292.

13. Lord Charteris of Amisfield, "The work of the National Heritage Memorial Fund," *JRSA*, 132 (1984), 326–7.

14. Kathleen Claar, curator of Last Indian Raid in Kansas Museum, quoted in Ian A. Frazier, "Authentic accounts of massacres," *New Yorker*, 19 March 1979, 61–76, ref. p. 69; Joseph Addison, *The Tatler*, no. 216 (26–28 Aug. 1710), 4 vols. (London, 1898–99), 4:110–13.

15. Martin Drury, "The restoration of Calke Abbey," *JRSA*, 136 (1988), 497.

16. Michael Herzfeld, *A Place in History* (Princeton, 1991), 34, 191–259; Mordecai Richler, *This Year in Jerusalem* (New York, 1994), 237–8; Mayor Bob Polipnick quoted in Thomas W. Sweeney, "Goodbye, Sinclair Lewis? Modernization threatens the original Main Street," *Historic Preservation News*, July-Aug. 1993, 14–15, 26.

17. Michael S. Roth, "Remembering and forgetting: *Maladies de la Mémoire* in nineteenth-century France," *Representations*, 26 (Spring 1989), 49–68.

18. John Patterson, "Conner Prairie refocuses its interpretive message to include controversial subjects," *History News*, 41:2 (March 1986), 12–15.

19. For most quotes see my "Nostalgia tells it like wasn't," in Christopher Shaw and Malcolm Chase, eds., *The Imagined Past* (Manchester, 1989), 18–32.

20. Jackie R. Donath, "The Gene Autry Western Heritage Museum," *AQ*, 42 (1991), 82–102.

21. Robert Hewison, "The heritage industry revisited," *Museums Journal*, 94:4 (1991), 23–6; idem, "Commerce and culture," in John Corner and Sylvia Harvey, eds., *Enterprise and Heritage* (London, 1991), 162–77; Stuart Cosgrove and Paul Reas, *Flogging a Dead Horse* (Manchester, 1993); John Martin Robinson, "Mind your Manors!" *Spectator*, 9 June 1990, 19–20.

22. Miles Kington, "Windfalls from the family tree," *Times*, 29 April 1985, 12.

23. Robert L. Kroon, "Court fight disputes legacy of Anne Frank," *IHT*, 15 Feb. 1996; Andy Croft, "Forward to the 1930s: The literary politics of anamnesis," in Shaw and Chase, *Imagined Past*, 161; David Mather quoted in "Wigan squares its account

with Orwell," *IHT*, 16 Sept. 1991, 14; Dan Matei quoted in "Hollywood Dracula pierces Romanian hearts," *Times*, 1 Feb. 1993, 8.

24. Hewison, "Commerce and culture," 175; Natalie Zemon Davis, "Who is the American Historical Association serving?" AHA *Perspectives*, 29:7 (Oct. 1987), 13–14.

25. Ada Louise Huxtable, "Inventing American reality," *NYRB*, 3 Dec. 1992; for Halley and Scott see my "Counterfeit art: Authentic fakes," *IJCP*, 1 (1992), 80–2.

26. Diane Ravitch, "History and the perils of pride," AHA *Perspectives*, 29:3 (March 1991), 12–14; idem, "Multiculturalism: an exchange," *American Scholar*, 60 (1991), 275.

27. Linda Shopes, "Some second thoughts on Disney's America," AHA *Perspectives*, 33:3 (March 1995), 7–8.

28. Davis, "Who is the American Historical Association serving?"; G. Donald Adams, "The changing museum audience," *History News*, 49:2 (Mar.–Apr. 1994), 30–1; Gertrude Himmelfarb, "Postmodernist history" (1992), in her *On Looking into the Abyss* (New York, 1994), 159; Hobsbawm, "New threat to history."

29. Julian Spalding, "Art galleries: church or funfair? Museums in a democracy," *JRSA*, 137 (1989), 581; Michael Kammen, *Mystic Chords of Memory* (New York, 1991), 667.

Chapter 5

1. Pendleton Herring (1948) cited in Peter Novick, *That Noble Dream: The "Objectivity Question" and the American Historical Profession* (Cambridge, 1988), p. 317.

2. Carl Becker, "Everyman his own historian" (1932), in Robin W. Winks, ed., *The Historian as Detective* (New York, 1969), 14–15.

3. Neal Ascherson, *Games with Shadows* (London, 1988), 12.

4. Lucian of Samosata [c. A.D. 170], "The way to write history," 132, and "The true history," 166, in his *Works* (Oxford, 1905).

5. Reinhart Koselleck, *Futures Past: On the Semantics of Historical Time* (Cambridge, MA, 1985), 20; Raynal and Diderot quoted in Anthony Pagden, *European Encounters with the New World* (New Haven, 1993), 86; H. A. L. Fisher, "Fustel de Coulanges," *English Historical Review*, 5, (1890), 1–6, ref. p.: 1; Joyce Appleby et al., *Telling the Truth about History* (New York, 1994), 56, 89.

6. Joseph M. Levine, *The Battle of the Books: History and Literature in the Augustan Age* (Ithaca, NY, 1991), 269–70, 301–14; Ruth Morse, *Truth and Convention in the Middle Ages* (Cambridge, 1991), 91, 113, 238.

7. Janet Coleman, *Ancient and Medieval Memories* (Cambridge, 1992), 321–4; Jeanette Beer, *Narrative Conventions of Truth in the Middle Ages* (Geneva, 1981), 48–9.

8. Morse, *Truth and Convention in the Middle Ages*, 132; William Wirt Henry (1893) quoted in Michael Kammen, *Mystic Chords of Memory* (New York, 1991), 195; Dorothy Ross, "Grand narrative in historical writing," *AHR*, 100 (1995), 655.

9. Lord Acton (1896) quoted in Paul Dukes, "Fin de siècle: A watershed in world history," *History Today*, 42 (Nov. 1992), 45–50; Moses Coit Tyler (1895–6) quoted in Gordon S. Wood, "A century of writing early American history: Then and now compared," *AHR*, 100 (1995), 678–96, ref. p. 684; Novick, *That Noble Dream*, 71–2.

10. Hans-Georg Gadamer, *Truth and Method* [1965], 2nd ed. (London, 1989), 298–303.
11. Michael Hunter, in Juliet Gardiner, ed., *The History Debate* (London, 1990), 99; J. H. Hexter, "Historiography: The rhetoric of history," *International Encyclopedia of the Social Sciences* (New York, 1968), 6:390.
12. David Cannadine, "British history past, present—and future?" *Past and Present*, 116 (1987), 178–9; National Parks spokesman Frank Barnes (1957) quoted in John Bodnar, *Remaking America* (Princeton, 1992), 196.
13. Roy Porter, "Healthy history," *History Today*, 40 (Nov. 1990), 8–11 (reprinted in Gardiner, *History Debate*, 13).
14. Numa Denis Fustel de Coulanges [1864], *The Ancient City* (New York, [c. 1960]), 170–1; Marc Ferro, *The Use and Abuse of History or How the Past Is Taught* (New York, 1984); Eric Williams, *History of the People of Trinidad and Tobago* (Port-of-Spain, Trinidad, 1962), vii–viii.
15. S. M. Solov'ev (1868–76) quoted in Mark Bassin, "Turner, Solov'ev, and the 'Frontier Hypothesis'": The nationalist signification of open spaces," *Journal of Modern History*, 65 (1993), 473–511, ref. p. 481; Langlois and Seignobos (1898) cited in Eugen Weber, *Peasants into Frenchmen* (London, 1979), 110; Emile Coornaert, *Destins de Clio en France depuis 1800* (Paris, 1977), ch. 3; Nora, "L'ère de la commémoration," in his *LM*, III.3:1005–9; Nicholas Tate and John Fines (chairman, Historical Association) quoted in John O'Leary, "Curriculum head urges schools to restore heroes," *Times*, 18 Sept. 1995, p. 5.
16. Frances FitzGerald, *America Revised* (New York, 1980), 178; American Legion and others quoted in James W. Loewen, *Lies My Teacher Told Me* (New York, 1995), 265–6, 278–9; Cary Carson, "Lost in the fun house: A commentary on anthropologists' first contact with history museums," *Journal of American History*, 81 (1994), 144.
17. Cannadine, "British history past, present—and future"? 190.
18. Arthur M. Schlesinger, Jr., *The Disuniting of America* (New York, 1992), 137; Ronald Takaki, "Teaching American history through a different mirror," 1, 9–12, and Robert K. Fullinwider, "Tensions within multiculturalism's ideals," 14, in AHA *Perspectives*, 32:7 (Oct. 1994).
19. Peter Burke, "History and social memory," in Thomas Butler, ed., *Memory: History, Culture and Mind* (Oxford, 1989), 98.
20. John Updike, *Memories of the Ford Administration* (London, 1993), 191. On the unavoidable limits of history see my *The Past Is a Foreign Country* (Cambridge, 1985), 214–19.
21. G. M. Young, *Victorian England: Portrait of an Age* [1936] (New York, 1954), 6; James to Sarah Orne Jewett, 5 Oct. 1901, *Selected Letters of Henry James* (London, 1956), 234–5.
22. Michael Baxandall, *Patterns of Intention: On the Historical Explanation of Pictures* (New Haven, 1985), 109; Peter Dickinson, *Death of a Unicorn* (New York, 1984), 25.
23. Arthur C. Danto, "The problem of other periods," *Journal of Philosophy*, 63 (1966), 566–77.
24. Matthew Parris, *Times*, 8 March 1993, 14; Bernard Bailyn, *On the Teaching and Writing of History* (Hanover, NH, 1994), 51–3.
25. Virginia Woolf, "I am Christina Rossetti" [1930], in her *The Common Reader: Second Series* (London, 1932), 237–44, ref. p. 236; Jeanette Winterson, *Oranges Are Not the Only Fruit* (New York, 1985), 95.

26. Arthur M. Schlesinger, Jr., "The historian as participant," in Felix Gilbert and Stephen W. Graubard, eds., *Historical Studies Today* (New York, 1972), 393–412, ref. p. 404; Colin Gordon, "The cloak of power," *New Internationalist*, 247 (Sept. 1993), 20–2.

27. Michael Schudson, *Watergate in American Memory* (New York, 1992), 216.

28. Indianapolis Children's Museum director Peter Sterling quoted in George Gonis, "History in the making," *History News*, 40:7 (July 1985), 12–15; Samuel S. Wineburg, "Probing the depths of students' historical knowledge," AHA *Perspectives*, 30:3 (March 1992), 19–24; idem, "On the reading of historical texts," *American Educational Research Journal*, 28 (1991), 501, 510–14 Loewen, *Lies My Teacher Told Me*, 280–1.

29. Simone de Beauvoir, *Memoirs of a Dutiful Daughter* [1958], trans. James Kirkup (London, 1963), 127; students quoted in Denis J. Shemilt, "Adolescent ideas about evidence and methodology in history," in Christopher Portal, ed., *The History Curriculum for Teachers* (Lewes, Sussex, 1988), 41–43; student quoted in Judy P. Hohmann, "Discovering documents," *History News*, 48:5 Sept.-Oct. (1993), 13–16.

30. Loewen, *Lies My Teacher Told Me*, 92–3, 5 (1991 student); Eric Foner, "A conversation [with] John Sayles," in Mark C. Carnes, ed., *Past Imperfect: History According to the Movies* (New York, 1995), 25.

31. Sterling quoted in Gonis, "History in the making."

32. Winterson, *Oranges Are Not the Only Fruit*, 93.

33. Penelope Lively, *Treasures of Time* (London, 1979), 134.

34. Robert R. Archibald, "From the president," *AASLH Dispatch*, May 1995; Jo Tollebeek and Tom Verschaffel, "The particular character of history," *H & M*, 4:2 (1992), 88–9.

35. Diodorus Siculus quoted in Pagden, *European Encounters*, 77; Kirsten Hastrup, "Uchronia and the two histories of Iceland, 1400–1800," in her (ed.) *Other Histories* (London, 1992), 113.

36. Becker, "Everyman his own historian," 13.

37. Sam Schrager, "What is social in social history?" *International Journal of Oral History*, 4 (1983), 76–98, ref. p. 78.

38. Leon Pompa, *Human Nature and Historical Knowledge* (Cambridge, 1990), 197–205, 222.

39. Finnish scholars (c. 1917) quoted in William A. Wilson, *Folklore and Nationalism in Modern Finland* (Bloomington, IN, 1976), 76–9; Alon Confino, "The nation as a local metaphor," *H & M*, 5:1 (1993), 42–86; Celia Applegate, *A Nation of Provincials: The German Idea of Heimat* (Berkeley, 1990), 94–9. 180–1, 235–9.

40. William Graham Sumner, *Folkways* [1906] (Boston, 1940), 636; Richard Cobb, *French and Germans, Germans and French* (Hanover, NH, 1983), xv.

41. Loewen, *Lies My Teacher Told Me*, 289; Libby Purves, "Pride, not prejudice," *Times*, 19 Oct. 1995.

42. Françoise Zonabend, *The Enduring Memory: Time and History in a French Village* (Manchester, 1984).

43. Becker, "Everyman his own historian," 23; Amos Elon, "The politics of memory," *NYRB*, 7 Oct. 1993, 3–5; Bernard Levin, "Compounding the evil," *Times*, 25 June 1993, 16.

44. Peter Laslett, "The way we think we were" [review of Lowenthal, *The Past Is a*

Foreign Country], *Washington Post* Book World, 30 March 1986, 5, 11; Denis Shemilt, *History 13–16 Evaluation Study* (Edinburgh, 1980), 21.

45. Wilbur Zelinsky, *Nation into State* (Chapel Hill, NC, 1988), 82–93; James R. Lehning, "The historical memories of students," AHA *Perspectives*, 30:8 (Nov. 1992), 15–18; "Asking questions about the past," *Mosaic* [Center for History-Making, Bloomington, IN], 1:2–3 (1992), 2–7, 8–9.

46. Lois Silverman, "Center piece: Heeding Calvin," *Mosaic*, 2:1 (1992), 1; Michael Eisner *Washington Post* interview (1994) in Ronald G. Walters, "In our backyard," AHA *Perspectives*, 33:3 (March 1995), 1; Carl Schorske, *Fin-de-Siècle Vienna* (New York, 1981), xvii.

47. Jean Piaget, *The Child's Conception of Time* [1927] (New York, 1982); Denis J. Shemilt, "Beauty and the philosopher: Empathy in history and classroom," in A. K. Dickinson et al., *Learning History* (London, 1984), 39–84; Samuel S. Wineburg, "The psychology of learning and teaching history," in R. C. Calfee and D. C. Berliner, eds., *Handbook of Educational Psychology* (New York, 1996), 15–24; Annie Dillard, *An American Childhood*, (London, 1988), 74.

48. Nicholas Merriman, *Beyond the Glass Case: The Past, the Heritage, and the Public in Britain* (Leicester, England, 1991); Frank Kermode, *History and Value* (Oxford, 1988), 126–7; Renato Rosaldo, "From the door of his tent: The fieldworker and the inquisitor," in James Clifford and George E. Marcus, eds., *Writing Culture* (Berkeley, 1986), 84–5.

49. Harry Dunlop, "Objects or relics? The development of the St Mungo Museum of Religious Art and Craft," Interpreting Religious Sites symposium, Strawberry Hill, Twickenham, England, 5 Dec. 1992; Christopher Mulvey, *Anglo-American Landscapes* (Cambridge, 1983), 18.

50. John Davis, "The social relations of the production of history," in Elizabeth Tonkin et al., eds., *History and Ethnicity* (London, 1989), 104.

51. John Dewey (1916) quoted in FitzGerald, *America Revised*, 174; Kansas court in Bodnar, *Remaking America*, 184.

52. Geoffrey Elton (1970) cited in Wineburg, "Psychology of learning and teaching history," 19; Peter N. Stearns, "The challenge of 'historical literacy,'" AHA *Perspectives*, 29:4 (April 1991), 21–3; Loewen, *Lies My Teacher Told Me*, 276–7; Billy Collins, "History Teacher," in his *Questions about Angels* (New York, 1991).

53. David Glassberg, "History and the public: Legacies of the Progressive era," *Journal of American History*, 73 (1987), 980; Christopher Chippindale, "Putting the 'H' in Stonehenge," *History Today*, 43 (April 1993), 5–8.

Chapter 6

1. Allen P. Slickpoo, Sr., and Deward E. Walker, Jr., quoted in Gertrude Himmelfarb, "Where have all the footnotes gone?" (1991), in her *On Looking into the Abyss* (New York, 1994), 130; Darcy McNickle and Robert Lewis cited in Robert E. Bieder, "Anthropology and history of the American Indian," *AQ*, 33 (1982), 309–26; Iowa State Senator Norpel quoted in Charles Phillips, "The politics of history," *History News*, 40:9 (Sept. 1985), 16–20.

2. Hanay Geiogamah quoted in "Disney assailed for Pocahontas portrayal," *IHT*, 27–28 May 1995; *Teaching Manual for U.S. High Schools* quoted in Greg Dening,

"Mutiny on the Bounty," in Mark C. Carnes, ed., *Past Imperfect: History According to the Movies* (New York, 1995), 100.

3. On Drake and the Armada celebration, see my "The timeless past: Some Anglo-American historical preconceptions," *Journal of American History*, 75 (1989), 1274.

4. Diane L. Good, "Sacred bundles: history wrapped up in culture," *History News*, 45:4 (July–Aug. 1990), 13–14, 27; Howard Creamer, "Aboriginal perceptions of the past," in Peter Gathercole and David Lowenthal, eds., *The Politics of the Past* (London, 1990), 130–40; Johan van der Dennen, "Ethnocentrism and in-group/out-group differentiation," in Vernon Reynolds et al., eds., *The Sociobiology of Ethnocentrism* (Athens, GA, 1987), 1–47.

5. Sigmund Freud, "Constructions in analysis" [1937], *Complete Works* (London, 1964), 23:268–9; Peter Munz, *Our Knowledge of the Growth of Knowledge* (London, 1985), 282–302.

6. Alessandro Portelli, "The time of my life: Functions of time in oral history," *International Journal of Oral History*, 2 (1981), 162–80; idem, "Uchronic dreams: Working-class memory and possible worlds," in Raphael Samuel and Paul Thompson, eds., *The Myths We Live By* (London, 1990), 143–60; on Derry, Brian Lacey quoted in Simon Tait, "Not afraid to face up to the facts," *Times*, 25 Oct. 1995.

7. Plato, *The Republic*, trans. Desmond Lee (2nd ed., London, 1974), 414c–415d, pp. 181–2.

8. William Graham Sumner, "War" (1903), in his *War and Other Essays* (New Haven, 1919), 36; Donna Merwick, "Comment [on James Hijawa, 'Why the West is lost']," *William & Mary Quarterly*, 51 (1994), 736–9.

9. Ernest Renan, "What is a nation?" (1882), in Homi K. Bhabha, ed., *Nation and Narration* (London, 1990), 11; Herbert Butterfield, *The Englishman and His History* (Cambridge, 1944), 7–9.

10. Alexandre Daguet (1872) quoted in Geneviève Heller, *D'Un Pays et du Monde*, Association du Musée de l'Ecole et de l'Education, exhibition text (Yverdon-les-Bains, Switzerland, 1993), 38; Charles Heimberg, *Un étrange anniversaire: Le centenaire du premier août* (Geneva, 1990), 61–3; Werner Meyer, *1291: L'histoire: Les prémices de la Conféderation suisse* (Zurich, 1991); idem, *Nos ancêtres les Waldstaetten: La Suisse centrale au XIIIe siècle: Mythes et histoire*, Musée Historique de Lausanne exhibition, 1994, 48; Olivier Pavillon, "Du débat à l'anathème," *Revue Suisse d'Histoire*, 44 (1995), 311–14.

11. Brendan Bradshaw, "Nationalism and historical scholarship in modern Ireland," *Irish Historical Studies*, 26 (1989), 348–9; Colm Toibin, "New ways of killing your father," *London Review of Books*, 18 Nov. 1993, 3–6; Briege Duffaud, *A Wreath upon the Dead* (Swords, County Dublin, 1993), 445.

12. Quoted in Richard Clogg, "The Greeks and their past," in Dennis Deletant and Harry Hanak, eds., *Historians as Nation-Builders* (London, 1988), 28; see Anna Collard, "Investigating 'social memory' in a Greek context," in Elizabeth Tonkin et al., eds., *History and Ethnicity* (London, 1989), 89–97.

13. James W. Loewen, *Lies My Teacher Told Me* (New York, 1995), 123.

14. Henry Cabot Lodge (1915) quoted in Michael Kammen, *Mystic Chords of Memory* (New York, 1991), 484; Josephine Tey, *The Daughter of Time* (London, 1954), 95.

15. Morvan Lebesque (1970) quoted in Ellen Badone, "Folk literature and the invention of tradition: The case of the *Barzaz-Breiz*," *Comparative Studies in Society and*

History, forthcoming; Jean-Yves Guiomar, "Le *Barzaz-Breiz* de Théodore Hersart de La Villemarqué," in Nora, *LM*, III.2:554.

16. Joseph Roth, *The Radetsky March* [1932] (London, 1974), 7–10.

17. Loewen, *Lies My Teacher Told Me*, 23, 285; British curriculum adviser Nicholas Tate (*Times*, 18 Sept. 1995); French culture ministry spokesman André-Marc Delocque-Fourcaud quoted in Ronald Koven, "National memory: The duty to remember, the need to forget," *Society*, 32:6 (1995), 52–8, ref. p. 57; Joyce Appleby et al., *Telling the Truth about History* (New York, 1994), 307.

18. David Lowenthal and Colin G. Clarke, "Slave breeding in Barbuda," *Annals of the New York Academy of Sciences*, 272 (1977), 510–35. See my *West Indian Societies* (London, 1972), 76.

19. David Lowenthal and Colin Clarke, "Common lands, common aims: The distinctive Barbudan community," in Malcolm Cross and Arnaud Marks, eds., *Peasants, Plantations and Rural Communities in the Caribbean* (Guildford, England, 1979), 142–59, ref. pp. 147, 157; Mark Porter, "Diana relaxes on a former Negro stud farm," *Sunday Express* (London), 31 Dec. 1995, p. 7.

20. Gordon S. Wood, "Jefferson at home," *NYRB*, 13 May 1993, 6–9.

21. Martii Ruutu (1941) quoted in William A. Wilson, *Folklore and Nationalism in Modern Finland* (Bloomington, IN, 1976), 119; Stephen Maly, "The Celtic fringe," Institute of Current World Affairs newsletter SM-10, 30 April 1990.

22. Roger Just, "Cultural certainties and private doubts," in Wendy James, ed., *The Pursuit of Certainty* (London, 1995), 294; Kent C. Ryden, *Mapping the Invisible Landscape* (Iowa City, 1993), 6–7; Michael Billig, "Collective memory, ideology and the British royal family," in David Middleton and Derek Edwards, eds., *Collective Remembering* (London, 1990), 74.

23. Warren Leon, "Some thoughts on museums and the Constitution," *Museum News*, 65:6 (1987), 25–6; Wilbur Zelinsky, *Nation into State* (Chapel Hill, NC, 1988), 244; Michael Kammen, *A Machine That Would Go of Itself: The Constitution in American Culture* (New York, 1987); Hearst Corp. survey in *The Humanities and the Nation*, cited *NYRB*, 11 Aug. 1994, p. 41; Karl Marx, "Critique of the Gotha Programme" (1875), in his *Collected Works* (London, 1989), 24:75–99, ref. p. 87.

24. Edith Wharton, "The angel at the grave," in her *Roman Fever and Other Stories* (London, 1983), 116, 119.

25. Michael Millgate, *Testamentary Acts* (Oxford, 1992), 160; Giorgio Vasari, *Lives of the Artists* [1551], 2 vols. (London, 1965), 1:419; on Thurgood Marshall, Linda Greenhouse, *New York Times*, 27 May 1993, p. 1; Garrigues (1898) quoted in Marc Ferro, *The Use and Abuse of History* (New York, 1984), 18.

26. Shelton Waldrep, "Monuments to Walt," in The Project on Disney, *Inside the Mouse: Work and Play at Disney World* (Durham, NC, 1995), 204–5.

27. Christina Cameron, "Commemoration: A moving target?" Place of History symposium, Hull, Canada, Nov. 1994; Tamar Katriel, "Remaking place: Cultural production in an Israeli pioneer settlement museum," *H & M*, 5:2 (1993), 113; idem, "Sites of memory," *Quarterly Journal of Speech*, 80 (1994), 5–6.

28. Mona Ozouf, "Le passé recomposé," *Magazine littéraire*, no. 307 (Feb. 1993), 22–25; Jacques Revel, "La cour," in Nora, *LM*, III.1:128–93; Graham Hood (1978) quoted in Eric Gable et al., "On the uses of relativism: Fact, conjecture, and black and white histories at Colonial Williamsburg," *American Ethnologist*, 19 (1992), 799.

29. Allan Hanson, "The making of the Maori: Culture invention and its logic," *American Anthropologist*, 91 (1989), 890–902; on Fiji, Bernard S. Cohn, "Anthropology and history in the 1980s," *Journal of Interdisciplinary History*, 12 (1981), 237–9.

30. Ernest Beaglehole (1944) quoted in Robert Borofsky, *Making History: Pukapukan and Anthropological Constructions of Knowledge* (Cambridge, 1987), 142–3.

31. Mark Leyner, "Eat at Cosmo's," *New Yorker*, 7 March 1994, 100.

32. Kammen, *Mystic Chords of Memory*, 129; Barry Schwartz, "Social change and collective memory: The democratization of George Washington," *American Sociological Review*, 56 (1991), 225–7.

33. John McPhee, "Travels of the Rock," *New Yorker*, 26 Feb. 1990, 108–17.

34. Charles Eliot Norton letter (1874) quoted in Curtis M. Hinsley, "From shell-heaps to stelae," in George W. Stocking, Jr., ed., *Objects and Others* (Madison, WI, 1985), 59.

35. Virginia Woolf, *Between the Acts* (New York, 1941), 174–5.

36. Lowenthal, "Timeless past," 1267.

37. C. H. K. Marten (1905) quoted in Raphael Samuel, "Continuous national history," in his *Patriotism* (London, 1989), 1:12.

38. Warren Rodgers, Stuhr Museum of the Prairie Pioneer, to the author, 19 Nov. 1980; Edwin Fenton, *The Americans* (1975), quoted in Frances FitzGerald, *America Revised* (New York, 1980), 162n; Bernard Bailyn, *On the Teaching and Writing of History* (Hanover, NH, 1994), 41–2.

39. Michael J. Smith, "Looking out and looking in," AASLH presidential address, *History News*, 45:6 (Nov.–Dec. 1990), 8; Eric Gable and Richard Handler, "Deep dirt: Messing up the past at Colonial Williamsburg," *Social Analysis*, 34 (1993), 13; Morris dancer quoted in Boyes, *The Imagined Village* (Manchester, 1993), 44–5; Padstow celebrant on "The Future of the Past," Channel 4 (U.K.) television program, 22 June 1986; D. R. Rowe cited in Jonathan Sale, "Rhubarb and customs?" *Times*, 4 Feb. 1995.

40. Mona Ozouf, "Le Panthéon," in Nora, *LM*, I:136–66.

41. Janet L. Nelson, "The Lord's anointed and the people's choice: Carolingian royal ritual," in David Cannadine and Simon Price, eds., *Rituals of Royalty* (Cambridge, 1992), 137–80, ref. pp. 149–50; Marie Tanner, *The Last Descendant of Aeneas* (New Haven, 1993), 107; Barry Schwartz, "The character of Washington," *AQ*, 38 (1986), 202–22.

42. Catherine A. Lutz and Jane L. Collins, *Reading National Geographic* (Chicago, 1993), 56; Joan Gero and Dolores Root, "Public presentations and private concerns: Archaeology in the pages of National Geographic," in Peter Gathercole and David Lowenthal, eds., *The Politics of the Past* (London, 1990), 31; John Bodnar, *Remaking America* (Princeton, 1992), 201–3.

43. Elizabeth Kastor, "Melina Mercouri: Dramatizing culture," *IHT*, 3 Feb. 1988; Michael Herzfeld, *A Place in History* (Princton, 1991), 15–17, 34–5, 57.

44. Ben Zion Dinur quoted in David N. Myers, "Remembering *Zakhor*," *H & M*, 4:2 (1992), 139–40; Edward T. Linenthal, "The U.S. Holocaust Memorial Museum," *AQ*, 46 (1994), 406–33.

45. Donald P. Spence, *Narrative Truth and Historical Truth* (New York, 1982).

46. John Fowles, *The French Lieutenant's Woman* [1969] (London, 1987), 87.

47. Marcus Bilson (1980) cited in Timothy Dow Adams, *Telling Lies in Modern American Autobiography* (Chapel Hill, NC, 1990), 130; Alphine W. Jefferson, in Jaclyn Jeffrey and Glenace Edwall, eds., *Memory and History* (Lanham, MD, 1994), 106;

Anthony Greenwald, "The totalitarian ego: Fabrication and revision of personal history," *American Psychologist*, 35 (1980), 615; Howard Schuman and Jacqueline Scott, "Generations and collective memories," *American Sociological Review*, 54 (1989), 360, 371–3.

48. Richard Wright, *Black Boy: A Record of Childhood and Youth* (New York, 1945); Adams, *Telling Lies*, 75–9; Richard Rodriguez, *Hunger of Memory* (New York, 1983), 179, 186.

49. Mamie Garvin Fields with Karen Fields, *Lemon Swamp and Other Places* (New York, 1983); Karen E. Fields, "What one cannot remember mistakenly," in Jeffrey and Edwall, *Memory and History*, 93, 96–8.

50. W. Walter Menninger, "Say, it isn't so: When wishful thinking obscures historical reality," *History News*, 40:12 (Dec. 1985), 12; J.-R. Staude (1950) quoted in Donald E. Polkinghorne, "Narrative and self-concept," *Journal of Narrative and Life History*, 1 (1991), 149; Jefferson Singer and Peter Salovey, *The Remembered Self* (New York, 1993), 143–57; Dan P. McAdams, "Personality, modernity, and the storied self," *Psychological Inquiry*, 7 (1996), in press.

51. Malcolm Bradbury, "Telling life: Some thoughts on literary biography," in Eric Homberger and John Charmley, *The Troubled Face of Biography* (London, 1988), 131–40; Millgate, *Testamentary Acts*, 127 (Hardy), 104–5 (James).

52. Henry James (1913) quoted in Adeline R. Tintner, "Autobiography as fiction," *Twentieth Century Literature*, 23 (1977), 242–4; Fields, "What one cannot remember mistakenly," 91; Philippe Lejeune, *On Autobiography*, trans. Katherine Leary (Minneapolis, 1989), 235.

53. Salman Rushdie, "'Errata': or, unreliable narration in *Midnight's Children*" (1983), in his *Imaginary Homelands* (London, 1992), 22–5. On the persistence of delusive self-memory see William F. Brewer, "What is autobiographical memory?" and Craig R. Barclay, "Schematization of autobiographical memory," in David C. Rubin, ed., *Autobiographical Memory* (Cambridge, 1986), 25–49 and 82–99.

54. Annie Dillard, "'To fashion a text," in William Zinsser, ed., *Inventing the Truth: The Art and Craft of Memoir* (Boston, 1987), 71.

55. James Fentress, in Fentress and Chris Wickham, *Social Memory* (Oxford, 1992), 198.

56. George Lipsitz, *Time Passages: Collective Memory and American Popular Culture* (Minneapolis, 1990), 163; *Roots* promoter quoted in Miles Orvell, *The Real Thing* (Chapel Hill, NC, 1989), xxiii.

Chapter 7

1. Jack Goody, "The time of telling and the telling of time in written and oral cultures," in John Bender and David E. Wellbery, eds., *Chronotypes* (Stanford, CA, 1991), 94; Robert A. Rosenstone, *Visions of the Past: The Challenge of Film to Our Idea of History* (Cambridge, MA, 1995), 78, 117.

2. W. Walter Menninger, "Say, it isn't so: When wishful thinking obscures historical reality," *History News*, 40:12 (Dec. 1985), 10–13; Patrick J. Geary, *Phantoms of Remembrance: Memory and Oblivion at the End of the First Millennium* (Princeton, 1995), 135–46.

3. James Fentress and Chris Wickham, *Social Memory* (Oxford, 1992), 59, 73; Geary, *Phantoms of Remembrance*, 147–53.

4. Mark L. Sargent, "The conservative covenant: The rise of the Mayflower Compact in American myth," *New England Quarterly*, 61 (1988), 233–51.

5. Johannes Magnus, *Historia de omnibus Gothorum Sveonumque* (1554), cited in Kurt Johannesson, *The Renaissance of the Goths in Sixteenth-Century Sweden* (Berkeley, 1991), 127–38; Patrick Wright, *On Living in an Old Country* (London, 1985), 164–5.

6. Bernard M. Zlotowitz, in "The issue of patrilineal descent—a symposium," *Judaism*, no. 133, 34:1 (1985), 130–3.

7. Susan Jeffers, *Brother Eagle, Sister Sky: A Message from Chief Seattle* (New York, 1991); Ted Perry quoted in John Lichfield, *Independent on Sunday*, 26 April 1992, 13; Susan Jeffers quoted in Timothy Egan, "Mother Earth? From the film, not the Indian," *IHT*, 22 April 1992, 2. See Gretchen M. Bataille and Charles L. P. Silet, eds., *The Pretend Indians: Images of Native Americans in the Movies* (Ames, IW, 1980).

8. Exhibit captions, American Indian Archaeological Institute [now Institute for American Indian Studies], Washington, CT, July 1987; Russell G. Handsman, "Material things and social relations," *Conference on New England Archaeology Newsletter* (Washington, CT, 1987), 5; Richard White, "The Last of the Mohicans," in Mark C. Carnes, ed., *Past Imperfect: History According to the Movies* (New York, 1995), 82–5. See Michael S. Nassaney, "An epistemological enquiry into some archaeological and historical interpretations of 17th century Native American–European relations," in Stephen J. Shennan, ed., *Archaeological Approaches to Cultural Identity* (London, 1989), 76–93.

9. Mandell Creighton, *The English National Character* (London, 1896), 8, 11, 14–18, 23.

10. Anne Pallister, *Magna Carta* (1971) and Joseph Story (1845) quoted in Michael Kammen, *A Machine That Would Go of Itself: The Constitution in American Culture* (New York, 1987), 36, xxiii.

11. Robert P. Morgan, "Tradition, anxiety, and the current musical scene," in Nicholas Kenyon, ed., *Authenticity and Early Music* (Oxford, 1988), 57–82; Harry Haskell, *The Early Music Revival* (London, 1988), 184.

12. Edmund Kean and others quoted in Lawrence W. Levine, "William Shakespeare and the American public" (1984), in his *The Unpredictable Past* (New York, 1993), 160–1; Rosenstone, *Visions of the Past*, 148–9, 206–7.

13. Margaret Thatcher interview, James Bishop, "Programme for the 1980s," *Illustrated London News*, May 1983, 23–5; Nicholas Tate quoted in David Charter, "Schools must not blur culture boundary, says syllabus chief," *Times*, 8 Feb. 1996; Michael Wallace, "Ronald Reagan and the politics of history," *Tikkun*, 2:1 (1987), 14; "It's a Great Country" quoted in James W. Loewen, *Lies My Teacher Told Me* (New York, 1995), 3.

14. James Oliver Horton and Spencer R. Crew, "Afro-Americans and museums," in Warren Leon and Roy Rosenzweig, eds., *History Museums in the United States* (Urbana, IL, 1989), 230–1; "National symbols: Presidential homes," *History News*, 45:1 (Jan.–Feb. 1990), 8–17; Mark Bograd, "Apologies accepted: Facing up to slave realities at historic house museums," *History News*, 47:1 (Jan.–Feb. 1992), 20–21.

15. Jonathan Raban, *Hunting Mister Heartbreak* (London, 1991), 218–19; Patrick Henry letter quoted in J. Franklin Jameson, *The American Revolution Considered as a Social Movement* [1926] (Boston, 1956), 23.

16. Eric Gable et al., "On the uses of relativism: Fact, conjecture, and black and white histories at Colonial Williamsburg," *American Ethnologist*, 19 (1992), 794, 802; James M. McPherson, "Glory," in Carnes, *Past Imperfect*, 131.

17. Michael Olmert, "The new, no-frills Williamsburg," *History News*, 37:5 (Oct. 1985), 26–33; Warren Leon and Margaret Piatt, "Living-history museums," in Leon and Rosenzweig, *History Museums in the United States*, 75.

18. This section is condensed from my "Memory and oblivion," *Museum Management and Curatorship*, 12 (1993), 171–82.

19. John Erskine (1927) quoted in Kammen, *Mystic Chords of Memory*, 497.

20. George de Scudéry, *Curia Politiae* (London, 1654), 98; Sheldon S. Wolin, *The Presence of the Past: Essays on the State and the Constitution* (Baltimore, 1989), 37–38, 142.

21. Suzanne Citron, *Le mythe national: L'histoire de France en question* (Paris, 1989), 183; Committee of Public Safety, An II, and Bertrand Barère, quoted in Robert Gildea, *The Past in French History* (New Haven, 1994), 32, 26; Gambetta quoted in Eugen Weber, *Peasants into Frenchmen* (London, 1979), 100; Renan, "What is a nation?" (1882), in Homi K. Bhabha, ed., *Nation and Narration* (London, 1990), 11; Pompidou (1971) quoted in Ronald Koven, "National memory: The duty to remember, the need to forget," *Society*, 32:6 (1995), 52–8, ref. p. 55.

22. Wilfred Laurier (1900) quoted in Louisbourg Heritage Society, *Heritage Notes*, no. 4 (Feb. 1994), 1.

23. David Freedberg, *Iconoclasts and Their Motives* (Maarssen, Netherlands, 1985); Jacques Le Goff, *History and Memory* (New York, 1992), 73; Marian Wenzel, "Bosnian history and Austro-Hungarian policy," *Museum Management and Curatorship*, 12 (1993), 127–42; panelists at Horyu-ji Temple site World Heritage inscription ceremony, Nara, Japan, 6 Nov. 1995.

24. Margaret Aston, *England's Iconoclasts: Laws against Images* (Oxford, 1988), 256, see also 2, 10; and Ann Kibbey, *The Interpretation of Material Shapes in Puritanism* (Cambridge, 1986), 47–50.

25. Judge Edward Ruzzo (1964) quoted in Loewen, *Lies My Teacher Told Me*, 289; Acton to Bishop Mandell Creighton quoted in Roland Hill, "Europe's last great liberal," *TLS*, 16 June 1995, 31.

26. Loewen, *Lies My Teacher Told Me*, 172; Holt, Rinehart and Winston editor (1982) in Joan DelFattore, *What Johnny Shouldn't Read* (New Haven, 1992), 131–2; publisher quoted in Diane Ravitch, "Decline and fall of teaching history," *New York Times Mag.*, 17 Nov. 1985, 56.

27. Jon Wiener, "Tall tales and true," *Nation*, 31 Jan. 1994, 133–5; Jackie Young, *Black Collectables* (West Chester, PA, 1988); Thomas C. Holt, "Marking: Race, race-making, and the writing of history," *AHR*, 100 (1995), 1–20.

28. James E. Young, *The Texture of Memory: Holocaust Memorials and Meaning* (New Haven, 1993), 27–48; Timothy W. Ryback, "Stalingrad: Letters from the dead," *New Yorker*, 1 Feb. 1993, 58–71; Jane Kramer, "The politics of memory: Letter from Germany," *New Yorker*, 14 Aug. 1995, 48–65, ref. p. 56.

29. Norwegian quoted in Hans Magnus Enzensberger, *Europe, Europe* (London, 1990), 26–7.

30. John P. Dickenson, "Nostalgia for a gilded past? Museums in Minas Gerais, Brazil," in Flora E. S. Kaplan, ed., *Museums and the Making of "Ourselves"* (London, 1994), 221–45; Ghislaine Lawrence, "Object lessons in the museum medium," in Susan

Pearce, ed., *Objects of Knowledge* (London, 1990), 103–24; Mike Wallace, "Razor ribbons, history museums, and civic salvation," *Radical History Review*, 57 (1993), 230; Robert Wagner-Pacifici and Barry Schwartz, "The Vietnam Veterans Memorial," *American Journal of Sociology*, 97 (1991), 388n; James Clifford, "Four Northwest Coast museums: Travel reflections," in Ivan Karp and Steven D. Lavine, eds., *Exhibiting Cultures: The Poetics and Politics of Museum Display* (Washington, 1991) 215, 244–5,

31. Edward T. Linenthal, "Can museums achieve a balance between memory and history?" *Chronicle of Higher Education*, 10 Feb. 1995, sec. B2, 1–2; Philip Nobile, ed., *Judgment at the Smithsonian: The Uncensored Script of the Smithsonian's 50th Anniversary Exhibit of the Enola Gay* (New York, 1995); Representatives Blute and Johnson quoted in Edward T. Linenthal, "Struggling with history and memory," *Journal of American History*, 82 (1995), 1094–1101, ref. p. 1100.

32. William Safire (1989) quoted in Michael Schudson, *Watergate in American Memory* (New York, 1992), 59.

33. Alon Confino, "On Disney's America," AHA *Perspectives*, 33:3 (March 1995), 10; Loewen, *Lies My Teacher Told Me*, 18; Leon F. Litwack, "The Birth of a Nation," in Carnes, *Past Imperfect*, 136–41; Pat Laughney, Library of Congress film division, in *IHT*, 30–31 Oct. 1993, 3.

34. David Glassberg, "Monuments and memories," *AQ*, 43 (1991), 146.

35. George Orwell, *Nineteen Eighty-Four* (London, 1954), 170–1; Deborah Lipstadt, *Denying the Holocaust* (New York, 1993); Elisabeth Domansky, "'Kristallnacht,' the Holocaust and German unity," *H & M*, 4:1 (1992), 60; Stephen Greenblatt, "Resonance and wonder," in Karp and Lavine, *Exhibiting Cultures*, 42–56.

36. Ian T. Ousby, *The Englishman's England: Taste, Travel, and the Rise of Tourism* (Cambridge, 1990), on Goldsmith (1760), 28–9, and on Shakespeare frauds, 39–55; Washington Irving, "Stratford-on-Avon" (1815), in his *The Sketchbook of Geoffrey Crayon, Gent* (London, n.d.), 253; Erik Cohen, "Authenticity and commoditization in tourism," *Annals of Tourism Research*, 15 (1988), 377, 383.

37. Martyn Welch quoted in George Hill, "A train not arriving at platform 2," *Times*, 25 Oct. 1990; Jean Little in discussion at "Travellers in Time," Children's Literature New England summer institute, Newnham College, Cambridge (England), August 1989; idem, *Little by Little: A Writer's Education* (Markham, Ontario, 1987), 103–4.

38. Carolly Erickson, "The Scarlet Empress," in Carnes, *Past Imperfect*, 88.

39. Nigel Nicolson, "Upstairs, downstairs," *Spectator*, 18 March 1995, 46.

40. Andrew Lass, "Romantic documents and political monuments: The meaning-fulfillment of history in 19th-century Czech nationalism," *American Ethnologist*, 15 (1988), 456–71.

41. Yael Zerubavel, "The death of memory and the memory of death: Masada and the Holocaust as historical metaphors," *Representations*, 45 (Winter 1994), 74–5; idem, *Recovered Roots* (Chicago, 1995), 60–76, 114–37, 192–213; Barry Schwartz et al., "The recovery of Masada," *Sociological Quarterly*, 27 (1986), 147–64; Neil Asher Silberman, *Between Past and Present: Archaeology, Ideology, and Nationalism in the Modern Middle East* (New York, 1989), 87–101; Amos Elon, "Politics and archaeology," *NYRB*, 22 Sept. 1994, 14–18.

42. Donna Morganstern and Jeff Greenberg, "The influence of a multi-theme park on cultural beliefs as a function of schema salience: Promoting and undermining the myth of the Old West," *Journal of Applied Social Psychology*, 18 (1988), 584–96;

Adrian Mellor, "Enterprise and heritage in the dock," in John Corner and Sylvia Harvey, eds., *Enterprise and Heritage* (London, 1991), 93–115; Shelagh Squire, "Meanings, myths and memories: Literary tourism as cultural discourse in Beatrix Potter's Lake District," Ph.D. thesis, University College London, 1991, 203–22.

43. Wallace, "Ronald Reagan and the politics of memory," 128n; Garry Wills, *Reagan's America* (New York, 1987), 375.

44. James R. Curtis, "The most famous fence in the world: Fact and fiction in Mark Twain's Hannibal," *Landscape*, 28:3 (1985), 8–13; William Zinsser, "They keep mixing fact and fiction in Hannibal, Missouri," *Smithsonian*, 9:7 (Oct. 1978), 155–63.

45. Evelyn Waugh, "A pleasure cruise in 1929," in his *When the Going Was Good* (Harmondsworth, England, 1951), 24; other refs. in my "Counterfeit art: Authentic fakes?" *IJCP*, 1:1, 85–6.

46. Henry James, "The Birthplace" (1903), in his *Selected Tales* (London, 1982), 335–6, 345; John Sayles, "A conversation [with] Eric Foner," in Carnes, *Past Imperfect*, 22.

47. D. W. Griffith cited in Pierre Sorlin, *The Film in History: Restaging the Past* (Oxford, 1980), viii–ix; Lowenthal, *Past Is a Foreign Country*, 230–1.

48. Kenneth Chorley (1941) quoted in Kammen, *Mystic Chords of Memory*, 373n; Cary Carson in "Who owns history? Conversations with William Styron and Cary Carson," *Humanities* [National Endowment for the Humanities], 16:1 (Jan.–Feb. 1995), 8–11, 50–3, ref. p. 9.

49. Peter Shaffer, *Lettice and Lovage* (London, 1988), 25; James, "Birthplace," 304, 307, 325; Alan Bennett, *Writing Home* (London, 1994), 211.

50. Israeli curator quoted in Tamar Katriel, "Remaking place: Cultural production in an Israeli pioneer settlement museum," *H & M*, 5:2 (1993), 109.

51. W. Richard West, Jr., quoted in AHA *Perspectives*, 32:8 (Nov. 1994), 20; Simon Jenkins, "Centre point," *Spectator*, 8 April 1995, 29.

52. Maurice Halbwachs, *The Collective Memory* [1950] (New York, 1980); Patrick H. Hutton, "The role of memory in the historiography of the French Revolution," *History and Theory*, 30 (1991), 58–9; Michael Kammen, "History is our heritage," in Paul Gagnon and the Bradley Commission, eds., *Historical Literacy* (Boston, 1989), 153.

53. Yael Zerubavel, "The historic, the legendary, and the incredible: Invented tradition and collective memory in Israel," in John R. Gillis, ed., *Commemorations: The Politics of National Memory* (Princeton, 1994), 105–23; idem, "The politics of interpretation: Tel Hai in Israel's collective memory," *Journal of the Association for Jewish Studies*, 16 (1991), 133–60; idem, *Recovered Roots*, 39–47, 84–95, 147–77.

54. Ronald G. Walters, "In our backyard," AHA *Perspectives*, 33:3 (March 1995), 3; John Bodnar in "A house divided: Historians confront Disney's America," OAH [Organization of American Historians] *Newsletter*, 22:3 (Aug. 1994), 11; Loewen, *Lies My Teacher Told Me*, 278.

55. Patrick H. Hutton, "The problem of memory in the historical writings of Philippe Ariès," *H & M*, 4:1 (1992), 112–13; Joyce Appleby et al., *Telling the Truth about History* (New York, 1994), 257–9.

56. Brendan Bradshaw, "The invention of the Irish," *TLS*, 14 Oct. 1994, 8–10.

57. Graeme Davison, "The meanings of 'heritage,'" in Davison and Chris McConville, eds., *A Heritage Handbook* (North Sydney, 1991), 12; Raphael Samuel, *Theatres of*

Memory (London, 1994), 268–78; Mark C. Carnes, "Introduction," in his *Past Imperfect*, 9.

58. Yigael Yadin quoted in Elon, "Politics and archaeology."

59. E. L. Doctorow quoted in Bruce Weber, "The creative mind: The myth maker," *New York Times Mag.*, 20 Oct. 1985, 24–26.

60. Laura McLemore, "Darwinian dilemma: Documenting recent history," *History News* (Mar.–Apr. 1993), 30; Alfred North Whitehead, *Symbolism: Its Meaning and Effect* (Cambridge, 1928), 104; George Orwell, *The Lion and the Unicorn* (1941), in his *Collected Essays* (London, 1968), 2:109.

61. Barry Schwartz, "Social change and collective memory: The democratization of George Washington," *American Sociological Review*, 56 (1991), 222, 232–4; idem, "The reconstruction of Abraham Lincoln," in Middleton and Edwards, *Collective Remembering*, 82–3, 104–5.

Chapter 8

1. Francis Bacon, *Advancement of Learning* [1605], ch. 23: para 36 (London, 1973), 199.

2. Mandell Creighton, *The English National Character* (London, 1896), 8.

3. Sabine MacCormack, "History, memory and time in Golden Age Spain," *H & M*, 4:2 (1992), 49; Walter E. Leitsch, "East Europeans studying history in Vienna (1855–1918)," in Dennis Deletant and Harry Hanak, eds., *Historians as Nation-Builders* (London, 1988), 145.

4. John Bodnar, *Remaking America* (Princeton, 1992), 71–2; Anthony Buckley, "'We're trying to find our identity': Uses of history among Ulster Protestants," in Elizabeth Tonkin et al., eds., *History and Ethnicity* (London, 1989), 183–97.

5. David Ben-Gurion quoted in Amos Elon, *Jerusalem: City of Mirrors* (New York, 1991), 242; Emanuel Anati, "Parks and museums at rock art and archeological sites," in *International Perspectives on Cultural Parks* (Washington, 1989), 107–9.

6. Robert A. Stafford, "Annexing the landscapes of the past: British imperial geology in the nineteenth century," in John M. MacKenzie, ed., *Imperialism and the Natural World* (Manchester, 1990), 76, 71.

7. Suzanne Citron, *Le mythe national* (Paris, 1989), 85; W. J. McCann, "'Volk und Germanentum': The presentation of the past in Nazi Germany," in Peter Gathercole and David Lowenthal, eds., *The Politics of the Past* (London, 1990), 81–3; Roger Just, "Cultural certainties and private doubts," in Wendy James, ed., *The Pursuit of Certainty* (London, 1995), 295.

8. J. B. La Curne de Sainte-Palaye (c. 1756) quoted in Jacques Le Goff, *History and Memory* (New York, 1992), 25; Krzysztof Pomian, "Francs et Gaulois," in Nora, *LM*, 3.1:40–105; Pierre Chaunu (1982) quoted in Peter Burke, "French historians and their cultural identities," in Tonkin et al., *History and Ethnicity*, 162; security guard interviewed in Michael Billig, *Talking of the Royal Family* (London, 1992), 51–2.

9. Johannes Goropius Becanus (1569) quoted in Henri Krop, "The antiquity of the Dutch language," *Geschiedenis van de Wijsbegeerte in Nederland*, 5 (1994), 1–8.

10. Yigael Yadin quoted in Amos Elon, "Politics and archaeology," *NYRB*, 22 Sept. 1994, 15; Yadin's own version in his *Bar Kokhba* (London, 1971), 15, is less eloquent.

11. William A. Wilson, *Folklore and Nationalism in Modern Finland* (Bloomington, IN, 1976), 59–60; on Pakistan, Eric Hobsbawm, "The new threat to history," *NYRB*, 16 Dec. 1993, 62–4; on Indonesia, Benedict Anderson, *Imagined Communities* (London, 1983), 19n.

12. Magen Broshi, "Religion, ideology and politics and their impact on Palestinian archaeology," *Israeli Museum Journal*, 6 (Spring 1987), 28.

13. David Lowenthal, *The Past Is a Foreign Country* (Cambridge, 1985), 53; Alex Haley quoted in Mark Ottaway, "Tangled roots," *Sunday Times Mag.*, 10 April 1977, 17–21.

14. Georgina Boyes, "Cultural survivals theory and traditional customs," *Folk Life*, 26 (1987–88), 5–11; see also her *The Imagined Village* (Manchester, 1993), 10, 64, 104–5.

15. Thomas Hauschild, "Making history in southern Italy," in Kirsten Hastrup, ed., *Other Histories* (London, 1992), 29–44.

16. Numa Denis Fustel de Coulanges, *The Ancient City* [1864] (New York, c. 1960), 170; Colette Beaune, *Naissance de la nation France* (Paris, 1985), 222–4.

17. Baron Dairoku Kikuchi, "The claim of Japan, by a Japanese statesman," *Encyclopaedia Britannica*, 11th ed. (1910–11), 5:273. See George Macklin Wilson, "Time and history in Japan," *AHR*, 85 (1980), 577–71.

18. Liah Greenfeld, *Nationalism* (Cambridge, MA, 1992), 94, 76; John Pocock, "England," in Orest Ranum, ed., *National Consciousness, History, and Political Culture in Early-Modern Europe* (Baltimore, 1975), 105–10.

19. Quotes from my "The past in the American landscape," in David Lowenthal and Martyn J. Bowden, eds., *Geographies of the Mind* (New York, 1976), 101–4.

20. Herbert Butterfield, *Christianity and History* (London, 1957), 98.

21. Edward W. Said, *Beginnings: Intention and Method* (New York, 1985), xvii.

22. Jane Brown Gillette, "A conversation with Roger Kennedy," *Historic Preservation*, Nov.-Dec. 1994, 49–51; see Roger Kennedy, *Greek Revival America* (New York, 1989); idem, *Hidden Cities: The Discovery and Loss of Ancient North American Civilization* (New York, 1994).

23. Rivka Sturman, Gurit Kadman, and Yemenite dancer quoted in Shalom Staub, "Folklore and authenticity," in Burt Feintuch, ed., *The Conservation of Culture* (Lexington, KY, 1988), 175–6.

24. Saul Dubow, *Scientific Racism in Modern South Africa* (Cambridge, 1995), 68–74; Nigel Worden, "Public history in the new South Africa," *AHA Perspectives*, 34:2 (Feb. 1996), 1, 5–8.

25. Thomas Jefferson (1785) quoted in Carl J. Richard, *The Founders and the Classics* (Cambridge, MA, 1994), 44; Bernard Levin, "Shakespeare—the history man," *Times*, 18 Sept. 1989, 16.

26. Cesare Baronio, *Annales Ecclesiastici* (1588–1607), quoted in Simon Ditchfield, *Liturgy, Sanctity and History in Tridentine Italy* (Cambridge, 1995), 283; Southern Historical Society (1873) quoted in Michael Kammen, *Mystic Chords of Memory* (New York, 1991), 111.

27. Alexander Kluge (1983) cited in Anton Klaes, *From Hitler to Heimat: The Return of History as Film* (Cambridge, MA, 1989), 133–4; Jules Michelet (1847–53) quoted in Citron, *Mythe national*, 19; Jean-François Chiappe, preface, in Henry Servieu, *Petite Histoire de la France* (Paris, 1989), 8; François Mitterand (1989) quoted in Robert Gildea, *The Past in French History* (New Haven, 1994), 112.

28. Ditchfield, *Liturgy, Sanctity and History*, 345–56, and personal communication, December 1995; Christophe Charle, "Les grands corps," in Nora, *LM,* III.2:230.

29. John Redwood (then secretary of state for Wales), "Why Jack Straw should be reading King Lear," *Times,* 12 Dec. 1994, 7; Creighton, *English National Character,* 14–15; Herbert Butterfield, *The Englishman and His History* (Cambridge, 1944), 113–14; "All our yesterdays," *English Heritage Mag.,* 3 (Oct. 1988), 3.

30. Harriet Ritvo, "Race, breed, and myths of origin: Chillingham cattle as ancient Britons," *Representations,* 39 (Summer 1992), 11; Michael Heseltine, "Wales, and a yard-square blaze of colour long ago," *The Field,* 272 (May 1990), 78–9; Howard Newby, "Revitalizing the countryside," *JRSA,* 138 (1990), 630–6; Stanley Baldwin, "The Classics" (1926), in his *On England* (London, 1927), 101.

31. F. M. Cornford, *Microcosmographia Academica* [1908] (Cambridge, 1953), 15.

32. Philadelphia *Public Ledger* (1837) quoted in Kammen, *Mystic Chords of Memory,* 53; David Lowenthal, "A global perspective on American heritage," in Antoinette J. Lee, ed., *Past Meets Future: Saving America's Historic Environments* (Washington, 1992), 157–63. See my *Past Is a Foreign Country,* 108–17.

33. A. L. Rowse, "What people has a better record?" *The Field,* 272 (May 1990), 79–80.

34. Nathaniel Hawthorne, *Doctor Grimshawe's Secret* (Boston, 1883), 229; Peter Tate, *New Forest* (London, 1979), 14.

35. Dan Vittorio Segre, *Memoirs of a Fortunate Jew* (London, 1988), 160; August Ludwig Schloezer quoted and Adam Müller cited in Greenfeld, *Nationalism,* 247, 367.

36. Marcus Garvey, "Who and what is a Negro?" (1923), in *The Philosophy and Opinions of Marcus Garvey* (London, 1967), part II, 19; Andreas of Spartohori quoted in Just, "Cultural certainties and private doubts," 287.

37. Bronislaw Baczko, "Le calendrier républicain," in Nora, *LM,* I:37–83.

38. Frederick von Raumer, *America, and the American People,* trans. William Turner (New York, 1846), 300; George P. Marsh, *The Goths in New-England* (Middlebury, VT, 1843), 34.

39. Ralph Waldo Emerson, "English traits" (1856), *The Portable Emerson* (New York, 1946), 370–1; James K. Paulding (1815) and Cadwallader D. Colden (1825) quoted in Lowenthal, "Past in the American landscape," 93.

40. Emerson, "Works and days" [1870], *Complete Works* (Boston, 1912), 7:177.

41. A 1980 survey quoted in Denis J. Shemilt, "Beauty and the philosopher: Empathy in history and classroom," in A. K. Dickinson et al., *Learning History* (London, 1984), 50.

42. John Updike, *S.* (London, 1988), 149; Dave Dame, "The role and responsibility of interpretation: protecting park resources," in *International Perspectives on Cultural Parks,* 227–9.

43. Karen Fog Olwig, "Defining the national in the transnational: Cultural identity in the Afro-Caribbean diaspora," 361–76; and Thomas Hylland Eriksen, "A future-oriented, non-ethnic nationalism? Mauritius as an exemplary case," 197–221, both *Ethnos,* 58 (1993).

44. Herbert Weiner (1954) quoted in Robert Paine, "Israel: The making of self in the 'pioneering' of the nation," *Ethnos,* 58 (1993), 234.

45. Ben Zion Dinur quoted in Uri Ram, "Zionist historiography and the invention of modern Jewish nationhood," *H & M,* 7:1 (1995), 94, 105, 116.

Chapter 9

1. Gabrielle M. Spiegel, "History, historicism, and the social logic of the text in the Middle Ages," *Speculum*, 65 (1990), 78–80; André Burguière, "La généalogie," in Nora, *LM*, III.3:20–2, 26–9.
2. Joel T. Rosenthal, *Fifteenth Patriarchy and Families of Privilege in Fifteenth Century England* (Philadelphia, 1991); Jeanne C. Fawtier Stone and Lawrence Stone, *An Open Elite? England 1540–1880* (Oxford, 1984), 105–34.
3. George P. Marsh, *Address, delivered before the New England Society of the City of New-York* (New York, 1845), 9; Alex Shoumatoff, *The Mountain of Names* (New York, 1990), 214.
4. Isaiah Berlin, *Vico and Herder* (London, 1976), 198; Dorothy Ross, "Historical consciousness in nineteenth-century America," *AHR*, 89 (1984), 918, 924; Harry H. Loughlin (1936) quoted in Stefan T. Kühl, *The Nazi Connection: Eugenics, American Racism, and German National Socialism* (New York, 1994), 87.
5. Ralph Waldo Emerson, "English traits" (1856), *The Portable Emerson* (New York, 1946), 362; Dale T. Knobel, *Paddy and the Republic: Ethnicity and Nationality in Ante-Bellum America* (Middletown, CT, 1986); Josiah C. Nott and George R. Gliddon (1854) quoted in Thomas F. Gossett, *Race: The History of an Idea in America* (Dallas, 1963), 65; Donald A. Grinde, Jr., "Teaching American Indian history," AHA *Perspectives*, 32:6 (Sept. 1994), 1, 11–16.
6. An 1851 quote in Reginald Horsman, *Race and Manifest Destiny* (Cambridge, MA, 1981), 155; J. S. Dunnett (1907–08) quoted in Henry Reynolds, "Progress, morality, and the dispossession of the Aboriginals," *Meanjin Quarterly*, 37 (1974), 312; Lenore Coltheart, "The moment of Aboriginal history," in Jeremy R. Beckett, ed., *Past and Present: The Construction of Aboriginality* (Canberra, 1988), 183; George M. Fredrickson, *The Black Image in the White Mind: The Debate on Afro-American Character and Destiny, 1817–1914* (New York, 1971), 241–59.
7. Saul Dubow, *Scientific Racism in Modern South Africa* (Cambridge, 1995), 91–2; Edward East (1927) and V. Gordon Childe (1926) quoted in Elazar Barkan, *The Retreat of Scientific Racism* (Cambridge, 1992), 148, 56.
8. Fredrickson, *Black Image*, 102–17; Arthur Riss, "Racial essentialism and family values in *Uncle Tom's Cabin*," *AQ*, 46 (1994), 513–44; Harriet Beecher Stowe, *Uncle Tom's Cabin, or, Life among the Lowly* [1852] (Harmonsworth, England, 1981), 608; Joan D. Hedrick, *Harriet Beecher Stowe: A Life* (New York, 1994), 209–10, 215; Alexander Crummell (1891) quoted in Paul Gilroy, *The Black Atlantic* (London, 1993), 98; Horace M. Kallen, "Democracy versus the melting pot," *Nation*, 100 (1915), 190–4, 217–20.
9. William H. Tucker, *The Science and Politics of Racial Research* (Urbana, IL, 1994), 41; animal breeders and Kansas Free Fair placard (1920) quoted in Dorothy Nelkin and M. Susan Lindee, *The DNA Mystique* (New York, 1995), 21–3.
10. David M. Schneider, *A Critique of the Study of Kinship* (Ann Arbor, MI, 1984), 175, 194–8; Edwin M. Yoder, Jr., "The hazard of stereotypes: History's many reminders," *IHT*, 26 Oct. 1994.
11. "Rose Peters" quoted in Mary C. Waters, *Ethnic Options* (Berkeley, 1990), 25.
12. Zofia Kossak-Szcucka (1936) quoted in Abraham Brumberg, "Enigma," *TLS*, 22 June 1995, 65; F. James Davis, *Who Is Black?* (University Park, PA, 1991), 25, 174; wildlife-park owner John Aspinall quoted in *Times*, 17 Feb. 1995.

13. Richard Rodriguez, "An American writer," in Werner Sollors, ed., *The Invention of Ethnicity* (New York, 1989), 10.

14. Louis Owens, *The Sharpest Sight* (Norman, OK, 1992), 20; Gerald M. Sider, *Lumbee Indian Histories* (Cambridge, 1993), 208; on the Sioux, Claudia J. Nicholson, "Advisors to partners: Bridging the cultural gap," *History News*, 50:4 (1995), 10–13.

15. Arthur W. Upfield, *Bony and the Kelly Gang* [1960] (New York, 1988), 63, 72, 99; idem, *Death of a Swagman* [1945] (New York, 1982), 26; Tom Griffiths, *Hunters and Collectors* (Melbourne, 1996), 263.

16. Simon Jenkins, "The House of Windsor is incorrigibly bourgeois," *Spectator*, 22 Oct. 1994, 36; William Rees-Mogg, "The best and the brightest," *Times*, 30 Nov. 1995.

17. Diana Forsythe, "German identity and the problem of history," in Elizabeth Tonkin et al., *History and Ethnicity* (London, 1989), 144; Harold James, *A German Identity 1770–1990* (London, 1989), 91–6; Jane Kramer, "Neo-Nazis: A chaos in the head," *New Yorker*, 14 June 1993, 52–70, ref. p. 67. Reunification has made ethnic Germans less welcome (see *IHT*, 27 March 1996, 2).

18. Heinrich Wiepking-Jürgensmann (1935) quoted in Gert Gröning, "The feeling for landscape—a German example," *Landscape Research*, 17 (1992), 108–15; Knut Haukelid (1946) quoted in Anne Eriksen, "The paper clip war—the mythology of the Norwegian resistance," colloquium on The Resistance and the North-Europeans, Brussels, 1994, 8, 10; Auberon Waugh, "It is often a mistake for exiles to return," *Spectator*, 29 Oct. 1994, 8; Takie Sugiyama Lebra, *Above the Clouds: Status Culture of the Modern Japanese Nobility* (Berkeley, 1993), 14–15.

19. Martin Bernal, *Black Athena*, 1 (London, 1987), 287–92; Michael Herzfeld, *Anthropology through the Looking-Glass* (Cambridge, 1987), 192; Nikos Kazantzakis (1961) quoted in Roger Just, "Triumph of the ethnos," in Tonkin et al., *History and Ethnicity*, 82.

20. Fani-Maria Tsigakou, *The Rediscovery of Greece* (London, 1981), 72; Virginia Woolf, "A dialogue upon Mount Pentelicus" [1906], *TLS*, 11–17 Sept. 1987, 979.

21. Godfrey Barker (1984) and Charles Moore (1984) quoted in Roger Just, "Cultural certainties and private doubts," in Wendy James, ed., *The Pursuit of Certainty* (London, 1995), 303 n14, 306 n43; Gavin Stamp, "Keeping our Marbles," *Spectator*, 10 Dec. 1983, 14–17.

22. Neal Ascherson, "Why German migrants torment the liberal spirit," *Independent on Sunday*, 30 May 1993, 25; Robert Henderson, "Is it in the blood?" *Wisden's Cricket Monthly*, 17:2 (July 1995), 9–10; Michael Cockerell, "Enoch Powell: The marketplace romantic," *Times* Weekend, 11 Nov. 1995.

23. Simon Jenkins, "It is time for Mr Straw to prove he is a man of more than his name suggests," *Spectator*, 10 Dec. 1994, 36.

24. Alan Ryan, "Apocalypse now?" *NYRB*, 17 Nov. 1994, 7–11; Ira Katznelson letter to the author, 10 Sept. 1992; quotes from John Larew in Mark Munro, "Class privilege," *Boston Globe*, 18 Sept. 1991, 43, 46; Michael Lind, *The Next American Nation* (New York, 1994), 168–71; on President Lowell, Harry Barnard, *The Forging of an American Jew: The Life and Times of Judge Julian W. Mack* (New York, 1974), 291–9.

25. On Madagascar, Maurice Bloch, "Literacy and enlightenment," in Karen Schousboe and Mogens Trolle Larsen, *Literacy and Society* (Copenhagen, 1989), 15–37, ref. 19–24; Gordon Marsden, in Juliet Gardiner, ed., *The History Debate* (London, 1990), 117; Schneider, *Critique of the Study of Kinship*, 114, 165–6.

26. Miri Rubin, *Corpus Christi: The Eucharist in Late Medieval Culture* (Cambridge, 1991); Paul Connerton, *How Societies Remember* (Cambridge, 1989), 86; Colette Beaune, *Naissance de la nation France* (Paris, 1985), 82; W. M. Thackeray, *Vanity Fair* [1847] (London, 1991), 427; Hugh Montgomery-Massingberd (1986) cited in Michael Billig, *Talking of the Royal Family* (London, 1992), 104–5.

27. Cape Codder (1887) quoted in Michael Kammen, *Mystic Chords of Memory* (New York, 1991), 249; E. A. Ross (1914) quoted in Gossett, *Race*, 293; David E. Whisnant, *All That Is Native and Fine* (Chapel Hill, NC, 1983), 87; Davis, *Who Is Black?* 10–11.

28. *Edinburgh Review* (1844) in Horsman, *Race and Manifest Destiny*, 60; Sen. Albert J. Beveridge (1900) quoted in Sider, *Lumbee Indian Histories*, 86.

29. Liah Greenfeld, *Nationalism* (Cambridge, MA, 1992), 321, 368–9; Robert N. Proctor, *Racial Hygiene: Medicine under the Nazis* (Cambridge, MA, 1988), 56, 110, 78–9 (quoting Eugen Stähle [1933]).

30. Proctor, *Racial Hygiene*, 149; Foster Rhea Dulles, *The American Red Cross: A History* [1950] (New York, 1970), 419–21.

31. Jane Kramer, "Bad blood," *New Yorker*, 11 Oct. 1993, 74–95.

32. Simon Blow, *Broken Blood: The Rise and Fall of the Tennant Family* (London, 1987), 4–5, 189, 192.

33. Toni Morrison, *Song of Solomon* (New York, 1987), 157; Nelkin and Lindee, *DNA Mystique*, 2, 8, 38, 20, 49.

34. Nelkin and Lindee, *DNA Mystique*, 38–42, 50, 57.

35. Ibid., 2; Harold Brooks-Baker quoted in Steve Lohr, "Bush: The 'royalty factor' means a blue-blooded lead," *IHT*, 5 July 1988, 3, and also in "General Powell 'is relative of Queen,'" *Times*, 16 Oct. 1995.

36. Andrew Kohut quoted in *IHT*, 2 May 1995; Nelkin and Lindee, *DNA Mystique*, 115 (Reaganite), 103 (Jeffries), 107 (Minnesotan).

37. Nelkin and Lindee, *DNA Mystique*, 1, 97, 146, 194, 198.

38. Jack D. Forbes, *Africans and Native Americans: The Language of Race in the Evolution of Red-Black Peoples*, 2nd ed. (Urbana, IL, 1993), 131–51; W. C. Spooner cited in Charles Darwin, *The Variation of Animals and Plants under Domestication* [1868], *Works*, vol. 20 (London, 1988), 64; *National Trust Mag.*, no. 77 (Spring 1996), 23.

39. Plutarch, "Pericles," in *The Rise and Fall of Athens: Nine Great Lives* (London, 1960), 203–4; Fredrickson, *Black Image in the White Mind*, 88, 188–91, 277.

40. Philippe le Bel (1302) quoted in Beaune, *Naissance de la nation France*, 218; Daniel Defoe, "The True-Born Englishman" [1701], in his *Selected Writings* (Cambridge, 1975), 51–81; C. R. Boxer, *The Portuguese Seaborne Empire 1415–1825* (London, 1969), 272; Luke Owen Pike (1866) quoted in Hugh A. MacDougall, *Racial Myth in English History* (Hanover, NH, 1982), 91.

41. Thomas Jefferson, *Notes on the State of Virginia* [1782] (Chapel Hill, NC, 1953), 143; Henry Hughes (1854) quoted in Ronald Takaki, *Iron Cages: Race and Culture in 19th-Century America* (New York, 1990), 49, 134; [John Quincy Adams], "Misconceptions of Shakespeare on the stage," *New England Mag.*, 9 (Dec. 1835), 435–40; idem, "The character of Desdemona," *American Monthly Mag.*, 7 (n.s. 1) (1836), 209–17; Australian half-caste aversion in Griffiths, *Hunters and Collectors*, 151, 188–91.

42. David G. Croly, *Miscegenation: The Theory of the Blending of the Races, Applied to the*

American White Man and Negro (1863), cited in David R. Roediger, *The Wages of Whiteness* (New York, 1991), 156; Sir Ralph Williams (1919) quoted in Roy May and Robin Cohen, "Race and colonialism: A case study of the Liverpool race riots of 1919," *Race and Class*, 16 (1974–75), 111–26, ref. p. 116; Theodore G. Bilbo, *Take Your Choice: Separation or Mongrelization* (Poplarville, MS, 1947), pref., 224.

43. Hollis R. Lynch, *Edward Wilmot Blyden* (London, 1967), 38–9, 53, 58ff, 105–12, 118, 139; Lawrence W. Levine, "Marcus Garvey and the politics of revitalization" (1982), in his *Unpredictable Past* (New York, 1993), 131–4; Edmund David Cronon, *Black Moses: The Story of Marcus Garvey and the United Negro Improvement Association* (Madison, WI, 1964), 190–3; W. E. B. Du Bois, *The Conservation of Races* (Washington, 1987); idem, *Dusk of Dawn* [1940] (New York, 1968), 99; Stanley Crouch, "Who are we? Where did we come from? Where are we going?" in Gerald Early, ed., *Lure and Loathing* (New York, 1993), 80–94, ref. pp. 83–6; David Levering Lewis, *W. E. B. Du Bois: Biography of a Race, 1868–1919* (New York, 1993), 136.

44. Jared Gardner, "'Our native clay': Racial and sexual identity and the making of Americans in *The Bridge*," *AQ*, 44 (1992), citing Jung (1930) and Hart Crane (1927), 25, 26; Arthur Groom, *I Saw a Strange Land* (1950), quoted in Griffiths, *Hunters and Collectors*, 188; Coolidge in *Good Housekeeping* (1921) quoted in Michael Lind, "American by invitation," *New Yorker*, 24 April 1995, 108.

45. Julian Huxley (1924) quoted in Barkan, *Retreat of Scientific Racism*, 182; C. B. Davenport and Morris Steggerda, *Race Crossing in Jamaica* (Washington, 1929), 469–75; H. B. Fantham (1927) and Gerrie Eloff (1933, 1938, 1942) quoted in Dubow, *Scientific Racism in Modern South Africa*, 136, 271–2.

46. Kühl, *Nazi Connection*, 60; Proctor, *Racial Hygiene*, 151, 137, 140, 112, 114, 197.

47. Paul Spickard, *Mixed Blood* (Madison, WI, 1989), 11, 329; Proctor, *Racial Hygiene*, 298–308; Leonard Thompson, *The Mythology of Apartheid* (New Haven, 1985), 44; Davis, *Who Is Black?* 17–27.

48. Dr. Cecil Cook quoted in Griffiths, *Hunters and Collectors*, 189–91; *Breiz Atao* (Brittany For Ever) members quoted in Maryon McDonald, *"We Are Not French!"* (London, 1989), 112; Marianne Heiberg, *The Making of the Basque Nation* (Cambridge, 1989), 99.

49. Zora Neale Hurston, *Dust Tracks on a Road: An Autobiography* [1942] (London, 1986), 235; John E. Bruce quoted in E. Franklin Frazier, *Black Bourgeoisie* (New York, 1965), 197; Itabari Njeri, "Sushi and grits: Ethnic identity and conflict in a newly multicultural America," in Early, *Lure and Loathing*, 13–40, ref. p. 25; Davis, *Who Is Black?* 57; John Langton Gwaltney, *Drysolong: A Self-Portrait of Black America* (New York, 1980), 80; Alice Walker, *In Search of Our Mothers' Gardens* (New York, 1983), 291–2.

50. Davis, *Who Is Black?* 3–4; Rena Owen quoted in David Robinson, "Warrior in the wasteland," *Times*, 13 April 1995.

51. Mestizo quoted in Jean Molesky-Poz, "Reconstructing personal and cultural identities," *AQ*, 45 (1993), 619; Gillett G. Griffin, "Ethics of collecting pre-Columbian art," in Phyllis M. Messenger, ed., *The Ethics of Collecting* (Albuquerque, NM, 1989), 113.

52. Arthur W. Upfield, *Man of Two Tribes* [1956] (New York, 1986), 57; idem, *Bony and the Kelly Gang*, 72; Olive Schreiner (1890–92) and J. M. Coetzee (1988) quoted in

Dubow, *Scientific Racism in Modern South Africa*, 187; Toni Morrison cited in Nelkin and Lindee, *DNA Mystique*, 118.

53. Charles Mingus (1971) quoted in Michael M. J. Fischer, "Ethnicity and the postmodern arts of memory," in James Clifford and George E. Marcus, eds., *Writing Culture* (Berkeley, 1986), 215; Lise Funderburg, *Black, White, Other: Biracial Americans Talk About Race and Identity* (New York, 1994), 84–5, 367.

54. Waters, *Ethnic Options*, 23–4.

55. W. B. Yeats, *Purgatory* [1939], in his *Plays* (London, 1966), 1049 [tense altered]; Julian Moynahan, *Anglo-Irish: The Literary Imagination in a Hyphenated Culture* (Princeton, 1995), 225–7.

56. Don D. Fowler, "Uses of the past: Archaeology in the service of the state," *American Antiquity*, 52 (1987), 235; John Collinson, *The Beauties of British Antiquity* (1779) excerpt in Ronald Jessup, comp., *Curiosities of British Archaeology* (Chichester, England, 1974), 186; Anthony Trollope, *The West Indies and the Spanish Main* [1860] (London, 1968), 64; Bernard Semmel, *George Eliot and the Politics of National Inheritance* (New York, 1994), 118–32; Emerson, "English traits," 363; Renan, "What is a nation?" (1882) in H. K. Bhabha, ed., *Nation and Narration* (London, 1990), 14. See Tzvetan Todorov, *On Human Diversity: Nationalism, Racism and Diversity in French Thought* (Cambridge, MA, 1993), 133–40.

57. Jefferson (1808) quoted in Takaki, *Iron Cages*, 58–9; Poesche and Goepp (1853) quoted in Horsman, *Race and Manifest Destiny*, 295–6.

58. Lord Rosebery, "The patriotism of the Scot" (1882), in his *Miscellanies: Literary and Historical* (London, 1921), 2:115; William Macneile Dixon (1938) quoted in Marilyn Strathern, *After Nature: English Kinship in the Late Twentieth Century* (Cambridge, 1992), 30–1, 36; Julian S. Huxley et al., *We Europeans: A Survey of "Racial" Problems* (London, 1935), 23–24, 277–8.

59. Proctor, *Racial Hygiene*, 21, 40; Spickard, *Mixed Blood*, 109, 112.

60. Increase Niles Tarbox (1864) quoted, and American Freedmen's Inquiry Commission report (1864) cited, in Fredrickson, *Black Image in the White Mind*, 123–5; David Glassberg, *American Historical Pageantry* (Chapel Hill, NC, 1990), 34–5, 61–5 (quoting William E. Bohn, 1914), 137.

61. Trollope, *West Indies and the Spanish Main*, 75, 64. For what follows, see my "Race and color in the West Indies," *Daedalus*, 96 (1967), 580–626; *West Indian Societies* (London, 1972); and "Free colored West Indians," in Harold E. Pagliaro, ed., *Racism in the Eighteenth Century* (Cleveland, 1973), 335–53. The classic comparative studies are Harmannus Hoetink, *The Two Variants in Caribbean Race Relations* (London, 1967); and Carl N. Degler, *Neither Black nor White: Slavery and Race Relations in Brazil and the United States* (New York, 1971).

62. Quoted in Levine, "Marcus Garvey and the politics of revitalization," 113; for the background see Gad J. Heuman, *Between Black and White: Race, Politics, and the Free Coloreds in Jamaica, 1792–1865* (Westport, CT, 1981).

63. R. David Edmunds, "Native Americans, new voices: American Indian history, 1895–1995," *AHR*, 100 (1995), 717–40; Gail Vines, "Genes in black and white," *New Scientist*, 8 July 1995, 34–7; Key WalkingStick, "Democracy, Inc.," *Artforum*, 30 (Nov. 1991), 20–1; Eustace Lewis quoted in Ian Katz, "The tribe that found a fortune," *Guardian*, 29 July 1995, p. 23.

64. Howard Creamer, "Aboriginality in New South Wales," in Beckett, *Past and Present*, 47–8; Griffiths, *Hunters and Collectors*, 229; Lind, *Next American Nation*, 120.
65. Davis, *Who Is Black?* 11–12, 21–2; Bernadine Simmons quoted in Gordon S. Wood, "Jefferson at home," *NYRB*, 13 May 1993, 8.
66. James McPherson, "Junior and John Doe," in Early, *Lure and Loathing*, 175–93, ref. 178–9; Wood, "Jefferson at home."
67. "The future of the colored race" (1866) and "The future of the Negro" (1884) in Philip Foner, ed., *The Life and Writings of Frederick Douglass*, 4 vols. (New York, 1950–55), 4:193–6 and 4:411–13; Wendell Phillips (1863) cited in Andrew Kull, *The Color-Blind Constitution* (Cambridge, MA, 1992), 60; George Tillman quoted in Lerone J. Bennett, *Before the Mayflower: A History of the Negro in America* (Chicago, 1964), 266.
68. Davis, *Who Is Black?* 58, 72, 139, 182–5; Funderburg, *Black, White, Other*, 15; Alex Haley and David Stevens, *Queen: the Story of an American Family* (New York, 1993); Shirlee Taylor Haizlip, *The Sweeter the Juice: A Family Memoir in Black and White* (New York, 1994), 212.
69. Lawrence Wright, "One drop of blood," *New Yorker*, 25 July 1994, 55, 48; *Newsweek* poll Feb. 1995; Funderburg, *Black, White, Other*, 375. See Gary B. Nash, "The hidden history of mestizo America," *Journal of American History*, 82 (1995), 941–62.
70. Walter Benn Michaels, "Race into culture," *Critical Inquiry*, 18 (1992), 655–85; idem, "The no-drop rule," *Critical Inquiry*, 20 (1994), 758–69; Njeri, "Sushi and grits," 24.
71. Walker, *In Search of Our Mothers' Gardens*, 295; *Autobiography of Malcolm X* (New York, 1966), 2, 202; Garvey quoted in Levine, "Marcus Garvey," 132; Molefi Kete Asante, "Racism, consciousness, and Afrocentricity," in Early, *Lure and Loathing*, 127–43, ref. pp. 139–40; Njeri, "Sushi and grits," 38.
72. Barbara Tizard and Ann Phoenix, *Black, White or Mixed Race?* (London, 1993), 31, 36, 3.
73. Schneider, *Critique of the Study of Kinship*, 165–75.
74. John Boswell, *The Kindness of Strangers: The Abandonment of Children* (London, 1988), 72–4, 139–42, 430–1.
75. Ibid., 81, 128, 389, 394; R. C. Lewontin et al., *Not in Our Genes* (New York, 1984), 18.
76. Mary Ann Mason, *From Father's Property to Children's Rights* (New York, 1994), 120–2, 188–91; Elizabeth Bartholet, *Family Bonds* (Boston, 1993), 34, 167, 173; Nelkin and Lindee, *DNA Mystique*, 154; Betty Jean Lifton, *Journey of the Adopted Self* (New York, 1994), 47, 128.
77. José Van Dyck, *Manufacturing Babies and Public Consent: Debating the New Reproductive Technologies* (London, 1995), 150–64; Janet L. Dolgin, "Just a gene: Judicial assumptions about parenthood," *UCLA Law Review*, 40 (1993), 681–7; "Status of a child genetically not Jewish," Responsa No. 41, Feb. 1984, in Walter Jacob, *Contemporary American Reform Responsa* (New York, 1987), 70–1.
78. Ivor Gaber, "Transracial placements in Britain: A history," in Gaber and Jane Aldridge, eds., *In the Best Interests of the Child* (London, 1994), 12–42, ref. p. 15; David Rosner and Gerald Markowitz, "Race and foster care," *Dissent*, 40 (1993), 233–7.

79. David S. Rossetenstein, "Custody disputes involving tribal Indians in the United States," in John Eekelaar and Peter Sarcevič, *Parenthood in Modern Society* (Dordrecht, Netherlands, 1993), 597–619.

80. John Small, "Transracial placements: Conflicts and contradictions," in Sonia Morgan and Peter Righton, eds., *Child Care* (London, 1989), 60; Owen Gill and Barbara Jackson, *Adoption and Race* (London, 1983), 64–5, 71–5, 81, 139.

81. Phil Cohen, "Yesterday's words, tomorrow's world: From the racialization of adoption to the politics of difference," 43–76, and Elizabeth Bartholet, "Race matching in adoption: An American perspective," 151–87, in Gaber and Aldridge, *In the Best Interests of the Child*; National Assn. of Black Social Workers quoted in Rita J. Simon and Howard Altstein, *Transracial Adoption* (New York, 1977), 45, 50, 108; Rita Simon, "Adoption of black children by white parents in the USA," in Philip Bean, ed., *Adoption* (London, 1984), 329–42; NABSW president (1988) quoted in Bartholet, *Family Bonds*, 104–5; Gill and Jackson, *Adoption and Race*, 64–5, 71–5, 81, 139; Tizard and Phoenix, *Black, White or Mixed Race?* 2, 48–65.

82. Gaber, "Transracial placements in Britain," 23; Jane Aldridge, "In the best interests of the child," 191; Children Act 1989 Practice Note 26, Children and Their Heritage (1991), 238, all in Gaber and Aldridge, *In the Best Interests of the Child*; Shama Ahmed, "Children in care: The racial assessment in social work assessment," in Morgan and Righton, *Child Care*, 216–18.

83. Malcolm Gladwell, "When the cries of racism drown out culture's color," *IHT*, 28 June 1994, 5.

84. Waters, *Ethnic Options*, 91; Richard Rodriguez, *Days of Obligation* (New York, 1992), 171.

85. Diane Ravitch, "Multiculturalism: E pluribus plures," *American Scholar*, 59 (1990), 339; Joan Laxson, "How 'we' see 'them': Tourism and Native Americans," *Annals of Tourism Research*, 18 (1991), 385.

86. Micaela di Leonardo, "Habits of the cumbered heart: Ethnic community and women's culture as American invented traditions," in Jay O'Brien and William Rosebery, eds., *Golden Ages, Dark Ages* (Berkeley, 1991), 240–1; Waters, *Ethnic Options*, 159–64.

87. Daniel A. Pollen, *Hannah's Heirs: The Quest for the Genetic Origins of Alzheimer's Disease* (New York, 1993), 7, 169.

88. W. David Kubiak, "E pluribus Yamato: The culture of corporate beings," *Whole Earth Review*, 93 (Winter 1990), 4–10; Nelkin and Lindee, *DNA Mystique*, 188.

89. Eytan Avital and Eva Jablonka, "Social learning and the evolution of behaviour," *Animal Behaviour*, 48 (1994), 1195–9.

90. Italo Calvino, *Time and the Hunter* (London, 1970), 77, 80.

Chapter 10

1. Thomas Traherne, "First century" [c. 1670], in his *Centuries, Poems, and Thanksgivings*, 2 vols. (Oxford, 1958), no. 29, 1:15

2. Parks Canada, *Cultural Resources Management Policy*, Presentation Perspectives, Feb. 1994, 7; National Initiative for a Networked Cultural Heritage, Washington, Mar. 1995; "The Banff Recommendations" [1985], in *Proc. 1st World Congress on Heritage Interpretation and Presentation* (Edmonton, Alberta, 1988), 366–8. See UNESCO,

Conventions and Recommendations . . . Concerning the Protection of Cultural Heritage (Paris, 1985), 61, 105, 152, 195.

3. Etienne Clément, "Some recent practical experience in the implementation of the 1954 Hague Convention," *IJCP*, 3 (1994), 11–25; Swedish visitor quoted in Alexander Frater, "Lasting lure of the stones," *Observer on Sunday*, 20 June 1993, 49–50.

4. Charles Butler (1895) quoted in Allison Lockwood, *Passionate Pilgrims: American Travelers in Great Britain, 1800–1914* (New York, 1981), 362–3; *New York Mail* (1913) quoted in Neil Harris, "Collective possessions: J. Pierport Morgan and the American imagination," in his *Cultural Excursions* (Chicago, 1990), 274.

5. Anthony D. Smith, "The problem of national identity: Ancient, medieval and modern," *Ethnic and Racial Studies*, 17 (1994), 375–99; Sándor Petöfi (c. 1847) quoted in Benedict Anderson, *Imagined Communities* (London, 1983), 97; Woodrow Wilson (1915) and Theodore Roosevelt (1917) quoted in Arthur M. Schlesinger, Jr., *The Disuniting of America* (New York, 1992), 35.

6. Peter Novick, *That Noble Dream* (Cambridge, 1988), 470.

7. Auberon Waugh (1987) quoted in David Lowenthal, "Durham: Perils and promises of a heritage," *Durham University Journal*, 81 (1989), 185–90, ref. p. 187; David Lowenthal and Hugh C. Prince, "The English landscape" and "English landscape tastes," *Geographical Review*, 54 (1964), 309–46, and 55 (1965), 186–222.

8. Gerhard von Rad, *Genesis: A Commentary* (London, 1961), 146–50; Vicki Frost (1983) parsed in Joan DelFattore, *What Johnny Shouldn't Read* (New Haven, 1992), 55, 14.

9. Michael Lind, *The Next American Nation* (New York, 1994), 271–2, 288; Jamaica Kincaid, *A Small Place* (New York, 1988), 24.

10. A. N. Wilson, "England, his England" [interview with Lord Denning], *Spectator*, 18 Aug. 1990, 8–10; *Daily Mail* editor Andrew Alexander quoted in Alexander Chancellor, "Diary," *Spectator*, 1 Sept. 1990, 6.

11. Robert Bridges, "The Society's work" (1925), in W. F. Bolton and D. Crystal, *The English Language*, 2 vols. (Cambridge, 1969), 1:88; Clifford H. Prator, "The British heresy in TESL [teaching English as a second language]," in Joshua A. Fishman et al., eds., *Language Problems of Developing Nations* (New York, 1968), 459–76, ref. p. 471; Peter Holland, "Shakespeare for everybody?" *TLS*, 2 Dec. 1994, 18–19.

12. Brinsley Samaroo, "The East as West: Indo-Caribbean heritage as tourism," Heritage Tourism and Caribbean Identity conference, Jamaica, March 1995; Derek Walcott, *The Antilles: Fragments of Epic Memory* (London, 1993), 6–7.

13. H. T. Buckle, *History of Civilization in England* (1857), 3 vols. (London, 1873), 1:232–5; Ralph Waldo Emerson, "English Traits" (1856), *Portable Emerson* (New York, 1946), 425; Mandell Creighton, *The English National Character* (London, 1896), 23, 11, 16, 17; Lord Chorley quoted in Paula Weidiger, *Gilding the Acorn: Behind the Façade of the National Trust* (London, 1994), 163–4; Jacques Darras, "Should we go on growing roses in Picardy?" *JRSA*, 138 (1990), 526.

14. Walter E. Leitsch, "East Europeans studying history in Vienna," 145, and Stanoje Stanojevic (1905) quoted in Charles Jelavich, "Milenko M. Vukicevic: From Serbianism to Yugoslavism," both in Dennis Deletant and Harry Hanak, eds., *Historians as Nation-Builders* (London, 1988), 113–14.

15. Peter Elfer (Early Childhood Unit, National Children's Bureau) quoted in *Times*, 16 June 1993, 17; Luigi Barzini, *The Europeans* (London, 1984), 258–9.

16. Johann G. von Herder quoted in William A. Wilson, "Herder, folklore and romantic nationalism," *Journal of Popular Culture*, 6 (1973), 822; Gershom Scholem quoted in Stéphane Moisès, "Scholem and Rosenzweig: The dialectics of history," *H & M*, 2:2 (1990), 113.

17. Abbott Gleason, "Republic of humbug: The Russian nativist critique of the United States 1830–1930," *AQ*, 44 (1992), 4–7; D. G. Boyce, "'The marginal Britons': The Irish," in Robert Colls and Philip Dodd, eds., *Englishness: Politics and Culture 1880–1920* (London, 1986), 248–9; Declan Kiberd, "The war against the past," in Audrey S. Eyler and Robert E. Garratt, *The Uses of the Past: Essays on Irish Culture* (Newark, DE, 1988), 37.

18. Maryon McDonald, *"We are not French!"* (London, 1989), 213; Victoria Razak, "Culture under construction: The future of native Arubian identity," *Futures*, 27 (1995), 447–59; Cajun Creole Cultural Center (Berkeley, CA), "Points to remember when in Southwestern Louisiana" (1992).

19. Neil Asher Silberman, *Between Past and Present: Archaeology, Ideology, and Nationalism in the Modern Middle East* (New York, 1989), 32; Amos Elon, "Politics and archaeology," *NYRB*, 22 Sept. 1994, 15.

20. Akbar Ahmed, "The history-thieves: Stealing the Muslim past?" *History Today*, 43 (Jan. 1993), 11–13; Ahmed Rashid and Raymond Whitaker, "Islam damns ancient city," *Independent on Sunday*, 8 March 1992, 16.

21. Patrick J. O'Keefe and Lyndel V. Prott, *Law and the Cultural Heritage, 3: Movement* (London, 1989); Patrick J. O'Keefe, personal communication, 5 March 1996; Patrick J. Boylan, *Review of the Convention for the Protection of Cultural Property in the Event of Armed Conflict* [UNESCO] (London, 1993), 118; Charles S. Maier, "A surfeit of memory?" *H & M*, 5:2 (1994), 147.

22. Benoît Pelletier, "The case of the treasures of l'Ange-Gardien', *IJCP*, 2 (1993), 371–82.

23. Tom Griffiths, *Hunters and Collectors* (Melbourne, 1996), 234–6; Jeremy R. Beckett, "The past in the present," in his (ed.) *Past and Present: The Construction of Aboriginality* (Canberra, 1988), 207–8; Matthew Spriggs, "God's police and damned whores: Images of archaeology in Hawaii," in Peter Gathercole and David Lowenthal, eds., *The Politics of the Past* (London, 1990), 118–29; Klara Bonsack Kelley and Harris Francis, *Navajo Sacred Places* (Bloomington, IN, 1994), 46–50.

24. Elias Simajoki (1923) quoted in Wilson, *Folklore and Nationalism in Modern Finland* (Bloomington, IN, 1976), 132; Józef Olszewski (1968) quoted in Marc Ferro, *The Use and Abuse of History* (London, 1984), 173; Johan van der Dennen, "Ethnocentrism and in-group/out-group differentiation," in Vernon Reynolds et al., *The Sociobiology of Ethnocentrism* (Athens, GA, 1987), 31.

25. William Graham Sumner, "War" [1903], in his *War and Other Essays* (New Haven, 1919), p. 37; Faisal Husseini quoted in Jim Hoagland, "Mideast: Weak David and weary Goliath give hope," *IHT*, 18 May 1995.

26. Jeanette Greenfield, *The Return of Cultural Treasures* (Cambridge, 1989), 276–8; John Henry Merryman, "The nation and the object," *IJCP*, 3 (1994), 64–7; Patrick J. Geary, *Furta Sacra: Thefts of Relics in the Central Middle Ages* (Princeton, 1990), xii–xiii, 109–15, 125–8, 133.

27. Basque quoted in Marianne Heiberg, *Making of the Basque Nation* (Cambridge, 1989), 229–30.

28. Ray W. Gonyea, "Give me that old time religion: A story of a successful wampum repatriation," *History News*, 48:2 (1993), 4–7.

29. Adrian Lyttleton, "The national question in Italy," in Mikulas Teich and Roy Porter, eds., *The National Question in Europe in Historical Context* (Cambridge, 1993), 82–3; W. G. Sumner, *Folkways* [1906] (Boston, 1940), 635; Barzini, *Europeans*, 258–9.

30. Avner Ben-Amos, "Monuments and memory in French nationalism," *H & M*, 5:2 (1993), 50–81; Michelet quoted in Robert Gildea, *The Past in French History* (New Haven, 1994), 138; Tony Judt, "Chauvin and his heirs," *TLS*, 9 July 1993, 11–12.

31. Adam Müller (1810) quoted, and J. G. Fichte cited, in Liah Greenfeld, *Nationalism* (Cambridge, MA, 1992), 364–7; Kathleen Neils Conzen, "Ethnicity and festive culture: Nineteenth-century German America on parade," in Werner Sollors, ed., *The Invention of Ethnicity* (New York, 1989), 54–5.

32. Dorothy Ross, "Historical consciousness in nineteenth-century America," *AHR*, 89 (1984), 909–28; idem, "Grand narrative in American historical writing," *AHR*, 100 (1995), 652; David Glassberg, "History and the public," *Journal of American History*, 73 (1987), 957–80; Senator Albert J. Beveridge (1900) quoted in James W. Loewen, *Lies My Teacher Told Me* (New York, 1995), 248; James Bryce, *The American Commonwealth*, 2 vols. (New York, 1907), 1:1.

33. Woodrow Wilson (1919) quoted in Loewen, *Lies My Teacher Told Me*, 80; John F. Kennedy (1961) quoted in James Oliver Robinson, *American Myth, American Reality* (New York, 1980), 272; on the Liberty Bell, Michael Kammen, *Mystic Chords of Memory* (New York, 1991), 165, and John Henry Merryman, "Two ways of thinking about cultural property," *American Journal of International Law*, 80 (1986), 837 n.21.

34. Edward Gibbon, *The Decline and Fall of the Roman Empire* (London, 1896–1900), ch. 38, 4:163.

35. Banister Fletcher, *A History of Architecture on the Comparative Method* (New York, 1950), 888; Hugh Trevor-Roper, *The Rise of Christian Europe* (London, 1965), 11; Martha Doerr Toppin, "I know who's going with me: Reflections on the fellowship of history," *Social Education*, 44 (Nov. 1980), 456–60; Schlesinger, *Disuniting of America*, 127.

36. Silberman, *Between Past and Present*, 7–8; Sally Price, *Primitive Art in Civilized Places* (Chicago, 1989), 76–9.

37. Nerys and Orlando Patterson, "Beyond the legends, St. Patrick belongs to us all," *IHT*, 17 March 1993, p. 17.

38. O'Keefe and Prott, *Law and the Cultural Heritage*, 846–7, 478–9.

39. Wallis Budge quoted in Brian M. Fagan, *The Rape of the Nile* (London, 1977), 304; "Who's heritage?" *Connoisseur*, no. 192 (June 1976), 178.

40. Ann M. Early, "Profiteers and public archaeology: Antiquities trafficking in Arkansas," 39–50, ref. pp. 44–7, and Lowell Collins quoted in Charles S. Koczka, "The need for enforcing regulations on the international art trade," 185–98, ref. pp. 190–1, both in Phyllis M. Messenger, ed., *The Ethics of Collecting Cultural Property* (Albuquerque, NM, 1989); Philip Allison (1973) quoted in Price, *Primitive Art*, 76.

41. Rupert Christiansen, "Brush up your har-mo-nee," *Spectator*, 10 June 1994, 46–8; Griffiths, *Hunters and Collectors*, 98–9.

42. P. J. O'Keefe, "Cultural agency/cultural authority: Poetics and politics of intellectual property in the post-colonial era," *IJCP*, 4 (1995), 388–96; Tom Wilkie,

"Whose gene is it anyway?" *Independent on Sunday Review* (London), 19 Nov. 1995, 75–6; Donna J. Haraway, "Universal donors in a vampire culture," in William Cronon, ed., *Uncommon Ground: Toward Reinventing Nature* (New York, 1995), 321–66, ref. pp. 353–6; Nigel Hawkes, "Tribal treasure," *Times*, 4 March 1996, 12.

43. Gibbon, *Decline and Fall of the Roman Empire*, ch. 62, 6:486; Virginia Woolf, "A dialogue upon Mount Pentelicus" [1906], *TLS*, 11–17 Sept. 1987, 979; other sources from my "Classical antiquities as national and global heritage," *Antiquity*, 62 (1988), 726–35.

44. British diplomat (1980) quoted in Richard Clogg, "Greek-bashing," *London Review of Books*, 18 Aug. 1994, 18; Roger Just, "Cultural certainties and private doubts," in Wendy James, ed., *The Pursuit of Certainty* (London, 1995), 299–300; Paul Theroux, *The Pillars of Hercules: A Grand Tour of the Mediterranean* (New York, 1995), 324–5. See Michael Herzfeld, "Romanticism and Hellenism," in his *Anthropology through the Looking-Glass* (Cambridge, 1987), 19–27; Bernard Knox, "On two fronts" (1980), in his *Backing into the Future: The Classical Tradition and Its Renewal* (New York, 1994), 306.

45. Just, "Cultural certainties," 290; Greenfield, *Return of Cultural Treasures*; David Lowenthal, "Conclusion: Archaeologists and others," in Gathercole and Lowenthal, *Politics of the Past*, 308–10; O'Keefe and Prott, *Law and the Cultural Heritage*, 802–923.

46. Anna Somers Cocks, "A dangerously politicized issue . . .," *Art Newspaper*, 52 (Oct. 1995), 27; Paul M. Bator, *The International Trade in Art* (Chicago, 1983), 37–43, 92–3; Jaime Litvak King, "Cultural property and national sovereignty," in Messenger, *Ethics of Collecting Cultural Property*, 199–208; John Henry Merryman, "Archaeologists are not helping," *Art Newspaper*, 55 (Jan. 1996), 26; Bernard Smith, "Art objects and historical usage," in Isabel McBryde, ed., *Who Owns the Past?* (Melbourne, 1985), 79–80; Geary, *Furta Sacra*, 40–2, 110–11.

47. Patrick J. Geary, *Living with the Dead in the Middle Ages* (Ithaca, NY, 1994), 177–218; Silberman, *Between Past and Present*, 129–30.

48. Henry James, *The Outcry* [1911] (New York, 1982), 44–5; Just, "Cultural certainties," 288.

49. Walter Benn Michaels, "Race into culture," *Critical Inquiry*, 18 (1992), 682.

50. Amos Elon, *The Israelis: Founders and Sons* (New York, 1971), 256–89; Tamar Katriel, "Remaking place: Cultural production in an Israeli pioneer settlement museum," *H & M*, 5:2 (1993), 104–35; Barry Schwartz et al., "The recovery of Masada," *Sociological Quarterly*, 27 (1986), 147–64; on Church Fathers, Anthony Kemp, *The Estrangement of the Past* (New York, 1991), 98–104; on Americans, my *The Past Is a Foreign Country* (Cambridge, 1985), 117–21, George B. Forgie, *Patricide in the House Divided* (New York, 1979), and Andrew Delbanco, *The Puritan Ordeal* (Cambridge, MA, 1989), 224–8.

51. Eric Gable and Richard Handler, "The authority of documents at some American history museums," *Journal of American History*, 81 (1994), 119–36. Mormons who buttress their faith with academic scholarship are similarly distressed by the dissonance between theology and history (Douglas Davies, "Mormon history, identity, and faith community," in Elizabeth Tonkin et al., eds., *History and Ethnicity* [London, 1989], 171–2).

SELECT BIBLIOGRAPHY
AND CITATION INDEX

The bibliography stresses publications that bear explicitly on topics discussed in this book. It mostly omits general works, fiction and nonfiction, from which I have merely drawn illustrative examples, along with brief magazine pieces. Numbers at the end of each item refer to chapters (in boldface) and references in which these works are cited.

Adams, Timothy Dow, *Telling Lies in Modern American Autobiography* (Chapel Hill, NC, 1990). **6**: 47, 48

Agulhon, Maurice, "Le centre et le périphérie," in Nora, *LM*, III. 1:824–49. **3**: 13, 52

American Historical Association *Perspectives*, 33:3 (March 1995), "Public history and Disney's America," 1–12. Essays (not separately listed) by Confino, **7**: 33; Shopes, **4**: 27; Walters, **5**: 46; **7**: 54

American Quarterly, special issue on "Multiculturalism," 45:2 (June 1993), 195–308. **3**: 56

Anderson, Benedict, *Imagined Communities: Reflections on the Origin and Spread of Nationalism* (London, 1983). **8**: 11; **10**: 5

Appleby, Joyce, Lynn Hunt, and Margaret Jacob, *Telling the Truth about History* (New York, 1994). **5**: 5; **6**: 17; **7**: 55

Applegate, Celia, *A Nation of Provincials: The German Idea of Heimat* (Berkeley, 1990). **5**: 39

Arlen, Michael, *Passage to Ararat* [1975] (Harmondsworth, England, 1982). **3**: 7, 41

Aston, Margaret, *England's Iconoclasts: Laws against Images* (Oxford, 1988). **7**: 24

Babcock, Barbara, "Taking liberties, writing from the margins and doing it with a difference," *Journal of American Folklore*, 100 (1987), 390–411. **2**: 56, 59

Baczko, Bronislaw, "Le calendrier républicain," in Nora, *LM*, I:37–83. **8**: 37

Badone, Ellen, "Folk literature and the invention of tradition: The case of the *Barzaz-Breiz*," *Comparative Studies in Society and History*, forthcoming. **6**: 15

Baldwin, Stanley, "The Classics" (1926), in his *On England and Other Addresses* (London, 1927), 99–118. **8**: 30

Bailyn, Bernard, *On the Teaching and Writing of History* (Hanover, NH, 1994). **5**: 24; **6**: 38

Barkan, Elazar, *The Retreat of Scientific Racism* (Cambridge, 1992). **9**: 7, 45

Bar-On, Daniel, *The Dark Side of the Mind: Encounters with Children of the Third Reich* (Cambridge, MA, 1989). **2**: 13

Bartholet, Elizabeth, *Family Bonds: Adoption and the Politics of Parenting* (Boston, 1993). (See also Gaber and Aldridge.) **2**: 21; **9**: 76, 81

Bator, Paul M., *The International Trade in Art* (Chicago, 1983). **10**: 46

Baxandall, Michael, *Patterns of Intention: On the Historical Explanation of Pictures* (New Haven, 1985). **5**: 22

Beaune, Colette, *Naissance de la nation France* (Paris, 1985). **8**: 16; **9**: 26, 40

Becker, Carl, "Everyman his own historian," *AHR*, 37 (1932), 221–36; in Robin W. Winks, ed., *The Historian as Detective: Essays on Evidence* (New York, 1969), 3–23. **5**: 2, 36, 43

Beckett, Jeremy R., ed., *Past and Present: The Construction of Aboriginality* (Canberra, 1988). Essays (not separately listed) by Beckett, **3**: 71; **10**: 23; Coultheart, **9**: 6; Creamer, **9**: 64; Deirdre F. Jordan, **3**: 71

Beer, Gillian, *Arguing with the Past: Essays in Narrative from Woolf to Sidney* (London, 1989). **2**: 36

Beer, Jeanette, *Narrative Conventions of Truth in the Middle Ages* (Geneva, 1981). **5**: 7

Ben-Amos, Avner, "Monuments and memory in French nationalism," *H & M*, 5:2 (1993), 50–81. **10**: 30

Bender, Barbara, "Stonehenge—contested landscape, medieval to present-day," in her (ed.) *Landscape: Politics and Perspectives* (Providence, RI, 1993), 245–79. **1**: 59

Berlin, Isaiah, *Vico and Herder: Two Studies in the History of Ideas* (London, 1976). **9**: 4

Bernal, Martin, *Black Athena: The Afroasiatic Roots of Classical Civilization*, 1, *The Fabrication of Ancient Greece 1785–1985* (London, 1987). **9**: 19

Besson, Jean, "Family land and Caribbean society," in Elizabeth M. Thomas-Hope, ed., *Perspectives on Caribbean Regional Identity* (Liverpool, 1983), 57–83. **2**: 3

Bichsel, Peter, *La Suisse du Suisse* (Lausanne, 1970). **3**: 32

Bieder, Robert E., "Anthropology and history of the American Indian," *AQ*, 33 (1982), 309–26. **6**: 1

Billig, Michael, "Collective memory, ideology and the British royal family," in Middleton and Edwards, *Collective Remembering*, 60–80. **4**: 7, **6**: 22

——— *Talking of the Royal Family* (London, 1992). **8**: 8; **9**: 26

Björklund, Ulf, "Armenia remembered and remade: Evolving issues in a diaspora," *Ethnos*, 58 (1993), 335–60. **1**: 17

Bodnar, John, *Remaking America: Public Memory, Commemoration, and Patriotism in the Twentieth Century* (Princeton, 1992). **5**: 12, 51; **6**: 42; **8**: 4

Borofsky, Robert, *Making History: Pukapukan and Anthropological Constructions of Knowledge* (Cambridge, 1987). **6**: 30

Boswell, John, *The Kindness of Strangers: The Abandonment of Children* (London, 1988). **2**: 38, 40; **9**: 74, 75

Bourdin, Alain, *La patrimoine reinventé* (Paris, 1984). **1**: 3; **3**: 52

Boyce, D. G., " 'The marginal Britons': The Irish," in Robert Colls and Philip Dodd, eds., *Englishness: Politics and Culture 1880–1920* (London, 1986). **10**: 17

Boyes, Georgina, "Cultural survivals theory and traditional customs," *Folk Life*, 26 (1987–88), 5–11. **8**: 14

——— *The Imagined Village: Culture, Ideology and the English Folk Revival* (Manchester, 1993). **6**: 39; **8**: 14

Bradbury, Malcolm, "Telling life: Some thoughts on literary biography," in Eric

Homberger and John Charmley, *The Troubled Face of Biography* (London, 1988), 131–40. **6**: 51

Bradshaw, Brendan, "Nationalism and historical scholarship in modern Ireland," *Irish Historical Studies*, 26 (1989), 329–51. **6**: 11

Brewer, John, and Susan Staves, eds., *Early Modern Conceptions of Property* (London, 1995). Essays (not separately listed) by Blum, **2**: 53; Somers, **2**: 4; Staves, **2**: 25, 43; Sugarman and Warrington, **2**: 52

Brodzinsky, David M., Marshall D. Schechter, and Robin Marantz Henig, *Being Adopted: The Lifelong Search for Self* (New York, 1992). **2**: 12, 56

Broshi, Magen, "Religion, ideology and politics and their impact on Palestinian archaeology," *Israeli Museum Journal*, 6 (Spring 1987), 17–32. **8**: 12

Buckley, Anthony, "'We're trying to find our identity': Uses of history among Ulster Protestants," in Tonkin et al., *History and Ethnicity*, 183–97. **8**: 4

Burguière, André, "La généalogie," in Nora, *LM*, III.3:18–51. **1**: 30; **2**: 54; **9**: 1

Burke, Peter, "French historians and their cultural identities," in Tonkin et al., *History and Ethnicity*, 157–67. **8**: 8

———— "History and social memory," in Thomas Butler, ed., *Memory: History, Culture and Mind* (Oxford, 1989), 97–113. **5**: 19

Butterfield, Herbert, *The Englishman and His History* (Cambridge, 1944). **1**: 8; **3**: 45; **6**: 9; **8**: 29

Cannadine, David, "British history past, present—and future?" *Past and Present*, 116 (1987), 169–91. **5**: 12, 17

Carnes, Mark C., ed., *Past Imperfect: History According to the Movies* (New York, 1995). Essays (not separately listed) by Carnes, **7**: 57; Greg Dening, **6**: 2; Carolly Erickson, **7**: 38; Eric Foner, **5**: 30; Leon F. Litwack, **7**: 33; James M. McPherson, **7**: 16; John Sayles, **7**: 46; Richard White, **7**: 8

Carson, Cary, "Lost in the fun house: A commentary on anthropologists' first contact with history museums," *Journal of American History*, 81 (1994), 137–50. **5**: 16

Charle, Christophe, "Les grands corps," in Nora, *LM*, III.2:194–235. **8**: 28

Charteris of Amisfield, Lord, "The work of the National Heritage Memorial Fund," *JRSA*, 132 (1984), 325–38. **4**: 13

Chase, Malcolm, "This is no claptrap, this is our heritage," in Shaw and Chase, *Imagined Past*, 128–46. **1**: 8

Chastel, André, "La notion du patrimoine," in Nora, *LM*, II.2:405–50. **1**: 19; **4**: 1

Chevalier, Jean-Claude, "L'*Histoire de la langue française* de Ferdinand Brunot," in Nora, *LM*, III.2:418–59. **3**: 31

Chippindale, Christopher, *Stonehenge Complete*, rev. ed. (London, 1994). **1**: 57

Chippindale, Christopher, et al., *Who Owns Stonehenge?* (London, 1990). **1**: 59

Choay, Françoise, *L'Allegorie du patrimoine* (Paris, 1992). **1**: 5

Citron, Suzanne, *Le mythe national: L'histoire de France en question*, 2nd ed. (Paris, 1989). **7**: 21; **8**: 7, 27

Clément, Etienne, "Some recent practical experience in the implementation of the 1954 Hague Convention," *IJCP*, 3 (1994), 11–25. **10**: 3

Clifford, James, "Four Northwest Coast museums: Travel reflections," in Karp and Lavine, *Exhibiting Cultures*, 212–54. **7**: 30

———— "Objects and selves—an afterword," in Stocking, *Objects and Others*, 236–46. **2**: 37

Clifford, James, and George E. Marcus, eds., *Writing Culture: The Poetics and Politics of Ethnography* (Berkeley, 1986). Essays by Fischer; Rosaldo.

Clive, John, "The use of the past in Victorian England," *Salmagundi*, 68–69 (1985–86), 48–65. **1**: 11

Clogg, Richard, "The Greeks and their past," in Deletant and Hanak, *Historians as Nation-Builders*, 16–28. **6**: 12

Cockshut, A. O. J., *The Art of Autobiography in 19th and 20th Century England* (New Haven, 1984). **2**: 33

Cohen, Erik, "Authenticity and commoditization in tourism," *Annals of Tourism Research*, 15 (1988), 371–86. **7**: 36

Cohen, Patsy, and Margaret Somerville, *Ingelba and the Five Black Matriarchs* (Sydney, 1990). **2**: 18, 58

Cohn, Bernard S., "Anthropology and history in the 1980s," *Journal of Interdisciplinary History*, 12 (1981), 227–52. **6**: 29

Cohn, Samuel K., Jr., *The Cult of Remembrance and the Black Death: Six Renaissance Cities in Central Italy* (Baltimore, 1992). **2**: 45, 48

Coleman, Janet, *Ancient and Medieval Memories* (Cambridge, 1992). **5**: 7

Collard, Anna, "Investigating 'social memory' in a Greek context," in Tonkin et al., *History and Ethnicity*, 89–97. **6**: 12

Colley, Linda, *Britons: Forging the Nation 1707–1837* (London, 1992). **3**: 5, 13, 23, 24

Compagnon, Antoine, "La *Recherche du temps perdu*, de Marcel Proust," in Nora, *LM*, III.2:926–67. **3**: 31

Compton-Burnett, Ivy, *A Heritage and Its History* (London, 1959). **2**: 3

Confino, Alon, "The nation as a local metaphor: Heimat, national memory, and the German Empire, 1870–1918," *H & M*, 5:1 (1993), 42–86. **5**: 39

Connerton, Paul, *How Societies Remember* (Cambridge, 1989). **3**: 14; **9**: 26

Conzen, Kathleen Neils, "Ethnicity as festive culture: Nineteenth-century German America on parade," in Sollors, *Invention of Ethnicity*, 44–76. **10**: 31

Cooper, J. P., "Patterns of inheritance and settlement by great landowners from the fifteenth to the eighteenth centuries," in Goody et al., *Family and Inheritance*, 192–327. **2**: 47

Coornaert, Emile, *Destins de Clio en France depuis 1800* (Paris, 1977). **5**: 15

Corner, John, and Sylvia Harvey, eds., *Enterprise and Heritage: Crosscurrents of National Culture* (London, 1991). Essays by Hewison; Mellor.

Cornford, F. M., *Microcosmographia Academica* [1908] (Cambridge, 1953). **8**: 31

Cosgrove, Stuart, and Paul Reas, *Flogging a Dead Horse* (Manchester, 1993). **4**: 21

Creamer, Howard, "Aboriginal perceptions of the past: The implications of cultural resource management in Australia," in Gathercole and Lowenthal, *The Politics of the Past*, 130–40. **6**: 4. See also Beckett.

Creighton, Mandell, *The English National Character*, The Romanes Lecture (London, 1896). **7**: 9; **8**: 2, 29; **10**: 13

Crocombe, Ron, "The continuing creation of identities in the Pacific islands," in Hooson, *Geography and National Identity*, 311–30. **1**: 18

Croft, Andy, "Forward to the 1930s: The literary politics of anamnesis," in Shaw and Chase, *Imagined Past*, 147–70. **4**: 23

Curtis, James R., "The most famous fence in the world: Fact and fiction in Mark Twain's Hannibal," *Landscape*, 28:3 (1985), 8–13. **7**: 44

Danto, Arthur C., "The problem of other periods," *Journal of Philosophy*, 63 (1966), 566–77. **5**: 23

Darras, Jacques, "Should we go on growing roses in Picardy? The future for our cultural heritages in Europe," *JRSA*, 138 (1990), 524–30. **1**: 47; **10**: 13

Davies, Douglas, "Mormon history, identity, and faith community," in Tonkin et al., *History and Ethnicity*, 168–82. **10**: 51

Davis, F. James, *Who Is Black? One Nation's Definition* (University Park, PA, 1991). **9**: 12, 27, 47, 49, 50, 59, 65, 68

Davis, John, "The social relations of the production of history," in Tonkin et al., *History and Ethnicity*, 104–20. **5**: 50

Davison, Graeme, "The broken lineage of Australian family history," in Donna Merwick, ed., *Essays in Honour of Greg Dening* (Melbourne, 1994), 333–51. **1**: 32; **2**: 16

—— "Cities and ceremonies: Nationalism and civic ritual in three new lands," *New Zealand Journal of History*, 24 (1990), 97–117. **3**: 55

—— "The meanings of 'heritage,'" in Graeme Davison and Chris McConville, eds., *A Heritage Handbook* (North Sydney, NSW, 1991), 1–13. **Introd**: 1; **1**: 6; **4**: 5; **7**: 57

Deletant, Dennis, and Harry Hanak, eds., *Historians as Nation-Builders: Central and South-Eastern Europe* (London, 1988). Essays by Clogg; Jelavich; Leitsch.

DelFattore, Joan, *What Johnny Shouldn't Read: Textbook Censorship in America* (New Haven, 1992). **7**: 26; **10**: 8

Dennen, Johan van der, "Ethnocentrism and in-group/out-group differentiation," in Vernon Reynolds et al., eds., *The Sociobiology of Ethnocentrism* (Athens, GA, 1987), 1–47. **6**: 4; **10**: 24

Dennis, Nigel, *Cards of Identity* [1955] (London, 1974). **4**: 7

Dickenson, John P., "Nostalgia for a gilded past? Museums in Minas Gerais, Brazil," in Flora E. S. Kaplan, ed., *Museums and the Making of "Ourselves"* (London, 1994), 221–45. **7**: 30

Dillard, Annie, *An American Childhood* (London, 1988). **5**: 47

—— "To fashion a text," in William Zinsser, ed., *Inventing the Truth: The Art and Craft of Memoir* (Boston, 1987), 53–76. **6**: 54

Dilworth, Leah, "Object lessons," *AQ*, 45 (1993), 257–80. **3**: 57

Ditchfield, Simon, *Liturgy, Sanctity and History in Tridentine Italy: Pietro Maria Campi and the Preservation of the Particular* (Cambridge, 1995). **8**: 26, 28

Dolgin, Janet L., "Just a gene: Judicial assumptions about parenthood," *UCLA Law Review*, 40 (1993), 637–94. **9**: 77

Domansky, Elisabeth, "'Kristallnacht,' the Holocaust and German unity," *H & M*, 4:1 (1992), 60–94. **7**: 35

Donath, Jackie, "The Gene Autry Western Heritage Museum: The problem of an authentic Western mystique," *AQ*, 43 (1991), 82–102. **4**: 20

Drury, Martin, "The restoration of Calke Abbey," *JRSA*, 136 (1988), 490–9. **4**: 15

Dubow, Saul, *Scientific Racism in Modern South Africa* (Cambridge, 1995). **8**: 24; **9**: 7, 45, 52

Dukes, Paul, "Fin de siècle: A watershed in world history," *History Today*, 42 (Nov. 1992), 45–50. **5**: 9

Durand, Georges, "La vigne et le vin," in Nora, *LM*, III.2:784–821. **3**: 33

Early, Gerald, ed., *Lure and Loathing: Essays on Race, Identity, and the Ambivalence of*

Assimilation (New York, 1993). Essays (not separately listed) by Asante, **9**: 71; Crouch, **9**: 43; James McPherson, **9**: 66; Njeri, **9**: 49, 70, 71

Eddy, John, and Deryck Schreuder, "The Edwardian empire," in their (eds.), *The Rise of Colonial Nationalism* (Sydney, 1988), 19–62. **3**: 5

Elon, Amos, *The Israelis: Founders and Sons* (New York, 1971). **1**: 49; **10**: 50

—— "Politics and archaeology," *NYRB*, 22 Sept. 1994, 14–18. **7**: 41, 58; **8**: 10; **10**: 19

Ely, David, *Time Out* (London, 1968). **1**: 54

Emerson, Ralph Waldo, "English traits" [1856], *The Portable Emerson* (New York, 1946), 353–488. **3**: 28; **8**: 39; **9**: 5, 56; **10**: 13

Enzensberger, Hans Magnus, *Europe, Europe* (London, 1990) **3**: 43, 44, 48; **7**: 29

Ergang, Robert R., *Herder and the Foundations of German Nationalism* [1931] (New York, 1966). **2**: 51

Eriksen, Thomas Hylland, "A future-oriented, non-ethnic nationalism? Mauritius as an exemplary case," *Ethnos*, 58 (1993), 197–221. **8**: 43

Ethnos, "Defining the national," special issue, 58:3–4 (1993). **8**: 44. Includes Björklund; Eriksen; Löfgren; Olwig; Paine

Evans-Pritchard, Deirdre, "How 'they' see 'us': Native American images of tourists," *Annals of Tourism Research,* 16 (1989), 89–105. **3**: 71

—— "The Portal case—Authenticity, tourism, traditions, and the law," *Journal of American Folklore*, 100 (1987), 287–96. **3**: 68

Fardon, Richard, ed., *Counterworks: Managing the Diversity of Knowledge* (London, 1995). Essays by Signe Howell; Salmond; Vitebsky.

Fast, Robin Riley, "Outside looking in: Nonnatives and American Indian literature," *AQ*, 46 (1994), 62–76. **3**: 65

Feintuch, Bert, ed., *The Conservation of Culture: Folklorists and the Public Sector* (Lexington, KY, 1988). Essays by Staub; Whisnant; Williams.

Fentress, James, and Chris Wickham, *Social Memory* (Oxford, 1992). **6**: 55; **7**: 3

Ferraro, Thomas J., "Blood in the marketplace: The business of family in the *Godfather* narratives," in Sollors, *Invention of Ethnicity*, 176–208. **3**: 56

Ferro, Marc, *The Use and Abuse of History or How the Past Is Taught* (New York, 1984). **3**: 48; **5**: 14; **6**: 25; **10**: 24

The Field, 272, no. 7028 (May 1990), "Being British, what it means to me," 76–85. Essays (not separately listed) by Gammon, **1**: 8; Heseltine, **8**: 30; Rowse, **8**: 33

Fields, Karen E., "What one cannot remember mistakenly," in Jeffrey and Edwall, *Memory and History*, 89–104. **6**: 49, 52

Fields, Mamie Garvin, with Karen Fields, *Lemon Swamp and Other Places* (New York, 1983). **2**: 5; **6**: 49

Fischer, Michael M. J., "Ethnicity and the post-modern arts of memory," in Clifford and Marcus, *Writing Culture*, 194–233. **9**: 53

FitzGerald, Frances, *America Revised: History Schoolbooks in the Twentieth Century* (New York, 1980). **5**: 16, 51; **6**: 38

Forsythe, Diana, "German identity and the problems of history," in Tonkin et al., *History and Ethnicity*, 137–56. **9**: 17

Fowler, Don D., "Uses of the past: Archaeology in the service of the state," *American Antiquity*, 52 (1987), 230–47. **9**: 56

Fredrickson, George M., *The Black Image in the White Mind: The Debate on Afro-American Character and Destiny, 1817–1914* (New York, 1971). **9**: 6, 8, 39, 60

Freedberg, David, *Iconoclasts and Their Motives* (Maarssen, Netherlands, 1985). **7**: 23

French, Sean, ed., *Fatherhood* (London, 1992). Essay by Jones French, "Introduction," 1–6. **2**: 55

Freud, Sigmund, *Complete Works*, trans. James Strachey (London, 1966–74):

————— "Constructions in analysis" [1937], 23:257–69. **6**: 5

————— "Family romances" [1909], 9:235–41. **2**: 55

————— *Moses and Monotheism* [1939], 23:1–173. **2**: 55

Fumaroli, Marc, "La conversation," in Nora, *LM*, III.2:679–743. **3**: 31

————— "La génie de la langue française," in Nora, *LM*, III.3:911–93. **3**: 31

Funderburg, Lise, *Black, White, Other: Biracial Americans Talk about Race and Identity* (New York, 1994). **9**: 53, 68, 69

Furet, François, "L'Ancien Régime et la Révolution," in Nora, *LM*, III.1:107–39. **1**: 10

Gaber, Ivor, and Jane Aldridge, eds., *In the Best Interests of the Child: Culture, Ideology, and Racial Adoption* (London, 1994). Essays (not separately listed) by Aldridge, **9**: 82; Bartholet, **9**: 81; Phil Cohen, **9**: 81; Gaber, **9**: 78, 82

Gable, Eric, and Richard Handler, "The authority of documents at some American history museums," *Journal of American History*, 81 (1994), 119–36. **10**: 51

————— "Deep dirt: Messing up the past at Colonial Williamsburg," *Social Analysis*, 34 (1993), 3–16. **1**: 25; **6**: 39

Gable, Eric, Richard Handler, and Anna Lawson, "On the uses of relativism: Fact, conjecture, and black and white histories at Colonial Williamsburg," *American Ethnologist*, 19 (1992), 791–805. **6**: 28; **7**: 16

Gadamer, Hans-Georg, *Truth and Method* [1965], 2nd ed. (London, 1989). **5**: 10

Gardiner, Juliet, ed., *The History Debate. A History Today Book* (London, 1990). Includes untitled essays by Michael Hunter, **5**: 11; Gordon Marsden, **9**: 25; Roy Porter, **5**: 13; Conrad Russell, **3**: 8.

Gardner, Jared, "'Our native clay': Racial and sexual identity and the making of Americans in *The Bridge*," *AQ*, 44 (1992), 24–50. **9**: 44

Gasnier, Thierry, "Le local: une et divisible," in Nora, *LM*, III.2:462–525. **3**: 52

Gathercole, Peter, and David Lowenthal, eds., *The Politics of the Past* (London, 1990). Essays by Creamer; Gero and Root; Lowenthal; McCann; Spriggs.

Geary, Patrick J., *Furta Sacra: Thefts of Relics in the Central Middle Ages*, rev. ed. (Princeton, 1990). **10**: 26, 46

————— *Living with the Dead in the Middle Ages* (Ithaca, NY, 1994). **Introd**: 2; **3**: 15; **10**: 47

————— *Phantoms of Remembrance: Memory and Oblivion at the End of the First Millennium* (Princeton, 1995). **2**: 59; **7**: 2, 3

Gero, Joan, and Dolores Root, "Public presentations and private concerns: Archaeology in the pages of National Geographic," in Gathercole and Lowenthal, *Politics of the Past*, 19–37. **6**: 42

Gershoni, Israel, "Imagining and reimagining the past: The use of history by Egyptian nationalist writers, 1919–1952," *H & M*, 4:2 (1992), 5–37. **3**: 38

Gildea, Robert, *The Past in French History* (New Haven, 1994). **3**: 5, 36, 40, 47, 51; **7**: 21; **8**: 27; **10**: 30

Gill, Owen, and Barbara Jackson, *Adoption and Race: Black, Asian and Mixed-Race Children in White Families* (London, 1983). **9**: 80, 81

Gillis, John R., ed., *Commemorations: The Politics of National Identity* (Princeton, 1994). Essays by Sherman; Zerubavel.

Gilroy, Paul, *The Black Atlantic* (London, 1993). **9**: 8

Glassberg, David, *American Historical Pageantry* (Chapel Hill, NC, 1990). **9**: 60

———— "History and the public: Legacies of the Progressive era," *Journal of American History*, 73 (1987), 957–80. **5**: 53; **10**: 32

———— "Monuments and memories," *AQ*, 43 (1991), 143–56. **7**: 34

Gleason, Abbott, "Republic of humbug: The Russian nativist critique of the United States 1830–1930," *AQ*, 44 (1992), 1–23. **10**: 17

Gonis, George, "History in the making," *History News*, 40:7 (1985), 12–15. **5**: 28, 31

Goody, Jack, *The Development of the Family and Marriage in Europe* (Cambridge, 1983). **2**: 46

———— "The time of telling and the telling of time in written and oral cultures," in John Bender and David E. Wellbery, eds., *Chronotypes* (Stanford, CA, 1991), 77–96. **7**: 1

Goody, Jack, Joan Thirsk, and E. P. Thompson, eds., *Family and Inheritance: Rural Society in Western Europe 1200–1800* (Cambridge, 1976). Essays by Cooper; Cicely Howell; Kiernan.

Gossett, Thomas F., *Race: The History of an Idea in America* (Dallas, 1963). **9**: 5, 27

Grafton, Anthony, *Forgers and Critics: Creativity and Duplicity in Western Scholarship* (Princeton, 1990). **3**: 46

Greenblatt, Stephen, "Resonance and wonder," in Karp and Lavine, *Exhibiting Cultures*, 42–56. **7**: 35

Greenfeld, Liah, *Nationalism: Five Roads to Modernity* (Cambridge, MA, 1992). **2**: 39; **3**: 13, 30; **8**: 18, 35; **9**: 29; **10**: 31, 45

Greenfield, Jeanette, *The Return of Cultural Treasures* (Cambridge, 1989). **10**: 26, 45

Greenwald, Anthony, "The totalitarian ego: Fabrication and revision of personal history," *American Psychologist*, 35 (1980), 603–18. **6**: 48

Griffiths, Tom, *Hunters and Collectors: The Antiquarian Imagination in Australia* (Melbourne, 1996). **1**: 34, 61; **2**: 29, 58; **3**: 71; **4**: 11; **9**: 15, 41, 44, 48, 64; **10**: 23, 41

Gröning, Gert, "The feeling for landscape—a German example," *Landscape Research*, 17 (1992), 108–15. **9**: 18

Guillaume, Marc, *La politique du patrimoine* (Paris, 1980). **1**: 16, 19, 24, 42; **3**: 10, 20

Guiomar, Jean-Yves, "Le *Barzaz-Breiz* de Théodore Hersart de La Villemarqué," in Nora, *LM*, III.2:526–65. **6**: 15

Hagestad, Gunnhild O., "Dimensions of time and the family," *American Behavioral Scientist*, 29 (1986), 679–94. **2**: 34

Haizlip, Shirlee Taylor, *The Sweeter the Juice: A Family Memoir in Black and White* (New York, 1994). **9**: 68

Halbwachs, Maurice, *The Collective Memory* [1950] (New York, 1980). **7**: 52

Hamilton, Paula, "The knife edge: Debates about memory and history," in Kate Darian-Smith and Paula Hamilton, eds., *Memory and History in Twentieth-Century Australia* (Melbourne, 1994), 9–32. **3**: 61

Handler, Richard, "On having a culture: Nationalism and the preservation of Quebec's *patrimoine*," in Stocking, *Objects and Others*, 192–217. **1**: 51. See also Gable.

Hanson, Allan, "The making of the Maori: Culture invention and its logic," *American Anthropologist*, 91 (1989), 890–902. **6**: 29

Harker, Dave, *Fakesong: The Manufacture of British "Folksong" 1700 to Present Day* (Milton Keynes, England, 1985). **3**: 18

Harris, Neil, "Collective possessions: J. Pierpont Morgan and the American imagination," in his *Cultural Excursions* (Chicago, 1990), 250–75. **1**: 50; **10**: 4

Harvie, Christopher, *The Rise of Regional Europe* (London, 1994). **3**: 50

Haskell, Harry, *The Early Music Revival: A History* (London, 1988). **7**: 11

Hastrup, Kirsten, "Uchronia and the two histories of Iceland, 1400–1800," in her (ed.) *Other Histories* (London, 1992), 102–20. **5**: 35

Hauschild, Thomas, "Making history in southern Italy," in Hastrup, *Other Histories*, 29–44. **8**: 15

Heaney, Seamus, "Past, pastness, poems," *Salmagundi*, 68–69 (1985–86), 30–47. **2**: 6

Heiberg, Marianne, *The Making of the Basque Nation* (Cambridge, 1989). **9**: 48; **10**: 27

Heimberg, Charles, *Un étrange anniversaire: le centenaire du premier août* (Geneva, 1990). **6**: 10

Hélias, Pierre-Jakez, *The Horse of Pride: Life in a Breton Village* [1975] (New Haven, 1978). **1**: 14; **2**: 28

Herzfeld, Michael, *Anthropology through the Looking-Glass: Critical Ethnography in the Margins of Europe* (Cambridge, 1987). **9**: 19; **10**: 44

——— *A Place in History: Social and Monumental Time in a Cretan Town* (Princeton, 1991), **4**: 16; **6**: 43

Hewison, Robert, "Commerce and culture," in Corner and Harvey, *Enterprise and Heritage*, 162–77. **4**: 1, 21, 24

——— *The Heritage Industry: Britain in a Climate of Decline* (London, 1987). **4**: 1

Hexter, J. H., "Historiography: The rhetoric of history," *International Encyclopedia of the Social Sciences* (New York, 1968), 6:368–94. **5**: 11

Himmelfarb, Gertrude, *The New History and the Old* (Cambridge, MA, 1987). **4**: 1

——— *On Looking into the Abyss: Untimely Thoughts on Culture and Society* (New York, 1994), 122–30. **4**: 28; **6**: 1

Hinsley, Curtis M., "From shell-heaps to stelae: Early anthropology at the Peabody Museum," in Stocking, *Objects and Others*, 49–74. **6**: 34

History & Memory, special issue, "Israeli historiography revisited," 7:1 (Spring/Summer 1995). Includes essays by Kimmerling; Ram.

Hobsbawm, Eric J., "Mass-producing traditions: Europe, 1870–1914," in Eric Hobsbawm and Terence Ranger, eds., *The Invention of Tradition* (Cambridge, 1983), 263–307. **3**: 19

——— *Nations and Nationalism since 1780: Programme, Myth, Reality* (Cambridge, 1990). **3**: 18

——— "The new threat to history," *NYRB*, 16 Dec. 1993, 62–4. **4**: 2, 28; **8**: 11

Hofer, Tamás, ed., *Hungarians between "East" and "West": Three Essays on National Myths and Symbols* (Budapest, 1994). [Katalin Sinkó, "Competing heroes and representation of Hungarian history"; Tamás Hofer, "Construction of the 'Folk Cultural Heritage in Hungary' and rival versions of national identity"; Eszter Kisbán, "From peasant dish to national symbol."] **3**: 37

Hollinger, David A., "How wide the circle of 'we'?" *AHR*, 98 (1993), 317–37. **3**: 1

Holt, Thomas C., "Marking: Race, race-making, and the writing of history," *AHR*, 100 (1995), 1–20. **7**: 27

Hooson, David, ed., *Geography and National Identity* (Oxford, 1994). Essays by Crocombe; Kristof; Takeuchi.

Horsman, Reginald, *Race and Manifest Destiny* (Cambridge, MA, 1981). **9**: 6, 28, 57

Horton, James Oliver, and Spencer R. Crew, "Afro-Americans and museums: Towards a policy of inclusion," in Warren Leon and Roy Rosenzweig, eds., *History Museums in the United States* (Urbana, IL, 1989), 215–36. **7**: 14

Howell, Cicely, "Peasant inheritance customs in the Midlands, 1280–1700," in Goody et al., *Family and Inheritance*, 112–55. **2**: 3

Howell, Signe, "Whose knowledge and whose power? A new perspective on cultural diffusion," in Fardon, *Counterworks*, 164–81. **3**: 62

Hutton, Patrick H., "The problem of memory in the historical writings of Philippe Ariès," *H & M*, 4:1 (1992), 95–122. **7**: 55

——— "The role of memory in the historiography of the French Revolution," *History and Theory*, 30 (1991), 56–69. **7**: 52

Huxtable, Ada Louise, "Inventing American reality," *NYRB*, 3 Dec. 1992, 24–9. **4**: 25

Huyssen, Andreas, "Monument and memory in a postmodern age," *Yale Journal of Criticism*, 6 (1993), 249–61. **4**: 1

Inglis, K. S., "Entombing unknown soldiers," *H & M*, 5:2 (1993), 7–31. **3**: 19

Isaacs, Harold R., *Idols of the Tribe* (New York, 1973). **3**: 6

Jackson, J. B., *The Necessity for Ruins, and Other Topics* (Amherst, MA, 1980). **3**: 19

James, Harold, *A German Identity 1770–1990* (London, 1989). **2**: 31; **9**: 17

James, Henry, "The Birthplace" [1903], in his *Selected Tales* (London, 1982), 284–351. **7**: 46

——— *The Outcry* [1911] (New York, 1982). **1**: 53; **2**: 1; **3**: 24; **10**: 48

Jeffrey, Jaclyn, and Glenace Edwall, eds., *Memory and History: Essays on Recalling and Interpreting Experience* (Lanham, MD, 1994). **6**: 47. Essays by Fields; Thompson.

Jelavich, Charles, "Milenko M. Vukicevic: From Serbianism to Yugoslavism," in Deletant and Hanak, *Historians as Nation-Builders*, 106–23. **10**: 14

Jochens, Jenny M., "The politics of reproduction: Medieval Norwegian kingship," *AHR*, 92 (1987), 327–49. **2**: 54

Johannesson, Kurt, *The Renaissance of the Goths in Sixteenth-Century Sweden: Johannes and Olaus Magnus as Politicians and Historians* [1982], trans. James Larson (Berkeley, 1991). **7**: 5

Jones, Mervyn, "Learning to be a father," in French, *Fatherhood*, 23–9. **2**: 35

Jordan, Cynthia, "'Old words' in 'new circumstances': Language and leadership in post-revolutionary America," *AQ*, 40 (1988), 491–513. **2**: 8

Jordanova, Ludmilla, "Gender, generation and science," in W. F. Bynum and Roy Porter, eds., *William Hunter and the 18th-Century Medical World* (Cambridge, 1985), 385–412. **2**: 54

Just, Roger, "Cultural certainties and private doubts," in Wendy James, ed., *The Pursuit of Certainty: Religious and Cultural Formulations* (London, 1995), 285–308. **6**: 22; **8**: 7, 36; **9**: 21; **10**: 44, 45, 48

——— "Triumph of the ethnos," in Tonkin, *History and Ethnicity*, 71–88. **9**: 19

Kammen, Michael, "History is our heritage: The past in contemporary American culture," in Paul Gagnon and the Bradley Commission, eds., *Historical Literacy: The Case for History in American Education* (Boston, 1989), 138–56, **7**: 52

——— *A Machine That Would Go of Itself: The Constitution in American Culture* (New York, 1987). **6**: 23; **7**: 10

——— *Mystic Chords of Memory: The Transformation of Tradition in American Culture* (New York, 1991). **1**: 7, 26, 35; **4**: 29; **5**: 8; **6**: 14, 32; **7**: 19, 48; **8**: 26, 32; **9**: 27; **10**: 33

Karp, Ivan, and Steven D. Lavine, *Exhibiting Cultures: The Poetics and Politics of Museum Display* (Washington, 1991). Essays by Clifford; Greenblatt.

Katriel, Tamar, "Remaking place: Cultural production in an Israeli pioneer settlement museum," *H & M*, 5:2 (1993), 104–35. **6**: 27; **7**: 50; **10**: 50

——— "Sites of memory: Discourses of the past in Israeli pioneering settlement museums," *Quarterly Journal of Speech*, 80 (1994), 1–20. **6**: 27

Kelley, Klara Bonsack, and Harris Francis, *Navajo Sacred Places* (Bloomington, IN, 1994). **10**: 23

Kemp, Anthony, *The Estrangement of the Past: A Study in the Origins of Modern Historical Consciousness* (New York, 1991). **10**: 50

Kermode, Frank, *History and Value* (Oxford, 1988). **5**: 48

Kiberd, Declan, "The war against the past," in Audrey S. Eyler and Robert E. Garratt, eds., *The Uses of the Past: Essays in Irish Culture* (Newark, DE, 1988), 24–54. **3**: 45; **10**: 17

Kiernan, V. G., "Private property in history," in Goody et al., *Family and Inheritance*, 361–98. **2**: 47, 62

Kimmerling, Baruch, "Academic history caught in the cross-fire: the case of Israeli-Jewish historiography," *H & M*, 7:1 (1995), 41–65. **4**: 3

Kincaid, Jamaica, *A Small Place* (New York, 1988). **1**: 47; **10**: 9

King, Thomas F., "Beneath the American mosaic: The place of archaeology," in Stipe and Lee, *American Mosaic*, 235–64. **1**: 20

Kirkpatrick, Sidney D., *Lords of Sipán* (New York, 1992). **1**: 43

Klaes, Anton, *From Hitler to Heimat: The Return of History as Film* (Cambridge, MA, 1989). **8**: 27

Koselleck, Reinhart, *Futures Past: On the Semantics of Historical Time*, trans. Keith Tribe (Cambridge, MA, 1985). **5**: 5

Kotre, John, *Outliving the Self: Generativity and the Interpretation of Lives* (Baltimore, 1984). **2**: 20

Kramer, Jane, "Bad blood," *New Yorker*, 11 Oct. 1993, 74–95. **9**: 31

Kristof, Ladis K. D., "The image and vision of the Fatherland: The case of Poland in comparative perspective," in Hooson, *Geography and National Identity*, 221–32. **3**: 44

Krop, Henri, "The antiquity of the Dutch language," *Geschiedenis van de Wijsbegeerte in Nederland*, 5 (1994), 1–8. **3**: 30; **8**: 9

Kühl, Stefan T., *The Nazi Connection: Eugenics, American Racism, and German National Socialism* (New York, 1994). **9**: 4, 46

Lass, Andrew, "Romantic documents and political monuments: The meaning-fulfillment of history in 19th-century Czech nationalism," *American Ethnologist*, 15 (1988), 456–71. **7**: 40

Laxson, Joan D., "How 'we' see 'them': Tourism and Native Americans," *Annals of Tourism Research*, 18 (1991), 365–91. **3**: 54, 61; **9**: 85

Lee, Antoinette J., "Cultural diversity in historic preservation," *Historic Preservation Forum*, 6:4 (1992), 28–41. **1**: 40

———— "Discovering old cultures in the New World: The role of ethnicity," in Stipe and Lee, *American Mosaic*, 179–205. **1**: 40

Lees-Milne, James, *People and Places: Country House Donors and the National Trust* (London, 1992). **1**: 1, 52; **4**: 8

Le Goff, Jacques, *History and Memory* [1977], trans. Steven Rendall and Elizabeth Claman (New York, 1992). **3**: 22, 39; **7**: 23; **8**: 8

Leitsch, Walter E., "East Europeans studying history in Vienna (1855–1918)," in Deletant and Hanak, *Historians as Nation-Builders*, 139–56. **8**: 3; **10**: 14

Lejeune, Philippe, *On Autobiography*, trans. Katherine Leary (Minneapolis, 1989). **6**: 52

Leon, Warren, and Margaret Piatt, "Living-history museums," in Warren Leon and Roy Rosenzweig, *History Museums in the United States* (Urbana, IL, 1989), 64–97. **7**: 17

Leonardo, Micaela di, "Habits of the cumbered heart: Ethnic community and women's culture as American invented traditions," in Jay O'Brien and William Rosebery, eds., *Golden Ages, Dark Ages: Imagining the Past in Anthropology and History* (Berkeley, 1992), 234–52. **3**: 56; **9**: 86

Levi, Carlo, *Christ Stopped at Eboli* [1947] (London, 1982). **3**: 13

Levi, Peter, "Knowing a place," in Richard Mabey, ed., *Second Nature* (London, 1984), 36–43. **3**: 26

Levine, Joseph M., *The Battle of the Books: History and Literature in the Augustan Age* (Ithaca, NY, 1991). **5**: 6

Levine, Lawrence W., *The Unpredictable Past: Explorations in American Cultural History* (New York, 1993). **7**: 12; **9**: 43, 62

Lewis, R. W. B., *The American Adam: Innocence, Tragedy, and Tradition in the Nineteenth Century* (Chicago, 1955). **3**: 2

Lewontin, R. C., Stephen Rose, and Leon J. Kamin, *Not in Our Genes: Biology, Ideology, and Human Nature* (Cambridge, MA, 1984). **2**: 59; **9**: 75

Lifton, Betty Jean, *Journey of the Adopted Self: A Quest for Wholeness* (New York, 1994). **2**: 12, 14, 23, 24; **9**: 76

Lind, Michael, *The Next American Nation: The New Nationalism and the Fourth American Republic* (New York, 1994). **9**: 24, 64; **10**: 9

Linenthal, Edward T., "Struggling with history and memory," *Journal of American History*, 82 (1995), 1094–1101 [in roundtable on "History and the public: what can we handle?" 1029–1144]. **7**: 31

———— "The U.S. Holocaust Memorial Museum," *AQ*, 46 (1994), 406–33. **6**: 44

Lipsitz, George, *Time Passages: Collective Memory and American Popular Culture* (Minneapolis, 1990). **6**: 56

Lipstadt, Deborah E., *Denying the Holocaust* (New York, 1993). **7**: 35

Lively, Penelope, *Oleander, Jacaranda: A Childhood Perceived* (London, 1994). **1**: 15.

Loewen, James W., *Lies My Teacher Told Me: Everything Your American History Textbook Got Wrong* (New York, 1995). **2**: 8, 61; **3**: 48; **5**: 16, 28, 30, 41, 52; **6**: 13, 17; **7**: 13, 25, 26, 33, 54; **10**: 32, 33

Löfgren, Orvar, "Materializing the nation in Sweden and America," *Ethnos*, 58 (1993), 161–96. **1**: 47

———— "The nationalization of culture," *Ethnologia Europaea*, 19 (1989), 5–25. **3**: 18

Lowenthal, David, "The bicentennial landscape," *Geographical Review*, 67 (1977), 253–67. **3**: 3; **4**: 4

——— "British national identity and the English landscape," *Rural History*, 2 (1991), 205–30. **3**: 35; **4**: 9

——— "Classical antiquities as national and global heritage," *Antiquity*, 62 (1988), 726–35. **10**: 43

——— "Conclusion," in Gathercole and Lowenthal, *Politics of the Past*, 302–14. **10**: 45

——— "Counterfeit art: Authentic fakes," *IJCP*, 1 (1992), 79–103. **4**: 25; **7**: 45

——— "Free colored West Indians," in Harold E. Pagliaro, ed., *Racism in the Eighteenth Century* (Cleveland, 1973), 335–53. **9**: 61

——— "Memory and oblivion," *Museum Management and Curatorship*, 12 (1993), 171–82. **7**: 18

——— "Nostalgia tells it like it wasn't," in Shaw and Chase, *Imagined Past*, 18–32. **4**: 19

——— "The past in the American landscape," in David Lowenthal and Martyn J. Bowden, eds., *Geographies of the Mind* (New York, 1976), 89–117. **3**: 2; **8**: 19, 39

——— *The Past Is a Foreign Country* (Cambridge, 1985). **1**: 50; **4**: 3; **5**: 20, 44; **7**: 47; **8**: 13, 32; **10**: 50

——— "The timeless past: Some Anglo-American historical preconceptions," *Journal of American History*, 75 (1991), 1263–80. **6**: 3, 36

——— *West Indian Societies* (London, 1972). **6**: 18; **9**: 61

Lowenthal, David, and Colin G. Clarke, "Slave breeding in Barbuda," *Annals of the New York Academy of Sciences*, 272 (1977), 510–35. **6**: 18

Lucian of Samosata, "The way to write history," 109–36, and "The true history," 136–73, in his *Works*, H. W. and F. G. Fowler, eds. (Oxford, 1905). **5**: 4

McBryde, Isabel, ed., *Who Owns the Past?* (Melbourne, 1985). Essays by Mulvaney; Bernard Smith; Wang Gungwu.

McCann, W. J., "'Volk und Germanentum': The presentation of the past in Nazi Germany," in Gathercole and Lowenthal, *Politics of the Past*, 74–88. **8**: 7

MacCannell, Dean, *Empty Meeting Grounds: The Tourist Papers* (London, 1992). **3**: 71

MacClancy, Jeremy, "At play with identity in the Basque arena," in Macdonald, *Inside European Identities*, 84–97. **3**: 63

MacCormack, Sabine, "History, memory and time in Golden Age Spain," *H & M*, **4**: 2 (1992), 38–68. **8**: 3

McCracken, Grant, *Culture and Consumption: New Approaches to the Symbolic Character of Consumer Goods and Activities* (Bloomington, IN, 1988). **2**: 27, 62; **3**: 16

McDonald, Maryon, *"We are not French!": Language, Culture and Identity in Brittany* (London, 1989). **3**: 51, 57; **9**: 48; **10**: 18

Macdonald, Sharon, ed., *Inside European Identities: Ethnography in Western Europe* (Providence, RI, 1993). Essays by MacClancy; McKechnie.

MacDougall, Hugh A., *Racial Myth in English History* (Hanover, NH, 1982). **9**: 41

McKechnie, Rosemary, "Becoming Celtic in Corsica," in Macdonald, *Inside European Identities*, 118–45. **3**: 58

McKendrick, Neil, John Brewer, and J. H. Plumb, *The Birth of a Consumer Society: The Commercialization of 18th-Century England* (London, 1982). **3**: 16

McKendrick, Scot, "'La vraye histoire de Troye la grant': Truth and romance in the late medieval story of Troy in literature and art," in Mark Jones, ed., *Why Fakes Matter: Essays on Problems of Authenticity* (London, 1992), 71–80. **3**: 41

McPhee, John, "Travels of the Rock," *New Yorker*, 26 Feb. 1990, 108–17. **6**: 33

Maier, Charles S., "A surfeit of memory? Reflections on history, melancholy and denial," *H & M*, 5:2 (1994), 136–52. **4**: 1; **10**: 21

Malcolm X, *Autobiography of Malcolm X* (New York, 1966). **9**: 71

Marris, Peter, *Loss and Change* (London, 1974). **2**: 16

Mason, Mary Ann, *From Father's Property to Children's Rights: The History of Child Custody in the United States* (New York, 1994). **9**: 76

Mellor, Adrian, "Enterprise and heritage in the dock," in Corner and Harvey, *Enterprise and Heritage*, 93–115. **7**: 42

Melman, Billie, "Gender, history and memory: The invention of women's past in the nineteenth and early twentieth centuries," *H & M*, 5:1 (1993), 5–41. **2**: 57

Menninger, W. Walter, "Say, it isn't so: When wishful thinking obscures historical reality," *History News*, 40:12 (Dec. 1985), 10–13. **6**: 50; **7**: 2

Merriman, Nicholas, *Beyond the Glass Case: The Past, the Heritage, and the Public in Britain* (Leicester, England, 1991). **5**: 48

Merryman, John Henry, "A licit international trade in cultural objects," *IJCP*, 4 (1995), 13–60. **1**: 45

———— "The nation and the object," *IJCP*, 3 (1994), 61–76. **1**: 4; **10**: 26

———— "Two ways of thinking about cultural property," *American Journal of International Law*, 80 (1986), 831–53. **1**: 9; **10**: 33

Messenger, Phyllis Mauch, ed., *The Ethics of Collecting Cultural Property: Whose Culture? Whose Property?* (Albuquerque, NM, 1989). Essays (not separately listed) by Ann M. Early, **10**: 40; Gillett G. Griffin, **9**: 51; Jaime Litvak King, **10**: 46; Charles S. Koczka, **10**: 40

Meyer, Werner, *1291: L'histoire: Les prémices de la Confédération suisse*, 3rd ed. (Zurich, 1991). **6**: 10

Michaels, Walter Benn, "The no-drop rule," *Critical Inquiry*, 20 (1994), 758–69. **9**: 70

———— "Race into culture: A critical genealogy," *Critical Inquiry*, 18 (1992), 655–85. **9**: 70; **10**: 49

Middleton, David, and Derek Edwards, eds., *Collective Remembering* (London, 1990). Essays by Billig; Radley; Schwartz.

Millgate, Michael, *Testamentary Acts: Browning, Tennyson, James, Hardy* (Oxford, 1992). **3**: 11; **6**: 25, 51

Milne, Christopher, *The Enchanted Places* (London, 1974). **2**: 33

Molesky-Poz, Jean, "Reconstructing personal and cultural identities," *AQ*, 45 (1993), 611–20. **9**: 51

Montaigne, Michel de, "On the affection of fathers for their children," in his *Complete Essays* [c. 1580–88], trans. M. A. Screech (London, 1991), 432–52. **2**: 32, 43, 44, 49

Morgan, Robert P., "Tradition, anxiety, and the current musical scene," in Nicholas Kenyon, ed., *Authenticity and Early Music* (Oxford, 1988), 57–82. **7**: 11

Morgan, Sally, *My Place* (Fremantle, Australia, 1987). **2**: 18

Morse, Ruth, *Truth and Convention in the Middle Ages: Rhetoric, Representation, and Reality* (Cambridge, 1991). **5**: 6, 8

Mosès, Stéphane, "Scholem and Rosenzweig: The dialectics of history," *H & M*, 2:2 (1990), 100–16. **10**: 16

Mote, F. W., "A millennium of Chinese urban history: Form, time, and space concepts in Soochow," *Rice University Studies*, 59:4 (1973), 49–53. **1**: 38

Mulvaney, D. J. "Past regained, future lost: The Kow Swamp Pleistocene burials," *Antiquity*, 65 (1991), 12–21. **1**: 60

———— "A question of values: Museums and cultural property," in McBryde, *Who Owns the Past?* 86–98. **1**: 60

Mulvey, Christopher, *Anglo-American Landscapes: A Study of Nineteenth-Century Anglo-American Travel Literature* (Cambridge, 1983). **5**: 49

Munz, Peter, *Our Knowledge of the Growth of Knowledge: Popper or Wittgenstein?* (London, 1985). **6**: 5

Murray, Les A., *Persistence in Folly: Selected Prose Writings* (London, 1984). **1**: 1, 6

Myers, David N., "Remembering *Zakhor*: A super-Commentary," *H & M*, 4:2 (1992), 129–46. **6**: 44

Naipaul, V. S., *A Bend in the River* (London, 1979). **1**: 46

Nelkin, Dorothy, and M. Susan Lindee, *The DNA Mystique: The Gene as a Cultural Icon* (New York, 1995). **9**: 9, 33, 34, 35, 36, 37, 52, 76, 88

Newby, Howard, "Revitalizing the countryside," *JRSA*, 138 (1990), 630–6. **8**: 30

Nora, Pierre, *Lieux de Mémoire*, I, II (3 vols.), III (3 vols.) (Paris, 1984–92). Essays by Agulhon; Baczko; Burguière; Charle; Chevalier; Compagnon; Durand; Fumaroli (2); Furet; Gasnier; Guiomar; Nora (5); Ory; Ozouf; Pomian (2); Revel; Vauchez.

———— "Entre mémoire et histoire: la problématique des lieux," in his *LM*, I: xv–xlii. **1**: 21

———— "L'ère de la commémoration," in his *LM*, III. **3**: 975–1012. **1**: 3, 28; **3**: 52; **5**: 15

———— "La génération," in his *LM*, III. 1:930–71. **2**: 41

———— "*L'Histoire de France* de Lavisse," in his *LM*, II. 1:317–75. **3**: 22

———— "Lavisse, instituteur national," in his *LM*, I: 247–89. **3**: 22

Novick, Peter, *That Noble Dream: The "Objectivity Question" and the American Historical Profession* (Cambridge, 1988). **2**: 57; **5**: 1, 9; **10**: 6

O'Keefe, Patrick J., and Lyndel V. Prott, *Law and the Cultural Heritage*, 3: *Movement* (London, 1989). **10**: 21, 38, 45

Olwig, Karen Fog, "Defining the national in the transnational: Cultural identity in the Afro-Caribbean diaspora," *Ethnos*, 58 (1993), 361–76. **8**: 43

Ortner, Sherry B., "Is female to male as nature is to culture?" in Michelle Z. Rosaldo and Louise Lamphere, eds., *Woman, Culture, and Society* (Stanford, CA, 1977), 67–88. **2**: 56

Ortoleva, Peppino, "Tradition and abundance: Reflections on Italian-American foodways," *Altreitalie*, 7 (June–July 1992), 53–70. **1**: 26

Orvell, Miles, *The Real Thing: Imitation and Authenticity in American Culture, 1880–1940* (Chapel Hill, NC, 1989). **6**: 56

Orwell, George, *The Lion and the Unicorn* [1941], in his *Collected Essays, Journalism and Letters* (London, 1968), 2:56–109. **3**: 35; **7**: 60

———— *Nineteen Eighty-Four* (London, 1954). **4**: 3; **7**: 35

Ory, Pascal, "La gastronomie," in Nora, *LM*, III.2:822–53. **3**: 33

Owen, Stephen, *Mi-Lou: Poetry and the Labyrinth of Desire* (Cambridge, MA, 1989). **2**: 35

Ozouf, Mona, "Le Panthéon," in Nora, *LM*, I:136–66. **6**: 40

Pagden, Anthony, *European Encounters with the New World: From Renaissance to Romanticism* (New Haven, 1993). **5**: 5, 35

Paine, Robert, "Israel: The making of self in the 'pioneering' of the nation," *Ethnos*, 58 (1993), 222–40. **8**: 44

Pascal, Roy, *Design and Truth in Autobiography* (London, 1960). **1**: 10

Pelletier, Benoît, "The case of the treasures of l'Ange-Gardien," *IJCP*, 2 (1993), 371–82. **10**: 22

Phillips, Charles, "The politics of history," *History News*, 40:9 (Sept. 1985), 16–20. **6**: 1

Plumb, J. H. *The Death of the Past* [1969] (Harmondsworth, England, 1973). **4**: 3, 5

Pocock, John, "England," in Orest Ranum, ed., *National Consciousness, History, and Political Culture in Early-Modern Europe* (Baltimore, 1975). **8**: 18

Polkinghorne, Donald E., "Narrative and self-concept," *Journal of Narrative and Life History*, 1 (1991), 135–53. **6**: 50

Pomian, Krzysztof, "Les archives: du Trésor des chartes au Caran," in Nora, *LM*, III.3:162–233. **3**: 20

———— "Francs et Gaulois," in Nora, *LM*, III.1:40–105. **8**: 8

Pompa, Leon, *Human Nature and Historical Knowledge: Hume, Hegel and Vico* (Cambridge, 1990). **5**: 38

Portelli, Alessandro, "Uchronic dreams: Working-class memory and possible worlds," in Raphael Samuel and Paul Thompson, eds., *The Myths We Live By* (London, 1990), 143–60. **6**: 6

Price, Sally, *Primitive Art in Civilized Places* (Chicago, 1989). **10**: 36, 40

Proctor, Robert N., *Racial Hygiene: Medicine under the Nazis* (Cambridge, MA, 1988). **9**: 29, 30, 46, 47, 59

Puymège, Gérard de, "Chauvin and chauvinism," *H & M*, 6:1 (1994), 35–72. **3**: 21

Raban, Jonathan, *Coasting* (London, 1987). **1**: 12, 31

Radley, Alan, "Artefacts, memory and a sense of the past," in Middleton and Edwards, *Collective Remembering*, 46–59. **2**: 32

Ram, Uri, "Zionist historiography and the invention of modern Jewish nationhood: The case of Ben Zion Dinur," *H & M*, 7:1 (1995), 91–124. **8**: 45

Ravitch, Diane, "Multiculturalism: E pluribus plures," *American Scholar*, 59 (1990), 337–54. **9**: 85

Ravitch, Diane, and Molefi Kete Asante, "Multiculturalism: An exchange," *American Scholar*, 60 (1991), 267–76. **4**: 26

Renan, Joseph Ernest, "What is a nation?" [1882], in Homi K. Bhabha, ed., *Nation and Narration* (London, 1990), 8–22. **3**: 39; **6**: 9; **7**: 21; **9**: 56

Revel, Jacques, "La cour," in Nora, *LM*, III.1:128–93. **6**: 28

Reynolds, Henry, "Progress, morality, and the dispossession of the Aboriginals," *Meanjin Quarterly*, 37 (1974), 306–12. **9**: 6

Richard, Carl J., *The Founders and the Classics: Greece, Rome, and the American Enlightenment* (Cambridge, MA, 1994). **8**: 25

Richler, Mordecai, "Inside/Outside," *New Yorker*, 23 Sept. 1991, 40–92. **3**: 41

———— *This Year in Jerusalem* (New York, 1994). **4**: 16

Riss, Arthur, "Racial essentialism and family values in *Uncle Tom's Cabin*," *AQ*, 46 (1994), 513–44. **2**: 39; **9**: 8

Ritvo, Harriet, "Race, breed, and myths of origin: Chillingham cattle as ancient Britons," *Representations*, 39 (Summer 1992), 1–22. **8**: 30

Rodriguez, Richard, "An American writer," in Sollors, *Invention of Ethnicity*, 3–13. **3**: 66; **9**: 13

—————— *Days of Obligation* (New York, 1992. **9**: 84

—————— *Hunger of Memory* (New York, 1983). **6**: 48

Rogan, Bjarne, "Things with a history—and other possessions," in *The Global and the Local: Consumption and European Identity*, Material Culture Studies SISWO (Amsterdam, 1993), 103–18. **2**: 6, 37

Rosaldo, Renato, "From the door of his tent: The fieldworker and the inquisitor," in Clifford and Marcus, *Writing Culture*, 77–97. **5**: 48

Rosenstone, Robert A., *Visions of the Past: The Challenge of Film to Our Idea of History* (Cambridge, MA, 1995). **7**: 1, 12

Rosenthal, Joel T., *Patriarchy and Families of Privilege in Fifteenth Century England* (Philadelphia, 1991). **9**: 2

Rosenzweig, Roy, "Marketing the past," in Susan Porter Benson, Stephen Brier, and Roy Rosenzweig, eds., *Presenting the Past: Essays on History and the Public* (Philadelphia, 1986), 21–49. **3**: 36

Ross, Dorothy, "Grand narrative in historical writing: From romance to uncertainty," *AHR*, 100 (1995), 651–77. **5**: 8; **10**: 32

—————— "Historical consciousness in nineteenth-century America," *AHR*, 89 (1984), 909–28. **9**: 4; **10**: 32

Rossetenstein, David S., "Custody disputes involving tribal Indians in the United States," in John Eekelaar and Peter Sarcević, eds., *Parenthood in Modern Society* (Dordrecht, Netherlands, 1993), 597–619. **9**: 79

Roth, Joseph, *The Radetsky March* [1932] (London, 1974). **6**: 16

Roth, Michael S., "Remembering and forgetting: *Maladies de la Mémoire* in nineteenth-century France," *Representations*, 26 (Spring 1989), 49–68. **4**: 17

Royce, Anya Peterson, *Ethnic Identity* (Bloomington, IN, 1982). **3**: 58

Rushdie, Salman, "'Errata': or, unreliable narration in *Midnight's Children*" (1983), in his *Imaginary Homelands* (London, 1992), 22–5. **6**: 53

Ruskin, John, *The Seven Lamps of Architecture* [1849] (New York, 1961). **3**: 29

Ryckmans, Pierre, *The Chinese Attitude towards the Past*, 47th George Ernest Morrison Lecture on Ethnology (Canberra, 1986). **1**: 37

Sadrin, Anny, *Parentage and Inheritance in the Novels of Charles Dickens* (Cambridge, 1994). **2**: 29, 30, 41, 64; **3**: 17

Said, Edward W., *Beginnings: Intention and Method*, rev. ed. (New York, 1985). **8**: 21

Salmagundi, "The literary imagination and the sense of the past," special issue, no. 68–69 (1985–86). Includes essays by Clive; Heaney.

Salmond, Anne, "Self and other in contemporary anthropology: Maori-European exchanges with the past," in Fardon, *Counterworks*, 23–48. **2**: 9

Samuel, Raphael, "Continuous national history," in his *Patriotism: The Making and Unmaking of British National Identity*. 1. *History and Politics* (London, 1989), 9–17. **4**: 7; **6**: 37

—————— *Theatres of Memory* 1. *Past and Present in Contemporary Culture* (London, 1995). **1**: 33; **3**: 53; **4**: 10, 12; **7**: 57

Santner, Eric L., *Stranded Objects: Mourning, Memory, and Film in Postwar Germany* (Ithaca, NY, 1990). **2**: 13

Schlesinger, Arthur M., Jr., *The Disuniting of America: Reflections on a Multicultural Society* (New York, 1992). **5**: 18; **10**: 5, 35

Schneider, David M., *A Critique of the Study of Kinship* (Ann Arbor, MI, 1984). **2**: 23, 56; **9**: 10, 25, 73

Schudson, Michael, *Watergate in American Memory: How We Remember, Forget, and Reconstruct the Past* (New York, 1992). **4**: 3; **5**: 27; **7**: 32

Schuman, Howard, and Jacqueline Scott, "Generations and collective memories," *American Sociological Review*, 54 (1989), 359–81. **6**: 47

Schwartz, Barry, "The character of Washington," *AQ*, 38 (1986), 202–22. **6**: 41

———— "Mourning and the making of a sacred symbol: Durkheim and the Lincoln assassination," *Social Forces*, 70 (1991–92), 343–64. **3**: 12

———— "The reconstruction of Abraham Lincoln," in Middleton and Edwards, *Collective Remembering*, 81–107. **7**: 61

———— "Social change and collective memory: The democratization of George Washington," *American Sociological Review*, 56 (1991), 221–36. **6**: 32; **7**: 61

Schwartz, Barry, Yael Zerubavel, and Bernice M. Barnett, "The recovery of Masada: A study in collective memory," *Sociological Quarterly*, 27 (1986), 147–64. **7**: 41; **10**: 50

Shaffer, Peter, *Lettice and Lovage* (London, 1988). **7**: 49

Shammas, Carole, Marylynn Salmon, and Michael Dahlin, eds., *Inheritance in America from Colonial Times to the Present* (New Brunswick, NJ, 1987). **2**: 31, 58, 62

Shaw, Christopher, and Malcolm Chase, eds., *The Imagined Past: History and Nostalgia* (Manchester, 1989). Essays by Chase; Croft; Lowenthal.

Sheehan, James J., "From princely collections to public museums," in Michael S. Roth, ed., *Rediscovering History* (Stanford, CA, 1994), 169–82. **3**: 18

Shemilt, Denis J., "Adolescent ideas about evidence and methodology in history," in Christopher Portal, ed., *The History Curriculum for Teachers* (Lewes, Sussex, 1988), 39–61. **5**: 29

———— "Beauty and the philosopher: Empathy in history and classroom," in A. K. Dickinson, P. J. Lee, and P. J. Rogers, eds., *Learning History* (London, 1984), 39–84. **5**: 47; **8**: 41

Sherman, Daniel J., "Art, commerce, and the production of memory in France after World War I," in Gillis, *Commemorations*, 186–211. **3**: 19

Shoumatoff, Alex, *The Mountain of Names: A History of the Human Family* (New York, 1990). **2**: 49, 59; **9**: 3

Sider, Gerald M., *Lumbee Indian Histories: Race, Ethnicity, and Indian Identity in the Southern United States* (Cambridge, 1993). **9**: 14, 28

Silberman, Neil Asher, *Between Past and Present: Archaeology, Ideology, and Nationalism in the Modern Middle East* (New York, 1989). **7**: 41; **10**: 19, 36, 47

Simon, Rita J., and Howard Altstein, *Transracial Adoption* (New York, 1977). **9**: 81

Small, John, "Transracial placements: Conflicts and contradictions," in Sonia Morgan and Peter Righton, eds., *Child Care: Concerns and Conflicts* (London, 1989), 50–66. **9**: 80

Smith, Anthony D., "The problem of national identity: Ancient, medieval and modern," *Ethnic and Racial Studies*, 17 (1994), 375–99. **10**: 5

Smith, Bernard, "Art objects and historical usage," in McBryde, *Who Owns the Past?* 74–85. **Introd**: 1; **1**: 19; **10**: 46

Smith, M. Estellie, "The process of sociocultural continuity," *Current Anthropology*, 23 (1982), 127–35. **3**: 69

Sollors, Werner, ed., *The Invention of Ethnicity* (New York, 1989). Essays by Conzen; Ferraro; Rodriguez.

Spalding, Julian, "Art galleries: Church or funfair? Museums in a democracy," *JRSA*, 137 (1989), 577–87. **4**: 29

Spence, Donald P., *Narrative Truth and Historical Truth* (New York, 1982). **6**: 45

Spickard, Paul R., *Mixed Blood: Intermarriage and Ethnic Identity in 20th-Century America* (Madison, WI, 1989). **9**: 47, 59

Spiegel, Gabrielle M., "History, historicism, and the social logic of the text in the Middle Ages," *Speculum*, 65 (1990), 59–86. **9**: 1

Spriggs, Matthew, "God's police and damned whores: Images of archaeology in Hawaii," in Gathercole and Lowenthal, *Politics of the Past*, 118–29. **10**: 23

Spring, Eileen, *Law, Land & Family: Aristocratic Inheritance in England, 1300 to 1800* (Chapel Hill, NC, 1993). **2**: 52

Stafford, Robert A., "Annexing the landscapes of the past: British imperial geology in the nineteenth century," in John M. MacKenzie, ed., *Imperialism and the Natural World* (Manchester, 1990), 67–89. **8**: 6

Staub, Shalom, "Folklore and authenticity," in Feintuch, *Conservation of Culture*, 166–79. **3**: 70; **8**: 23

Stipe, Robert E., and Antoinette J. Lee, eds., for US/ICOMOS, *The American Mosaic: Preserving a Nation's Heritage* (Washington, 1987). Essays by King; Lee.

Stocking, George W., Jr., ed., *Objects and Others: Essays on Museums and Material Culture* (Madison, WI, 1985). Essays by Clifford; Handler; Hinsley; Wade.

Stone, Jeanne C. Fawtier, and Lawrence Stone, *An Open Elite? England 1540–1880* (Oxford, 1984). **3**: 23; **9**: 2

Strathern, Marilyn, *After Nature: English Kinship in the Late Twentieth Century* (Cambridge, 1992). **3**: 9; **9**: 58

Sumner, William Graham, *Folkways* [1906] (Boston, 1940). **5**: 40; **10**: 29

——— "War" (1903), in his *War and Other Essays* (New Haven, 1919), 3–40. **6**: 8; **10**: 25

Takaki, Ronald, *Iron Cages: Race and Culture in 19th-Century America* (New York, 1990). **9**: 41, 57

Takeuchi, Keiichi, "Nationalism and geography in modern Japan, 1880s to 1920s," in Hooson, *Geography and National Identity*, 104–11. **3**: 13

Tanner, Marie, *The Last Descendant of Aeneas* (New Haven, 1993). **3**: 30; **6**: 41

Taylor, Robert M., Jr., and Ralph S. Crandall, "Historians and genealogists: An emerging community of interest," in their (eds.) *Generations and Change: Genealogical Perspectives in Society and History* (Macon, GA, 1986). **1**: 30

Teich, Mikulas, and Roy Porter, eds., *The National Question in Europe in Historical Context* (Cambridge, 1993). Essays (not separately listed) by Lyttleton, **10**: 29; Tomaszewski, **3**: 13

Terdiman, Richard, "The mnemonics of Musset's *Confession*," *Representations*, 26 (Spring 1989), 26–48. **1**: 10

Thoden van Velzen, Diura, "The world of Tuscan tomb robbers," *IJCP*, 5 (1996) 111–26. **1**: 45

Thompson, Paul, "Believe it or not," in Jeffrey and Edwall, *Memory and History*, 1–16. **2**: 29

Tintner, Adeline R., "Autobiography as fiction: 'The usurping consciousness' as hero of James's memoirs," *Twentieth Century Literature*, 23 (1977), 239–60. **6**: 52

Tizard, Barbara, and Ann Phoenix, *Black, White or Mixed Race? Race and Racism in the Lives of Young People of Mixed Parentage* (London, 1993). **9**: 72, 81

Tollebeek, Jo, and Tom Verschaffel, "The particular character of history," *H & M*, 4:2 (1992), 69–95. **5**: 34

Tonkin, Elizabeth, *Narrating Our Pasts: The Social Construction of Oral History* (Cambridge, 1992). **2**: 56

Tonkin, Elizabeth, Maryon McDonald, and Malcolm Chapman, eds., *History and Ethnicity* (London, 1989). Essays by Burke; Collard; Davies; Davis; Forsythe; Just.

Trollope, Anthony, *The West Indies and the Spanish Main*, 2nd ed. [1860] (London, 1968). **9**: 56, 61

UNESCO, *Conventions and Recommendations of Unesco Concerning the Protection of Cultural Heritage* (Paris, 1985). **1**: 4; **10**: 2

Unruh, David R., "Death and personal history: Strategies of identity preservation," *Social Problems*, 30 (1983), 340–51. **2**: 32

Van den Berghe, Pierre L., *The Ethnic Phenomenon* (New York, 1981). **3**: 62

Van Dyck, José, *Manufacturing Babies and Public Consent: Debating the New Reproductive Technologies* (London, 1995). **9**: 77

Vauchez, André, "La cathédrale," in *LM*, III.2:90–127. **3**: 33

Vitebsky, Piers, "From cosmology to environmentalism: Shamanism as local knowledge in a global setting," in Fardon, *Counterworks*, 182–203. **3**: 64

Wade, Edwin L., "The ethnic art market in the American Southwest, 1880–1980," in Stocking, *Objects and Others*, 167–91. **3**: 68

Wagner-Pacifici, Robert, and Barry Schwartz, "The Vietnam Veterans Memorial: Commemorating a difficult past," *American Journal of Sociology*, 97 (1991), 376–420. **7**: 30

Walcott, Derek, *The Antilles: Fragments of Epic Memory*, The 1992 Nobel Lecture (London, 1993). **10**: 12

Waldrep, Shelton, "Monuments to Walt," in The Project on Disney, *Inside the Mouse: Work and Play at Disney World* (Durham, NC, 1995), 199–229. **6**: 26

Walker, Alice, "If the present looks like the past, what does the future look like?" in her *In Search of Our Mothers' Gardens* (New York, 1983), 290–312. **9**: 49, 71

Wallace, Michael, "Razor ribbons, history museums, and civic salvation," *Radical History Review*, 57 (1993), 221–41. **7**: 30, 43

—— "Ronald Reagan and the politics of history," *Tikkun*, 2:1 (1987), 13–18, 127–31. **7**: 13

Walsh, Kevin T., *The Representation of the Past: Museums and Heritage in the Post-Modern World* (London, 1992). **1**: 6

Wang Gungwu, "Loving the ancient in China," in McBryde, *Who Owns the Past?* 175–95. **1**: 37

Waters, Mary C., *Ethnic Options: Choosing Identities in America* (Berkeley 1990). **3**: 56; **9**: 11, 54, 84, 86

Weber, Eugen, *Peasants into Frenchmen: The Modernization of Rural France 1870–1914* (London, 1979). **3**: 13, 22; **5**: 15; **7**: 21

Weidiger, Paula, *Gilding the Acorn: Behind the Façade of the National Trust* (London, 1994). **3**: 25; **10**: 13

Wenzel, Marian, "Bosnian history and Austro-Hungarian policy," *Museum Management and Curatorship*, 12 (1993), 127–42. **7**: 23

Wharton, Edith, "The angel at the grave," in her *Roman Fever and Other Stories* [1911–16] (London, 1983), 114–33. **6**: 24

Whisnant, David E., *All That Is Native and Fine: The Politics of Culture in an American Region* (Chapel Hill, NC, 1983). **9**: 27

———— "Public sector folklore as intervention," in Feintuch, *Conservation of Culture*, 233–47. **3**: 55

Williams, Michael Ann, "The realm of the tangible," in Feintuch, *The Conservation of Culture*, 196–205. **1**: 39

Wills, Garry, *Reagan's America: Innocents at Home* (New York, 1987). **7**: 43

Wilson, William A., *Folklore and Nationalism in Modern Finland* (Bloomington, IN, 1976). **5**: 39; **6**: 21; **8**: 11; **10**: 24

———— "Herder, folklore and romantic nationalism," *Journal of Popular Culture*, 6 (1973), 819–35. **10**: 16

Wineburg, Samuel S., "On the reading of historical texts: Notes on the breach between School and Academy," *American Educational Research Journal*, 28 (1991), 495–519. **5**: 28

———— "The psychology of learning and teaching history," in R. C. Calfee and D. C. Berliner, eds., *Handbook of Educational Psychology* (New York, 1996), 15–24. **5**: 47, 52

Wolin, Sheldon S., *The Presence of the Past: Essays on the State and the Constitution* (Baltimore, 1989). **7**: 20

Wood, Gordon S., "Jefferson at home," *NYRB*, 13 May 1993, 6–9. **6**: 20; **9**: 65, 66

———— *The Radicalism of the American Revolution* (New York, 1992), **2**: 8; **3**: 2

Woolf, Virginia, "A dialogue upon Mount Pentelicus" [1906], *TLS*, 11–17 Sept. 1987, 979. **9**: 20; **10**; 43

Wright, Lawrence, "One drop of blood," *New Yorker*, 25 July 1994, 46–55. **2**: 55; **9**: 69

Wright, Patrick, *On Living in an Old Country: The National Past in Contemporary Britain* (London, 1985). **4**: 1; **7**: 5

Young, James E., *The Texture of Memory: Holocaust Memorials and Meaning* (New Haven, 1993). **7**: 28

Zelinksy, Wilbur, *Nation into State: The Shifting Symbolic Foundations of American Nationalism* (Chapel Hill, NC, 1988). **5**: 45; **6**: 23

Zengotita, Thomas de, "Speakers of being: Romantic refusion and cultural anthropology," in G. W. Stocking, Jr., ed., *Romantic Motives: Essays on Anthropological Sensibility* (Madison, WI, 1989). **3**: 18

Zerubavel, Yael, "The death of memory and the memory of death: Masada and the Holocaust as historical metaphors," *Representations*, 45 (Winter 1994), 72–100. **7**: 41

———— "The historic, the legendary, and the incredible: Invented tradition and collective memory in Israel," in Gillis, *Commemorations*, 105–23. **7**: 53

———— *Recovered Roots: Collective Memory and the Making of the Israeli National Tradition* (Chicago, 1995). **7**: 41, 53

———— "The politics of interpretation: Tel Hai in Israel's collective memory," *Journal of the Association for Jewish Studies*, 16 (1991), 133–60. **7**: 53

Zonabend, Françoise, *The Enduring Memory: Time and History in a French Village* (Manchester, 1984). **5**: 42

Addendum

Tunbridge, J. E., and G. J. Ashworth, *Dissonant Heritage: The Management of the Past as a Resource in Conflict* (New York, 1996), came to my notice just as this book went to press. Tunbridge and Ashworth, like me, view heritage and history as linked but disparate enterprises and stress the possessive rivalries innate to heritage ("all heritage is someone's heritage and therefore logically not someone else's" [p. 21]) in detailed case-studies of Canada, the Netherlands, eastern Europe, and South Africa.

ACKNOWLEDGMENTS

THE RANGE OF COUNTRIES AND CONCERNS covered in this book magnifies my manifold indebtedness. I am grateful to the Research Institute for the Study of Man for a Landes Senior Fellowship on comparative national heritage; the Leverhulme Trust for an Emeritus Fellowship on minority heritage; the British Council for specialist heritage tours in Australia, Norway, and Greece; and the Nuffield Foundation for aid to seminars on "The Uses of the Past," as well as the Warburg Institute and University College London for hosting those seminars.

My knowledge of many heritage issues—notably cultural identity and conservation, authenticity, and landscape legacies—owes much to the liberality of the World Heritage Organization (UNESCO), the International Council on Monuments and Sites (ICOMOS); the Council of Europe; the Getty Conservation Institute; national trusts in Australia, the United Kingdom, and the United States; park services of the United States and Canada; the Dahlem Foundation (Free University of Berlin); the Centre National de la Recherche Scientifique (Paris); Heritage Interpretation International; the World Archaeological Congress; English Heritage; Victoria & Albert Museum, British Museum, and Science Museum; the International Cultural Property Society; the Association of Living History and Farm Museums; Pennsylvania Heritage Parks; the Yale Center for British Art; the Rutgers Center for Historical Analysis; Lessico Intellettuale Europeo (Rome); the Landscape Research Group (U.K.); the Locarno International Conferences; and the Cambridge University Department of Archaeology.

For stimulus from students and staff I am indebted to more universities than can be named here, notably the Warburg Institute (London);

humanities research centers at Odense (Denmark) and Canberra; the universities of Bergen, Lund, Warsaw, Lausanne, Aberdeen, Washington, and St. Mary's at Strawberry Hill, England; and the Architectural Conservation summer school at West Dean, England.

For insight, debate, hospitality, and sources over many years I am especially grateful to Ken Craik, Peter Gathercole, Tom Griffiths, Pat O'Keefe, Norman Palmer, Lyndel Prott, Herb Stovel, Samuel Wineburg, and Geneviève Heller-Racine, who has steadily supplied books and papers from Switzerland, as has Christian Girault from Paris. Peter Quartermaine read an early text draft with strict and benevolent care; Gillian Bridge, Hugh Prince, and Gordon Wood amplified and rectified particular chapters. "Uses of the Past" colleagues Peter Burke, Malcolm Baker, Robert Bud, Craig Clunas, Simon Ditchfield, Nicholas James, and Charles Saumarez Smith have been ever accessible, authoritative, and, when needed, admonitory.

Generous with advice and data, smoothing travel and travail, and offering special stimuli were Ran Aaronsohn, Eva Abraham, Michael Ames, Robert Anderson, Leena Arkio, Helen Armstrong, Ellen Badone, Ian Bell, Mike Bell, Barbara Bender, Ray Betts, Richard Bosworth, Georgina Boyes, Brendan Bradshaw, Christina Cameron, Cary Carson, Frank Carter, Malcolm Chase, Chris Chippindale, Françoise Choay, Sue Clifford, Anna Somers Cocks, Erik Cohen, Paul Connerton, Sheila Cooper, Denis Cosgrove, Eleni Cubitt, Douglas Davies, Natalie Davis, Graeme Davison, John Dickenson, Joan and Serge Domicelj, Harry Dunlop, Anne Eriksen, Elizabeth Estève-Coll, Deirdre Evans-Pritchard, Karen Fields, Linda Finan, Magnus Fladmark, John Foster, Jonas Frykman, Mary Fulbrook, Joan Gero, John Gillis, Carolyn Gilman, David Glassberg, Honor Godfrey, Christopher Grayson, Richard Handler, Dolores Hayden, Esben Hedegaard, Michael Herzfeld, Gad Heuman, Robert Hewison, Tamás Hofer, David Hooson, John Iddon, Tim Ingold, Peter Jackson, Nuala Johnson, Alun Jones, Mark Jones, Michael Kammen, Tamar Katriel, Bernard Kaukas, Harvey Kaye, Henri Krop, W. E. Krumbein, Marc Laenen, Knut Larsen, Heather Lechtman, Antoinette Lee, James Lees-Milne, Penelope Lively, James Loewen, Orvar Löfgren, Richard Longstreth, Eleanor Lowenthal, John Lunn, Nils Marstein, Brian Matthews, John Merryman, Hugh Miller, Nora Mitchell, Donna Morganstern, Françoise Morin, Dag

Myklebust, Ernst Nolte, Pierre Nora, Peter Novick, Dusan Ogrin, Kenneth and Karen Olwig, Robert Oresko, Mary V. Orna, Yiannis Papadakis, Helen Paterson, Michael Petzet, Krzysztof Pomian, Dominique Poulot, Colin Renfrew, Harriet Ritvo, Bjarne Rogan, Dolores Root, Pierre Ryckmans, Raphael Samuel, Barry Schwartz, George Seddon, Yossi Shilhav, Catherine Shoard, Per Kristian Skulberg, Al Solnit, Simon Spalding, Gaby Spiegel, Jean Starobinki, Shalom Staub, Geoffrey Stillwell, Marilyn Strathern, Barbara Szacka, Diura Thoden van Velzen, Yi-Fu Tuan, Sandra Wallman, Jill Paton Walsh, Mary Waters, Ernst van de Wetering, Patrick Wright, Ken Yellis, Wilbur Zelinsky, and Yael Zerubavel.

To Judith Flanders at Viking/Penguin I am grateful for sagacious support; and at the Free Press to Norah Vincent for invaluable critiques, judicious paring and reshaping, and unswerving editorial encouragement; and to Bruce Nichols for serene faith in a sometimes fractious author.

INDEX

Aachen, Germany, xvi

Aborigines (Australia), 16, 182; Aboriginal Protection Act, 207; art, 87, 243; defined, 87, 182, 217; dreamtime, 128, 183; extinction, 83, 90, 195; genealogy, 51; land claims, 181, 236; race and half-castes, 209–11; relics and sites, 29, 236, 243; removal and return of children, 37, 83, 222; in Tasmania, 217

Acropolis (Greece), 68, 142, 176, 228, 244; *see also* Elgin Marbles; Greece

Acton, John Emerich Edward Dalberg-, Lord, 108, 158

Adams, Henry, 141

Adams, John, 45

Adams, John Quincy, 207

Adamsville, R.I., 135

Addison, Joseph, 95

Admiralry Arch (London), xiii

adoption, 35–6, 38–9, 219–35; of Argentine "disappeareds", 37; of Chinese children, 223; Church curbs on, 46; color and race in, 221–3; Jewish law and, 199; natural children and, 35, 219–23

Africa, Africans: French Africa, 23; heritage of, 75, 77; historyless, 119; human origins, 175, 176, 182; rock art, 175; slavery, 132, 229

African-Americans, 121, 142–4; and adoption, 221–3; at Colonial Williamsburg, 154; and Gold Coast dungeons, 229; legacies, 75, 77, 86; mendacity required, 142–3; perception of Africa, 188; and race, 161–2, 207, 209–13, 217–19, 223; roots, 34, 210–12

afterlife, belief in, 46–8, 52, 61–3

AIDS, 152, 204

Alamo, the (San Antonio, Texas) 165

Alamo, The (film), 165

Albigensians, 75, 77, 82

Alexander III, Pope, xvi

Alford, Violet, 178

All Souls College (Oxford), 186

Allen, Woody, 53

amalgamation, of bones, 58; of past periods, 137–9; of races, 207–11; *see also* miscegenation

America(n), character, 55; concept of, 182; heritage, nature of, 231; history, relevance of, 123–4; *see also* United States

American Heritage Foundation, 93

American Indians, antiquity of, 117, 179, 181–3; Canadian, 5, 181–2, 208; in Brazil, 160; and casinos, 87; child adoption, 222; crafts, 86–7, 216; dual identity, 86–7, 216, 224; ecological virtues, 81, 150–1; exclusion of outsiders, 128; growth of, 84, 216; heritage pride, 127, 168, 224; "innate" traits, 194–5, 197–8, 202, 208, 224; negative images, 159, 194–5; nomadic image, 131; raid (Kansas), 95; repatriation of relics, 29–30; as role models, 81–5, 150–1, 159, 182, 197, 210; Spanish and, 78, 211; vanishing, 194–5; as victims, 83–4, 168, 216, 222, 224; *see also* First Nations; indigenes; mestizo; Native Americans; specific tribal names

Amherst College (Mass.), 159

Amish (U.S.), 203

amnesia, genealogical, 51; motives for,

319